Distributed Systems

ACM PRESS

Editor-in-Chief:

Peter Wegner, *Brown University*

ACM Press books represent a collaboration between the Association for Computing Machinery (ACM) and Addison-Wesley Publishing Company to develop and publish a broad range of new works. These works generally fall into one of four series.

Frontier Series. Books focused on novel and exploratory material at the leading edge of computer science and practice.

Anthology Series. Collected works of general interest to computer professionals and/or society at large.

Tutorial Series. Introductory books to help nonspecialists quickly grasp either the general concepts or the needed details of some specific topic.

History Series. Books documenting past developments in the field and linking them to the present.

In addition, ACM Press books include selected conference and workshop proceedings.

Distributed Systems

Edited by

Sape Mullender

ACM Press
New York, New York

Addison-Wesley Publishing Company
Wokingham, England • Reading, Massachusetts • Menlo Park, California
New York • Don Mills, Ontario • Amsterdam • Bonn
Sydney • Singapore • Tokyo • Madrid • San Juan

AMC Press Frontier Series

Copyright © 1989 by the ACM Press. A Division of the Association for Computing Machinery, Inc. (ACM).

Cover designed by Marshall Henrichs
and printed by The Riverside Printing Co (Reading) Ltd.
Reproduced by Addison-Wesley from camera-ready copy supplied by the editor.
Printed and bound in Great Britain by TJ Press (Padstow) Ltd, Cornwall.

First printed in 1989.

British Library Cataloguing in Publication Data

Distributed systems.
   1. Distributed computer systems
   I. Mullender, Sape
   004'.36

   ISBN 0–201–41660–3

Library of Congress Cataloging in Publication Data

A CIP catalogue record for this book is available from the Library of Congress

PREFACE

In July of 1988, the world's northernmost university, the University of Tromsø in Norway, was the host of the international Advanced Course on Distributed Systems, Arctic '88. Thanks to the university's generous hospitality and the students' enthusiasm, the lecturers — Birman, Herbert, Mullender, Needham, Satyanarayanan, Schroeder, Spector, and Weihl — decided that they would enjoy teaching the course again. As a result, Fingerlakes '89 will be held at Cornell University in July of 1989. This book is a combination of the lecture notes for Arctic '88 and Fingerlakes '89.

The contributors to this volume are all experienced researchers in the field of distributed systems and this book presents their views on those aspects of the field in which they are most experienced. The purpose of the book is not to give an overview of distributed systems, nor is it a tutorial. It is an attempt by the authors to share the experience gained in many years of distributed systems research. The authors' own systems are taken as examples throughout.

This book is intended for people in universities and industry interested in distributed systems. People teaching systems can use this book to refresh their knowledge of distributed systems. Ph.D. students can use it to get acquainted with the field and as a source of references to other work. Distributed systems designers and builders can use it to find descriptions of other systems and methods and solutions to many of the problems they will encounter during the course of their work. It can be used in post-graduate distributed systems courses. It is aimed at graduate students in computer science: the reader should have a good general knowledge of computer organization, computer networks, and operating systems.

The book contains seven parts, roughly grouping the work presented and each part has a small introduction which puts the work presented in it in context.

Part I is an introduction to distributed systems. The field is defined, and general techniques for building distributed systems and requirements for distributed applications are discussed. Chapter 1 is based on the excellent introductory lecture given by M. D. Schroeder at the Arctic '88 Course in Tromsø. Although I have written the words, most of the credit for this chapter should go to him. Chapter 2 defines the goals of distributed programs and explains implementation techniques to achieve those goals. A. Z. Spector, too, was inspired by his lectures in Tromsø when he wrote it.

Part II is about communication in distributed systems. Chapters 2 and 3 discuss communications support and language support for remote procedure call mechanisms.

The subject of Part III is naming and security, finding objects and services, controlling access to them, and authenticating communicating parties. Chapter 4 discusses the problems of designing very large, scalable name spaces. Chapters 5, 6 and 7 each describe a different aspect of computer security. Chapter 5 covers authentication. Chapter 6 describes another aspect of security in distributed systems: protecting objects from unauthorized access. Chapter 7 describes how accounting and resource control work in the Amoeba system.

The title of Part IV is Data Storage. The subject of data storage in distributed systems really encompasses both distributed file systems and distributed database systems. In this book we examine only distributed file systems. In Chapter 8, the Andrew file system is described after an overview of issues in distributed file system design and current work in the area.

In Part V, several aspects of transaction management are presented. Chapter 10 contains an introduction to transaction-processing techniques in distributed systems. How to use transactions is the subject of Chapter 11. Chapter 12 gives the theoretical background of nested transactions.

Part VI presents two viewpoints on replication. In Chapter 13, problems and solutions are discussed for maintaining replicated data consistent during network-partition failures. Chapters 14 and 15 introduce the notion of using reliable broadcast mechanisms for ordering events in a distributed system, such that each relevant site observes the same order of events.

In Part VII, Chapter 16 describes a methodology for program specification. After a simple example, a specification is discussed for the Grapevine system. Chapters 17, 18, and 19 are all about the Advanced Networked Systems Architecture, an architectural structure for distributed systems.

Part VIII concludes the book.

This book would not have been written if the Arctic '88 course had not been held. The programme committee for the course consisted of Otto Anshus of Tromsø University, Andrew Herbert, Sape Mullender and Liba Svobodova. They brought the team of lecturers together.

Teaching the course was made especially pleasant by the excellent local organization. The efforts of the local organization committee, Magnar Antonsen (the chairman), Tore Larsen, Dag Johansen, Otto Anshus and Terje Fallmyr.

Ken Birman also deserves to be mentioned. He organized the successor to Arctic '88, Fingerlakes '89 held at Cornell University. Fingerlakes '89 gave us the incentive to improve or rewrite the lecture notes for Arctic '88 and to finish the book quickly.

CONTENTS

Authors' Biographies

Kenneth P. Birman
Kenneth P. Birman is an Associate Professor of Computer Science in the Department of Computer Science at Cornell University. His main research interests are in the areas of distributed computing and fault-tolerance. As the head of the ISIS project, he developed a toolkit for distributed programming that is now in use at more than 200 sites worldwide. He has also worked extensively on medical computing problems, and developed systems for automated interpretation of human electrocardiograms, machine processing of radiology images, and medical database management.

Birman received his B.S. from Columbia University in 1978 and his Ph.D. from the University of California, Berkeley, in 1981. He worked as a visiting scientist with the Cardiology clinic of the University Hospital in Vienna for several months prior to joining Cornell in 1982. In 1988, Birman founded ISIS Distributed Systems, a small company providing software development and consulting services and support for the ISIS system, where he is currently President and CEO.

Susan B. Davidson
Susan B. Davidson received the B.A. degree in mathematics from Cornell University, Ithaca, NY, in 1978, and the M.A. and Ph.D. degrees in electrical engineering and computer science from Princeton University, Princeton, NJ, in 1980 and 1982 respectively. She is currently an Assistant Professor in the Department of Computer and Information Science at the University of Pennsylvania, Philadelphia, PA, where she has been since 1982. Her research interests in reliable distributed systems include database systems as well as real-time systems.

In distributed database systems, she has been concerned with maintaining the consistency of data, both during normal transaction processing and in the face of failures that partition the network into sets of nodes that cannot communicate. She has also developed an approach to generate approximate responses to queries when data is missing or incomplete, *e.g.*, in the presence of partition failures. The results are being applied to an ongoing project in heterogeneous distributed database systems, and also have application in time-constrained database systems.

Recently, she has collaborated in spearheading a real-time project in the Distributed Systems Lab at the University of Pennsylvania. The project includes developing models to capture the timing behavior of distributed processes, as well as developing a programming system for writing consistent, distributed real-time programs.

Andrew Herbert

Andrew J. Herbert heads the ANSA Project, a Cambridge-based industry consortium developing an Advanced Networked Systems Architecture. Prior to joining ANSA, he headed the Mayflower project and was a developer of the Cambridge Ring system in the Computer Laboratory at Cambridge University, where he is a Fellow of Wolfson College.

Andrew Herbert received his PhD from Cambridge University in 1978; his thesis was 'A Microprogrammed Operating System Kernel' and discussed a typed capability system, memory management and ipc in microcode on the CAP computer.

From 1978 to 1984, he was a Lecturer at the Cambridge University Computer Laboratory working on the implementation of the Cambridge Distributed System. A book on that system was written with Roger Needham. Herbert was responsible for initial versions of the Processor Bank management software and the Mayflower project (Concurrent CLU and RPC). Other interests were secure operating systems and object management for programming environments.

From 1985 to 1988, Andrew Herbert was Chief Architect of the UK Alvey Advanced Networked Systems Architecture Project. In 1989 he became Chief Architect of the ESPRIT II Integrated Systems Architecture Project and also Technical Director ESPRIT II Multiworks Project. He is a director of APM Ltd, a member of BCS, ACM, IEEE, the City of London Company of Information Technologists and a member of ISO/IEC JTC1 SC21 WG7 — the working group developing a reference model for Open Distributed Processing.

Sape J. Mullender

Dr. Sape J. Mullender studied at the Vrije Universiteit in Amsterdam. He received his Ph.D. there and was a faculty member from 1978 until 1983. Since 1984 he is the head of the distributed systems and computer networks research group at the Centre of Mathematics and Computer Science (CWI) in Amsterdam. With Prof. Andrew S. Tanenbaum, he designed the Amoeba distributed operating system. Amoeba is now a joint project of VU and CWI.

Sape Mullender is particularly interested in high-performance distributed computing and the design of scalable fault-tolerant services. He is also concerned about organization and protection in distributed systems that can span a continent.

In 1986—7 he was a visiting scientist at DEC's Systems Research Center in California, where he worked with Michael D. Schroeder on fast RPC protocols for the Firefly multiprocessor. He was a visiting research fellow at Cambridge University in 1987—8, where the foundations were laid for collaboration with the Cambridge University Computer Laboratory based on Amoeba.

He has published papers on file systems, high-performance RPC protocols, and locating migratable objects in computer networks, and protection mechanisms, and has lectured in more than a dozen countries. He is vice-chairman of the ACM Special Interest Group on Operating Systems.

Roger Needham

Roger M. Needham FRS is Professor of Computer Systems and Head of the Computer Laboratory at the University of Cambridge, England. He was an undergraduate in Mathematics and Philosophy at Cambridge, taking a conversion course, then called the Diploma in Numerical Analysis and Automatic Computing, in 1956—7. Since then he has been what is now known as a Computer Scientist.

In 1961 he obtained the Ph.D. Degree for work on the application of computers to problems of classification and grouping, and since then has worked in the systems area. He worked until 1968 on the Titan system, an early mutiple-access system which first provided integrated on-line and off-line working; he was involved all the way from the design automation for building the machine to planning the gross characteristics of the operating system and implementing parts of it. He has been credited with the idea, at that period, of storing password files under the protection of a one-way function.

Subsequently he led the CAP project, which designed and constructed a capability-based computer and operating system, in order to investigate techniques and effects in memory protection. In the course of this work he was promoted Reader in Computer Systems in 1973. The machine and system were completed by 1977, in which year he spent a sabbatical at Xerox PARC. While there he worked on authentication, leading to a well-known paper with M. D. Schroeder, and on the early planning and implementation of the Grapevine message system.

On returning to Cambridge he led the project to make the Cambridge Distributed Computing System, which relied on a processor bank rather than entirely on individual workstations. It is an idea more fashionable now than then. This was followed by Project Universe, which interconnected Cambridge Ring LAN's at various places by satellite, and Project Unison which interconnected geographically diverse LAN's by means of a pilot ISDN, giving very early experience of ATM communication. In 1981 he was promoted Professor, and was elected to the Royal Society in 1985. Since its foundation in 1984 he has been a regular visitor to the DEC Systems Research Center in Palo Alto Ca, and had the satisfaction in 1987 of completing there, together with M. Burrows and M. Abadi, some theoretical work on Authentication the need for which had been foreshadowed ten years earlier.

Mahadev Satyanarayanan

Mahadev Satyanarayanan is an Associate Professor of Computer Science at Carnegie Mellon University. His research addresses the problem of data sharing in large-scale distributed systems. His current work on the Coda File System investigates techniques to provide high availability without significant loss of performance or usability. Earlier, he was one of the principal architects and implementors of the Andrew File System, a location-transparent distributed file system that addressed issues of scale and security. His work on Scylla explored access to relational databases in a distributed workstation environment. His previous research included the design of the CMU-CFS file system, measurement and analysis of file usage data, and modelling of storage systems.

Professor Satyanarayanan received the Ph.D. in Computer Science from Carnegie Mellon, after a Bachelor's degree in Electrical Engineering and a Master's degree in Computer Science from the Indian Institute of Technology, Madras. He is a member of the ACM, IEEE, and Sigma Xi, and has been a consultant to industry and government. He received the NSF Presidential Young Investigator award in 1987.

Alfred Z. Spector

Dr. Alfred Z. Spector is an Associate Professor of computer science at Carnegie Mellon University. He obtained a Ph.D. in computer science at Stanford on the topic of multiprocessing architectures for local area computer networks and received an A.B. in applied mathematics from Harvard. Dr. Spector's interests are in operating systems, distributed systems, and database systems — particularly those requiring high reliability and availability. He helped to design the AFS file system and led the TABS Project, which focussed on distributed reliability. Dr. Spector also led the development of Camelot — the Carnegie Mellon Low Overhead Transaction System. Camelot runs on the Mach, Unix-compatible, operating system and provides support for a variety of applications requiring high data integrity and availability. Camelot provides most of the run-time environment for the Avalon language extensions, which further simplify the expression of reliable distributed programs.

In 1988, Dr. Spector directed CMU's Information Technology Center. While at the ITC, he focused on wide area file systems, which can provide multiple organizations with shared access to files. He also worked closely with the team developing object-oriented user interface toolkits.

Previously, Dr. Spector led a joint CMU-IBM contract on distributed systems and artificial intelligence; he was also a co-editor of the Communications of the ACM Case Studies Department and Program Chairman of the 1987 Symposium on Operating Systems. Currently, Dr. Spector is a member of the US Army Science Board, and he lectures widely. He is a member of ACM and IEEE.

William E. Weihl

William E. Weihl received the S.B. degree in Mathematics in 1979, the S.B. and
S.M. degrees in Computer Science in 1980, and the Ph.D. degree in Computer
Science in 1984, all from the Massachusetts Institute of Technology. In 1984 he
joined the faculty of the Massachusetts Institute of Technology, where he is
currently an Associate Professor of Computer Science and Engineering.

Dr. Weihl was one of the principal designers of the Argus programming
language and system, which is designed to support the construction of reliable
distributed systems, and the Mercury communications system, which is designed
to support efficient, flexible communication in heterogeneous distributed systems.
He has made significant contributions to the theory of atomic transactions, particularly in the design of highly concurrent type-specific concurrency control and
recovery algorithms. In joint work with Nancy Lynch, Michael Merritt, and
Alan Fekete, he has developed a theoretical framework for describing and
analyzing nested transaction systems.

Dr. Weihl's current research interests focus on parallel and distributed computing, particularly in the areas of programming methodology, programming
languages, specification techniques, synchronization, and fault-tolerance.

PART I

Introduction

Chapter 1

Introduction

S. J. Mullender

Based on a Lecture by

M. D. Schroeder

The first four decades of computer technology are each characterized by a different approach to the way computers were used. In the 1950s, programmers would reserve time on the computer and have the computer all to themselves while they were using it. In the 1960s, batch processing came about. People would submit their jobs which were queued for processing. They would be run one at a time and the owners would pick up their output later. Time-sharing became the way people used computers in the 1970s so that users could share a computer under the illusion that they had it to themselves. The 1980s are the decade of personal computing: people have their own dedicated machine on their desks.

The evolution that took place in operating systems has been made possible by a combination of economic considerations and technological developments. Batch systems could be developed because computer memories became large enough to hold an operating system as well as an application program; they were developed because they made it possible to make better use of expensive computer cycles. Time-sharing systems were desirable because they allow programmers to be more productive. They could be developed because computer cycles became cheaper and computers more powerful. Very large scale integration and the advent of local networks has made workstations an affordable alternative to time sharing, with the same guaranteed computer capacity at all times.

Today, a processor of sufficient power to serve most needs of a single person costs less than one tenth of a processor powerful enough to serve ten. Time sharing, in fact, is no longer always a satisfactory way to use a computer system: the arrival of bit-mapped displays with graphical interfaces demands instant visual feedback from the graphics subsystem, feedback which can only be provided by a dedicated, thus personal, processor.

The workstations of the 1990s will be even more powerful than those today. We foresee that a typical workstation will have a high-resolution colour display, and voice and video input and output devices. Network interfaces will allow communication at rates matching the requirements of several channels of real-time video transmission.

A time-sharing system provides the users with a single, shared environment which allows resources, such as printers, storage space, software and data to be shared. To provide users access to the services, workstations are often connected by a network and workstation operating-system software allows copying files and remote login over the network from one workstation to another. Users must know the difference between local and remote objects, and they must know at what machine remote objects are held. In large systems with many workstations this can become a serious problem.

The problem of system management is an enormous one. In the time-sharing days, the operators could back up the file system every night; the system administrators could allocate the available processor cycles where they were most needed, and the systems programmers could simply install new or improved software. In the workstation environment, however, each user must be an operator, a system administrator and a systems programmer. In a building with a hundred autonomous workstations, the operators can no longer go round making backups, and the systems programmers can no longer install new software by simply putting it on the file system.

Some solutions to these problems have been attempted, but none of the current solutions are as satisfactory as the shared environment of a time-sharing system. For example, a common and popular approach consists of the addition of network-copy commands with which files can be transferred from one work-station to another, or — as a slightly better alternative — of a *network file system*, which allows some real sharing of files. In all but very few solutions, however, the user is aware of the difference between local and remote operations. The real problem is that the traditional operating systems which still form the basis of today's workstation software were never designed for an environment with many processors and many file systems. For such environments a *distributed operating system* is required.

The 1990s will be the decade of distributed systems. In distributed systems, the user makes no distinction between local and remote operations. Programs do not necessarily execute on the workstation where the command to run them was given. There is one file system, shared by all the users. Peripherals can be shared. Processors can be allocated dynamically where the resource is needed most.

A distributed system is a system with many processing elements and many storage devices, connected together by a network. Potentially, this makes a distributed system more powerful than a conventional, centralized one in two ways. First, it can be more reliable, because every function is replicated several times.

When one processor fails, another can take over the work. Each file can be stored on several disks, so a disk crash does not destroy any information. Second, a distributed system can do more work in the same amount of time, because many computations can be carried out in parallel.

These two properties, *fault tolerance* and *parallelism* give a distributed system the potential to be much more powerful than a traditional operating system. In distributed systems projects around the world, researchers attempt to build systems that are fault tolerant and exploit parallelism.

1.1 Symptoms of a distributed system

The fundamental properties of a distributed system are *fault tolerance* and the possibility to use *parallelism*. What does a system have to have in order to be 'distributed'? How does one recognize a distributed system?

Definitions are hard to give. Lamport was once heard to say: 'A distributed system is one that stops you from getting any work done when a machine you've never even heard of crashes.' More seriously, Tanenbaum and van Renesse (1985) give the following definition:

> A *distributed* operating system is one that looks to its users like an ordinary centralized operating system, but runs on multiple, independent CPUs. The key concept here is *transparency,* in other words, the use of multiple processors should be invisible (transparent) to the user. Another way of expressing the same idea is to say that the user views the system as a 'virtual uniprocessor', not as a collection of distinct machines.

According to this definition, a *multiprocessor operating system*, such, as versions of Unix for Encore or Sequent multiprocessors would be distributed operating systems. Even dual-processor configurations of the IBM 360, or CDC number crunchers of many years ago would satisfy the definition, since one cannot tell whether a program runs on the master or slave processor.

Tanenbaum and van Renesse's definition gives a necessary condition for a distributed operating system, but I believe it is not a sufficient one. A distributed operating system also must not have any *single points of failure* — no single part failing should should bring the whole system down.

This is not an easy condition to fulfill in practice. Just for starters, it means a distributed system should have many power supplies; if it had only one, and it failed, the whole system would stop. If you count a fire in the computer room as a failure, it should not even be in one physical place, but it should be geographically distributed.

But one can carry failure transparency too far. If the power fails in our building, I can tolerate my system failing, provided it fails cleanly and I don't lose the work I have just been doing — one can't work very well in the dark anyway.

It is dangerous to attempt an exact definition of a distributed system. Instead, Schroeder gave a list of *symptoms* of a distributed system. If your system has all of the symptoms listed below, it is probably a distributed system. If it does not exhibit one or more of the symptoms, it probably isn't one.

A distributed system has to be capable of continuing in the face of single-point failures and of parallel execution, so it must have

● *Multiple processing elements,*

that can run independently. Therefore, each processing element, or *node* must contain at least a CPU and memory.

There has to be communication between the processing elements, so a distributed system must have

● *Interconnection hardware*

which allows processes running in parallel to communicate and synchronize.

A distributed system cannot be fault tolerant if all nodes always fail simultaneously. The system must be structured in such a way that

● *Processing elements fail independently.*

In practice, this implies that the interconnections are unreliable as well. When a node fails, it is likely that messages will be lost.

Finally, in order to recover from failures, it is necessary that the nodes keep

● *Shared state*

for the distributed system. If this were not done, a node failure would cause some part of the system's state to be lost.

To see more clearly what constitutes a distributed system, we shall look at some examples of systems.

Multiprocessor computer with shared memory
A shared-memory multiprocessor has several of the characteristics of a distributed system. It has multiple processing elements, and an interconnect via shared memory, interprocessor interrupt mechanisms and a memory bus. The communication between processing elements is reliable, but this does not in itself mean that a multiprocessor cannot be considered as a distributed system. What disqualifies multiprocessors is that there is no independent failure: when one processor crashes, the whole system stops working. However, it may well be that manufacturers, inspired by distributed systems research, will design multiprocessors that are capable of coping with partial failure; to my knowledge, only Tandem manufactures such machines, currently.

Ethernet with packet-filtering bridges
A bridge is a processor with local memory that can send and receive packets on two Ethernet segments. The bridges are interconnected via these segments and they share state which is necessary for routing packets over the internet formed by the bridges and the cable segments. When a bridge fails, or when one is

added to or removed from the network, the other bridges detect this and modify their routing tables to take the changed circumstances into account. Therefore, an Ethernet with packet-filtering bridges *can* be viewed as a distributed system.

Diskless workstations with NFS† file servers

Each workstation and file server has a processor and memory, and a network interconnects the machines. Workstations and servers fail independently: when a workstation crashes, the other workstations and the file servers continue to work. When a file server crashes, its client workstations do not crash (although client processes may hang until the server comes back up). But there is no shared state: when a server crashes, the information in it is inaccessible until the server comes back up; and when a client crashes, all of its internal state is lost. A network of diskless workstations using NFS file servers, therefore, is *not* a distributed system.

1.2 Why build distributed systems?

People are distributed, information is distributed

Distributed systems often evolve from networks of workstations. The owners of the workstations connect their systems together because of a desire to communicate and to share informations and resources.

Information generated in one place is often needed in another. This book illustrates the point: it was written by a number of authors in different countries who needed to interact by reading each other's material and discussing issues in order to achieve some coherence.

Performance/cost

The cost of a computer depends on its performance in terms of processor speed and the amount of memory it has. The costs of both processors and of memories are generally going down. Each year, the same money, buys a more powerful workstation. That is, in real terms, computers are getting cheaper and cheaper.

The cost of communication depends on the bandwidth of the communication channel and the length of the channel. Bandwidth increases, but not beyond the limits set by the cables and interfaces used. Wide area network cables have to be used for decades, because exchanging them is extremely expensive. Communication costs, therefore, are going down much less rapidly than computer costs.

As computers become more powerful, demands on the man-machine bandwidth go up. Five or ten years ago, most computer users had a terminal on their desk, capable of displaying 24 lines of text containing 80 characters. The communication speed between computer and terminal was 1000 characters per second at most. Today, we consider a bit-mapped display as normal, even a colour display is hardly luxury any more. The communication speed between

† NFS stands for SUN Microsystems' Network File System.

computer and screen has gone up a few orders of magnitude, especially in graphical applications. Soon, voice and animation will be used on workstations, increasing the man-machine bandwidth even more.

Man-machine interfaces are also becoming more interactive. Users want instant visual (or audible) feedback from their user interface, and the latency caused by distances of more than a few kilometres of network is often too high already.

These effects make distributed systems not only economic, but necessary. No centralized computer could give the required number of cycles to its customers and the cost of the network technology that gets the required number of bits per second out to the user's screen is prohibitive.

Modularity
In a distributed system, interfaces between parts of the system have to be much more carefully designed than in a centralized system. As a consequence, distributed systems must be built in a much more modular fashion than centralized systems. One of the things that one typically does in a distributed system is to run important services on their own machines. The interface between modules are usually remote procedure call interfaces, which automatically impose a certain standard for inter-module interfaces.

Expandability
Distributed systems are capable of incremental growth. To increase the storage or processing capacity of a distributed system, one can add file servers or processors one at a time.

Availability
Since distributed systems replicate data and have built-in redundancy in all resources that can fail, distributed systems have the potential to be available even when arbitrary (single-point) failures occur.

Scalability
The capacity of any centralized components of a system imposes a limit for the system's maximum size. Ideally, distributed systems have no centralized components, so that this restriction on the maximum size the system can grow to does not exist. Naturally, there can be many other factors that restrict a system's scalability, but distributed system designers do their best to choose algorithms that scale to very large numbers of components.

Reliability
Availability is but one aspect of reliability. A reliable system must not only be available, but it must do what it claims to do correctly, even when failures occur. The algorithms used in a distributed system must not behave correctly only when the underlying virtual machine functions correctly, they must also be capable of recovering from failures in the underlying virtual machine environment.

1.3 The complexity of distributed systems

The main reason that the design of distributed systems is so hard is that the enormous complexity of these systems is still well beyond our understanding. However, we now understand many aspects of distributed systems and many sources of complexity. We also know how to deal with quite a few of these sources of complexity, but we are still a long way from really understanding how to design and build reliable distributed systems. What causes the extraordinary complexity of distributed systems?

One can answer this question to some extent by comparing distributed computer systems to the railway system, another 'distributed system' that most people are familiar with. The railway system as we know it today has taken a century and a half to develop into a safe and reliable transport service. It took time before the complexity of the railway system was understood. The development of its safety has been at the cost of errors and mistakes that have cost many lives. It is often the case that, only after the fact, it is discovered that an accident was caused by a perfectly obvious design oversight — yet nobody had seen it beforehand.

Distributed computer systems have only been around for a decade or so, but they are every bit as complicated to design as national railway networks and it will take many generations of distributed systems before we can hope to understand how to build one properly. Just as the railway system has become safe only at the cost of many accidents, so distributed systems only become reliable and fault-tolerant at the cost of many system crashes, discovering design bugs and learning about system behaviour by trial and error.

The basic source of the complexity of distributed systems is that an interconnection of well-understood components can generate new problems not apparent in the components. These problems then produce complexity beyond our limits of methodical understanding. Much of this complexity is apparent though the unexpected behaviour of systems that we believe we understand.

As an illustration of unexpected behaviour consider the well-known fairness of the token ring network (Saltzer and Pogran (1980)). In this network, a station may obtain the token to send one packet at a time; then the other stations get an opportunity to send a packet if they have one. It would appear that station A sending a large, multi-packet message to a server S cannot lock out B from sending a message simultaneously. It turned out the unexpected behaviour had nothing to do with the principle of the token ring, but with the design of the token-ring interface board. Sventek et al. (1983) discovered that the receive circuitry of the interface board misses a packet when it immediately follows another one. This leads to the following scenario.

1. A sends the first packet of a message to S, which is received successfully.

2. B sends the first packet of a message to S, immediately behind A's packet, but it is ignored because it is too close behind the previous packet.

3. *A* sends the second packet immediately behind *B*'s first packet. Again, *A*'s packet is received, because *S* has recovered from *A*'s first packet by now.

4. *B* sends the second packet or retransmits the first (token rings often have a *packet-seen* bit which tells the sender whether the receiving interface has accepted the packet). In either case, *S* ignores the packet again because it immediately follows *A*'s second packet.

This goes on, of course, and the effect is that *B* is totally locked out from sending because the intended fairness of the token ring actually guarantees that *A* and *B* send alternate packets; *A*'s packets are always received and *B*'s packets are never received.

The above example nicely illustrates the sort of problems to which combinations of well-understood components can lead. In this case, the token protocol was well understood and the receive interface too, but the combination of the two caused an effect that wasn't foreseen by the designers.

In some cases, formal methods can be used to help predict what will happen when two systems are interconnected. However, these methods are only of limited help, especially when we don't understand the systems or the interconnection incompletely, or when we do not have the tools to describe them formally.

Complexity limits what we can build. Schroeder calls the problems caused by this complexity *systems problems*. Some examples of systems problems are:

- **Interconnection**: A very large number of systems problems come about when components that previously operated independently are interconnected. This has been very visible when various computer networks for electronic mail were interconnected (the Unix mail system, the Bitnet mail system, X.400, to name a few). Interconnection problems also had to be solved when it became desirable to connect the file systems of different Unix machines.

- **Interference**: Two components in a system, each with reasonable behaviour when viewed in isolation, may exhibit unwanted behaviour when combined. The problem in the token-ring example above is an example of unexpected interference of the properties of the token-passing protocol and the receive circuitry of the network interfaces.

- **Propagation of effect**: Failures in one component can bring down a whole network when system designers aren't careful enough. Two examples from the ARPANET can serve to illustrate this. A malfunctioning IMP (a message-processing node of the network) announced to its neighbours that it had zero delay to every other node in the network. Within minutes, large numbers of nodes started sending all their traffic to the malfunctioning node, bringing the network down. Another time, an east-coast node, due to an error, used the network address of a west-coast node, causing major upheaval in the network. Obviously, design effort is required to localize the effect of failures as much as possible.

- **Effects of scale**: A system that works well with ten nodes may fail miserably when it grows to a hundred nodes. This is usually caused by some resource that doesn't scale up with the rest of the system and becomes a bottleneck, or by the use of algorithms that do not scale up. The Grapevine system, developed at Xerox PARC (Birrell *et al.* (1982)), is an excellent example of a system that grew to the limits imposed by its design, and perhaps a little beyond. This is described in Birrell *et al.* (1984).

- **Partial failure**: The fundamental difference between traditional, centralized systems and distributed systems is that in a distributed system a component may fail, but the rest of the system continues to work. In order to exploit the potential fault tolerance of a distributed system, it is necessary that a distributed application is prepared to deal with partial failures. Needless to say, this is a considerable source of additional complexity in the design of fault-tolerant applications.

To some extent, all of these problems exist in all computer systems, but they are much more apparent in distributed systems: there are just more pieces, hence more interference, more interconnections, more opportunities for propagation of effect, and more kinds of partial failure.

1.3.1 Functional requirements as a source of complexity

Distributed systems are complex because what they have to do is complex. To illustrate this, we return to our railway example: Just outside Mike Schroeder's office in Palo Alto, California is the Palo Alto station on the San Francisco to San Jose line, which caters to commuter traffic in the Bay Area. The schedule for these trains is a straightforward one to design: the trains run at a frequency that depends primarily on the average number of travellers at each time of day.

My institute, the Centre for Mathematics and Computer Science in Amsterdam, Netherlands, commands a view of a railroad switching yard and the Amsterdam to Amersfoort line. This line forms part of a dense national railway network with hundreds of stations on dozens of lines. Here, the train schedules are complicated by a few orders of magnitude by the requirement that passengers have to change trains to reach their destination and that they usually expect that connecting trains are synchronized to within a few minutes.

The Dutch railway system has more demanding functional requirements (people travel in a two-dimensional mesh network rather than on a straight line) and therefore a more complex train schedule. The difference in complexity is enormous; it increases much more rapidly than linear with the number of lines.

As another example, consider three file systems, one for a stand-alone personal computer, one for a time-sharing system and one for a highly-available distributed system.

Designing the PC file system involves a certain amount of complexity, of course, but designing the time-sharing system file system involves a large amount of additional complexity. Here, there are issues of authentication, access control, maintaining quota, concurrency control for read/write sharing, and many others.

The distributed file system has to be more complex again so that it can meet the additional requirements of a highly available fault-tolerant file system: mechanisms for file location, coordination of replicated server state, recovery mechanisms from partitions or partial failure, and so forth.

Again, a longer list of functional requirements causes a large increase in complexity of the resulting system. The complexity of distributed systems stems to a large extent from the requirements of fault-tolerance, availability, scalability and performance which we impose.

1.3.2 Economic necessity as a source of complexity

Another source of complexity is that the simple solution cannot always be used: sometimes it is too expensive. Again, the railway serves to illustrate the notion of complexity caused by economic necessity. A single-track railroad through the mountains has a high uni-directional capacity — one can probably run a train every fifteen minutes — but a very long latency to reverse flow. Before a train can go in the other direction, the track must be empty. If the railroad is a long one, this can take many hours.

There are two ways to reduce the time needed to reverse traffic and increase the bi-directional capacity. The simple one is to double the tracks from beginning to end. Traffic in one direction is then independent of the traffic in the other direction. In fact, the operation of the line becomes even simpler than before: reversing traffic does not require co-ordination between the end points in order to know how many trains are still on the way.

Laying double tracks along the length of a mountain line is extremely expensive, so the most economic solution is to build a number of passing sidings in the track. This complicates the operation of the line considerably, however. The trains have to be carefully scheduled, signals are needed to tell the train drivers when they can go, there are limits on the length of trains, there is a risk of deadlock and there is a higher risk of collision.

Examples of complexity for reasons of economy abound in computer systems as well. Most time-sharing computer systems have paged virtual memory, because real memory for peak demand is too expensive; real memory for the working sets of active programs is affordable.

Long-haul networks are usually mesh networks, because fully interconnected networks are very much more expensive. Again the price is increased complexity: routing algorithms have to be designed, buffering is necessary to manage merging traffic, and flow-control mechanisms must prevent traffic between two nodes from blocking traffic between other nodes.

1.4 Useful techniques for building a distributed system

This chapter ends with a list of techniques that are important in building distributed systems. The list is by no means complete — we have probably missed some essential ones — but it is a useful list of techniques that may be applied where appropriate.

Replicate to increase availability
Once it is stated in black and white, *'replicate to increase availability'*, it becomes obvious. A single copy of something is not available when the machine it is on is down. The only way to make a service, a data item, or a network connection available across machine crashes and network failures is to replicate it.

Replicating non-changing data or stateless services is trivial. The data item can be copied any number of times, and one can bring up as many servers as one pleases. Since the data item is immutable, and the service is stateless, no information needs to be exchanged between the replicas when they are accessed.

Unfortunately, data often does change, and nearly all useful services have state. Even so-called stateless file servers (SUN's NFS is an example) have state: the contents of the files. The statelessness refers to protocol state, not file state. When one replica changes without the others, they become *inconsistent*. Accessing one replica is no longer the same as accessing another. This may or may not be a problem, but it certainly needs a system designer's attention.

Guaranteeing consistency while at the same time maintaining a large degree of availability is a very difficult problem. The most trivial algorithm for maintaining consistency is to lock every replica before an update, to update every replica and to unlock each one again, but obviously, this makes availability worse than that of a single copy — every replica must be working in order to make progress. Part VI is devoted to replication and the consistency versus availability problem is addressed there.

Trade off availability against consistency
There is a trade off between availability and consistency. In some cases, it is all right to sacrifice some availability to achieve absolute consistency — one often has to, anyway — while in other cases some (controlled) inconsistencies can be allowed to achieve better availability.

An example of a service where some consistency may be sacrificed for better availability is the electronic equivalent of the phone book: a network name service. Phone books are out of date by the time they land on the doormat, but people can live with them quite comfortably — if the number in the phone book turns out to be invalid, one can always call directory information. The same applies to the network name service. It usually maps things like mailboxes to machine addresses, and, if someone moves from one machine to another, the change of address does not reach all replicas of the directory simultaneously. But this doesn't matter: when an old address is used, there is usually a forwarding address to the correct site, and if there isn't, other, more up-to-date versions of the directory service can be consulted, or an enquiry can even be broadcast to all name servers.

Cache hints if possible
One of the most useful examples of a trade off between availability and consistency is a cache of hints. A hint is the saved result of some operation that is stored away so that carrying out the operation again can be avoided by using the hint. There are two additional important things to note about hints:

1. A hint may be wrong (obsolete), and

2. When a wrong hint is used, it will be found out in time (and the hint can be corrected).

Since the operation that was saved as a hint can always be redone, hints can safely be cached. When a hint is dropped from the cache, the operation will just have to be redone to reproduce the hint.

The telephone directory mentioned earlier is an excellent example of a whole book full of hints. The number behind someone's name has all the properties of a hint: It may be wrong, but when it is used, one finds out that it's wrong. The correct number can then be found through a forwarding address or directory information.

In distributed systems, there are many examples of hints. The current network addresses of all sorts of services are often kept as hints (which become obsolete when a server crashes or migrates). The absence of a carrier on a broadcast network cable is a hint that the cable is free and that no other station is currently sending. If this hint proves wrong, there will be a collision.

Hints are often very easy to use and can result in staggering performance improvements in distributed systems. This makes hints a vital technique in designing and building high-performance distributed systems.

Use stashing to allow autonomous operation
The word *stash* was first used by Birrell and Schroeder at the 1988 ACM SIGOPS workshop in Cambridge. I quote from Schroeder's position paper:

> 'Stashing' is just a name for a class of techniques many of us have used in our systems over the years. It simply refers to keeping local copies of key information for use when remote information is not available. By recognizing the general technique, however, we can discover systematic ways to apply it.
>
> The application of stashing I know so far is naming and authentication information. To stash name server information, a client always tries the remote service first. When the service is available (the usual case), then the answer is remembered locally in a stash. Whenever the service fails to respond, the local stash is used instead, even though it may be out of date.

> So a stash is like a cache, except it has strange replacement policy. For small, slowly changing information, like the rootiest information from a global naming hierarchy, stashing would be easy to manage.

When stashing is used, a client machine can continue to make some useful progress when it is separated from normally essential network services (such as authentication service, file service, name service). The client machine cannot always proceed — files that are not stashed are not accessible when the file service is down — but at least some work can continue while the machine is cut off from networked services.

Exploit locality with caches

The cache is yet another way of keeping local copies of remote data. Stashed information may be stale and hints may be wrong, but cached information has to be correct. A cache is a local copy of remote data. Sometimes the remote data is updated more slowly than the cached data; sometimes both remote data and cache are updated simultaneously. This depends on the nature of the data, the way the data is shared and the frequency of updates.

Caching, stashing and using hints are three techniques for improving system performance by avoidance of remote accesses. Without them, distributed systems are almost necessarily painfully slow: a distributed system does more than a centralized one and the data and services are farther away. With caching, remote data can be accessed with virtually the same efficiency as local data.

When information is used from the cache, one has to make sure that the cached information is up to date. Cache-coherence protocols are used for this. Depending on the expected amount of sharing and the expected kinds of sharing, different cache-coherence protocols may be appropriate. In Part IV about file systems and Part VI about replication, caching and cache coherence will be discussed further.

Use timeouts for revocation

There are many cases in distributed systems where a process locks up some resource while using it. When the process or its host crashes, the resource may be rendered inaccessible to others. As a general principle, it is a good idea to use timeouts on the locking up of resources. Clients must then refresh their locks periodically or they will lose them. The refresh frequency must be short enough and the timeout period long enough that the likelihood of having the lock taken away before it can be renewed is negligible.

One example where such a mechanism is useful is in servers using caching. Timers can be used in several ways in this context. One way is to give a caching client a shared read lock or an exclusive write lock, depending on whether it makes read or write accesses (Burrows (1988)). If the client crashes, the locks automatically break, allowing other clients to access the file. If the server crashes, the client will notice when trying to refresh its lock. It can then stash the file until the server comes back to life. If another client attempts to set a conflicting lock, a refresh from the first client could be denied.

Another way of using timers in a caching server is to use timers on the expiration of validity of cached data (Lampson (1986)). Essentially, the service tells a caching client: 'This data is good until such-and-such a time.' This is not very useful in a file system, but works quite well in a name server that, for instance, maps human names to mailboxes.

Use a standard remote invocation mechanism ·
There are many ways of invoking remote services. Current Unix systems illustrate this abundantly. One can do remote login, run a single command on a remote machine, invoke a file transfer to or from a remote machine, or invoke a specialized service by sending a message to a *daemon* on the remote machine (for example, *finger, rwho, ruptime*).

This not only leads to security flaws (see the 'worm' incident described in Chapter 20), but also to ineffective interfaces and complicated systems. Distributed systems usually provide only a few remote invocation mechanisms, and some provide only one.

Mike Schroeder and I both work on a system with a single remote invocation mechanism, remote procedure call, and believe that it is sufficient. RPC is simple and can be made to run very efficiently (van Renesse, van Staveren, and Tanenbaum (1988)).

Only trust programs on physically secure machines
Machines that are not physically secure can be tampered with. They can be made to bootstrap a version of the operating system that has been tampered with (if the boot ROM should incorporate an authentication mechanism, the boot ROM can be replaced; then the system can be brought up from a boot server running on the machine of a malicious user). Unfortunately, no secure bootstrap protocols have been designed for diskless workstations yet, so, for the time being, any diskless machine that is not on a physically secure network is in danger of being bootstrapped by a malicious user's kernel, even if the machine itself is in a physically secure place.

When a corrupted operating system runs on a machine, no process running on that machine is safe. Processes can be traced and keys used for authentication or data encryption can be found. This is why trusted servers must always run on trusted machines, and trusted machines must always be kept in physically secure places.

Use encryption for authentication and data security
Anything that appears on the network stops being a secret unless it is encrypted. Most local network interfaces allow machines to set their own network address and to receive every packet on the network. Thus, network addresses cannot be used to authenticate services (even if they run on a secure machine), and passwords for authentication can only be used once, because they stop being secret the moment they are used. Authentication protocols have to be used which use encryption to protect shared secrets from becoming public knowledge.

Try to prove distributed algorithms
Formal correctness proofs are gaining popularity. A variety of techniques now exists, some of which can deal with quite complicated algorithms. Reasoning about the correctness of a sequential algorithm is hard, but reasoning about the correctness of a parallel algorithm is virtually impossible. Examples of formal methods can be found in this book. In Chapter 5, Needham describes the use of formal methods in proving the correctness of authentication algorithms. In Chapter 11, a theory of nested transactions is presented by Weihl. In Chapter 15, Weihl then discusses specification methods for distributed programs.

But correctness proofs by themselves are not sufficient to guarantee that distributed programs are correct. After all, algorithms deal with an idealized world; the program has to deal with the real world. The boundary conditions used in a proof may not correspond to the real thing. Unexpected failures may occur, which the model did not take into account.

Building a reliable distributed system requires a combination of techniques; using formal methods is one of them, but testing is another that must always be used.

Capabilities are useful
The almost universal standard for academic computing these days is Unix. It uses access control lists (ACLs) for protection. When one is used to this model for protection, the alternative model, capability lists, does not come readily to mind. Yet, there is much to be said for using capability lists in distributed systems, especially if capabilities are objects managed in user space.

One benefit of using capabilities is that by holding a capability a client proves certain access rights to an object without any need for further authentication. Another, even greater benefit is that, in a capability system, a protection mechanism comes readily made with each service that is implemented. Server code needs only check a capability presented to it for validity — which can be done by a standard library package — before carrying out an operation. No separate authentication procedures need be carried out, nor need a service keep records of who can access what objects and how.

1.5 References

A. D. Birrell, R. Levin, R. M. Needham, and M. Schroeder (1982). 'Grapevine: An Exercise in Distributed Computing'. *Communications of the ACM* **25**: 260—274, April 1982.

A. D. Birrell, R. Levin, R. M. Needham, and M. Schroeder (1984). 'Experience with Grapevine: The Growth of a Distributed System'. *ACM Transactions on Computer Systems* **2**: 3—23, Feb. 1984.

M. Burrows (1988). *Efficient Data Sharing*. Ph.D. Thesis, Cambridge University Computer Laboratory, September 1988. (Also available as Technical Report No. 153, December 1988.)

B. Lampson (1986). 'Designing a Global Name Service'. *Proceedings 5th ACM Symposium on Principles of Distributed Computing*: 1—10, Calgary, Canada, Aug. 1986. (1985 Invited Talk.)

J. H. Saltzer and K. T. Pogran (1980). 'A Star-Shaped Ring Network with High Maintainability'. *Computer Networks* 4: 239—244, 1980.

J. Sventek, W. Greiman, M. O'Dell, and A. Jansen (1983). *Token Ring Local Networks — A Comparison of Experimental and Theoretical Performance*. Lawrence Berkeley Laboratory Report 16254, 1983.

A. S. Tanenbaum and R. van Renesse (1985). 'Distributed Operating Systems'. *ACM Computing Surveys* 17 (4): 419—470, December 1985.

R. van Renesse, H. van Staveren, and A. S. Tanenbaum (1988). 'Performance of the World's Fastest Distributed Operating System'. *Operating System Review* 22 (4): 25—34, October 1988.

Chapter 2

Achieving Application Requirements on Distributed Systems Architectures

A. Z. Spector

In this chapter the primary goals that distributed applications aim to meet, and some of the major implementation techniques that they use are described. Also described are the characteristics of the underlying distributed system architecture that most influence the implementation of distributed programs. Overall, this chapter is a start toward categorizing application goals, distributed programming paradigms, and architectural constraints. This categorization is done by presenting a collection of axes that categorize the space of distributed systems architectures, a list of key distributed application requirements, and a partial list of key distributed programming paradigms. These include parallel decomposition, data sharing, function shipping, and replication.

2.1 Introduction

This chapter defines the primary goals for distributed programs and lists some of the major implementation techniques used to achieve those goals. It also describes how the characteristics of an underlying distributed system architecture influence the implementation techniques used in distributed programs. Overall,

This research was sponsored by IBM and the Defense Advanced Research Projects Agency (DOD), ARPA Order No. 4864 (Amendment 20), under contract F33615-87-C-1499 monitored by the Avionics Laboratory, Air Force Wright Aeronautical Laboratories, Wright-Patterson AFB.

The views and conclusions contained in this chapter are those of the authors and should not be interpreted as representing the official policies, either expressed or implied, of any of the sponsoring agencies or the United States government.

this chapter attempts to provide insight as to how systems designers fulfill particular application requirements given particular system constraints. The chapter
is based on the belief that, first, practicing system designers categorize applications and underlying systems along a few simple dimensions and, second, that
systems designers use this categorization to select among a number of programming paradigms.

Of course, it is theoretically possible to implement any distributed programming paradigm on almost any base distributed architecture. Knowledge of communication and memory primitives is sufficiently good that almost any abstractions that a program may need can be synthesized. For example, procedure
calls and message passing can be implemented in terms of each other (Lauer
and Needham (1979)). The same holds true for shared memory and message
passing (Young *et al.* (1987)). But realistically, application requirements can
only be met if distributed programs have a structure that is well matched to the
underlying hardware architecture. The term 'well matched' has previously been
used to describe the situation where a parallel and distributed program is able to
execute efficiently on particular base architecture (Jones and Schwarz (1980);
Spector (1981)).

Consider the effect of a communication mechanism with high latency — that
is, a large delay between when an inter-node message is sent and received. High
delays tend to make many types of synchronous communication very costly,
since the sender must wait the duration of the round-trip communication before
continuing. This, in turn, can render many applications requiring fine-grained
synchronization or real time response impractical. This chapter will discuss
issues such as these in greater detail, though not quantitatively. (The exact performance impact is difficult to describe generally, since it depends greatly on the
specifics of the application and the underlying architecture.)

This analysis will proceed using a very simple model that contains two primary layers (Figure 2.1):

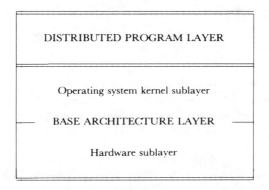

Figure 2.1 Distributed system model.

- **A base architecture layer**, which is further decomposed into a hardware layer, comprising processing nodes and inter-node communication; and an operating system kernel layer, supporting threads of control, address spaces, processor multiplexing, inter-process communication, and the like.

- **A distributed program layer**, which implements distributed and non-distributed algorithms necessary to meet application specifications.

Usually, both the operating system kernel and distributed programming layers are further subdivided. Here, this subdivision is unnecessary since this chapter explores only the relationship between the distributed computing paradigms of the one layer and the functions/performance of the other. (See Spector (1989) for a more complete architectural decomposition of distributed systems.)

Section 2.2 defines the base architecture and its most important characteristics. Section 2.3 summarizes the common requirements of distributed applications. Section 2.4 describes a collection of distributed program paradigms that permit application requirements to be met on various hardware architectures. Section 2.5 summarizes the lessons of this analysis.

2.2 Base architecture

The hardware base comprises processing nodes and a communication network, as illustrated in Figure 2.2. Processing nodes are a single failure domain, that is, a node crashes and is restarted as a whole. (Failures that are masked within the operation of a processing node are not considered.) Processing nodes may or may not be fail-fast; if they are, they will halt rather than perform erroneous computations. Processing nodes may be either uni- or multiprocessors. Multiprocessors may use either shared memory or message passing.

In general, there may be many types of processing node on the same distributed system. Processing nodes may or may not have independent failure modes. The hardware base may be packaged within a single cabinet, geographically dispersed around the globe, or anything in between.

All processing nodes have volatile storage — where portions of objects reside when they are being accessed. Nodes may also have non-volatile storage — where objects reside when they have not been accessed recently, and stable storage — memory that is assumed to retain information despite failures. The contents of volatile storage are lost after a system crash, and the contents of non-volatile storage may also be lost, though with lower probability. Volatile and non-volatile storage failures may or may not fail in a detectable fashion. Stable storage can be implemented using two non-volatile storage units on a node (Lampson (1981)) or using a network service (Daniels, Spector, and Thompson (1987)).

The hardware base also includes a communication network, that provides a peer-to-peer delivery service; for example, a Level 4 datagram-oriented service such as the Arpanet IP protocol (Postel (1982)). The network comprises both

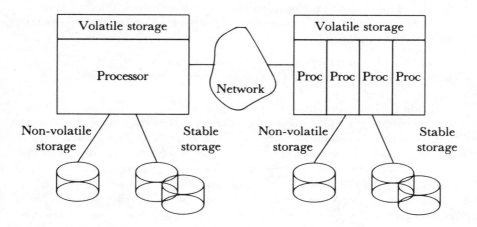

Figure 2.2 This figure shows the components of the hardware base. Non-volatile and stable storage may not be present on some nodes. Stable storage and non-volatile storage do not necessarily have to be implemented on local disks.

long-haul and local components (including, perhaps, a specialized local interconnection mechanism such as that of a Tandem Node or a VAXcluster (Bartlett (1981); Kronenberg, Levy, and Strecker (1986))). I shall assume the network provides full connectivity. Network partitions may occur with varying probabilities, depending on how the network is implemented.

The operating system kernel layer implements protected address spaces, threads of control, local synchronization, and local and remote communication between threads of control. Examples of such kernels are the Amoeba, Mach, Quicksilver, and V kernels (Accetta *et al.* (1986); Cheriton (1984); Haskin *et al.* (1988); Mullender (1985)). I shall assume that the operating system kernel supports both synchronous and asynchronous calls to protected objects, both local and remote. These may be protected procedure calls, remote procedure calls, remote procedure calls having no response, etc. (Gifford and Glasser (1988); Spector (1982)). Base architectures can be characterized along a number of axes, which describe performance, reliability, and functionality. Below, I list the axes that have the greatest influence on the design of distributed programs. Individual points on the axes are often vectors, which characterize various subcases (for example, local versus distributed operation) or probability distributions, which describe stochastic behavior (such as delays on networks).

1. **Communication-related axes**

    a. *Processor overhead for calling another thread of control* describes the overhead for inter-thread communication, whether local or remote. It describes

the processor overhead for local or inter-node messages, remote procedure calls (RPCs), and accesses to a multiprocessor's shared memory.
Note that the performance of shared memories may differ greatly from
the performance of local memories, due to differences in interconnection
and memory caching. Shared memory performance is also affected by
special processing in the kernel layer, such as extra translation look-
aside buffer flushes.

b. *Elapsed time for synchronously calling another thread of control* includes Item 1a,
but also includes asynchronous I/O transfer times across a network or
memory system. The variance in this measure also affects the ability to
provide clocks which are synchronized on all nodes of a distributed system. (Some distributed systems could use a specialized, low latency network for disseminating time information.)

c. *Communication bandwidth* characterizes the available data transmission
throughput between any two communicating threads, local or remote.

d. *Network distance* describes the geographic distances over which nodes can
be spread. It is of interest in addition to Item 1b, because it characterizes the ability to support sharing over large distances. The distance
over which nodes are spread can also affect failure independence (Item
2c) and the need for processing node autonomy (Item 5b).

2. **Failure-related axes**

a. *Failure and repair rate* describes the failure rates of processing nodes and
their communication network. Failure and repair rates are often
characterized by probability distributions which describe the mean time
between failures and the mean time to repair. Failures include crashes,
data lost from non-volatile or volatile memory, lost packets, and network partitions.

b. *Processor and storage integrity* specifies whether processor nodes are fail-fast
and whether storage fails only in detectable ways.

c. *Failure independence* specifies how failures affect the operation of the system, for example, whether a single failure can cripple multiple processing nodes or all communication.

d. *Availability of stable storage* specifies whether processing nodes have storage
available that survives all anticipated failures.

3. **Processing parallelism-related axes**

a. *Number of processors on a processing node* is a measure of the available CPU
parallelism on a node.

b. *Number of nodes on the network* is a measure of the available inter-node parallelism on a network. The number of nodes also influences the feasibility of replication.

4. **Other performance-related axes**

a. *Performance of processing nodes* describes the performance of processors and their primary memory capacity.

b. *Access latency and bandwidth of stable storage* describes the delay associated with synchronous reads or writes, and the feasible streaming data rates.

c. *Access latency and bandwidth of other secondary storage* describes the delay associated with synchronous read or write requests, and the feasible streaming data rates.

5. **Other axes**

a. *Homogeneity of processor nodes* describes the degree to which processor nodes are substitutable for each other, and the extent to which they use the same data representation.

b. *Processing node autonomy* specifies the degree to which processing nodes and associated data/devices can be under the control of separate organizational entities.

c. *Physical security* specifies which, if any, processing nodes and network components are physically secure.

2.3 Application requirements

In the model used in this chapter, clients makes collections of requests to distributed applications that execute on the base architecture. Logically, a client merely calls an abstract interface on a distributed abstract object, implemented by a distributed program. Internal to that object, there may be local and remote processing and substantial inter-thread communication. However, the application is insulated from these implementation details by a well-defined interface.

The requirements of distributed applications are taken from among the following:

● *Performance and modular growth.* A distributed program may have shorter response times and higher throughput if it can be decomposed into threads that execute simultaneously. If a program is decomposed into separate threads of execution, it may be possible to use additional processing nodes to provide enhanced functions or higher performance.

- *Availability.* A distributed program may use multiple processing nodes so that it can continue to make computational progress in spite of failures.

- *Reliability.* A distributed program may use redundant resources so that it can survive failures without storing or returning incorrect data.

- *Bounded response time.* A distributed program having interactive or real time uses may have bounds on how long it should take to service particular requests. (This is related to general performance and availability concerns.)

- *Sharing of physically separated resources.* A distributed program may need to perform proximate computations on data or other resources that are physically removed to permit sharing, increased efficiency, or more autonomous administrative control.

- *Autonomous control.* A distributed program may need to permit separate organizations to control subsets of the data and nodes on which it operates. Additionally, a program may still need to operate on all the data and nodes, regardless of the entity which controls them.

- *Security.* A distributed program may achieve enhanced security by isolating certain processing or data on particular processing nodes.

Affecting many of these application requirements is the degree to which *consistency* is required. Consistency specifies the degree to which the the application must uniformly store or return data that reflects all previous updates.

2.4 Distributed program paradigms

In this section, I consider the various requirements for distributed applications and how these can be met on base architectures. References to 'items' are to those axes described in Section 2.2.

2.4.1 Performance and modular growth

The decomposition of a distributed application into threads of control that execute in parallel is the central programming paradigm of distributed systems — and multiprocessing. Parallel decomposition permits an application to utilize multiple processors on a processing node and multiple processing nodes on a network. This decomposition also permits modular growth by allowing the use of additional processors or processing nodes. Multiple threads are also a convenient structuring mechanism even in a uniprocessor environment as they allow concurrency in the face of synchronous I/O operations, such as page faults.

Parallelism can be used within a single request to permit that request to be serviced faster. A single distributed SQL statement can often use intra-request parallelism to decrease response time by performing joins in parallel on multiple processing nodes. More typically, parallelism is used to permit more requests to be processed at once. This inter-request parallelism is very common in, for example, most large commercial transaction processing systems.

One key to determining how to decompose a distributed application into parallel threads arises from analysing the *available parallelism* on a particular base architecture. Parallelism arises from the overlap of synchronous I/O and processing, and from the use of multiple processors, either on a multiprocessor or on multiple processing nodes. There is little benefit in over-decomposing a problem, except to prepare for future systems that may have more parallel processing capability. The amount of available parallelism in the base architecture is substantially determined by Items 1a, 1b, 3a, 3b, and 4a—4c.

The term *locality of reference* holds the other key to determining how to decompose a distributed application into parallel threads of control. Locality of reference is defined as the propensity of a single thread of control to access the same data repetitively without intervening access by other processes. Locality of reference permits processing and data to be co-located, and allows processing to proceed asynchronously and without interference from other threads of control. In general, locality of reference lowers the latency and bandwidth demands on a communication network, reduces shared memory requirements on a multiprocessor, and permits load balancing since processing can be periodically moved to a new locus.

Certainly, decomposition of a distributed application into separate threads of control is easiest when there is near-perfect locality of reference. For example, the tens of millions of unconnected personal computers world-wide support many users and provide a system with modular growth.

When there is little locality of reference, it is problematical as to whether a distributed application can be accommodated on a given base architecture. It depends primarily on the bandwidth and latency of the communication mechanism (Items 1a-1d). In the limit, distributed applications with little locality of reference tend to require execution on a multiprocessor with shared memory attached by a cross-bar.

There are two different cases where there is partial locality of reference:

1. When there is *slowly changing* locality of reference, data can be shipped to the site of the processing, under the assumption that the data will be used there for a while. This is called *data sharing*. While data sharing is the classic multiprocessing paradigm, it can be implemented successfully in distributed systems as well. This technique is the basis of almost all distributed file systems, such as NFS and AFS (SUN (1986); Spector and Kazar (1989)), in which client nodes use volatile or non-volatile storage to cache data. Data sharing may be difficult in a heterogeneous distributed system when different processors use different data representations (Item 5a). In file systems this tends not be a problem, since most non-program data is stored in a machine-independent fashion. Data sharing for other applications benefits from executing on a homogeneous network.

2. When a thread has *substantial* locality of reference for some data, but other threads occasionally access it, the data can be stored near the thread that references it the most. Other threads must ship their requests to that remote thread for execution. This is called *function shipping*. This is the classic distributed system paradigm — the basis of the client-server model (Watson (1981)) and the remote procedure call (Birrell and Nelson (1984)). The distributed ET-1 banking benchmark (Anonymous *et al.* (1985)) is an example of the use of function shipping. In it, automated banking teller applications typically make fast, local RPCs to verify and update account balances at their local branch, but they make slower, remote RPCs to another randomly chosen branch with a probability of 15 per cent.

Whether function shipping or data sharing can be used depends not only on the structure of the distributed application but also on the CPU overhead, latency of inter-thread communication, and cost of shipping the data (Items 1a—1d). If there is sufficient communication bandwidth and only gradually changing locality of reference, data sharing may make sense, since data can be efficiently bulk transferred, and a program can compute autonomously on the retrieved data. On the other hand, if there is low processor overhead and latency in inter-thread communication and rapidly changing locality, function shipping may make sense. In ET-1, for example, it would cost more to ship the data than to ship a request to decrement an account, and there would be no benefit to data sharing, since a processing node would be unlikely to reference the (remote) account again soon.

In addition to basic data sharing and function shipping, there are a number of special cases that need to be considered: Read-only data can be easily distributed to the threads of control that use it, since there is no difficulty in maintaining its consistency. (Locality of reference is unnecessary in read-only data.) Read-mostly data can also be easily replicated for easy access by multiple threads — in the infrequent event that the data is updated, all holders of replicas can be notified to obtain a new copy. The AFS distributed file system uses this technique to permit clients to read file and directory data without having to contact servers; a 'call-back' is maintained on file servers indicating which clients are counting on their cache to be up-to-date. As described at the end of Section 2.3, some applications may not require absolutely consistent data, so multiple data copies may be kept only approximately up-to-date, thus reducing communication. Another technique for reducing communication is the batching of writes into single, larger write requests. This occurs in the X window system library: The X library buffers many updates, and sends them to the X server all at once. In another guise, this technique is also the basis for write-ahead logging. Many updates are forced to a stable storage log at once; usually, the updates are spooled asynchronously, but they may be written synchronously if a recently modified page of data is about to be written to permanent storage.

To consider the effect of the base architecture on a particular decomposition of a distributed application, one must analyse the interplay of most of the items in Section 2.2 — Items 1a—1d, 3a—3b, 4a—4c, 5a. I believe that back-of-the-envelope calculations are often sufficient to estimate the bandwidth required by a particular application's decomposition, as well as the resulting performance.

2.4.2 Reliability and availability

If processing nodes are fail-fast and have stable storage (Items 2b, 2d), transaction processing techniques coupled with the standard coding (such as cyclical redundancy checks) and retransmission of messages can provide reliability in the face of hardware malfunction (Gray (1980); Schwarz and Spector (1984)). That is, computations can occur within transactions which have serializability, failure atomicity, and permanence of effect properties. Transactions record all important state changes in stable storage, so non-catastrophic failures cause only delays. The access latency and bandwidth of stable storage (Item 4b) potentially limit performance, so these effects need to be considered to understand a system's performance and throughput.

Without fail-fast processing nodes or stable storage, multiple processors and memories are needed to perform computations and store data. (Independent failure modes are assumed.) Either hardware of software must perform voting to determine which computations are correct. Many fault-tolerant real time systems take this approach. For example, the space shuttle onboard computer system uses a combination of hardware and software voting (Spector and Gifford (1984)). Hence, Items 2b—2d have a major effect on the design of reliable systems.

The overall reliability of basic hardware components (Item 2a) provides some indication as to the error recovery techniques that should be used. The more reliable the underlying components, the coarser grained the error recovery can be. This is stated by the *end-to-end* principle (Saltzer, Reed, and Clark (1984)), which argues as follows: Since failure recovery mechanisms have to be done at the application level anyway (for example, to permit recovery from logical failures), one can dispense with failure recovery at lower system levels. For example if an ET-1 deposit can abort due to a deadlock condition, the same abort technique can be used to recover from a lost or corrupted message. In the case of a transaction system, all partial work can be undone and the entire unit of work can be retried.

Whether the end-to-end principle can be applied depends on the likelihood of failures occurring at levels below the contemplated level of recovery. For example, if the mean time to failure of the communication network or processing nodes (Item 2a) is less than the expected processing time of a particular application, it is necessary to perform low-level recovery to mask these failures. Otherwise, the application is unlikely to run to completion. For example, on the Carnegie-Mellon branch of the DARPA Internet, typical packet loss rates are at least two per cent. With error rates this high, application-level retry would occur too often if there were not automatic retries in the communication system.

Availability can be achieved either by using hardware that is less prone to failure or by using distributed replication. Stratus, for example, generally follows the former approach and constructs (virtual) reliable processors and non-volatile memories from two or more less reliable processors or memories. The Stratus techniques tend to guarantee high hardware availability, but they may not prevent down-time due to software failure.

Distributed replication techniques (Alsberg and Day (1976); Gifford (1979)) store state information on enough processing nodes for the state to remain accessible despite the failures of some of the nodes. Though all availability techniques utilize redundancy, the redundancy here is more likely to be at a logical level, than the replication of disk sectors that occur in more hardware-oriented fault-tolerance approaches.

Logical replication provides benefits of a number of types. The replicas can permit parallel processing on multiple nodes, particularly when the replicated data is read-mostly. Since the replicas are stored on separate processing nodes, a replica can be temporarily removed from service, improved (or re-implemented), and then reinstalled — provided that its abstract interface remains the same. Software reliability is often enhanced since transient software faults are often timing-dependent and they affect one replica but not another.

To summarize, many items from Section 2.2 influence the choice of reliability and availability techniques. Communication performance and limitations (Items 1a—1d) substantially influence the cost of replication, particularly for data that is commonly updated. The reliability of components and whether they can be assumed to fail independently (Items 2a, 2c) influence the redundancy that is needed in a system. If nodes are not fail fast or storage fails undetectably (Item 2b), voting techniques are needed on computation and data reads, respectively. Transaction processing techniques can be used if there is processor/storage integrity and stable storage (Items 2b, 2d). Transaction processing overhead is effected by the cost of writing to stable storage (Item 4b) as well as communication performance (Item 1a—1d). Node autonomy (Item 5b) improves system reliability and availability, since it reduces the likelihood that any single organization can disable an entire system, through either malice or negligence.

2.4.3 Bounded response time

Reducing the variance in processing and communication times is key to the successful implementation of real-time applications. Implementors of real-time applications will even tolerate decreased average case performance in return for guarantees that the worse case performance meets certain requirements. Virtual memory with uncertain performance due to page faults, communication networks with potentially high delay due either to contention or failures (Items 1a—1d, 2a—2c), and logical delays due to synchronization exacerbate the difficulty of building real-time systems.

To reduce variance, real-time applications may choose not to apply the end-to-end argument. Instead, they may be programmed to detect a failure as soon as possible in order that the least amount of work is discarded, and hence the least delay. Real-time applications also tend not to use virtual memory and communication systems having potentially unbounded communication delays (for example, contention buses like the Ethernet).

2.4.4 Sharing of physically separated resources

To allow sharing of physically separated resources such as remote file servers or printers, the communication component of the system must permit communication over wide area networks (Item 1d). Sharing is simplified when there is *network transparency*. If there is network transparency, a distributed program can often use communication primitives (such as procedure calls) that are the same, regardless of whether it is communicating locally or remotely.

2.4.5 Autonomous control

To allow different organizations to control different nodes on a network, the processing nodes must admit to autonomous control (Item 5b). That is, the individual processing nodes need to be separate computer systems on a network, rather than special-purpose nodes connected to a backplane.

In addition to the physical makeup of the hardware base, the computational paradigms in the distributed application must permit organizations to exert autonomous control over resources. For example, function shipping paradigms give greater control to a site owning data, since an owner can decide which requests to accept and which to reject. With data sharing, data is transmitted to the site where it is to be used. Once there, the data can be manipulated any way the user wants. As another example, distributed transaction-processing techniques provide substantial autonomy during execution of a distributed transaction, since sites are free to abort the transaction they are executing. However, during the commit phase, processing nodes must agree to abide by a particular commit or abort decision.

2.4.6 Security

A hardware base with processing nodes that are autonomous (Item 5b) is a good base for developing secure systems. For reasons similar to those in the previous section, function shipping can provide greater security than data sharing techniques.

The physical security of processing nodes and networks (Item 5c) influences how security must be implemented. Without physical network security, the ability to perform encryption algorithms efficiently (a special case of Item 4a) is crucial. Without physical security of nodes, encryption can be used to keep data private, but data can be deleted maliciously. If one can argue that the physical security of a percentage of processing nodes can be maintained, there are some potentially useful, probabilistic algorithms for storing data. These algorithms store replicas, which are by themselves are impenetrable, but, in combination, permit the reconstruction of the original data. These algorithms are also fault tolerant in the sense that they can regenerate the original data despite the absence of some number of replicas.

2.5 Discussion

As the field of distributed systems becomes better understood, computer scientists will becoming better at explaining (a) the constraints that most affect how a problem can be solved, (b) the application requirements that most affect how an application should be implemented, and (c) the key paradigms that permit application requirements to be met, given particular constraints. This chapter is a start toward categorizing these architectural constraints, application requirements, and distributed programming paradigms. It is only a start because the task is enormous, the understanding of our field is still growing, and my own perspective is insufficiently wide.

However, I have no doubt that the various base architecture characteristics itemized in Section 2.2 have a substantial impact on the design of distributed programs. I also believe that the list of application requirements of Section 2.3 and the paradigms of Section 2.4 are valuable. The central considerations are unquestionably parallel decomposition, replication, and error-recovery. I should note that much of my categorization of distributed systems also applies to multiprocessing as well. Issues of communication and I/O performance underlie both multiprocessing and distributed processing.

Perhaps, the most important part of this chapter is the treatment of important programming paradigms — particularly parallel decomposition. To understand distributed systems, one must understand the tension between decomposing problems into parallel threads (for performance, reliability, autonomy, etc.), and ensuring that inter-thread communication requirements are met. This balance between parallelism and communication is clearly a fundamental design paradigm in the field of computer science, and probably just as important as the more highly studied trade offs, such as space versus time.

Acknowledgements

I learned much from (Watson (1981)) and (Jones and Schwarz (1980)). I also benefited enormously from the discussion that accompanied my lecture on this topic at Tromsø. Since the initial draft, I have incorporated a number of issues that were raised by my fellow faculty members and students.

2.6 References

M. Accetta, R. Baron, W. Bolosky, D. Golub, R. Rashid, A. Tevanian, and M. Young (1986). 'Mach: A New Kernel Foundation for UNIX Development'. *Proceedings of the Summer Usenix Conference*, Atlanta, GA, July 1986.

P. A. Alsberg and J. D. Day (1976). 'A Principle for Resilient Sharing of Distributed Resources'. *Proceedings of the Second International Conference on Software Engineering*: 562—570, San Fancisco, CA, October 1976.

Anonymous *et al.* (1985). 'A Measure of Transaction Processing Power'. *Datamation* **31** (7), April 1985. (Also available as Technical Report Technical Report 85.2, Tandem Corporation, Cupertino, California, January 1985.)

J. Bartlett (1981). 'A NonStop Kernel'. *Proceedings Eighth Symposium on Operating System Principles*, 1981.

A. D. Birrell and B. J. Nelson (1984). 'Implementing Remote Procedure Calls'. *ACM Transactions on Computer Systems* **2** (1): 39—59, February 1984.

D. R. Cheriton (1984). 'The V Kernel: A Software Base for Distributed Systems'. *IEEE Software* **1** (2): 186—213, April 1984.

D. S. Daniels, A. Z. Spector, and D. Thompson (1987). 'Distributed Logging for Transaction Processing'. *Sigmod '87 Proceedings*, May 1987. (Also available as Technical Report CMU-CS-86-106, Carnegie-Mellon University, June 1986.)

D. K. Gifford (1979). 'Weighted Voting for Replicated Data'. *Proceedings of the Seventh Symposium on Operating System Principles*: 150—162, December 1979.

D. K. Gifford and N. Glasser (1988). 'Remote Pipes and Procedures for Efficient Distributed Communication'. *ACM Transactions on Computer Systems* **6** (3): 258—283, August 1988. (Also available as MIT LCS TR-384.)

J. N. Gray (1980). *A Transaction Model*. Report RJ2895, IBM Research Laboratory, San Jose, California, August 1980.

R. Haskin, Y. Malachi, W. Sawdon, and G. Chan (1988). 'Recovery Management in QuickSilver'. *ACM Transactions on Computer Systems* **6** (1): 82—108, February 1988.

A. K. Jones and P. Schwarz (1980). 'Experience using Multiprocessor Systems — A Status Report'. *ACM Computing Surveys* **12** (2): 121—166, June 1980.

N. P. Kronenberg, H. M. Levy, and W. D. Strecker (1986). 'VAXclusters: A Closely-Coupled Distributed System'. *ACM Transactions on Computer Systems* **4** (2): 130—152, May 1986. (Presented at the Tenth Symposium on Operating System Principles, Orcas Island, Washington, December, 1985.)

B. Lampson (1981). 'Atomic transactions'. In Goos and Hartmanis (Ed.), *Distributed Systems — Architecture and Implementation*, Volume 105, pages 246—265. Springer-Verlag Lecture Notes in Computer Science, Berlin, 1981.

H. C. Lauer and R. M. Needham (1979). 'On the Duality of Operating System Structures'. *Operating Systems Review* **13** (2): 3—19, April 1979.

S. J. Mullender (1985). *Principles of Distributed Operating System Design*. Ph. D. Thesis, Vrije Universiteit, Amsterdam, October 1985.

J. B. Postel (1982). 'Internetwork Protocol Approaches'. In P. E. Green, Jr. (Ed.), *Computer Network Architectures and Protocols*, pages 511—526. Plenum Press, 1982.

SUN (1986). *Networking on the SUN Workstation.* 800-1324-03, Sun Microsystems, Inc, Mountain View, California, 1986.

J. H. Saltzer, D. P. Reed, and D. D. Clark (1984). 'End-to-End Arguments in System Design'. *ACM Transactions on Computer Systems* 2: 277—278, Nov. 1984.

P. M. Schwarz and A. Z. Spector (1984). 'Synchronizing Shared Abstract Types'. *ACM Transactions on Computer Systems* 2 (3): 223—250, August 1984. (Also available in Stanley Zdonik and David Maier (Eds.), *Readings in Object-Oriented Databases.* Morgan Kaufmann, 1988, and as Technical Report CMU-CS-83-163, Carnegie Mellon University, November 1983.)

A. Z. Spector (1981). *Multiprocessing Architectures for Local Computer Networks.* Ph.D. Thesis, Stanford University, 1981. (Available as Stanford Report STAN-CS-81-874.)

A. Z. Spector (1982). 'Performing Remote Operations Efficiently on a Local Computer Network'. *Communications of the ACM* 25 (4): 246—260, April 1982.

A. Z. Spector and D. K. Gifford (1984). 'The Space Shuttle Primary Computer System'. *Communications of the ACM* 27 (9): 875—900, September 1984.

A. Z. Spector (1989). 'Modular Architectures for Distributed and Database Systems'. *Proceedings Eighth SIGACT News-SIGMOD-SIGART Symposium on Principles of Database Systems*, Philadelphia, PA, March 1989.

A. Z. Spector and M. L. Kazar (1989). 'Wide Area File Service and The AFS Experimental System'. *Unix Review* 7 (3), March 1989.

R.W. Watson (1981). 'Distributed System Architecture Model'. In B. W. Lampson (Ed.), *Distributed Systems — Architecture and Implementation: An Advanced Course*, Volume 105, pages 10—43. Springer-Verlag Lecture Notes in Computer Science, 1981.

M. Young, A. Tevanian, R. Rashid, D. Golub, J. Eppinger, J. Chew, W. Bolosky, D. Black, and R. Baron (1987). 'The Duality of Memory and Communication in the Implementation of a Multiprocessor Operating System'. *Proceedings of the Eleventh Symposium on Operating System Principles*: 63—76, Austin, TX, 8-11 November 1987. (In *ACM Operating Systems Review* 21:5.)

PART II
Communication

Interprocess-communication mechanisms in distributed systems have been developed almost independently of the interprocess communication mechanisms in networked systems or in Open Systems Interconnection (OSI). In distributed systems, the focus has been primarily on performance, whereas in OSI, it has been mainly on standardization and operating-system independence.

Chapters 3 and 4 discuss communications support and language support for Remote Procedure Call (RPC) mechanisms. RPC is by no means the only communication paradigm in distributed systems, but it is certainly the predominant one.

Chapter 3 is based for a large part on the author's experience with the Amoeba distributed operating system and concentrates on methods to achieve efficiency and speed. Chapter 4 builds on Weihl's experience with the MIT Argus and Mercury projects. Argus is a programming language supporting fault-tolerant distributed applications. Mercury is an efficient RPC system supporting multi-lingual distributed applications in an environment of heterogeneous hardware.

Chapter 3

Interprocess Communication

S. J. Mullender

In this chapter problems and solutions concerning interprocess communication in distributed systems are described. Communication in local networks receives the most coverage, since most distributed systems run exclusively over these. Considerable attention is given to issues of high-performance communication at the expense of giving an incomplete overview of the field.

For a more general treatment of computer networks and interprocess communication protocols, Tanenbaum (1988) is recommended.

3.1 The nature of communication in distributed systems

When designing efficient mechanisms for interprocess communication in a distributed system, it is necessary to know something about how interprocess-communication mechanisms are used. It is, for instance, useful to know the distribution of the sizes of data transfers in order to optimize the transport protocols. It is useful to know how often processes exchange data with each other in order to know whether to cache associations between processes. It is useful to know how exchanges between processes are structured in order to structure the communication protocols.

In this section these issues will be examined so that the information presented here can be used to design optimally efficient interprocess communication mechanisms.

3.1.1 Structure of process interaction

System and application software usually has a layered and modular structure, ideally structured as shown in Figure 3.1. System software usually resides in the lower layers while application software typically occupies the higher layers. Naturally, the exact division between system software and application software is

| 3.1 | 3.2 | 3.3 | Layer 3 |

| 2.1 | 2.2 | 2.3 | Layer 2 |

| 1.1 | 1.2 | 1.1 | Layer 1 |

Figure 3.1 Idealized representation of modular software.

fuzzy and depends very much on one's personal viewpoint. In a distributed system, a structured application may be distributed over a number of processors by splitting it up in a number of processes. Obviously, one very natural way of splitting up a large application into processes is by splitting it up by layer and module boundary.

When this is done, we have two classes of interfaces between processes: interfaces between processes in different layers and interfaces between processes in the same layer. We shall look at each in turn.

In traditional, non-distributed systems, interfaces between layers include the operating system interface (usually including the file system interface as a subset), the interface to various libraries, and the interface to a window-management system. The latter, in fact, is already familiar to us as an interface between processes communicating over a network: both MIT's X windows (Scheifler and Gettys (1986)) and SUN's NeWS (SUN (1986)) define interfaces in terms of a network protocol.

In most interlayer interfaces we see an *active* upper layer and a *passive* lower layer. The lower-layer software acts on commands from the upper-layer software. The interface can be viewed as a procedural interface with the upper layer as the caller and the lower layer as the callee.

It is also common that a layer provides a *service* to the layers above it. The layer defines a certain class of objects and operations on the objects. The examples mentioned earlier illustrate this: the operating system provides process objects, file objects, directory objects; the X-window system provides a window object, a bitmap object; a mathematical library provides a matrix object, a complex number object, and so on.

In traditional systems, interlayer interfaces can usually be implemented as true procedural interfaces: Library interfaces are almost exclusively procedural; operating system interfaces usually have procedure stubs. It is in distributed systems that layer interfaces usually become more involved.

Early distributed systems were structured on the viewpoint that a network interface was just another I/O device and that any interface that happened to go across a network had to be structured like other I/O. This led to the *'file model'* for network I/O. The idea here is that a connection is *opened*, then *read* or *written* for some time, and finally *closed*. This model still persists in the Open Systems Interconnection model as advocated by the International Standards Organization (see Section 3.3). This has led to very involved network service interfaces.

Today, procedure-like interfaces are *bon ton* again for distributed systems. In its simplest form (as implementation), the interface consists of a *request* message from a *client* process to a *server* process, followed by a *reply* message in the opposite direction. We refer to the underlying model as the *client/server* or the *remote operation* model.

When requests and replies are adorned with a procedural syntax such that the client calls a *stub* routine which sends input arguments in a request message, sends it, waits for a reply message and returns output arguments and function results, we have a *remote procedure call* (RPC) model. RPC is discussed in the next chapter.

The remote-operations model captures most client/server interfaces quite adequately, but there are, of course, examples where the model cannot be used. Think, for instance, of an alarm service which sends a wakeup signal to a client at a prearranged moment. At first glance a possible implementation might send the wakeup command in a request and the wakeup signal in the accompanying reply, but, since in most remote-operation models, client processes block until a reply is received, this would stop the client process from making progress while a wakeup call is outstanding. Exception handling (hardware exceptions and software interrupts) is another case where special mechanisms are required.

Fortunately, many distributed systems provide the possibility of having multi-threaded processes, which allows client processes to reserve a special thread for dealing with *upcalls*, remote operations from server to client. In the single-threaded world, exception handling is a mess at the best of times and it only becomes worse in a distributed system.

Making general observations about the structure of horizontal communication between peer modules in a distributed application is much harder than about vertical communication between layers. The kinds of interactions between processes in a distributed application depend very much on the application. A glance at any book describing distributed algorithms will confirm this.

Most distributed applications, however, require reliable communication, so, no matter how the distributed algorithm works, acknowledgements are needed to inform the sender that a message has safely arrived. This is why the request/reply paradigm is quite suitable for peer communication between modules, even though there is only need for reliable point-to-point message passing. The roles of client and server are then dynamically determined and processes must often be prepared to act both as client and server.

But some applications remain where request/reply is not a suitable communication model. In Chapters 14 and 15, for instance, Birman describes algorithms for synchronizing events in a distributed system in a way that tolerates failures. He uses algorithms that achieve reliable broadcast using ordinary unreliable message passing. Another example of an application that may need different communication paradigms is a real-time system. When sensor readings must be transmitted to the machine that processes them, there is often no point in making communication reliable by means of retransmissions: it is better just to use the next — fresher — reading. A third example of a special kind of transmission facility is that of digital sound or video. Here, end-to-end delay must be constant and very low, but an occasional packet may be lost without significant loss of signal quality.

The request/reply model has become the norm for interprocess communication in spite of these examples. Most distributed systems have request/reply (often augmented by RPC mechanisms) as their standard transport protocol, but many provide escape hatches for specialized protocols for certain applications as well.

3.1.2 Data transfer size

Traditionally, data processing consisted of sequential processing of large files. A large file would be updated once in a while, by collecting the changes, sorting them, and then updating the file while copying it. This method is rapidly becoming obsolete. By and large, computer systems will mostly be used interactively. Large (sorted) files have disappeared in favour of databases which provide more possibilities and can be updated in place. Techniques are being developed in the database world to minimise network traffic by optimum allocation of the data and judiciously choosing the locations where queries are resolved. Modern interactive data base systems mostly use short transactions; large bodies of data need seldom be transferred.

To get an idea of the maximum size of things transferred between processes in a distributed system, we can examine the distribution of file sizes. After all, if a large body of data is transferred, the data must have been stored somewhere, and the file system is where the data usually is. As an example of the typical sizes of the files in a computer system, we have examined the file systems of the five time-sharing systems running BSD-4.3 Unix at the Centre for Mathematics and Computer Science (CWI) in Amsterdam. The systems at CWI are used for research, program development and text processing, and measurements showed that half the 450,000 or so files are less than two kilobytes in size and that 90 per cent of the files are smaller than 24 kilobytes (see Figure 3.2). Only one file in a thousand is larger than a megabyte — 0.08 per cent, to be exact.

Similar measurements were carried out on other file systems and these confirm that the overwhelming majority of files is small (Mullender and Tanenbaum (1984); Ousterhout et al. (1985)).

Typically, a number of processes will process data that originate from a file, is passed around, modified, and ends up on another file. Many files are read piecemeal or not sequentially, which results in smaller chunks of data on the network. The numbers presented above, therefore, give a good indication of the typical sizes of larger data transfers, while on average the transfers will be much smaller.

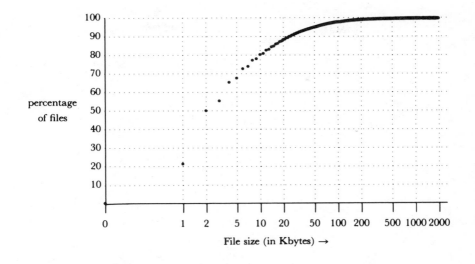

Figure 3.2 Percentage of files smaller than or equal to the indicated length (CWI, January, 1989).

The graph in Figure 3.2 might be used to claim that there is hardly any need for a transport protocol that can handle very large messages. After all, half of the files fit in a single network packet; in the future, faster networks will only provide larger maximum packet sizes, so things are only going to get better. The data of Figure 3.2 can be presented differently by plotting what percentage of disk storage is used for files less than or equal to a certain size. This has been done in Figure 3.3 and the picture comes out quite differently. Only 5 per cent of the storage is used for files of less than two kilobytes. The 10 per cent files of more than 24 kilobytes take up more than 60 per cent of the disk space and the 0.1 per cent files of more than a megabyte still consume 17 per cent of the disk space.

If all the files are read equally often, more than 95 per cent of the time file data is sent would be spent sending data belonging to files of more than one network packet (assuming a packet size of less than two kilobytes). In practice, only a fraction of the time will be spent in whole-file transfer, so that the percentage of real time spent doing large transfers is significantly lower.

What these numbers show, in conclusion, is that it is important to design transport protocols that are both good at transferring small things and big things. The time spent preparing for a transfer (reserving network resources in advance to obtain better throughput, for instance) must be small because most transfers are small making the overhead of such a thing rather significant. But the efficiency of sending large files must be good, because the transmission of large files takes up a large fraction of the total time.

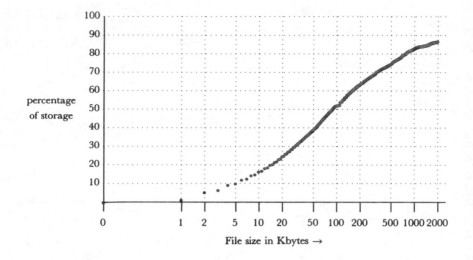

Figure 3.3 Percentage of disk storage in files that are less than or equal to the indicated size (CWI, January, 1989).

It might be argued that two kinds of protocol are needed, one for the transport of small things with minimal delay, and one for the transport of large things with maximal throughput. This is, in fact, exactly what the international standardization community has done. There are two main classes of standard transport mechanisms, *connection-oriented* for large things, and *connectionless* for small things. Many distributed systems show, however, that a single transport mechanism — provided it is well designed — can do both very efficiently (Cheriton (1986); van Renesse, van Staveren, and Tanenbaum (1988)). In this chapter, the design of high-speed transport protocols suitable both for very small messages and very large files will be discussed.

3.2 Communication models

3.2.1 Packet switching, message switching and circuit switching

A network is made connection-oriented or connectionless by the communication protocols used in it. On virtually every network, the hardware transports the transmitted data in *packets*. In this section, different strategies for transporting the packets that make up logical messages through a network are discussed.

In a *packet-switched network*, the sender must give to the network a series of packets. Each packet has a well-defined (maximum) size and each packet is sent to its destination independently of all other packets. The destination may be several hops away. The receiver gets the packets separately as well, not necessarily in the order they were sent. Occasionally, a packet may even get lost. Sender and receiver must agree on a protocol to recover from lost packets and to place the packets back in order.

In a *message-switched network*, the sender gives to the network a logical message. Messages have no fixed size, although there may be a maximum message size. The message is then sent to its destination as one unit, although it may have to be split up into packets when being transmitted over a communication link. At each intermediate node, however, the message is reassembled before it can be sent on to the next node. In many networks, message transmission is made reliable; that is, protocols are put in place that see to it that messages do not get lost unless the network breaks or a node crashes. In networks where message transmission is not made totally reliable, messages are often called *datagrams*.

In a *circuit-switched network*, before sending data, a connection is established. This sets up state and reserves resources at all intermediate nodes, so that the data can be sent through the network efficiently. After opening the circuit, the sender can write data into the connection and the receiver can read data from the connection much like writing or reading a Unix pipe.

In a store-and-forward network, these different styles of communication result in different end-to-end delays as illustrated in Figure 3.4. The picture presents a much simplified model of the actual protocols involved — acknowledgement packets and retransmission packets are not shown — but the figure still represents the essential characteristics of packet switching, message switching and circuit switching: processing time at the forwarding nodes and the sequence in which data is sent.

For choosing the best communication protocol, the most important considera-tion is usually minimizing end-to-end delay. In Figure 3.4, the end-to-end delay has been indicated by the dotted lines. For small amounts of data, such as illus-trated, packet switching is clearly optimal in terms of end-to-end delay, and cir-cuit switching is clearly worst. But consider what this figure will look like when a very large amount of data has to be transmitted. The per-packet processing time in circuit switching is less than that in packet switching because the routing decisions have been made in advance, so circuit switching will become better than packet switching when the amount of data is large enough.

But what about message switching? It doesn't work well for small amounts of data — this is clearly visible in Figure 3.4 — and it won't work well for large amounts of data either, because there can be no overlap between sending from *A* to *B* and from *B* to *C*. In local networks, however, which are usually not store-and-forward, message switching is very useful. If *B* were the final destination in Figure 3.4, instead of *C*, message switching would actually have resulted in a better end-to-end delay than either packet switching or circuit switching. This is caused by the shorter per-packet processing time and is illustrated in Figure 3.5.

In heterogeneous networks, such as internetworks consisting of local and wide-area networks, message switching also has a prominent place. Packet switching has problems in these environments, because of incompatible packet

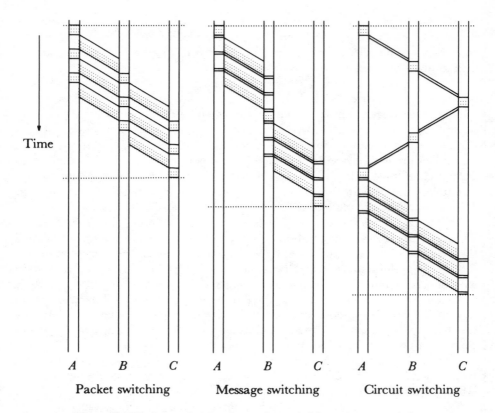

Time

A	B	C
Packet switching	Message switching	Circuit switching

Figure 3.4 End-to-end delay for packet switching, message switching and circuit switching

sizes on different networks. For instance, an Ethernet has a 1500-byte packet, while a public X.25 network offers circuit switching with 128-byte packets. Sending Ethernet packets of only 128 bytes would be an enormous waste of Ethernet bandwidth, and splitting up and re-merging packets at the connections between networks is not possible in a packet-switched network where each packet is supposed to be routed independently. When circuit switching is used, packets can be simply split up and joined again, but this requires some processing at switching nodes. Circuit switching also suffers from the usual problem of circuit setup which is inefficient for short communications. Message switching is often the simplest and also most efficient solution for heterogeneous networks.

And heterogeneity is where the world will go: typically, wide-area store-and-forward networks will connect local-area networks. Sometimes, an intermediate level network is present in the form of a campus-wide backbone network.† The

---

† See, for instance, Figure 8.2 which shows the Carnegie-Mellon Internet.

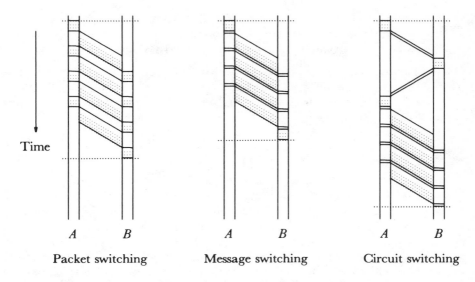

Time

A   B   A   B   A   B

Packet switching   Message switching   Circuit switching

Figure 3.5 End-to-end delay for packet switching, message switching and circuit switching in local networks.

properties of wide-area networks and local networks are radically different. Wide-area networks have long signal propagation delays and low bandwidth compared to local networks, and error rates that are an order of magnitude higher than those of local networks. Efficient transmission protocols for local and wide-area networks, therefore, are usually radically different. To exploit the best of both worlds, *protocol conversion* at the boundaries between local and wide-area networks is needed. The machine that carries out protocol conversion at this boundary is usually called a *gateway*.

In internetworks, it is necessary to distinguish at least two levels of protocol: the protocols used in each of the constituent networks, and the protocol used in the internetwork. The internetwork protocol makes use of the constituent-network protocols to deliver its data. The internetwork is typically a three-hop store-and-forward network: one hop from source machine over a local network to a wide-area network gateway, one hop over the wide-area network to another wide-area network gateway, and one hop over another local network to the destination machine.

Since local networks are often message-switching networks, it makes a lot of sense to use a message-switching protocol for the internet protocol as well, because:

1. The internet protocol can also be used for local traffic since it can be implemented as a *null* protocol in this case. There need be no distinction between local network traffic and wide-area network traffic this way.

2.   Wide-area networks are usually an order of magnitude slower than local
      networks. The delay incurred by collection of the whole message at each
      gateway is only a small fraction of the total delay.

3.   Wide-area networks are often circuit-switched networks run by the PTTs for
      profit. Since idle open virtual circuits cost money, it is necessary to open a
      circuit only when there is traffic and to close it again when traffic ceases.
      This can only be sensibly done on a message-switching basis.

3.2.2 Sessions

When processes communicate, several things have to be arranged in order to
ensure that the communication goes well. It is of some importance that communicating parties can establish that the party at the other end of the communication channel is not an impostor but really is the intended party. Sometimes it
is necessary to find at what network address the other party resides before communication can commence. Byte-order problems may have to be resolved when
communication starts. Once communication has begun, both parties have to
maintain state to ensure that all the data arrives exactly once.

To realize all this, associations between processes need to be structured properly, and both parties must maintain state for the duration of the association.
We call these associations *sessions* and in this section we shall go into some of the
issues of session management.

The most fundamental issue in this area is that of *naming*. In order to communicate with something, one must be able to tell the system which something it
is that one wants to communicate with. That names are needed is perfectly
obvious, but what kinds of names to choose is one of the most difficult problems
of distributed systems research.

In distributed systems, names often refer to *services*, abstract entities which
respond to requests of a certain type. A client, for instance, may want to send a
request to a distributed file service to read a file. The client should not have to
know how file service is implemented, how many server processes there are,
where they run and which one to contact to read a file. Given the name of a
service, selecting a server process and establishing communication with it is part
of the starting of a session. The selection may depend on a multitude of factors,
such as load of the servers, 'distance' of the servers to the client, which servers
actually hold copies of the file data, and so on. Session setup may involve both
client and service. Chapter 5 discusses naming issues in detail.

Before sending sensitive data to a file server, a client process will naturally want
to have some assurance that the server process at the other end of the communication channel really is the server and not some impostor. To make sure that
processes communicate with the desired parties and no others, *authentication mechanisms* are needed. Usually, the authentication procedure results in the establishment of a *session key* known only to the two communicating processes and no others, which is used for the duration of the session to encrypt all data exchanged.

In distributed systems using remote operation protocols, each remote operation could be considered a separate session. The session protocol (or remote operations protocol), at the beginning of each remote operation would have to choose a server process to handle the operation, send the operation request to it and make sure a reply is returned. In practical implementations, the session state will usually be *cached* between remote operations. This prevents expensive lookup operations and authentication procedures on each individual operation. If session state is lost between two remote operations, however, a new session can automatically be established for the next operation.

3.2.3 Blocking versus non-blocking protocols

One of the goals of distributed systems is the exploitation of *parallelism*. And a very natural way to obtain parallelism is to provide *asynchronous* or *non-blocking* communication primitives. There is a variety of non-blocking communication primitives. The ones for *sending* are easy. The primitive tells the system to send a message off-line. The sending process continues to compute while the message is being sent. Non-blocking *receive* is harder. Some systems provide non-blocking send and blocking receive: the receive primitive blocks until a message has been received. Others provide an additional primitive with which one can see if a message is waiting. If so, it can be received without blocking. Others again have a non-blocking receive operation which tells the system where to put received messages; another primitive or an interrupt is then used to find out about the arrival of a message. Finally, there are systems where an upcall is used when the system receives a message for a process. The process merely specifies the procedure to be called when a message arrives.

In systems with blocking communication protocols, all this is much simpler. A process making a call to receive always blocks until a message has arrived. Many systems (Cheriton and Zwaenepoel (1983); Mullender and Tanenbaum (1986)) provide one call for clients to do remote operations and two calls for servers: one to receive a request for a remote operation and one to return the reply. All these calls block until they are complete.

In systems with blocking calls, parallelism must be obtained in some other way. This way is often by providing *light-weight processes*, or *threads*. In such systems, a process consists of an address space, and one or more threads of control. Each thread has its own program counter, general registers and stack, but all threads share the address space. Often the threads are independently scheduled, in which case the system usually provides synchronization primitives. Sometimes, the threads have control over the way they are scheduled.

To make the difference clear between blocking communication with threads and non-blocking communication, consider a file server. A file server receives requests from many clients to read and write files. A single client request is typically handled as follows. A request to do some file operation will come in, the file server will check the request for permissions and check whether a disk access is required. If not, the reply can be sent immediately. If there is, a disk request will be queued and the file server will wait for it to complete. When it is complete, a reply is sent to the client.

When there are multiple, simultaneous clients, it will be necessary to overlap the execution of client requests. Otherwise, the performance of the server will be unacceptable. In a system with non-blocking calls, the way to do this is to have the file server work on several requests simultaneously. It will become event-driven: after queueing a request for the disk, the server will test an event queue. On this queue the server will find new client requests and completed disk operations.

The server will have to be operated like an enormous state machine, with entries for every outstanding client request. Whenever a disk operation completes, the appropriate piece of client state must be retrieved to find out how to continue carrying out the request.

In a system with blocking calls and threads, each incoming request is handled by a different thread. The state of a request being carried out is thus simply stored on the stack of the associated thread. Threads can either be created dynamically, whenever a request comes in, or a pool of threads can be created at start-up time to deal with as many simultaneous requests as there are threads. Data structures in memory shared by all threads are usually protected by semaphores or other synchronization devices.

Threads have become very popular in distributed systems, because of the simplicity of using them. A few systems provide a threads package in user space, implemented on top of non-blocking communication calls and single-threaded processes. Within the threads package, communication calls are then blocking. Other systems implement threads in the kernel. Communication system calls can then be blocking.

3.3 Communications standards

3.3.1 The seven layers of ISO

The International Standards Organization (ISO), recognizing that there is an increasing need for digital communication between different computers belonging to different organizations, has proposed a suite of protocols for what is called *Open System Interconnection*, or OSI (Zimmermann (1980)). These protocols deal with data transport over individual links, authentication of communicating entities, mechanisms for file transfer, remote terminal access and a host of other issues.

The OSI suite of protocols has been arranged as a pile of seven layers, called the *reference model*, where lower layers provide service to higher layers, each layer improving on the quality of the layers below in some way. Each layer in the seven layer cake performs a well-defined set of functions. The layer structure is shown in Figure 3.6. We shall now briefly describe the function of each layer.

	Machine A	Store-and-forward node		Machine B	
7	Application			Application	7
6	Presentation			Presentation	6
5	Session			Session	5
4	Transport			Transport	4
3	Network	Network		Network	3
2	Data link	Data link		Data link	2
1	Physical				1

Figure 3.6 The ISO OSI reference model

- *The physical layer*
  The physical layer deals with the issues of getting raw bits over a transmission medium: how bits are coded, the electrical levels used, pin assignments on the connectors, the definition of frames, and so on.

- *The data link layer*
  The data link layer is responsible for providing reliable transmission over the raw transmission medium. To this end, the data is split up into *data frames* which are sent while *acknowledgement frames* are sent back to indicate the undamaged receipt of the frames. When frames are damaged or lost, they are retransmitted.

- *The network layer*
  The network layer deals with the transport of data through the network. Issues of routing and congestion control are dealt with in this layer. The network layer accepts data from one host and delivers it to another network host.

- *The transport layer*
  The transport layer is concerned with the end-to-end transport of data between hosts. Where the network layer is usually operated by the carrier, the transport layer is typically under control of the network user. The store-and-forward nodes of a public network, therefore, do not generally provide transport services, but only the bottom three layers of service.

- *The session layer*
  The session layer is used for negotiating connections between processes in a computer network. It must deal with authentication of the communicating parties, choose the right sort of transport service, deal with accounting and repair broken transport connections.

- *The presentation layer*
  Network services that are sufficiently general are often provided by the presentation layer. Examples of such services are file transfer, text

compression, encryption, terminal handling, network window systems, electronic mail, and remote execution.

- *The application layer*
  The application layer is where applications that use the OSI suite of protocols are based. Applications can use presentation services or bypass them and interface directly to the session layer to communicate with other applications.

An enormous international standardization effort is in progress to define standards for each of the seven layers of the OSI cake. Many standards are now in place for the bottom four layers; some standards exist for the session and presentation layers, while work is still going on to define more.

3.3.2 Relevance of OSI to distributed systems

The OSI suite of protocols is intended for interconnection of *open systems*. It allows communication between sites without having to negotiate the implementation of communications protocols beforehand. ISO has already done the negotiations. All that remains to be done is for two sites to start sending messages.

OSI was never intended to provide standards for distributed computing. Distributed systems are generally designed from the ground up by a team of people working in close collaboration; every machine usually runs a copy of the same distributed-operating-system kernel; a client process sending requests to a server knows exactly what format requests have to be in and servers know exactly what to expect. International standards are — of necessity — much too heavy-weight for efficient communication in a distributed system.

Yet, considerable pressure is applied on distributed systems projects to use ISO OSI protocols. This pressure is greatest in Europe and comes primarily from funding organizations, such as Esprit, and, to a lesser degree, from industry. The term OSI has magic qualities in political circles, because standardization is considered a wonderful thing and the OSI standards are the only ones available.

This pressure to use OSI protocols regardless of their suitability for the goal at hand did not come from the standards organizations themselves, however. In fact, an international standardization effort is now starting to produce standards for *Open Distributed Processing*. This work has been pushed by the European Computer Manufacturers Association (ECMA), the International Standards Organization, and the Advanced Networked Systems Architecture Project (ANSA) in the UK. But work is only just starting in this area and it will probably take a while before proposals for standards for open distributed processing appear.

3.4 Protocol design issues in distributed systems

Up to this point, the discussion of communication issues has been fairly general. However, in this section, the impact of the specialized nature of communication in distributed systems on protocol design will be discussed.

The first consideration is that distributed systems usually run over local-area networks. These networks often consist of a single broadcast medium and sometimes a local backbone network connecting several local networks. Most network traffic in distributed systems stays within a single local network. Even when the network is so large that there has to be a backbone connecting several local networks, the designers of the system usually try to arrange it so that local traffic dominates.

Another consideration is that most communication is intended for carrying out *remote operations*: a process asks a server process to carry out some task (such as reading a file or creating a window on a screen) and awaits the result. Usually, the size of these requests and replies is very small. Since the process that wants the remote operation carried out usually depends on the result of the operation for further execution, it is important to minimize the delay in getting the message across.

A third consideration has to do with errors and faults. Errors were discussed earlier: data may get corrupted in the course of transmission, frames may get lost, or be delivered out of order. Network protocols often deal with these matters, so they are considered to be of little importance in the area of distributed computing. Faults are serious failures of the system. Machines may crash, communication links may fail, partitioning the network, bugs may cause processes to get into an infinite loop. It is easy to recover from errors; retransmission usually does this without any problems — but it is much harder to recover from faults. If a server crashes, it is hard to decide whether the last request was executed or not; if the network partitions, it is difficult to know whether it was the network that failed or the server that crashed.

The OSI protocols put reliable transmission (error recovery) in the network and transport layers, but fault recovery has been put in the session layer. In distributed systems, which run primarily over highly reliable local networks, the frequency of errors is of the same order of magnitude as that of faults; it is not worth while having one mechanism to deal with errors and another to deal with faults.

At the highest level of protocol — in the application itself — there must always be a check for the success of any remote operation, because every remote operation can fail at the application level through a process or machine crash. Error recovery in the lower levels of protocols is only useful for purposes of increasing efficiency. This is the end-to-end argument, which has been familiar to people working in the distributed systems area for a long time (Saltzer, Reed, and Clark (1984)).

3.5 Issues in high-performance communication protocols

In this section we shall identify a number of design principles which contribute to the implementation of fast interprocess communication protocols. Many of

the recommendations in this section apply primarily to local-area networks, but
some are applicable to wide-area networks as well.

3.5.1 Integrating protocol and scheduler

It was argued earlier that minimizing round-trip delay is an important consideration in protocol design. After all, it is fairly typical that a client, asking a
server for some service, is impatiently waiting for the answer to its question. The
system most familiar to the author and which he helped develop is the Amoeba
distributed system at Vrije Universiteit and CWI in Amsterdam (Mullender
(1985); Mullender and Tanenbaum (1986)). The Amoeba round-trip delay of
1.4 ms for a null call† is roughly built up of 400 μs 'network hardware time',
500 μs 'protocol time' and another 500 μs 'scheduler time', where *network
hardware time* is the wire time for the packets plus time to transfer packets to and
from primary memory plus hardware-interrupt latency, *protocol time* is the time
spent executing protocol code, and *scheduler time* is the time spent scheduling the
client and server processes.

These numbers show that scheduling delays take up a significant portion of
the total round-trip time. Before a request arrives, the intended recipient is typically a server process or thread which is in a *suspended* state — the process is
blocked waiting for the request to arrive. When it does arrive on the server
machine (heralded by a *receive interrupt* from the hardware), protocol code must
check whether the received packet is a legal one, for which process it is intended
and if that process must be awoken to process the received request (the request
may consist of several packets). When the process becomes runnable, it must be
scheduled. Assuming no other process is running, this requires that the process's
memory map must be loaded, its registers restored and the process started.

All this takes a significant amount of time, and — if the interface between
protocol code and scheduler is not designed properly — it takes even longer.
So, what can we do to make the interaction between scheduler code and protocol code as smooth and efficient as possible?

It will not work to let the protocol code run as a separate network process. It
might appear very elegant to do this, but it is not efficient enough: the network process would have to be scheduled on each receive-complete or transmit-complete
interrupt — an unacceptable overhead. Neither will it work to let the protocol code
be part of the receiving and sending processes. Although this reduces the number of
context switches a little, a large number still remain because each packet causes
two, one for sending and one for receiving. Also, before any process can be
scheduled, the protocol code has to run in order to determine the receiving process.

The protocol code has to run as part of the operating system kernel, and in
the interrupt routines where possible. This way the number of context switches
is kept down to a minimum. We shall say more about this when discussing
large messages.

† Measured with client and server on different SUN 3/50s connected by Ethernet.

There must be a direct path from the protocol code into the scheduler code — when the protocol code wraps up and makes the receiving process runnable, it must call the scheduler to schedule that process. Setting the process to 'runnable' and waiting for the scheduler to find the process later is not good enough, even if the scheduler is hunting for runnable processes in a fairly tight loop.

A very useful concept to speed scheduling up is to allow processes to *spin*. A process, waiting in kernel mode for a message to arrive, can be made to wait in a tight loop for a process to become runnable. If the process is another one, the scheduler is called to schedule it. But usually, it will be the process itself that becomes runnable in which case it can return to user space without the need to set the memory map or load the registers. Spinning is useful in uniprocessors, but can give spectacular results in multiprocessors where, usually, one or more of the processors are available for spinning.

3.5.2 Rate control

The mechanism that prevents a sender from flooding a receiver is called a *rate control* mechanism. Fast local networks, where the per-packet processing time exceeds the packet interarrival time, need such a mechanism. On a typical 10 Mbps local network with 1 to 3 MIPS machines, the interarrival time of full 1500-byte packets is 1.2 ms, allowing the protocol code some 1000 to 3000 instructions per packet. This is usually plenty, so rate control is not strictly necessary here, but if networks become ten times faster† there will not be enough time to process the packets of the same size.

Networks in which the interfaces are not capable of receiving *back-to-back* packets form another example of networks where rate control is needed. In Stanford's V system (Cheriton (1984)) it was discovered that a fast sender could overrun a slower receiver: the next packet would be on the cable before the receiving hardware had recovered from the previous packet. To deal with this requires, a sender has to introduce a small delay between packets to give the receiver time to get ready for the next packet.

In a new version of V's communication protocols, the *Versatile Message Transport Protocol* (VMTP), Cheriton (1986) proposed a rate control mechanism based on *packet blasts*. A large datagram is split up in groups of at most 32 packets. Each packet in a group is labelled by a 32-bit sequence number consisting of a single one bit. At the receiving end, the sequence numbers of the received packets of a group are OR-ed together. When a whole group arrives intact, the resulting value will be a 32-bit number consisting of all ones. If packets are missing, some of the bits will be zero. This number is sent back to the sender, allowing the sender to carry out *selective retransmission*.

Suppose now that a sender can send faster than a receiver can receive. When a packet group is sent, the first packet will be received successfully, but the

† FDDI networks are planned to run at 100 Mbps; the Cambridge Fast Ring already runs at 75 Mbps.

second packet will be lost because the receiver has not yet recovered. Every second packet will be lost. The selective retransmission mechanism will retransmit the even packets in another blast, but every fourth packet still won't make it across. Fortunately, VMTP does not work this way. It has an additional notion of an *interpacket gap*, a small delay between packets. Initially, the interpacket gap is set to zero by the sender, but when an acknowledgement with every second bit missing arrives, the interpacket gap is increased until packets are no longer lost.

Optimum values for the length of interpacket gaps must range in the neighbourhood of several hundred microseconds — an awkward value, because it is too long for a timed loop in the transmit interrupt routine and too short for using interrupts from the hardware clock. Cheriton suggested that network interfaces should be equipped with a mechanism to specify an interpacket gap.†

I feel that a network interface that is not capable of receiving back-to-back packets has not been designed correctly. Interfaces should not be made more complex by introducing interpacket gaps, but the incorrect interfaces should be put right.

Amoeba uses a rate control mechanism based on stop-and-wait at the individual packet level. Each packet is acknowledged separately and the next packet is sent only when the acknowledgement from the previous packet has been received. This seems a crude way to do rate control, but it works extremely well, especially on a busy Ethernet, for example, where packet blasts would cause many collisions. By doing stop-and-wait, the Amoeba protocols cause remarkably few: two, three or four pairs of machines exchanging large datagrams at maximum rate can transport 8 Mbps worth of useful data, an 80 per cent utilization of the Ethernet, which, within limits, seems independent of the number of communicating machines.

In wide-area networks, rate control is hardly an issue. The speeds of wide-area networks are nothing special, so machines are always fast enough to cope with incoming traffic. Flow control *is* an issue, of course, but we consider flow control outside the scope of distributed systems research; it is a network research problem that has to be solved by the carriers.

3.5.3 Using large datagrams

Designing protocols and interfaces that require only minimal moving of data is an excellent way of reducing delay. It is easy to see why this is when one realizes that internal memory-to-memory copying in a workstation typically goes at one or two megabytes per second, only marginally faster than a 10 Mbps network. Avoiding copying is thus an important factor contributing to good end-to-end delay.

---

† The interface would automatically introduce the interpacket gap between adjacent packets bound for the same destination.

Circuit-switching protocols often require extra copying because writes to the circuit and reads from the circuit need not be aligned to packet boundaries. Message-passing protocols can usually be made more efficient in this respect. Since most distributed systems are message-oriented anyway, we will only consider those.

Most network interfaces today have a mechanism by which a packet can be sent consisting of a header and a body that are in different places in memory. This capability is called *scatter-gather* and it is extremely useful when sending large datagrams. When there is no scatter-gather and a datagram has to be split up into packets, each of these packets has to be copied to append it to a packet header.

Scatter-gather is also useful for speeding up remote operations for file I/O. When data is written to a file by sending a request to a file server, a message has to be constructed containing the operation code (*write*), the file name, the position in the file, and so on, plus the data. This usually means that all this information, including the file data, has to be copied to a buffer and that the buffer is transmitted as a datagram. The Amoeba protocols allow a client to specify two buffers: one intended for parameters and the other for data. The transmitter's scatter-gather mechanisms combine the two into one packet. For a file-read or file-write operation of a kilobyte, the gain is at least half a millisecond (a total of 3 ms in Amoeba, assuming the file is cached at the server).

Avoiding copying on send is much easier than avoiding it on receive. On receive, the problem is that, before the packet is actually in memory for the protocol code to examine, it is not known where the packet will have to go. One way to avoid copying could be to allocate the receiver's buffers on page boundaries and to demand that user processes do the same. The data can then be copied by swapping pages. Although this method gains some speed, it is a moot point whether it should be advocated. It makes memory management more complicated — compilers will be needed that allocate the buffers in the right place, and packets can only be filled with an integral number of pages worth of data.

By allowing datagrams to be very large, system-call overheads can be significantly reduced, as only one is needed to send (or receive) a whole datagram. Additionally, the transmission protocol running in the kernel can do a good job of streamlining the transfer of large datagrams, for instance, by using packet blasts.

3.5.4 Sweep timers

Communication protocols need timers to recover from certain failures. After sending a packet, for instance, a retransmission timer is usually started which, when it goes off, causes the packet to be resent. In most cases, some sort of acknowledgement arrives and the timer is cancelled. There are three observations that we can make about timers that are useful in making protocols run faster.

1. *Starting and stopping timers costs time.* Pending timeouts are usually kept on a sorted list (sorted on expiration time), so setting a timer requires allocating an entry and going through a linked list to insert it. Cancelling requires hunting the entry down and removing it. While the tables are manipulated, the clock interrupt routine must be locked out.

2. *Timers seldom go off.* Timers only go off when something has gone awry, for instance, when a machine has crashed or a packet got lost.

3. *Timer values are only used to recover from errors.* They do not have to be very accurate.

Realizing this, one can omit the code to set and reset timers from the protocol code itself and replace it with a separate kernel thread which wakes up periodically and makes a *sweep* of all protocol data structures. It can compare the state of the protocol to the previous state to see if any progress was made. If the protocol has not made any progress for some time, the timer thread can initiate some appropriate action (such as retransmitting a packet).

The sweep timer thread is scheduled at fairly low priority to run effectively in the background. This makes timing inaccurate, but that is not a problem when the timers are only used for error recovery.

The only special arrangement needed in the kernel is that the protocol's data structures are allocated in a place where the timer thread can find them (in an array of state structures, for instance).

3.6 Detailed example: The Amoeba protocols

The Amoeba Distributed Operating System was designed and implemented by distributed systems groups at the Free University and the Centre for Mathematics and Computer Science, both in Amsterdam (Mullender (1985); Mullender and Tanenbaum (1986); van Renesse, van Staveren, and Tanenbaum (1988)). An Amoeba typically has five components:

1. Workstations that are used to provide a high-level user interface. Currently, workstations have a processor, several megabytes of memory, a bit-mapped display, keyboard and mouse; in the future, the plan is to equip workstations with devices for voice and video I/O as well.

2. A *processor pool*, consisting of a number of powerful processors and multiprocessors, each with many megabytes of memory for executing most of the application software in Amoeba.

3. Server machines, including file servers, directory servers, authentication servers, and accounting servers.

4. Gateways, for communication with other Amoebas over wide-area networks.

5.   A fast local network connecting all the components together.

On each of the machines runs a copy of the Amoeba Kernel, which has been kept as small as possible. The Amoeba Kernel is responsible for providing multithreaded processes, each with a segmented virtual address space, and highly efficient interprocess communication. Other traditional operating system services are all provided by user-space services.

The interprocess communication facilities of Amoeba are intended to support *remote operations*. All communication takes place between (threads in) processes taking on the roles of *clients* making requests to *servers* to carry out operations. The act of sending a request to a server and receiving a reply is called a *message transaction*.

A client invokes a message transaction by a call to

```
trans(reqhdr, reqbuf, reqlen, rephdr, repbuf, replen);
```

where reqhdr, reqbuf and reqlen specify the request to be sent and rephdr, repbuf and replen specify a buffer for the reception of the reply. The request header (reqhdr) contains the name of the object and the operation and there is room for some parameters. The reply header (rephdr) contains the results of the operation, also optionally accompanied by some parameters. Both requests and replies may have an additional buffer (reqbuf or repbuf) which contains data associated with the request or reply. The length field (reqlen or replen) specifies the length of the buffer.

The reason that the header and buffer are specified separately is one of efficiency: it allows the system to transmit data directly from where it is kept in memory or to receive it directly where it has to go in memory. If the header and buffer formed one data structure, the buffer contents would nearly always have to be copied.

At the server end, the call to receive a request is

```
getrequest(server, reqhdr, reqbuf, reqcnt);
```

where server is the name of the service. After the request has been carried out, a reply is returned with

```
putreply(rephdr, repbuf, repcnt);
```

A server thread can only carry out one request at a time, so there is no ambiguity about what message transaction the putreply refers to.

Both trans and getrequest are *blocking* calls; that is, trans blocks the calling thread until a reply arrives (or until the message transaction fails), and getrequest blocks the calling thread until a request comes in. Putreply blocks a thread until the system has removed the reply from the calling address space. Depending on the implementation, this may be until the receipt of the reply has been acknowledged by the client's kernel, or until the header and data have been copied into system space.

3.6.1 Naming

Processes cannot communicate unless there is a *naming* mechanism by which one can specify who talks to whom. In Amoeba, names refer to *services*. A service implements an *abstract data type*. The instances of the type are the *objects* that the service manages. The service defines the set of values that objects may assume and the operations allowed on them. Upon request of a client, the service carries out these operations.

Amoeba objects are named using *capabilities*. When a client provides the service that manages an object with a capability for that object, it proves to the service that it has the right to carry out the set of operations on the object specified by the capability. Capabilities were first described by Dennis and Van Horn (1966).

Amoeba capabilities consist of two parts as follows. The first part specifies the service that manages the object to which the capability refers, and the second part specifies the object itself plus the set of operations that the capability allows the holder to invoke. The layout of a capability is shown in Figure 3.7.

The name of a service is a *port*, essentially a 64-bit random number. Clients can only talk to a service if they know the port of that service. When a good random-number generator is used, the chances of guessing a service's port are very slim indeed. Ports can therefore be viewed as capabilities: having a port of a service in one's possession gives one the right to talk to that service.

A service can be represented by many server processes and all server processes receiving requests on the service's port are deemed to be equivalent. When a client process sends a request to a service, the system is responsible for delivering it to exactly one server process. In the next sections, the mechanisms for locating a server process and delivering requests to it will be shown.

Naming services by a 64-bit number and naming objects by a 256-bit number is very inconvenient for humans. Amoeba therefore provides a service that maps ordinary Unix-like *path names* onto capabilities (and thus also on ports). This service, called Directory Service, is an ordinary user-space service. Amoeba users who are dissatisfied with the Amoeba Directory Service can design and build their own and several directory services can live peacefully together.

Normally, the invocation of a service involves taking an ASCII path name to the directory service, which yields a capability containing the service's port. The port must then be mapped somehow to a *network address* of one of the server processes for the service. This is called *locating* a server process.

Before describing the details of the locate process, it is necessary to point out

64 bits	64 bits	128 bits
Service Port	Location Hint	Object + Rights

Figure 3.7 Layout of an Amoeba capability

that processes can *migrate*. This means that it is possible that, during the course of a message transaction, a client or server process can change its address. This makes it possible that, when sending a reply, for instance, the system where the client once resided will claim never to have heard of the addressed process. When this happens, the server's kernel must re-locate the client in order to deliver the reply.

Server and client processes, therefore, have an additional *unique port* (also known as *FLIP port*, for reasons which will become clear below) which can be used to locate a specific server or client process. If this port was not there, it would be possible, when a process migrates, for retransmissions to be sent to another server, with the effect that a request may be carried out twice.

There are thus two types of locate operations, one that maps a service port onto a FLIP port and a current network address, and one that maps a FLIP port onto a current network address. The first type of locate is only allowed at the beginning of a new message transaction.

A locate operation essentially works as follows. Each Amoeba machine keeps a cache of mappings of the form {*port*, *FLIP port*, *network address*}. When a client calls `trans`, the system first examines the cache. If there is an entry for the port, the system uses that. Otherwise, it broadcasts a locate request containing the port; if there is a server for that port, its kernel will return a message containing the server's FLIP port and network address. This information is then entered in the cache and used for as long as the information in the cache remains correct. If the server crashes, or if it migrates, there will either be no response, or an error message saying 'this port doesn't live here any more.'

When a cache entry proves to be invalid during a transaction, the kernel will attempt to locate the FLIP port again. If this fails, the message transaction fails.

Astute readers may have noticed the *location hint* in the discussion of capabilities. This is used to locate objects on wide-area networks over which broadcast is infeasible. Essentially, the location hint is a capability for the gateway to the remote Amoeba holding the object that the capability refers to.

3.6.2 The protocols

Amoeba provides two layers of protocol. The bottom layer provides a rate-controlled, secure, but not totally reliable datagram service. These datagrams can carry a whole request or reply; they can vary in size from a header only to a header and one gigabyte of data. (In practice, however, messages of one gigabyte do not occur, since no machine has enough memory to send or receive one.) The protocol at this layer is called the *Fast Local Internet Protocol*, or FLIP.

FLIP has been designed for *local internets*. A local internet consists of several local networks, connected by gateways of bridges. The FLIP layer in the gateways forwards datagrams from one network to the other, if necessary.

FLIP layer addresses are the *FLIP ports* mentioned earlier. The FLIP layer maintains a cache of {*FLIP port*, *network address*} pairs.

The top layer, called the *transaction layer*, provides a reliable remote-operations service. The interface at the top of this layer consists of the calls `trans`, `getrequest` and `putreply` (and one or two others, actually).

The reason for this somewhat peculiar layering is one of efficiency. Large datagrams have to be split up into packets for transmission over a local network; by doing this splitting at a low level of protocol, it is possible to streamline the sending of the individual packets in the device handler, so that kernel scheduling does not have to take place for every packet.

3.6.3 FLIP implementation

FLIP is responsible for transporting large datagrams from one FLIP address to another over a local internet. As shown in Section 3.2.1, depending on the size of the datagram to be sent, either packet switching or circuit switching gives the best results over a store-and-forward network (which a local internet is). Amoeba currently uses packet switching, but a new design is in the works that uses a special form of circuit switching.

FLIP uses stop-and-wait at the packet level: A large datagram is fragmented into packets and fragments are only sent when the acknowledgement packet for the previous fragment has arrived. Some experimentation showed that acknowledging the last fragment of a request message was a bad idea: it would often delay the transmission of the reply message. FLIP now acknowledges the last fragment of replies and of retransmissions of a request. Note that in most remote operations, a message consists of just one fragment.

When a fragment arrives at a machine and there is no process receiving on the destination FLIP port, a *not-here* packet is returned. This causes the sender to try to re-*locate* the FLIP port on the assumption that the receiver has probably migrated. If the FLIP port cannot be located, an error is reported to the transaction layer.

3.6.4 Transaction layer implementation

To provide reliable transactions, the transaction layer uses timeouts and retransmissions. Each message transaction receives a *transaction sequence number* which is incremented per transaction for every FLIP-port pair. After a crash, all FLIP ports will be regenerated to prevent requests from being accidentally accepted twice.

When a client makes a call to *trans*, the transaction layer checks its cache to see if it knows a FLIP port for the service port. If it does not, it broadcasts a 'locate-server-port request.' When the reply comes in, containing a FLIP port for a server, the cache is updated. The request is then passed to the FLIP layer for transmission. The FLIP layer then consults its cache of {*FLIP port, network address*} pairs to see to which machine to send the message. This cache will normally always hit, because incoming messages — which include incoming responses to locate requests — will automatically update the cache.

When the request arrives at the server, the transaction layer does not send an acknowledgement. Experience has shown that acknowledgements get in the way of replies which are often sent almost immediately. Only when a retransmitted request is received is an acknowledgement generated.

When a process — and thus a FLIP port — migrates, the FLIP layer deals with re-locating the FLIP port. The extra layer of naming using FLIP ports is needed to ensure that, upon migration, the same server *process* is re-located. After all, the transaction layer state resides with individual server process and, if that state is lost, a transaction will fail.

3.7 Other examples

3.7.1 VMTP

The *Versatile Message Transaction Protocol* (Cheriton (1986)), known as VMTP, is a protocol designed for the V system (Cheriton (1984)). Cheriton (1987) describes VMTP thus:

> VMTP is a transport protocol specifically designed to support the transaction model of communication, as exemplified by remote procedure call. In particular, a major design objective is to support high-performance communication for distributed operating system services, including time, naming, file access, remote execution and distributed programming. The full function of VMTP, including support for security, real-time, asynchronous message exchanges, streaming, multicast and idempotency, provides a rich selection to the VMTP user level while the subsettability allows the VMTP module for particular clients and servers to be specialized and simplified to the services actually needed.

The basic protocol for VMTP is a request/response protocol. A message (a request or response) is sent as one or more *packet groups*. The data in a packet group represents up to 16 kilobytes of data, or 32 *segment blocks*. A network packet (such as an Ethernet packet) can contain one or several segment blocks. A bit map of 32 bits, called the *delivery mask*, indicates which segment blocks of a packet group are in a network packet.

When a packet group is received, the delivery masks for the individual packets can be OR-ed together to obtain a bit map indicating which segment blocks are still outstanding. An acknowledgement packet contains this bit map and the sender can use *selective retransmission* for the missing segment blocks.

VMTP makes a special effort to deal with *overruns*. An overrun occurs when a faster machine sends packets to a slower machine so quickly that the slower machine misses some of the packets. This problem shows up with interfaces that cannot receive packets back-to-back. A typical consequence of overrun is that every second packet needs to be retransmitted. To prevent this from happening, VMTP uses *interpacket gaps* to allow sufficient time between packets for a slow receiver to get ready for the next packet in time. The VMTP protocol uses a feedback mechanism to adjust the interpacket gap for communication between machines automatically.

Large messages consist of several packet groups. A sequence of packet groups is called a *run*. Effectively, VMTP uses stop-and-wait on packet groups to transmit runs. This provides a flow-control mechanism.

VMTP has several extras intended to make the protocol more efficient or to improve the functionality. We mention the important ones.

A server can label a response to indicate that a message transaction was *idempotent*. This means that a client can repeat the transaction any number of times without there being any side effects. Requesting the time-of-day is a typical idempotent operation, but transferring money from one bank account to another clearly is not. By labelling responses as idempotent, VMTP does not have to make arrangements for retransmitting the response when it is lost; the server can reproduce the response when the request is retransmitted. When a response is not idempotent, VMTP must prevent the server from executing a request more than once.

A server identifier can indicate an individual server process or a *group* of server processes. When a request is sent to a *group identifier*, VMTP multicasts the request to all the members of the group. This is done on a *best effort* basis: the request is retransmitted until at least one response is received.

For real-time communication, VMTP provides *datagrams* (messages that do not require a response so they don't block the sender) and four levels of priority for messages. In addition there is also an option that allows VMTP to discard packets when the intended receiver is not ready for them.

Secure message transport is another option in VMTP. Each transaction can be made secure individually. The security mechanisms guard against wire tapping, tampering with messages, replays and impostors. Security is obtained by encrypting packets and using an authentication server. The mechanism is based on one described by Birrell (1985).

3.7.2 Mercury

The Mercury project at MIT's Laboratory for Computer Science studies the problems of heterogeneous computing. The communication mechanisms in Mercury (Liskov *et al.* (1987)) aim for high performance and flexibility. The research that led to these mechanisms was triggered by the following considerations.

Remote procedure call (Birrell and Nelson (1984)) is a convenient paradigm for structuring distributed programs. RPC has an important disadvantage, however. The caller blocks while the request is being sent, while the call executes and while the results are being sent back. The overhead of sending two packets and making three system calls per RPC is significant and could be avoided in many cases.

RPC does not allow any parallelism between caller and callee. For communication between a program and the X-window system, for instance, this is a disadvantage. Most RPC calls are intended to write strings to the screen and the performance of the window system could benefit dramatically if the calls were streamed.

The Mercury communication system attempts to do this streaming of calls in such a way that in the absence of errors, to the programmer, it *appears* as if all RPC calls are made consecutively, while *in reality* two streams are maintained, one from caller to callee and one from callee to caller with streams of calls and results that are only synchronized when necessary.

Calls to unrelated servers need not be synchronized at all, but the system cannot detect that two streams are unrelated without a mechanism for the program to tell it. This mechanism exists in the form of *ports* and *groups* of ports. A port is provided by a receiving entity and gives a caller a destination for remote procedure calls. Ports are strongly typed, *e.g.*,

port (int) **returns** (real) **signals** (e1 (char), e2)

By grouping ports, streams that have to be synchronized with respect to each other are indicated.

Some language support for streams exists. The *promises* mechanism (Liskov and Shrira (1988)) in Argus (Liskov (1984)) allows exception handling even when calls are asynchronous. Language veneer for the support of streams is also available for Lisp and C.

3.8 References

A. D. Birrell and B. J. Nelson (1984). 'Implementing Remote Procedure Calls'. *ACM Transactions on Computer Systems* 2 (1): 39—59, February 1984.

A. D. Birrell (1985). 'Secure Communication Using Remote Procedure Calls'. *ACM Transactions on Computer Systems* 3: 1—14, Feb. 1985.

D. R. Cheriton and W. Zwaenepoel (1983). 'The Distributed V Kernel and its Performance for Diskless Workstations'. *Proceedings Ninth Symposium on Operating System Principles*: 128—140, New York, October 1983.

D. R. Cheriton (1984). 'The V Kernel: A Software Base for Distributed Systems'. *IEEE Software* 1 (2): 186—213, April 1984.

D. R. Cheriton (1986). 'VMTP: a transport protocol for the next generation of communication systems'. *Proceedings of SIGCOMM '86*, Aug 5-7, 1986.

D. R. Cheriton (1987). *VMTP: Versatile Message Transaction Protocol.* Stanford University Computer Science Dept. Report, January 1987.

J. B. Dennis and E. C. Van Horn (1966). 'Programming Semantics for Multi-programmed Computations'. *Communications of the ACM* 9 (3): 143—155, 1966.

B. Liskov (1984). *Overview of the Argus Language and System*. MIT Laboratory for Computer Science Programming Methodology Group Memo, 1984.

B. Liskov, T. Bloom, D. Gifford, R. Scheifler, and W. Weihl (1987). *Communication in the Mercury System*. Programming Methodology Group Memo 59-1, MIT LCS, Cambridge, Ma 02139, Oct. 1987.

B. Liskov and L. Shrira (1988). 'Promises: Linguistic Support for Efficient Asynchronous Procedure Calls in Distributed Systems'. *Proceedings of the ACM SIGPLAN '88 Conference on Programming Language Design and Implementation*, 1988.

S. J. Mullender and A. S. Tanenbaum (1984). 'Immediate Files'. *Software-Practice and Experience* **14** (4): 365—368, April 1984.

S. J. Mullender (1985). *Principles of Distributed Operating System Design*. Ph. D. Thesis, Vrije Universiteit, Amsterdam, October 1985.

S. J. Mullender and A. S. Tanenbaum (1986). 'The Design of a Capability-Based Distributed Operating System'. *The Computer Journal* **29** (4): 289—300, 1986.

J. Ousterhout, H. Da Costa, D. Harrison, J. Kunze, M. Kupfer, and J. Thompson (1985). 'A Trace-Driven Analysis of the Unix 4.2 BSD File System'. *Proceedings of the Tenth Symposium on Operating System Principles*, 1985.

SUN (1986). *NeWS Technical Overview*, Volume . Sun Microsystems, Inc, 1986.

J. H. Saltzer, D. P. Reed, and D. D. Clark (1984). 'End-to-End Arguments in System Design'. *ACM Transactions on Computer Systems* **2**: 277—278, Nov. 1984.

R. W. Scheifler and J. Gettys (1986). 'The X Window System'. *ACM Transactions on Graphics* **5** (2): 79—109, 1986.

A. S. Tanenbaum (1988). *Computer Networks*, Volume . Prentice-Hall, Englewood Cliffs, N.J. 07632, 1988. (2nd edition.)

R. van Renesse, H. van Staveren, and A. S. Tanenbaum (1988). 'Performance of the World's Fastest Distributed Operating System'. *Operating System Review* **22** (4): 25—34, October 1988.

H. Zimmermann (1980). 'OSI Reference Model—The ISO Model of Architecture for Open Systems Interconnection'. *IEEE Transactions on Communication* **COM-28**: 425—432, April 1980.

Chapter 4

Remote Procedure Call

W. E. Weihl

Procedure call is a well-understood control mechanism used in many sequential programming languages. The basic idea of remote procedure call (commonly called *RPC*) is to extend the use of procedure calls to a distributed environment. In a simple scenario, when a remote procedure is invoked, the caller is suspended, a message containing the arguments is constructed and passed to the remote machine, and the procedure is executed there. When the procedure finishes, the results are passed in a message back to the calling machine, and the caller resumes as if the procedure had run locally. RPC is attractive as the primary communication mechanism for distributed programs because it is simple, familiar (because of its similarity to local calls), general (consider the number of single-machine applications that are implemented using local procedure call as the primary control mechanism), and can be implemented efficiently.

RPC can simplify the construction of distributed programs by abstracting away from details of communication, transmission errors, and failures. Ideally, a remote call would have the same semantics as a local call, so that the distributed nature of the program would not affect its (functional) behavior. (It will almost surely have an effect on performance.) In practice, this ideal is difficult to achieve. One reason for this is that failures are hard to mask completely. In addition, differences in data types and the need to send data in messages (instead of, for example, passing a pointer on the stack) typically result in RPC having a parameter passing semantics that either restricts or is different from local calls.

Many RPC systems have been built over the last decade. Notable work includes Nelson's PhD thesis (1981), Courier in the Xerox NS family of protocols (Xerox Corporation (1981)), the Cedar RPC system (Birrell and Nelson (1984)), Sun RPC (Sun Microsystems (1985)), Argus (Liskov and Scheifler (1983)), and the HRPC system developed at the University of Washington (Bershad *et al.* (1987)). Argus is unique among these systems in integrating a transaction mechanism (see

Chapter 11) with RPC. Some of these systems (for example, Argus and Cedar RPC) were initially designed to work with a single language, while others were explicitly designed for a multi-language or multi-machine environment.

While the simplicity of RPC makes it attractive as the primary paradigm for communication in distributed programs, the performance provided by RPC is not adequate for some applications. In particular, most RPC systems are designed to minimize latency (so individual calls are fast). In some applications, throughput is more important than latency. An RPC system could be designed to provide high throughput instead of low latency, but then it would not provide good performance for the applications that need low latency calls. An alternative, currently being explored in the Mercury system at MIT, is to allow the programmer to choose a low latency or high throughput implementation for each call.

In the remainder of this chapter, we discuss some of the issues involved in designing and building an RPC system, and then present two examples, Argus and Mercury. Argus is a programming language and system designed to support the construction of highly reliable distributed applications. Mercury is a system designed to support the construction of heterogeneous (multi-language and multi-machine) distributed programs.

4.1 Issues

In this section we discuss several issues that arise in the design of an RPC system:

- *Binding.* How does a caller name the procedure to be called, and how does the caller find the procedure?

- *Heterogeneity.* How does the system deal with multiple machine types and programs written in different programming languages?

- *Transparency.* To what extent do the semantics of an RPC match that of a local procedure call?

- *Concurrency.* What mechanisms are provided for obtaining concurrency, and how do they interact with the communication mechanism?

There are a number of implementation issues that we will not discuss here — for example, minimizing the latency of calls, minimizing the overhead of context swaps, and avoiding expensive connections. A good discussion of implementation issues, along with a description of an implementation optimized for low latency, can be found in Birrell and Nelson (1984).

4.1.1 Binding

An RPC system, like a system for building single-machine programs, must provide some mechanism for connecting the calling program with the called procedure. The calling program contains a name for the procedure to be called; this name must be *bound* to an actual value for the procedure. In addition, it is important to check that the caller and the callee agree on the interface (or type) of the procedure. Abstractly, the situation with remote procedures is identical to the situation for local procedures.

Binding can be accomplished in a variety of ways. A simple approach, taken in the MLP system (Hayes and Schlichting (1987)), is to extend the static *linker* to accommodate multi-machine programs. Alternatively, binding can be done each time a program is run using some sort of *dynamic linker*. The most flexible approach, taken in Argus and Mercury, is to allow binding to be done under program control: a program contains *procedure variables*, and assigns procedure values to the variables using some arbitrary computation (for example, looking up the names in some dynamic name space). The Cedar system provides support for all three approaches, though the second approach is the primary mechanism.

4.1.2 Heterogeneity

Current distributed systems exhibit a substantial degree of heterogeneity: many different kinds of machines are attached to the same network, and the programs running on those machines are often written in different programming languages. In addition, the different machines may be running different operating systems. An important problem is to permit programs running in a heterogeneous environment of this sort to communicate. To do so, it is necessary to define the semantics of communication in a language- and machine-independent manner.

Many RPC systems permit communication among heterogeneous program components by relying on static *declarations* of the interfaces of remote procedures. An interface declaration serves several purposes. First, the caller and callee must agree on the types of the arguments and results of a procedure; the interface declaration documents this agreement. (Some systems also permit remote procedures to signal *exceptions*; the types of exceptions should also be documented in an interface description.) Second, the interface declaration serves as a basis for type-checking, allowing both the caller and the body of the called procedure to be checked for type-correctness. Third, the representation for data at the two ends may be different; the interface declaration can be used as the basis for automatically generating the appropriate conversion code.

Inherent in the above discussion is the assumption that we have an appropriate notion of data type. Since different programming languages have different notions of data types, the types used in messages will in general be different from the types used locally in each program. To support heterogeneity, the types used in interface descriptions for remote procedures must be defined independently of any particular programming language.

If the types used in messages are different from the local types used in programs, we need a way of converting between the two kinds of types. Even if the types are the same (for example, in a single language system), different communicating modules may use different representations for the same type, and some form of conversion is needed here too. Many RPC systems use automatically generated *stubs* to perform such conversions.

Stubs were introduced in Nelson's thesis. To call a remote procedure, a client program makes a local procedure call to a *client stub* for that remote procedure. The client stub places an appropriate representation of the arguments in a message (a process commonly called *marshalling*), and then initiates a message exchange with the server machine. At the server, messages are dispatched to a *server stub*, which uses the incoming message to reconstruct the arguments and then passes them to the desired procedure. When the procedure returns, the process is reversed: the server stub marshals the results, and sends them back to the client stub; the client stub reconstructs the results and then returns to the calling program. The stubs encapsulate all details of conversion and communication; the caller does a local procedure to the client stub, and the server procedure is called via a local call from the server stub.

In many systems, stubs are generated automatically from the description of the remote interface. (Obviously, there needs to be a different stub generator for each language.) If the types used in messages are different from the local types used in programs, the stub generator must determine from the interface description what local types should be used in the stubs. For example, suppose a remote procedure has an interface indicating that it takes a sequence of integers as its only argument. In some languages, the client stub might have a single array argument. In other languages, the client stub might take a pointer to the array as an argument. This works fine as long as the correspondence between the types in messages and local types is reasonably obvious. If a language has no types that correspond naturally to a given message type, or if it has several, some mechanism must be provided for the programmer to override the defaults built into the stubs.

The problem of converting between different representations can be solved in several ways. One way is to define a single standard representation for each message type, and to require each sender and receiver to perform a conversion if its local representation does not match the standard. When the local representation matches the message representation, this approach is quite efficient, since it may be possible to use efficient block copy instructions, or at least to avoid the overhead of translating the data as it is copied. When the local representation does not match the message representation, however, the overhead of conversion can be substantial. For example, if the sender and the receiver have the same local representation, but their local representation is different from the message representation, two conversions will be performed when in fact none is necessary. Whether this is a problem depends on the amount of data transmitted with each call, and what fraction of the total time for a call is spent doing the conversions.

An alternative approach is for the sender to send its data using its local representation (with some sort of tag identifying the representation being used), and to have the receiver convert it if necessary. This has the problem that the receiver must be prepared to accept and convert any local representation (which causes problems as new machines and languages are added to the system). In addition, in some applications (for example, a heavily used server) it is better for the sender to perform any necessary conversion. Some systems handle low-level machine differences (such as byte order) in this way, but use a standard representation for most data types (for example, arrays).

Another problem is how to handle arguments that contain pointers. Many systems prohibit certain types, such as pointers, from being used for arguments and results of RPCs. Other systems, such as Argus and Mercury, allow pointers, but may impose some restrictions on them or provide semantics that differ from those in local calls. The issue of pointers will be discussed in more detail below.

Heterogeneity shows up at the implementation level as well. For example, different RPC systems use different network protocols to implement the same or similar semantics. The HRPC system at the University of Washington (Bershad *et al.* (1987)) allows a client program to call servers using different underlying protocols; the appropriate protocol is determined at binding time for each call.

4.1.3 Transparency

A basic goal of many RPC systems is to make the semantics of a remote call as close as possible to that of a local call. Some differences, however, are almost impossible to avoid.

First, the possibility of communication and site failure affects the semantics of remote calls. Different systems handle failures in different ways, resulting in a variety of calling semantics. Perhaps the weakest semantics are to provide no guarantees when a failure occurs. An invocation might result in the actual procedure being called zero, one, or more times; each call might run to completion or might fail part way through. These semantics push the job of coping with failures almost entirely on the application, but is quite cheap to implement.

Achieving stronger semantics can be difficult. The most difficult problem involves calls that have external effects, causing some action (such as dispensing money or opening a valve) to occur in the world outside the computer. Several alternative semantics have been explored. For example, the Cedar RPC system provides *at-most-once* execution: an invocation will result in the actual procedure running no more than once; if a response is received by the caller, the procedure ran exactly once, while if no response is received, the procedure might or might not have run (for example, the response could have been lost), or might have run partially. The Argus system provides *zero-or-one* semantics: each call appears to execute either zero or one times, and the response returned to the caller indicates whether or not the call was successful. A nested transaction mechanism (see Chapter 11) is used to implement these semantics. Note that the response returned to the caller applies only to internal effects; a call could have external effects and then abort, in which case the caller would receive a response indicating that the call never ran. Zero-or-one semantics make it much easier to keep internal data consistent in the presence of failures, but careful design is still necessary to cope with external effects.

A second area in which transparency is difficult to achieve is parameter passing. As discussed above, the data types used in messages (at least in a heterogeneous system) are not the same as the types used in programs. As a result, many RPC systems restrict the set of data types that can be used in remote procedures, for example, by prohibiting the use of pointers or procedures. Alternatively, types such as pointers may have different semantics when used in arguments and results of remote calls than in local calls. In Argus, for example, pointer structures are copied from the client to the server in an RPC, so that the client and server do not share data directly. If the call were local, the caller and the called procedure would share the same storage for the structure; no copy would be made.

Most RPC systems also pass arguments and results *by value*. As a result, they typically restrict the range of parameter passing semantics available to local calls, precluding the use of call-by-reference.

A final area in which transparency can be difficult to achieve is exception handling. Different languages provide a variety of exception handling mechanisms, ranging from a simple termination model as in CLU to a more complicated resumption model as in Mesa. An RPC system will either have to restrict the power of the mechanism in some languages, or provide a way of coping with the more complex mechanisms in languages that do not support it.

4.1.4 Concurrency

In many RPC systems, an RPC *blocks*: the caller is suspended until the called procedure returns a result. This can lead to problems if servers and clients are single-threaded. For example, a client may have other work that could be done while an RPC is being executed at a server. Also, a server may make calls to other servers as part of servicing a request from one client, and could service other clients while waiting for responses from the sub-calls.

A lightweight process facility provides a nice solution to many of the problems caused by blocking RPC. A server can run calls from multiple clients concurrently, each in separate processes. Similarly, a client can create several processes to perform work concurrently; if one blocks (perhaps waiting for an RPC to return), the others can continue. A good discussion of the interactions between calling mechanisms and support for concurrency can be found in Liskov, Herlihy, and Gilbert (1986).

4.2 Argus

Argus is a programming language and system that was designed to support the implementation of reliable distributed applications. In this section we provide a brief summary of the main features of Argus; more detailed descriptions can be found in Liskov and Scheifler (1983) and Liskov *et al.* (1987).

An Argus program consists of a collection of *guardians*. Each guardian resides at a single site, although multiple guardians may reside at the same site. Each guardian is a separate address space that contains data and a number of light-weight processes. A process in one guardian cannot access the data in another guardian directly. Instead, each guardian provides some number of *handlers*, which are operations that can be called by processes in other guardians. A handler call is a remote procedure call with zero-or-one semantics (achieved through the use of a transaction mechanism).

Binding is accomplished dynamically by passing guardian and handler names as arguments and results of handler calls. In addition, there is a system-wide 'catalog' that maps user-friendly names (such as 'printer') to data of various types. A guardian can store its name or the names of its handlers in the catalog; other guardians can look it up and retrieve the stored handlers. In this way, the catalog acts as a name service for exporting services.

When a process makes a handler call, it blocks until the results are returned. Concurrency is achieved by explicitly creating multiple processes. Each guardian starts running with a single background process. Any process can create other processes through the use of the *coenter* statement, which creates a dynamically determined number of subprocesses and waits for them to complete. In addition, a process can fork a completely independent process. Finally, a new process is created to run each handler call that arrives at a guardian.

Argus was initially designed as a single-language system so many of the issues involved with data types in a multi-language system did not arise. For example, the data types used in messages are the same as those used locally within a guardian. However, parameter passing for handler calls differs from parameter passing for local calls: parameters to local procedure calls are passed by sharing (similar to call-by-reference), while parameters to handler calls are passed by value.

Argus permits the programmer to define new, abstract data types. To permit such types to be used as argument and result types of handler calls, the programmer must define an *external representation*, or *xrep*, which is used to represent values of the type in messages. Each implementation of the type must then provide procedures to translate between the implementation's internal representation and the xrep. In this way, a type can be implemented in different ways in different guardians. This is important for the built-in data types, since differences in hardware may necessitate differences in representations for data types such as *integer*. In addition, it may be important for some abstract data types, since which of several implementations of a data structure is most efficient might depend on the patterns of access, and this may be different in different guardians.

Data local to a guardian is stored in objects in a garbage-collected heap. One object, such as an array, never contains another object, such as a record, directly; instead, the first object will contain a pointer to the second.† When an object is sent as an argument or result of a handler call, the system preserves the sharing relationships among the sub-objects. This is done by keeping track,

---

† The implementation optimizes small immutable objects, such as integers, to avoid using pointers.

during the construction of a message, of which objects have been encountered; if an object is encountered again, a reference to the earlier part of the message in which its value can be found is used instead of copying the object again. When a message is received, these references are used to reconstruct the pointer structure in the receiver's heap. Details can be found in Herlihy and Liskov (1982).

Preserving sharing is useful when the sharing relationships among objects encode meaningful semantic information. In many applications, however, pointers provide a convenient way of structuring the representation of some objects, but there is no actual sharing (or the sharing has no semantic meaning, such as when the shared objects are immutable). Since preserving sharing can be expensive — it requires frequent checks during the process of constructing and receiving messages — it would be nice to avoid the cost when it is not needed. The Mercury system, described below, is designed to preserve sharing when it is needed, but avoids the cost at other times.

4.3 Mercury

As mentioned earlier, RPC alone may not provide adequate performance for applications that require high throughput. These performance problems can be addressed using lower-level mechanisms, but such mechanisms can be hard to use. In addition, the use of lower-level mechanisms complicates server interfaces, and can result in a loss of flexibility because a server designed to be used via RPC would not be usable via a lower-level mechanism, and vice-versa.

The communication mechanism developed in the Mercury system generalizes and unifies RPC and byte stream communication mechanisms. The mechanism is high level, yet at the same time supports efficient communication for a broader class of application than is supported by either RPC or byte stream protocols alone. It is also simpler than the other mechanisms, because of its uniformity: it is not necessary to use two distinct mechanisms to achieve adequate performance. As a result, server interfaces will be more regular, which will permit applications to be plugged together more directly.

An important aspect of our mechanism is its flexibility. The builder of an application that provides a service to clients need not choose a communication paradigm (RPC or byte streams) in advance. Instead, the programmer of a client can decide for each call whether to optimize the call for high throughput or low latency, and thus use of the service can be tailored to meet individual needs. The result is better performance.

Our mechanism is programmer-oriented in the sense that it provides primitives that are easy for programmers to use. It is also language-independent. To make the mechanism usable within a particular language, some extensions to that language are needed; we call these the *language veneer*. Our initial prototype includes veneers for three languages, Argus, C and Lisp. (We have veneers for two versions of Lisp: Zetalisp, which runs on Symbolics Lisp Machines, and Elisp, the extension language for Gnu Emacs.)

4.3.1 Requirements

Before describing our mechanism, we will examine the requirements and goals of the mechanism in more detail. A uniform and flexible communication mechanism must support a wide range of applications. As discussed earlier, RPC is appealing because it is simple to use and understand. From work on sequential programming languages, we have a deep understanding of what procedure calls mean and how to reason about programs that use them. It is attractive to be able to benefit from these advances in distributed programs, which are already more difficult to implement than centralized systems.

In a distributed system, however, procedure calls have a serious disadvantage: they prevent the caller from running in parallel both with message passing and with the callee. In a centralized system, this might not be an important issue, since there may be only a single processor, so there may be little to be gained from such concurrency. In a distributed system in which the caller and the callee run on different machines, and in which the transmission delay for a message is significant, the loss of this concurrency can have a significant impact on performance.

For example, consider the use of a window system such as X (Scheifler and Gettys (1986)). To display information in a window, a program sends data to X, typically in small increments such as strings or lines, such as:

```
put(string1);
put(string2);
change_color("red");
put(string3);
```

Here string1, string2 and string3 are simply three strings that are intended to be displayed in an X window. Ideally, we would like to do each call as soon as the argument string is ready, without waiting for the reply to the previous call. If a lengthy computation or communication with another remote site such as a file system is needed to produce the next string, doing this work in parallel with the call and its processing will improve program performance. If the time to produce the next string is small, not waiting for replies improves performance and also allows the strings to be displayed without pauses in between. Of course, if one call is invoked before the previous one is complete, the order of the calls must be preserved so that, for instance, string3 is displayed in red, and the characters appear on the screen in the proper order.

We can illustrate why supporting high throughput communication is important by computing the performance improvement that it provides. Our analysis here is only approximate — for example, we ignore contention of multiple clients for a single server — but it should serve to give a rough idea of the potential savings. Consider a sender and a receiver, with the sender making calls to the receiver. Assume that the time for the sender to compute the arguments of a call is A, as is the time for the receiver to process a call and compute results, and for the sender to process the results. (Obviously, such uniformity is unlikely to occur in a real system, but it greatly simplifies our analysis.)

Let K be the time it takes to make the kernel call for sending or receiving a message, and let T be the transmission delay. Suppose the sender makes N calls in sequence.

If the sender must wait until the results of one call have been processed before making another call, it is easy to see that the time for N calls is $(3A + 4K + 2T)N$. Each call involves computing the arguments, processing the call, and processing the results $(3A)$, and sending and receiving two messages $(2K + T$ per message equals $4K + 2T)$. Now, suppose that the sender can start computing the arguments of one call immediately after sending the message for the previous call, and, similarly, that the receiver can receive a call as soon as the results for the previous call have been sent. If N is sufficiently large, the time for N calls is $2(A + K)N$. The sender can be kept busy all the time, first computing arguments and sending all the calls, and then receiving replies and processing the results. (For smaller N, or when the times for the various activities are not uniform, it may not be possible to keep the sender busy all the time.) Thus, as long as N is sufficiently large, the transmission delay is no longer a factor, since the sender runs in parallel with message transmission. (For simplicity, we are assuming the network has infinite buffer capacity.) In addition, the computation time on the receiving side drops out of the equation since the sender and the receiver can run in parallel.

The ability to make a call without waiting for the results of a previous call imposes a kind of pipeline structure on distributed computations. Viewing the computation in this way provides another way of understanding its performance. The maximum throughput is limited by the delay through the slowest stage in the pipeline — in the analysis above, the slowest stage turns out to be the sender. In addition, the throughput is not affected by the length of the pipeline; this is why the transmission delay is not a factor in the maximum throughput.

The transmission delay for a local area network is quite short, and, for many applications, may not have a significant impact on performance for blocking RPC. However, if the sender and receiver are on different local area networks, so that messages between them have to pass through one or several gateways, the transmission delay can become large, and can cause throughput for blocking RPC to drop significantly. One advantage of the pipelining structure outlined above is that it makes applications less sensitive to these differences in network topology.

There is one other important way in which we can improve throughput. Sending a network message typically has a fairly high fixed cost, independent of the size of the message. If calls are small, we can improve throughput significantly by buffering the calls, aggregating many calls in a single message. Buffering allows us to amortize the fixed cost of a message over many calls. For example, suppose that B calls or replies can be sent in a single message. The time for N calls is then $2(A + K/B)N$. Particularly for small calls, such as those that might be used to communicate with a window system like X, the performance advantages of this kind of buffering can be enormous.

In the example of the use of X above, the calls had no results; the only purpose of the reply was to indicate that processing of the call was complete. However, similar savings can be obtained for calls with results, provided that the result of one call is not needed to compute the arguments to the next. For example, suppose an editor is using X and needs to begin by obtaining some information about fonts:

```
for i from 1 to 20 do
    font[i] := get_font(a[i])
end
```

Here information is needed about twenty fonts corresponding to the elements of the array a. There is no real reason why the second call of get_font should wait until the first finishes since it does not depend on the results of the first. Notice that the above calls could run concurrently, since they are completely independent. Doing the calls sequentially is more convenient, however, because the program can maintain the correspondence between a font and what it represents in an easy way, and need not synchronize access to the font array.

Avoiding delays due to calls is not always important, but occasionally it is critical. Our experience with X indicates that adequate support for interaction with a remote display requires that delays be avoided. Another place where delays are a problem is in bulk data communication where we would like to be able to send a portion of the data while preparing the next for transport. A good example of the latter is query processing: if a query has many results, we can improve throughput significantly by overlapping the processing of one result at the caller while later results are being computed. This technique has been used in the Community Information System developed by Dave Gifford's group at MIT.

Of course, the programmer can cope with the above performance problems by clever programming. If the data items sent in each call are too small, they can be grouped together at the program level to reduce the number of messages sent, so only N/B calls need be made. If producing the next increment should be done in parallel with the previous call, the program can fork a process to make the call and wait for the result while it produces the increment; it would join with the forked process before making the next call. If the next call should be made immediately, rather than waiting for the reply, but it is important that the calls be done in order, an application level protocol could be invented so that the receiver will know the proper order. However, these structures are, for the most part, unattractive and ought to be avoided. The structures are particularly ugly when application level protocols are involved as they lead to more complicated interfaces.

Another possibility is to develop special mechanisms to solve specific problems. However, it is more attractive to generalize a single mechanism instead so it can be used everywhere. An important advantage of a single general mechanism is that applications other than those considered originally may be able to take advantage of the mechanism to improve their performance. In the following section such a mechanism is described.

4.3.2 Call streams

The mechanism is a *call-stream,* or *stream* for short. A call-stream connects two entities within a distributed program. One of these entities is the *sender*; the other is the *receiver*. The sender can make calls to the receiver over the stream, and the next call can be made before the reply to the previous call has been received. The call-stream guarantees that the calls will be delivered to the receiver in the order they were made and that the replies from the receiver will be delivered to the sender in the order of the corresponding calls. If this is not possible, the stream *breaks* as described in more detail below. However, a stream only breaks after the system has tried hard to deliver the messages and there is no point in the sender repeating the call at that point.

Streams permit senders to make three kinds of calls: *ordinary RPCs*, in which the sender receives the reply to the call before making another call; *stream calls*, in which the sender may make more calls before receiving the reply; and *sends*, in which the sender is not interested in the reply (assuming the call terminates normally). The application program at the receiver, however, need not distinguish between the three kinds of calls. The underlying system takes care of buffering messages where appropriate, and of delivering calls to the receiver in the proper order. Thus, the receiver provides a single interface, and clients can choose independently how to use it.

RPCs and their replies are sent over the network immediately, to minimize the delay for a call. Stream calls and sends are buffered and sent when convenient. In this way the overhead of kernel calls and the transmission delays for messages can be amortized over several calls, especially for small calls and replies. In addition, normal replies for sends need not be sent at all. We provide a 'flush' primitive that can be used to terminate a sequence of calls and replies and force the system to send out their messages, and a special form of RPC called a 'synch', which does a 'flush' and delays the caller until processing of all earlier calls is complete.

More precisely, this guarantee is (in the absence of failures):

1. *Exactly once delivery*. Each call request is delivered to the user code at the receiver exactly once and each reply is delivered to the user code at the sender exactly once. By *user code* we mean code corresponding to a program written by a user of our system, as opposed to the *system code* we provide ourselves.

2. *Ordered delivery*. The request for call $n + 1$ is delivered to the user code at the receiver only after the request for call n has been delivered to it. Similarly, the reply to call $n + 1$ is delivered to the user code at the sender only after the reply to call n has been delivered to it.

Notice that implicit in these requirements is a promise of delivery: calls and replies will be delivered in good condition.

Using a stream, the sender can do a sequence of calls with the same effect as if it waited to receive the *n*th reply before doing the $n + 1$st call. The system helps out by delivering calls in the proper order. The receiver is responsible for doing the processing properly. In particular, if call n has a side effect that ought to affect call $n + 1$, the receiver must ensure that this happens properly. For example, the `change_color` command must affect the color of subsequent displayed characters. A common approach might be for the receiver to execute call n to completion before receiving call $n + 1$; in this case it is easy for it to ensure the proper order of processing. A more sophisticated program at the receiver might process calls (such as queries and updates of a database) in parallel. In this case, it must synchronize the processing to ensure the required order.

Of course, the guarantees above cannot be realized completely because of problems such as site crashes and network partitions. If the system is unable to live up to the guarantees, it *breaks* the stream. It does so only after trying hard. For example, if the system notifies the user that delivery is not possible, there should be no point in the user trying again immediately, since the problem that prevented delivery is serious. We will discuss breaking streams in more detail below. One result of breaking a stream, however, is that user code at the sender is notified of the break.

In the remainder of this section, streams are discussed in more detail. We begin by defining the receiving end of a stream and go on to describe the sending end. Next, some ways of redefining streams dynamically are examined. Finally, we discuss the failure semantics.

A distributed program is composed of distinct *entities* that communicate with one another using streams. Each entity must reside entirely at a single site, since it would otherwise be very difficult to implement the ordering requirement. An entity has a unique name that is interpreted by the system. In particular, the system can find an entity given its name. We plan to allow entities to move, so we will need some sort of location service for finding entities. However, in our current prototype, entities cannot move, and the address of an entity is included as part of its name to make it easy to find the entity.

It is up to users to define what entities are. Entities will be implemented by different mechanisms in different languages. For example, in Argus, a guardian would be an entity, while in Ada, it is probable an entity would be a task. Our communication mechanism is independent of how entities are implemented; the neutral word 'entity' emphasizes this independence. In addition, we do not depend on the size of the entities or on how frequently they communicate. It is expected they are relatively large and need to communicate with one another relatively infrequently since remote calls are likely to be more expensive than local calls. However, in certain environments it may be more sensible to have smaller entities that communicate more frequently.

A receiving entity provides one or more *ports*. These are procedures that can be called remotely from other entities. It is not necessary that all communication between entities occur via ports. Entities could, for example, share data directly. However, the call-stream system supports communication only through calls on ports. In particular, no way is provided for references to data in one entity to be sent to other entities: all communication is by value. The only inter-entity sharing supported is of the entities themselves and their ports. Of course, entities could define application-level ways of referring to each others' data.

A receiving entity typically provides many operations that clients can use. For example, a mail repository back end provides operations to read and send mail, to create mailboxes for new users, and to destroy mailboxes for former users. Similarly, X provides many different operations for putting strings and graphics onto the display. For each operation it provides, a receiving entity creates a *port*. Some ports are created when the entity first comes into existence; others can be created dynamically. Ports are transmissible and can be sent as arguments and results of remote calls.

A call of a port can pass zero or more arguments. As mentioned above, these are passed by value. The termination model of exception handling developed for CLU (Liskov *et al.* (1977)) is used; thus, a call can terminate normally or in one of a number of named exceptions. In each case (normal or exceptional), zero or more results can be returned. A port is strongly typed, and its type contains information about the types of its arguments and results, for example,

```
port(INT32) returns(FLOAT64) signals(e1(CHAR), e2);
```

(The types used in interface descriptions for ports are in capital letters to distinguish them from the local types used in programs.) Here the port expects a 32-bit integer argument. If it terminates normally, it returns a floating point number. It can also terminate by raising the exception e1 or the exception e2; if e1 is raised it returns a character. The information in a reply is sent in a message as a discriminated union, and can be used in whatever way is appropriate in the programming language of the sender. Thus, in Argus the sender will use the built-in exception handling mechanism; in other languages the reply might be passed back using a kind of variant record. Our type system is described in more detail in the next section.

As mentioned above, any of our three calls (call, stream-call, and send) can be done to any port. Thus, a send can be done to a port that signals an exception. Our experience in distributed systems indicates that almost all calls have exceptions that can be raised. If sends to ports with exceptions were not permitted, many situations where sends would be useful would be ruled out. However, if an exception is raised by the processing of a send, the sender may want to know about it. This is provided for at the receiver by sending back an exception reply, just as we would for calls and stream-calls. It is up to each language veneer to determine how such information will be made available to the program.

One of the difficult issues in designing a language veneer for streams involves expressing stream calls and sends. Since the results of a stream call (or an exception raised by the processing of a send) are not available when the call is made, a mechanism must be provided for the calling program to pick up the results of the call some time after the call is made. We have designed one mechanism, which we call a *promise*, for the Argus veneer. Promises are similar to 'futures' in Multilisp (Halstead (1985)), except that they are strongly-typed, where the type includes the exceptions that can be raised by the promise. A stream call can be made to a port, creating a promise whose type indicates the result type and possible exceptions of the call. At some later point, the program can *claim* the promise, obtaining the results of the call, or any exception it raised, if the call has completed. If the call has not completed, an attempt to claim the promise blocks. Promises are described in Liskov and Shrira (1988).

As an example of this, a window system might provide a port that is used to create a new window. This port would be created when the window system comes into existence and registered in a catalog so that client entities can find it. (The catalog provides a mapping from user-friendly service names to ports that provide the named service; thus, it supports dynamic binding.) A group of ports might be created to serve as the user's handle on the window once it is created. Thus we have

```
create_window: port(...) returns(window)
window = struct [
    putc: port(char),
    putl: port(string),
    change_color: port(string),
    ...
]
```

To create a window, a user calls the `create_window` operation. This operation returns newly-created ports that can be used to interact with the new window; information about the window — its position and so on — need not be passed as arguments to these operations because it is bound into the window system code that processes the calls.

Ports are grouped together for sequencing purposes; as discussed below, all calls to ports in the same group from a single sender are sequenced. All ports in a group must belong to the same entity. Ports are placed in a group when they are created; in addition, as discussed further below, the grouping can be changed later. Groups of ports define the receiving ends of streams.

It is assumed that entities can survive crashes, although user code, not system code, is responsible for any state that needs to be saved and recovered. After a crash, an entity must reregister at its site to inform the system that it is again a possible source or sink for messages. Ports can also survive crashes, but again the system is not responsible for their survival. Instead, interested entities must remember ports on some stable device (Lampson (1981)). If the owner of the port crashes, it must reregister the port after a crash to notify the system that the port is again a legitimate target for messages. As discussed further below, no guarantees are made about whether or not messages sent to the reregistered port before the crash survive.

We assume that there may be concurrent execution within an entity. In some languages or systems, concurrency might be expressed directly in terms of parallel processes. In other languages, an entity might contain a single process that multiplexes its activities among a number of tasks.

Whatever the form of concurrency, users need the ability to use separate streams for separate concurrent activities. For example, suppose an entity is acting as a front end to a mail repository. It carries out conversations with several users concurrently, and communicates with back ends of the mail repository to carry out user requests. It would be wrong to use the same stream to send messages for more than one user because streams impose additional synchronization. If message n were for user u and message $n + 1$ were for user v, this would imply that message $n + 1$ could not be delivered until after message n, and furthermore, should not be processed until message n's effects are known. Delaying delivery of message $n + 1$ delays v unnecessarily, and might even lead to a deadlock, for example, if the process sending the message to v already held a lock on u's mailbox.

Although user code could get around these problems, by, for example, having replies just indicate message arrival, a more straightforward solution is to use different streams for different users. We permit this by allowing an entity to define *agents*. Each agent has a unique name and belongs to a single entity. Presumably, there will be a separate agent for each concurrent activity within an entity (although we do not require or rely on this).

Agents define the sending ends of streams. An agent and a port group together define a single stream: all calls sent by the agent to ports in the port group are sent on the same stream, and thus are sequenced. Calls made by different agents to ports in the same group are sent on different streams, as are calls made by one agent to ports in different groups.

As mentioned above, the sequencing provided by streams must typically be supplied for several ports at once. For example, a window system might provide several ports, including one to put a character in a window and one to move the cursor. Calls to these various ports must arrive in order or the user will not get the effect he desires. As discussed above, calls sent by a single agent to ports in the same port group are sequenced. We group ports by using a *group identifier*, or *group-id* for short. A group-id is a unique identifier. Every port contains a group-id, and all ports with the same group-id must belong to the same entity. Thus, the group-id identifies the port group.

A group-id is associated with a port when the port is created; thus a receiving entity decides how its ports are grouped. In the most common case, clients of the entity will accept this original grouping. However, it is also possible for clients to change the grouping. For example, consider two windows created by separate calls of `create_window`, where `create_window` returns a record of ports for manipulating a window:

```
w1 := create_window(...)
w2 := create_window(...)
```

Suppose that the ports returned by a single call of `create_window` all have the same group-id, but each call to `create_window` provides ports with different group-ids. Thus, calls to ports of w1 will be sequenced and calls to ports of w2 will be sequenced, but the two windows will be used asynchronously. Now suppose that the client wishes the uses of the two windows to be sequenced. To do this, we regroup the ports, e.g.,

```
g: group-id :=  % assign appropriate value
w3 := regroup(w1, g)
w4 := regroup(w2, g)
```

The two calls of `regroup` cause new ports containing the new group-id `g` to be created; these ports, however, have the same names and types as those in `w1` and `w2`, and the window system is still their owner. Now calls by the agent to both windows will be sequenced, so that in

```
w3.putc(c); w4.putc(c);
```

the character `c` will appear in the window referred to by `w4` after it appears in the window referred to by `w3`.

In the discussion above, the semantics of streams have been explained in the absence of failures. Now we consider what happens when parts of the system fail, for example, a site crashes or messages are lost.

The semantics of streams requires exactly-once, ordered delivery of requests. If either of these properties cannot be guaranteed, the stream *breaks*. In addition, a receiver can break a stream involving one of its ports. Messages cannot be sent on a broken stream. However, the sending end of the stream can *restart* it and then send more messages.

We can view a stream as a sequence of *incarnations*. Each time the stream breaks, its present incarnation is discarded, in the sense that no more messages can be sent on it. Each time a stream is restarted, a new incarnation is created. Each incarnation has a 'prefix' property: the sender is guaranteed that some prefix of the calls made in an incarnation were executed. The last call in the prefix might have been executed partially (if the receiver crashes while processing the call, for instance). However, any call for which the sender received a reply is guaranteed to have executed to completion. Thus, the sender knows that all calls up to the last one for which a reply was received were executed to completion, and some prefix of the remaining calls were executed, with the last call of that prefix possibly having executed only partially.

The system breaks a stream only because of crashes of the sender or receiver, or serious communication problems. It tries hard to deliver messages before breaking a stream, so if a stream is broken there is no point in the caller doing the call again immediately.

The system can break the stream at either the sending or receiving side. When the system breaks a stream at the sending side, it refuses to accept further calls for the current stream incarnation and also 'cancels' all outstanding calls on the incarnation for which it has not yet received a reply by terminating them with the *broken* exception. This exception has a string argument that explains the reason for the break.

A break at the receiving side causes the receiver to refuse to accept more calls on the stream incarnation. Eventually, the system at the sending end will discard the incarnation, either independently, or because communication from the receiver informs it of the break. It then terminates all outstanding calls as described above.

Breaks made by the system are asynchronous in that they happen independently of particular calls. User code at the receiver can also cause a stream to break. It might break a stream because it is unable to process a particular call, so it cannot process future calls on the stream properly. (Recall that the communication mechanism guarantees ordered delivery; the receiver is responsible for ensuring that the calls appear to be processed in order.) Such a break is synchronous because it happens as the result of processing a call. The break causes the system at the receiver to refuse further calls on the current stream incarnation, and thus user code at the receiver will not see them. The system sends a reply message back to the sender; the reply indicates that the incarnation has been discarded, and also contains an argument indicating what the problem is. The system at the sending side will then discard the incarnation and cause any outstanding calls for which it has not already received replies to terminate with the 'broken("receiver broke stream")' exception; these calls will necessarily come after the one that broke the stream.

User code on the sending end of a stream can discover that the stream is broken the next time it tries to use it, when it tries to receive a reply or make another call. (Other mechanisms might also be provided, depending on the programming language.) It responds to information about a break in an application-dependent way. The stream can be made usable again by restarting it. The sender can restart a stream at any time, not just after a break. A restart causes the system at the sender to discard the current incarnation, thus 'cancelling' any outstanding calls on it by giving them the result 'broken("stream restarted")', and to create a new incarnation. The system at the receiver is informed about the restart before (or as part of) the first call sent over the new incarnation. At that point it can discard any calls on the old incarnation that have not yet been given to user code for processing.

4.3.3 Data types

We intend that ports always be used in a type-correct manner; we are providing facilities to store information about the types of interfaces and to do type checking at either compile time, link time or run time (depending on the language). Even so, type correctness cannot be enforced since all the entities that might send messages to ports cannot be controlled. Instead, we will take a constructive approach to this problem; we make it easy for senders to provide correct data by supplying translation functions (as part of stubs) that do the right thing. Also, we attempt to detect arriving messages containing information of the wrong type. It is not the intention that each piece of data in a message is self-describing (contain its own type), however, so the checks will only validate such things as the proper size of an argument, and that the sender and receiver of a message were compiled using the same interface description. Notice that even with self-describing data, it is impossible to be certain that the data is of the type described.

To distinguish between the data types used in Mercury messages and those used locally in programs, we have adopted the term 'vspace' (short for 'value space') for the types used in messages. This emphasizes that what is important about a type used in a message is simply the set of values that belong to the type, and how they are represented. This differs from data types in some languages (particularly those that permit the programmer to define abstract data types), in which a type is characterized also by the *operations* that can be used to manipulate objects of the type.

Our type system contains a fairly typical set of base vspaces and constructors, including integers and floating point numbers of several different sizes, union types, records, and arrays. In addition, there is a vspace constructor for ports that defines a port vspace for each possible list of argument and result vspaces. There are no restrictions on the use of the constructors; for example, an array of ports can be sent as an argument of a call.

In addition to the vspaces mentioned above, there is also support for preserving sharing in pointer structures in messages. This is accomplished using a special vspace constructor called a *container*. A container can be thought of as a box containing a value; a 'pointer' to the box is a value that can itself appear in other values. For example, a value of the vspace

```
RECORD[x, y: ARRAY[CONTAINER[INT32]]]
```

would consist of a record value with two components. Each component of the record would be an array. The components of the arrays would be pointers to containers, with an integer inside each container. Different components of the arrays could point to the same container. Thus, sharing of array elements is represented by introducing containers. However, the two arrays in the record, since they are not in containers, are not shared: they are distinct array values.

The CONTAINER constructor provides a simple mechanism for encoding sharing structure in a message. The process of encoding and decoding messages with containers is similar to the process used in Argus. The CONTAINER constructor has two advantages: the cost of preserving sharing must be paid only when it is really needed, and the places where sharing is important are explicitly documented.

There are several options for integrating remote calls and vspaces into a programming language. The simplest is to define a mapping from vspaces to types in the language, so that for each vspace there is exactly one type that corresponds to it. This is essentially the approach taken in most RPC systems today. The advantage of this approach is that it is easy to automate the stub generation process. Given an interface description, the corresponding local type for each argument and result position is uniquely defined. Building a stub generator then involves defining the translation functions between each vspace and its corresponding type.

The disadvantage of the simple approach of having a single type corresponding to each vspace is that it is inflexible. For example, in a language like Argus there are several record-like types, struct, record, and atomic_record. All three are records, in that their objects consist of several named fields, but they differ in that struct objects are immutable, meaning that once they are created they cannot be modified, while the record type provides operations to modify fields of a record, and the atomic_record type provides synchronization and recovery to ensure that transactions are atomic. While these three types provide different operations for manipulating their objects, there is no difference in the values of their objects: all can be viewed as a mapping from field names to associated values. The differences in the types lie in whether the value of an object can change over time, and in whether objects of the type can be shared among concurrent transactions.

Suppose a restriction is imposed, limiting a single type to each vspace. For example, suppose that the Argus struct type is selected to be the type corresponding to the Mercury RECORD vspace. Then an Argus program calling a port that expects a RECORD argument must supply a struct object. If the way in which the object is used locally in the program requires it to be mutable, the program would need to use a record locally, and then copy the record into a struct to make the call on the port. Such extra copies are potentially expensive, and also require cluttering the program with unnecessary code.

A more flexible system could permit several types to correspond to each vspace. It might also be useful to allow there to be several vspaces corresponding to a single type. For example, suppose there are vspace constructors for fixed-length sequences and for variable-length sequences. It would be useful to permit a program to supply an array to a remote procedure that expects a fixed-length sequence, and also to a remote procedure that expects a variable-length sequence.

Further flexibility can be achieved by allowing multiple translations between a given type and vspace. For example, there are two natural translations from a stack type to a sequence vspace: one that puts the top of the stack at the front of the sequence, and one that puts it at the back.

Several options are currently being studied for providing greater flexibility. One option is to enhance the stub generators: rather than generating stubs merely from an interface description (which simply describes the argument and result vspaces), we could annotate the interface description with the desired corresponding type for each argument and result position, and generate stubs from the annotated description. In a language like Argus, in which the compiler acts as a stub generator, we could integrate vspaces more directly into the language. As one might expect, providing greater flexibility sometimes results in greater complexity, requiring the programmer to supply more information as input to the stub generation process. However, this must be balanced against the costs of the restrictive approaches, in terms of both efficiency and programmer convenience.

4.4 References

B. N. Bershad *et al.* (1987). 'A Remote Procedure Call Facility for Interconnecting Heterogeneous Computer Systems'. *IEEE Transactions on Software Engineering* **SE-13** (8): 880—894, 1987.

A. D. Birrell and B. J. Nelson (1984). 'Implementing Remote Procedure Calls'. *ACM Transactions on Computer Systems* **2** (1): 39—59, February 1984.

R. H. Halstead (1985). 'Multilisp: A Language for Concurrent Symbolic Computation'. *ACM Transactions on Programming Languages and Systems* **7** (4): 501—538, 1985.

R. Hayes and R. D. Schlichting (1987). 'Facilitating Mixed Language Programming in Distributed Systems'. *IEEE Transactions on Software Engineering* **SE-13** (12): 1254—1264, 1987.

M. Herlihy and B. Liskov (1982). 'A Value Transmission Method for Abstract Data Types'. *ACM Transactions on Programming Languages and Systems* **4** (4): 527—551, 1982.

B. Lampson (1981). 'Atomic transactions'. In Goos and Hartmanis (Ed.), *Distributed Systems — Architecture and Implementation*, Volume 105, pages 246—265. Springer-Verlag Lecture Notes in Computer Science, Berlin, 1981.

B. Liskov and R. Scheifler (1983). 'Guardians and Actions: Linguistic Support for Robust, Distributed Programs'. *ACM Transactions on Programming Languages and Systems* **5** (3): 381—404, July 1983.

B. Liskov, M. Herlihy, and L. Gilbert (1986). 'Limitations of synchronous communication with static process structure in languages for distributed computing'. *Proceedings of the Thirteenth Annual ACM Symposium on Principles of Programming Languages*: 150—159, 1986.

B. Liskov and L. Shrira (1988). 'Promises: Linguistic Support for Efficient Asynchronous Procedure Calls in Distributed Systems'. *Proceedings of the ACM SIGPLAN '88 Conference on Programming Language Design and Implementation*, 1988.

B. Liskov *et al.* (1977). 'Abstraction Mechanisms in CLU'. *Communications of the ACM* **20** (8): 564—576, 1977.

B. Liskov *et al.* (1987). *Argus Reference Manual*. MIT-LCS-Technical Report-400, MIT Laboratory for Computer Science, 1987.

B. J. Nelson (1981). *Remote Procedure Call*. CSL-81-9, Xerox Palo Alto Research Center, 1981.

R. W. Scheifler and J. Gettys (1986). 'The X Window System'. *ACM Transactions on Graphics* **5** (2): 79—109, 1986.

Sun Microsystems (1985). *Remote Procedure Call Protocol Specification.* Sun Microsystems, Inc, 1985.

Xerox Corporation (1981). *Courier: The Remote Procedure Call Protocol.* Xerox System Integration Standard XSIS-038112, Stamford, Connecticut, 1981.

PART III

Naming and Security

If you want to identify an object in a computer system, you have to be able to name it. There are several aspects to naming in distributed systems that are different from naming in centralized systems.

A name can refer to a local object or to an object on another machine. The system has to be able to find *where* an object is, given its name. When objects can move about in the system, finding where objects are becomes even more difficult, especially when the system is very large. In Chapter 5, Needham shares his experience with designing very large scalable name spaces and making them work as well.

Security is closely related to naming. Chapters 6, 7 and 8 each describe a different aspect of computer security. The subject of Chapter 6 is authentication: making sure that two communicating parties can both satisfy themselves that they are really communicating with who they think they are; making sure that the party at the other end of a communication channel corresponds to its name. Needham is an expert in the field of authentication. The logic for authentication developed by Burrows, Abadi and Needham (1988) has already helped to expose design errors in several published authentication protocols, including the draft ISO standard for authentication.

Chapter 7 describes another aspect of security in distributed systems: protecting objects from unauthorized access. In this chapter, Mullender discusses general issues and methods, after which he gives a detailed description of the protection mechanisms in the Amoeba distributed system.

The subject matter of Chapter 8 is also related to Amoeba. It describes how accounting and resource control work in the Amoeba system, which is possibly the only distributed system about whose accounting system published material exists.

Chapter 5

Names

R. M. Needham

What's special about naming in distributed systems? If you read Saltzer (1979) on naming and binding there doesn't seem to be very much that depends on the system being centralized, and there doesn't seem to be very much either that needs adding to that excellent exposition. The material that has to be stored to do with naming is of course not all in the same place in a distributed context, but there is a separate subject called distributed database, and, on the face of it, that handles all we need to do. In fact, it is worth talking about naming in distributed systems, because it isn't really that simple.

5.1 Naming in general

Names have several purposes in computer systems. One is to facilitate sharing. If various computations want to act upon the same object, they are enabled to do so by each containing a name for the object. When such a name comes to be resolved, so that the shared object may be used, it has to be arranged that the names themselves and the contexts used to resolve them all give the same result. It is not at all necessary that the same name be used in all instances, though it will often turn out that way. This is because names are frequently used for communication about objects; if they are to achieve this correctly then they must either be valid in a universal context, or they must be accompanied by a representation of the context in which they are to be resolved, or it must be certain that the context will turn out to be identical wherever the names are to be resolved. The fact that names are used to refer to objects does not mean that names are bound whenever they are found. It is a perfectly legitimate use of names to arrange that several computations will, when executed, share an object, although we do not yet know which object that is. One must distinguish here between the use of names which have been bound to an object of as yet unknown value — typically a container which will at the appropriate time have some bits put in it — and names which have not been bound at all.

Another use of names is exemplified by unique identifiers, which are usually particular members of some large set, such as the integers up to $2^{128} - 1$. It is arranged that names of this form are never reused, so that a particular 128 bit pattern refers either to nothing or, if it refers to anything, to the same thing at all times. In practice, such names are never found unbound, and their function is largely to provide location independence. If we wish to have the flexibility to move the representation of an object from one place to another and still have it satisfactorily shared between computations, the names used by these computations must be, or resolve into, a form of name that is location independent and which can itself be resolved to find the current physical location information. Names of this form are sometimes used for a security-related purpose. If the proportion of possible names in a name space that actually refer to objects is sufficiently small, and if there is no general way of predicting which names will be used, then the names may be used as tickets of permission to access the objects. A computation that presents a valid name may be assumed to have been given it deliberately rather than to have guessed or invented it. This is an example of the use of protected names or capabilities, one of the classical approaches to access control management.

The last paragraph has implicitly referred to another distinction relevant to names. This is between human-sensible names such as RMN/ANIMALS/PIG and names intended for internal use only such as #257A 9B3F CD45 B1C8. This distinction is often made, and it is not a particularly helpful one (except, of course, if you have to remember the names or type them in). A more serious distinction is between pure names and other names. A pure name is nothing but a bit-pattern that is an identifier, and is only useful for comparing for identity with other such bit-patterns — which includes looking up in tables in order to find other information. The intended contrast is with names which yield information by examination of the names themselves, whether by reading the text of the names or otherwise. For example, a human-sensible name like RMN/ANIMALS/PIG may, in a suitable context, be interpretable to say that if it is a valid name at all, there is a directory called RMN and it contains an entry for a sub-directory called ANIMALS. Something that is less obviously penetrable like #257A 9B3F CD45 B1C8 may, if it is the unique identifier of a file from the Cambridge File Server (Needham and Herbert (1982)), be known to contain the identity of the disc pack on which the file resides.

Such impure names all carry commitments of one sort or another which have to be honoured if the names are to retain their validity. Looking at the previous examples, the former commits one to having, among other things, a directory called RMN, and the latter commits one not to move the file from one disc pack to another. Pure names are very attractive because they commit one to nothing. Of course, like most good things in computer science, pure names help by putting in a extra stage of indirection; but they are not much use for anything else.

5.2 Naming in distributed systems

What's different about distributed systems? That they are not centralized. If, in a system, there is anywhere that has global information about all instances of anything, then it isn't a real distributed system but a centralized one made of funny components. This rather gross statement has to be interpreted; we should really have said 'anywhere that *necessarily has to have* global information,' otherwise one could stop a system being distributed by storing a list of its components on a disc somewhere. We also have to be careful in principle about the definition of 'having global information'. In some distributed systems, one may approach any instance of a service to perform a task the correct execution of which requires that information from in a general way anywhere must be used. We do not deny that Grapevine (Birrell *et al.* (1982)), in which one may send a message anywhere from any message server, is distributed on these grounds. To pursue this point further would take us out of technology and into philosophy.

We must first consider some characteristics and consequences of distribution.

5.2.1 Bindings

A first and obvious consequence of distribution is that there is, in some sense, more naming because there is more binding. By this I mean that, by comparison with centralized systems, there is more that can change — consider

> binding machines to addresses
>
> binding services to machines

neither of which has a very obvious analogue in a centralized system. It is the conventional wisdom of distributed computing that in any cases of this sort early binding is extremely wicked, and every opportunity must be taken to allow for variability. To describe a system designer as the kind of person who would embed machine addresses in his code is considered to be not merely critical but downright offensive. In practice, the conventional wisdom is rarely followed as well as it should be, because of the practice of programmers of omitting code that they think they do not need. In order to preserve efficiency of operation it is necessary to cache bindings that are frequently required, and in many cases these bindings change very rarely indeed. The Cambridge File Servers had ring addresses 1B and 6C from their inception and retained these until they were abandoned. It is extremely likely that many programs which made use of them did not include reconsultation of the name server in their outermost retry loop, which, strictly speaking, they should have done. If someone had changed these numbers at three o'clock one morning, and updated the name server accordingly, it may confidently be expected that parts of the distributed world would have been found not to be working by nine. Clients of the file service would have behaved as if it were down. This in fact corresponds to behaviour in other aspects of life; if I call a friend on the telephone and get 'number unobtainable' I tend to assume that his phone is broken, not that he has moved. Eventually, though, I shall call enquiries just in case.

5.2.2 Interpreting names

As was made clear in an earlier section, the purpose of names is to identify values, usually by being looked up in collections of names to yield the values from a table. In a distributed system complications arise. The lookup tables, or directories as they are often called, are frequently replicated for a variety of reasons including system robustness and, often more importantly, ease of access in the sense of being able to find an instance of desired material geographically close by. Replication, however, has its own complexities to do with distribution of updates. (Phone books are an everyday example of replication for easy access.) Also, given a name to look up, it is necessary to be able to find the directory to use, which may not be obvious. (Consider what it would be like to find a phone number for J. W. Tailcheck, 19 Gossamer Gardens, which is quite likely a unique identification — or to establish that such a person did not exist.)

This last point indicates why pure names are not much good in distributed systems, the point being that you don't know where to look them up, and pure names have to be looked up to be of any use at all. The nearest you can get to pure naming, in practice, is to accompany the name with a hint as to where abouts it may profitably be used; if the hint fails, global search may, in principle, be needed. How disastrous this is depends on the size of the network, how likely the need for such a search is, how good broadcast facilities there are, and how clever network components such as gateways are. The Amoeba system seeks to tackle this problem (Mullender and Tanenbaum (1986)).

5.2.3 Consistency — immediate

A common objective of distributed database technology is to arrange that when a request for the value associated with some name or definite description is put to some manifestation of a database, the reply, should one be forthcoming, will be correct in the sense that it reflects the most recent information that there is (anywhere). Systems that achieve goals of this type do so at a cost, incurring one or both of two penalties:

(a) One can't do an update because insufficient of the places at which it must be made are accessible

(b) One can't do a read because the material to be read isn't stable yet, or because insufficient replicates are accessible.

The bodies of data representing name lookup tables are sufficiently fundamental to practical distributed computing that it usually believed that there should be no compromise about accessibility. It is more important to get an answer than to be guaranteed to get the absolutely latest answer. It would not be considered tolerable for me to be unable to look up someone at MIT to find their mailbox because not all the replicates of the relevant directory in South America were known to be up to date. This attitude depends for its justification on a selection of assumptions, each of which is capable of discussion and argument:

(a) Naming data doesn't change very fast, so inconsistencies will be rare

(b) You will find that something doesn't work if you try to use obsolete naming data, so you can attend to it

(c) Even if you don't find out, and use obsolete data, it doesn't matter much *sub specie æternitatis.*

The first assumption seems to be fairly true. A great bulk of the contents of a naming database concerns people, who do not change their names very often, who do not change their organisational affiliations on a daily basis, who do not change their passwords or their mailbox sites all that often. There is in fact not a great deal of solid evidence for this assumption; people who maintain naming databases have in general not kept many statistics. In the vicinity of Cambridge, UK, it seems that something like a quarter of the entries in the telephone book change each year, or, more precisely, that there are about 5000 changes a week to a database of about a million entries. However, it is easy to assume too much. The Grapevine Registration Servers started off in life as repositories for the information needed to translate between people's names and mailbox sites. They were also used for translating the names of distribution lists, i.e. for recording the contents of the lists. The assumption of slow change, at any rate, was not true for some of the distribution lists, and algorithmic changes needed to be made because of the resulting inconvenience. If a naming implementation has been designed on the assumption of low update traffic one must beware of adding applications which break the assumption.

The second assumption is fairly true too, with, interestingly, a cognate exception to the first. In many contexts the use of out-of-date naming data is self-detecting. You can't log in with a new password if the system at the other end only knows an old one for you, you can't connect to a service which is now on a different machine from where you thought it was, and you can't connect to a machine which is now at a different network address. If this property applied universally, a very attractive implementation technique comes at once to mind. Anyone may keep copies of parts (or the whole) of a naming database. Perhaps it is circulated on a CD-ROM from time to time. Certainly no attempt is made to propagate changes to it by pushing from the centre. Use of obsolete data will be detected, authority consulted, and the newer data cached for use until the next updated edition appears. The reader will recognize the technique adopted by the world's phone companies. The authority for consultation may logically be regarded as centralized though it would certainly have a distributed implementation; the point about it is that its implementation is orders of magnitude smaller than the naming database as a whole, and it may perfectly well be susceptible to standard methods of treatment such as quorum-consensus. Unfortunately, using an obsolete value of a list isn't that easily detected. It may only become apparent for reasons outside the system and after a long time. It certainly is not a basis for a visit to central authority and the caching of a new value; lists are, in a way, the Achilles' heel of the second assumption as well as of the first.

The third assumption is of a rather different status. If it is the case that, in almost all circumstances, changes to the naming data propagate very quickly to all stations, then one can argue that a use made of the data in place A at about the same time as it was being changed in place B has an essentially indeterminate result; as long as a half-changed state is never seen then all is as well as may reasonably be hoped for. After all, the user of the data might have asked for it a second or so sooner. Independent and unsynchronized activities are going to give indeterminate results and we should not futilely complain about this rather obvious fact. This may even be believed if propagation time is long. It is clearly deplorable for avoidable error to be made, but having people killed in battle in eighteenth century India because it was impossible for the British or French to tell the combatants instantly when they kissed and made up for a few years wasn't avoidable.

A point that is most naturally made in the context of consistency is that the issue may be fudged to some extent if what the naming system is used for is predominantly convergent. Grapevine is again our example, since its naming scheme was designed explicitly to support message delivery. The case in point is the translation from names to mailbox sites. If, because of the lack of propagation of an update in that system, a message is sent to the wrong message server, it is forwarded rather than rejected. Out-of-dateness is transformed from a correctness issue to a performance issue. Evidently, not every application can be expressed in a convergent way; it is not clear what characterizes the set of applications that can be so expressed. At any rate, there is here a prime example of making the substrate simpler by taking advantage of certain properties of an application.

Another consequence of the abandonment of transactional consistency for naming databases worth mentioning has to do with client blunders. If an attempt is made to look up an erroneous name, that is, something to which no entry corresponds, the answer should strictly be 'Either the name you have presented is wrong or it is as yet unknown to this instance of the service which is only guaranteed up-to-date to time t'. We are, once again, familiar with this topic from the world of the phone book. If I fail to find an entry for a company that I believe to have existed for some years, I shall look for an ad or a letterhead to check how they spell themselves rather than call enquiries and ask about new listings. I am not aware of any experience of this sort with computer name services.

5.2.4 Consistency — long-term

While there may be room for argument about how much effort should be devoted to obtaining very rapid consistency of an updated naming database, there is no room for argument about the desirability of avoiding long-term inconsistencies developing among what are supposed to be replicates of a single directory. This topic falls into two parts, one of which is germane to our present subject-matter and one of which is not. The latter, concerned with how one propagates updates among replicates of a naming database, whether it should be done by deterministic methods or by stochastic methods for example, is a fascinating subject in itself but cannot really be covered here. See Lampson (1986) and Demers and Sturgis (1987) for details of two very different approaches. The former part concerns the representation of values and updates in a naming database, and is directly relevant to us here.

A naming database is the aggregate effect of the changes or updates that were made to an initially empty state. In a centralized system, without replication and with all changes being entered at a common place, there is little conceptual difficulty in deciding what the database ought to contain at a particular time. One way of defining it would be as the result of taking a journal of all keystrokes at the origination site of the update and applying it to an empty state. In a distributed system things are not so straightforward for the reasons discussed in the last section, and no simple conceptual model like replaying journalized keystrokes will do. All the quirks and glitches that occurred in the network would have to be updated, which is not possible.

Updates are distributed by sending messages containing them to sites which are believed to be interested. The message delivery mechanism is never completely reliable, and it may have a deliberate element of randomness in its application. The result of this is that messages about differing or conflicting updates to the same value may arrive at a site in an arbitrary order, and it is essential that this does not affect the final result. We have to be a little careful about how we specify the desirable property since the most obvious way of doing it involves a counterfactual conditional:

> If the supply of updates stopped, then there would eventually be a glorious uniformity

where there is no reason to suppose that the supply would ever stop for long enough for the assertion to be tested. Attempts to deal with this are treated in some detail in Lampson's paper referenced above.

5.2.5 Scaling

In a centralized system there is usually some a priori idea about how large the set of names to be dealt with is liable to get. In many, if not in most, distributed systems this is not true, and it is good design to assume that it never is. Our image should rather be of an indefinite number of machines each providing

some part of a name lookup service of indefinite size which is managed by a
great number of more or less autonomous administrators. The whole business
should never have to be subject to radical redesign simply because it has grown.
The relevant topic here is the management of the name-space rather than the
avoidance of scale disasters in the implementation, and a prominent feature is
the use of measures to avoid confusion resulting from accidental non-uniqueness
of naming. Of course, it is easy enough to generate unique names as, for example, by prepending the time from a wall-clock to the serial number of the
machine on which the name is being generated. Such names are not quite as
useless as pure names are, because they do contain a reference to one machine,
but we would not usually want to give the creating machine so special a status
as would be implied by that approach, or to have to keep a machine in
existence as long as all objects it had ever named. (There is a slightly arcane
point here to do with trust. We could be trusting machines to use their own
serial numbers rather than someone else's.)

The more customary way to control uniqueness is the use of hierarchy. Most
reasonable suggestions for distributed naming make use of a hierarchic division
of a name-space leading to the use of multi-part names reminiscent of (and thus
to be carefully distinguished from) the familiar names for files in a garden
variety operating system such as UNIX. If people are responsible for a small
part of a hierarchic name-space they have no difficulty in maintaining uniqueness, which is only required within a directory. In real life the account just
given is a little glib, and there is a buried issue that ought to be exposed. Early
in these notes it was emphasized how many uses of naming there were in distributed systems. It has implicitly been assumed that these can and should all be
catered to by the same naming structure and probably by a common naming
mechanism. This is far from necessarily so, and the point warrants discussion.

That a certain machine is being prepared to offer a particular service by
RPC, may very well be indicated by an entry in a name server relating the
name of the service offered to the name or to the address of the offering
machine. At some level, this is identical to the operation that relates the name
of a user to his mailbox site, but, at another level, it is very different. One way
of seeing this is to compare it with a different form of electronic mail, namely
fax. It is, in principle, perfectly capable of integration into a workstation world,
in which context I would have on my screen something like

John Evans, Nocturnal Aviation Ltd, Cambridge Science Park, 0223 234567 *

and would copy the appropriate number into the destination field. Assume that,
in a very slight update of current fax practice, a digitally coded line is sent so
that the whole line marked * appears at the destination machine-readably. It is
reasonable to expect that a computer at the receiving end routes the material to
Evans, or, if his screen won't produce it, prints it and tells him, or, if the matter
isn't resolved, passes the decision as to what to do to a (human) clerk.

The foregoing is very like the way paper mail is dealt with in an organization
such as the Computer Laboratory where I work, and is also very like the way

Telex communications were handled in a place where I worked some years ago. It is very unsuitable, of course, for RPC binding and things like that, but is arguably more suitable for mail than the presently customary methods. Generality has its price, which is often much higher than one first thinks. In the present instance, the final name used — the phone number — is managed in a much flatter way than is usual with computer names, and is also administered in a much less intelligent manner, which is a good thing, since the less we rely on intelligence the better.

5.3 Examples

In conclusion, two examples are presented of approaches to naming, where rather different emphases occur.

5.3.1 The DEC global name service

The following discussion is based on the system described in Lampson (1986), of which the author was one of the design group. Here we concern ourselves not with the mechanism for handling distribution but with the structure an interpretation of the naming system itself. Those of its goals relevant to the present discussion are:

- Long life, during which many changes will occur in the organization of the name space and the components that implement the service

- Large size, to handle an essentially arbitrary number of names and serve an arbitrary number of administrative organizations.

Hierarchy is used to manage name-creation and the user sees a multipart name looking much like a file-name in an ordinary operating systems such as Unix. The purpose of the name service is to map names to values and values themselves may be structured. Suppose (and the examples are in the main taken from Lampson's paper) that there is a hierarchical directory structure rooted in a node called *ANSI*† and a substructure of values within a directory, as illustrated in Figure 5.1.

Directories have unique identifiers known as DIs and the directory tree is stuck together by giving in a directory the DIs of its juniors; an arc labelled with a DI is a *directory reference* (DR). In this design there is a concept of *full name*, which has to be distinguished from a similar notion in filing systems. In a filing system we may consider a full name as starting from a well-known and unique *root*. A full path name will resolve correctly in any environment where the root is correct. In the

---

† The paper avoids the common American view that the US is the root of everything and does not itself need a name. This will be seen also in electronic mail systems, where there are domains such as UK, FR, and so on but not one called US. This has the odd consequence that UK domains have to be given different names from American ones, despite the apparent hierarchic structure. This is why US names for businesses begin COM and UK names for businesses begin CO.

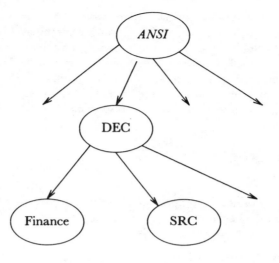

Figure 5.1

present context a full name is any name starting with a DI. Such a name will resolve correctly wherever it is encountered; pedantically one might say that it will never resolve incorrectly, since inability to find the directory with the given DI will prevent resolution occurring at all. In the examples given above, the head node ANSI was put in italics to make a distinction which can now be appreciated: the string *ANSI* refers to the DI of the *ANSI* directory. If the DI of the directory *ANSI*/DEC/SRC is #783, then #783/Lampson is as good a full name as is *ANSI*/DEC/SRC/Lampson.

We may thus see that it is as if there were two trees among directories: one based on their text names as full names starting from a root such as ANSI, and another very flat one with a hypothetical super-root, which consists simply of a list of all the DIs.

Why should one go to all this complication? It is in order to be able to grow and combine pieces of name-space in response to organizational needs. There is no problem if a name service grows downwards and outwards from a fixed root; the manager of any directory may create entries in it for individuals or for new directories without having to engage in any outside consultation, and the best sort of full names will start with the local root. Suppose however that it is required to bring together under a common root the trees for DEC and IBM, wherein full names *DEC*/SRC/x or *IBM*/TJW/y. Notice first that these names will still work correctly, being full names the first component of which is a DI, provided that one can physically find the directory with the required DI. In order to get help with this, it is possible to place in the common root directory an entry of a different kind. Suppose the common root is *ANSI* = #999,

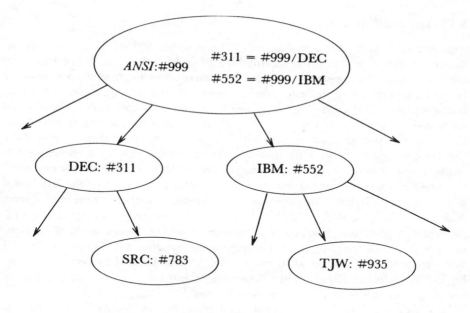

Figure 5.2

DEC = #311, *IBM* = #552. We may then place in the ANSI directory translation entries for well-known directories such as DEC and IBM, of the form
'#311 → #999/DEC,' and similarly '#552 → #999/IBM.' It will thus be possible to go to the new root ANSI with an old name DEC/SRC/x and have the
correct result. The process is illustrated by Figure 5.2

It should be emphasized that these devices are not required in order to maintain
the correctness of the naming system. They are there to make it possible to use
names in contexts where they would formerly not have worked because of the
unavailability of a root directory, or perhaps one should say of the first directory
in a full name.

Similar manœuvres can occur if the change is one of subsumption, for
instance, if DEC buys IBM. Names of the form ANSI/IBM/X/Y will *prima
facie* no longer work, because IBM is no longer an immediate child of ANSI. It
is only necessary to insert in ANSI an entry of the form 'IBM → #999/-
DEC/IBM' and all will be well.

It is perhaps worth mentioning that it is not compulsory for a client of this naming service to utter nothing but full names. The standard helpful but confusing
devices, familiar from filing systems, in which working directories, local roots, and
what have you, are all available. They are nothing more than syntactic devices
for prepending standard material to a quoted name; they have the effect of permitting a user to type less at the cost of having more hidden context, change to
which may hamper correct name resolution in other places or at other times.

5.3.2 The Stanford design

This approach (Cheriton and Mann (1989)), is characterized by a strong desire to avoid location problems having anything to do with the structure of a naming facility. They deal in objects managed by managers — to cause an operation to be performed on an object one sends a request to the manager and, subject to access controls and so on, the manager does the required work. An object's name determines its manager, and the primary task is to discover where physically the manager of a given object is. An object has a multi-part name with the same resemblance to a file name as in the system described earlier, but a name of that form is bound directly to the object; it is not bound to some internal name or unique identifier that is itself bound to the object (see the DIs in the last example). Indeed, the contrast goes further. Suppose there are names A/B/C, A/B/D, A/B/E, A/B/F, and so on. In the earlier system this would have presupposed the existence of a directory object A/B with a DI of its own, being a first-class member of the progeny of the hypothetical super-root. In the Stanford system there is no such implication. It may be, and indeed is, useful to be aware of clusters of names like the example, but there is no ontological commitment. An outline of the mechanisms follows.

It is assumed that there is a single root, and that any named object has an absolute name depending on that single root. The manager of any object will know the name of any object managed, and it is up to a client that depends upon an object to know where its manager is. It is envisaged that clients will typically have extensive caches of object names and their managers, and that if cache lookup fails, either because there is no entry or because no response is received from what is presumably an obsolete manager address then a new attempt is made by multicast (or even broadcast) to find a manager. Since it is certain that any attempt to have an object managed by an agency other than the manager will fail, there is no need to inform all clients which may have cached information about a manager's location that the manager has moved.

It is legitimate to record what Cheriton and Mann refer to as a context, and to use it as a hint in looking up a name. A context is the result of a partial lookup; for example to look up A/B/C/D we may look up C/D in the context provided by having antecedently looked up A/B. A context is rather a low-level notion, such as a process identifier and some numbers. It was said earlier that the existence of a number of objects of the form A/B/X/Y where X and Y vary does not presuppose that there is an object A/B which we should think of as a directory. The use of contexts does not violate this, because a context is just a hint. If on reference to a cache a client needing to interpret A/B/C/D finds a context for A/B, then it is quite legitimate for it to send to the appropriate place the context and C/D. If the operation does not succeed, then one multicasts with A/B/C/D.

As one would expect, there are arrangements for handling 'current contexts' which have no surprising properties.

5.3.3 Commentary

The two approaches outlined differ markedly. In the Stanford approach the path-name from the root is the only canonical name for an object, which makes for a level less of organization and some simplicity. A Stanford name as presented relative to a context may look very like a DEC name presented relative to a DI — they may even be bitwise identical, but the DI is the frozen truth and the context is just a hint. Accordingly, the Stanford design lacks the features which facilitate gross restructuring of the name-space by punning the use of DIs. These questions of gross readjustment are not yet the subject of reported experience.

This chapter has attempted to study naming in distributed systems as a function to be provided rather than to consider in detail how, in particular, replication is effected.

5.4 References

A. D. Birrell, R. Levin, R. M. Needham, and M. Schroeder (1982). 'Grapevine: An Exercise in Distributed Computing'. *Communications of the ACM* **25**: 260—274, April 1982.

D. R. Cheriton and T. P. Mann (1989). 'Decentralizing a Global Naming Service for Efficient Fault-tolerant Access'. *ACM Transactions on Computer Systems* **7** (2), May 1989. (Also available as Stanford Report STAN-CS-86-1098.)

A. Demers and H. Sturgis (1987). 'Epidemic Algorithms for replicated Database Maintenence'. *Proceedings Sixth ACM Symposium on Principles of Distributed Computing*, 1987.

B. Lampson (1986). 'Designing a Global Name Service'. *Proceedings 5th ACM Symposium on Principles of Distributed Computing*: 1—10, Calgary, Canada, Aug. 1986. (1985 Invited Talk.)

S. J. Mullender and A. S. Tanenbaum (1986). 'The Design of a Capability-Based Distributed Operating System'. *The Computer Journal* **29** (4): 289—300, 1986.

R. M. Needham and A. J. Herbert (1982). *The Cambridge Distributed Computing System*. Addison Wesley, Reading, MA, 1982.

J. H. Saltzer (1979). 'Notes on Database Operating Systems'. In R. Bayer, R. M. Graham, and G. Seegmuller (Eds.), *Operating Systems — An Advanced Course*, Volume 60. Springer-Verlag, Lecture Notes in Computer Science, 1979.

Chapter 6

Using Cryptography for Authentication

R. M. Needham

Cryptography has come into use in practical computing in close association with the advent of distributed computer systems. There are several reasons for this. One is an enabling change. Distributed systems tend not to have dumb terminals but workstations, even if simple ones. These workstations are capable of encrypting and decrypting material and of playing a part in encryption-based protocols. The other principal reason is a requirements matter; the networks on which distributed systems are based are typically insecure by their nature, and the only way to avoid data being readily accessible to all is to encrypt it. There is not any obvious analogue to the protection achieved between jobs or processes in a time-shared system, in which physical or logical separation is not too difficult. The tradition of protection by address-space management becomes almost wholly irrelevant.

6.1 What and why

Encryption is a process of transforming data, usually referred to as plain text, into cipher text in a manner such that the cipher text can only be turned back into plain text by the use of a particular key and an appropriate algorithm. We first introduce some terminology.

6.1.1 Conventional encryption

This is the term used for cryptosystems in which the same key is used for the encryption and the decryption. Thus we have

103

$Ciphertext$ = Encrypt($Message, Key$)

$Message$ = Decrypt($Ciphertext, Key$).

For such a system to be useful, the Key must be a shared secret between the originator of the message and the interpreter of it; shared because both need to know it, and secret because otherwise nothing is achieved. The best known conventional cryptosystem today is the US *Data Encryption Standard* (DES). It uses a key of 56 bits to encrypt blocks of 64 bits of data. Being a standard it is thoroughly described in the literature, National Bureau of Standards (1977) for example. It was designed for convenient hardware implementation, and many chips have been made to do this. However, in many parts of the world there are substantial legal or official obstacles to the ready use of DES hardware; software implementations of doubtful legal standing and mediocre performance are common. Relatively little appears to have been done on conventional encryption algorithms suitable for software implementation — Wheeler (1987) is an example.

At the heart of DES lies a method for building encryption out of key-controlled one-way functions. Suppose a block to be encrypted consists of two equal parts L_0 and R_0. These may be replaced as follows:

$$L_1 = R_0$$
$$R_1 = L_0 \oplus \text{OWF}(K, R_0).$$

This has of course not encrypted R_0 at all, which is one reason why multiple rounds of encryption are needed. DES has 16. Decryption works backwards in an obvious way.

6.1.2 Public-key encryption

This is the term used for cryptosystems in which different keys are used for encryption and decryption. Thus we have

$Ciphertext$ = Encrypt($Message, Key$ 1)

$Message$ = Decrypt($Ciphertext, Key$ 2).

It is assumed that in a usable algorithm knowing one key gives no clue as to the value of the other. It is then possible that there is, associated with a principal, a key which is well-known to all, *Key* 1, called the public key, and a secret known only to the owning principal, *Key* 2, called the secret key. Anyone may communicate securely with the principal in question by encrypting using *Key* 1.

The attractions of public-key encryption were first noticed by Diffie and Hellman (1976) and the most satisfactory practical algorithms are due to Rivest, Shamir, and Adleman (1978). The RSA approach depends upon the extreme difficulty of factorizing huge composite numbers of maybe 150 or 300 decimals which have only a few factors, such as two, each of which is itself vast. The existence of the RSA method has given a great fillip to the factorizing industry, and it is considered prudent to use very large numbers indeed for encryption keys that are meant to last.

One should think of using a key of maybe 500 bits, which then turns into the size of the block to be encrypted. This is quite large. The encryption and decryption operations are computationally heavy, consisting of taking the message and raising it to an immense power modulo a vast number. RSA is not therefore usually considered suitable for the encryption of bulk data.

RSA has the extremely helpful property that the two keys function in either order. That is to say, in the example above, we could successfully encrypt with Key 2 and decrypt with Key 1. This is not necessary in order to justify the 'public key' title, but it is a very valuable feature in practice.

6.1.3 Assumptions

All use of encryption in distributed computing relies upon various assumptions that are not always carefully set out, and which may in fact only be valid in special circumstances.

(a) The encryption is perfect: you cannot decrypt without knowing the appropriate key, nor can you find the key from the cipher text or from a combination of cipher text and plain text. This is in principle simply false, but may, in practice, be adequately true if one interprets 'cannot' as meaning 'cannot with a reasonable amount of computing'.

(b) You can recognize whether a message has been decrypted with the correct key or not. This is another theoretically shaky assumption, and, if it is to be treated as valid, considerable constraints are placed on what is communicated and how. One must not, for example, ever have a message which is completely unpredictable to the recipient, for he will not know whether it has been decrypted with the right key. The requirement is that there must be at least as much redundancy in the message as there are bits in the key. This is often achieved by devices such as knowing that the message consists of ASCII text.

(c) If 'Encrypt(Message A, Key K) = Encrypt(Message B, Key L)' then Message A = Message B and Key K = Key L. This is in fact very like (b).

(d) Accidents don't happen. If you decrypt a set of bits and get the Ten Commandments, someone encrypted them — yet another version of the same point.

All these assumptions enter into the design of protocols for the use of encryption, and it is right that designers should be aware of what they are assuming.

6.2 Threats

The most obvious use of cryptography is to maintain secrecy of information, that is, to make it difficult or impossible for an unauthorized person or a program operating on such a person's behalf to comprehend data that should not be comprehensible. The way to achieve this is to arrange that the data in question is encrypted in such a manner that only the intended recipient(s) can decrypt it. This is a response to the evident fact that in most forms of network there is little that can be done to prevent data flowing over the network being physically copied by anyone. If you cannot prevent copying you had better prevent comprehension.

A logically different use of cryptography is to maintain integrity of information. Suppose that we have a body of data consisting of an ordered chain of blocks; one way of compromising its integrity would be to alter the ordering. If you cannot, because of ignorance of keys, compute what the correct block 5 would look like in position 6, then you have a much harder task in interfering by exchanging blocks 5 and 6. In general, one use of encryption is to tie pieces of information together. This can be done separately from secrecy considerations, as the following example shows. Suppose that block 5 of the data is represented by the following:

> The characters of the data itself; the string 'FIVE'; the string 'FIVE' prepended to a 32-bit checksum CS of the data and encrypted using a key K.

To place that block in position 6 one would need to be able to encrypt using K the checksum with 'SIX' prepended, which is impracticable if you don't know K. The data is public.

Note that in this example we carefully arranged that the material to be encrypted fitted into one DES-sized block. All the bits of the cipher block depend on all the bits of the clear block, and hence the two pieces of data are held together. If there is more material than will fit in one block one has to do something extra to hold the blocks together, by having part of the clear block of one dependent on the other, or similar devices. For a comprehensive treatment of these topics in a context of communications security, see Voydock and Kent (1983); here we simply introduce some of the notions and terminology.

If, given a quantity of material to be encrypted and sent, we simply chop it into lengths appropriate to our favourite block encryption algorithm, encrypt them, and send them, we are working in what is known as Electronic Codebook Mode (ECB). This is considered to have a number of disadvantages for general use. On the face of it, there is no defence against permutation of blocks as a means of interfering with the message, though this depends upon the choice of level of protocol at which encryption is done. Perhaps more seriously, identical blocks will appear identically in an encrypted message, potentially betraying structural or pattern information.

It is possible to deal with these problems by using Cipher Block Chaining (CBC), which works as follows. The nth block is X-ORd with the encrypted version of the $n - 1$st block before itself being encrypted. Since we shall presumably have decrypted the $n - 1$st block before attempting to handle the nth, we shall have the $n - 1$st block of cleartext to hand for the required X-OR after decrypting the nth block of ciphertext. Such an operation must start somewhere, and both parties must have and agree on an initial vector which may be thought of as the encrypted version of block 0. It is advisable for the IV to be private, and it can reasonably be sent using ECB encryption. If a message being sent by the CBC method suffers change to part of the ciphertext on the way, more of the received plaintext will be corrupted.

It is evidently necessary for the two participants in the use of an encrypted message to share knowledge of the key to be used (conventional encryption) or alternatively to know the appropriate key-pair(s) in the other case. It has already been mentioned that public-key algorithms are computationally rather heavy; one practical use for them is the distribution of keys for conventional encryption which is much faster. It is the conventional wisdom, indeed, that keys of a long-term character should not be used for the encryption of bulk data but only for the protection of the keys needed for that data. We must accordingly consider the question of how pairs of communicants are put in possession of a shared key, since it is impracticable for every pair of potential communicants to have a statically shared secret key — there would simply be too many. Practical means require the use of what were originally called *key distribution centres* but which are now perhaps more often referred to as *authentication services*. The change of name is not accidental: it reflects the fact that if A and B need to engage in a secure communication they almost invariably also need assurance as to each other's identity. Equally, procedures for Authentication tend to leave the participants in possession of a shared secret which may very usually be suitable for use as a key.

6.3 Authentication and its logic

The remainder of this chapter concerns procedures for authentication and the means for reasoning about such procedures. The principles appear quite simple. If I believe that only Joe and I know a certain (conventional) key K, and I receive some material encrypted with key K, and I didn't do the encryption myself, then perhaps I ought to believe that Joe did. Notice here that it is crucial that I should know that the material was encrypted with K; this relies on the assumptions discussed above. It should also be added that believing that Joe did the encryption is not the same as believing that he did it recently. Much of the complexity of cryptographic authentication protocols is concerned with establishing timeliness of messages, that is, that they are not replays of old ones.

We here discuss authentication based on the use of conventional encryption; this is not as large a limitation as one might suppose because the main use of public-key encryption in this context is to facilitate the possession by the partners of a shared secret key for conventional encryption. Our treatment here will make use of recently published work by Burrows, Abadi, and Needham (1988) but will, however, illustrate a long-standing protocol for authentication.

Authentication protocols as discussed here guarantee that, by the end of a successful run of the protocol, if the principals involved really are who they say they are then they will end up in possession of one or more shared secrets. What is meant by the phrase if the principals involved really are who they say they are? If we are talking of people then we may at the end of the day be making an anatomical remark to do with retinal patterns, finger-prints, genetic traits, and so on. But these anatomical things are not readily checked by the average workstation (or at all) and some principals are not people but services such as file servers or indeed authentication servers which do not have fingers. In the result most authentication is not done anatomically but on the basis of pre-existing shared secrets set up on the authority of managers who have recognized principals directly. In this context we are talking about the phrase 'if the principals involved really are who they say they are' meaning if the principals know certain pre-existing secrets shared with authority.

6.3.1 Notation

To study authentication protocols we need a formalism and some postulates. We have chosen quite a sparse logic which has no notion of negation (or thus of falsehood) and no connective between propositions other than conjunction. The following definitions are taken from the paper referred to:

$P \models X$ — P believes X. Principal P is prepared to act as though X were true.

$P \hspace{0.2em}\vert\!\!\sim X$ — P once said X. The principal P at some time sent a message including the statement X. It may have been long ago or very recently, but it is known that P believed X when he sent the message.

$P \Rightarrow X$ — P has jurisdiction over X. P is the authority on X and should be trusted on the matter. This construct is used when a principal has delegated authority over some statement or set of statements. A common example concerns statemants to the effect that encryption keys have been carefully devised.

$P \overset{K}{\leftrightarrow} Q$ — P and Q may properly communicate using the good key K. K will never be discovered by any principal except P or Q or one trusted by both of them.

$\{X\}_K$ — X encrypted using key K. It is really an abbreviation for an expression of the form $\{X\}_K$ signed P. The signature of P appears when the encryption is used, but it is unreadable by everyone else. Note that a host can be assumed to recognize its own messages.

$P \lhd X$: $\quad$ P sees X. Principal P has received a message containing X and P can read X, maybe after some decryption. Thus P is able to use X in other messages.

$\#(X)$: $\quad$ Formula X is fresh, that is, X has not been sent before the current run of the protocol. This is commonly true of nonces, quantities invented for the purpose of being fresh, but there may be other ways of guaranteeing freshness.

6.3.2 Postulates

1. The message meaning rule tells us how to interpret encrypted messages:

$$\frac{P \models Q \overset{K}{\leftrightarrow} P, \; P \lhd \{X\}_K}{P \models Q \mid\!\sim X}$$

It is assumed that P recognizes that X is not of his own making. P believes that Q once said X, whether recently or long ago is not known.

2. Nonce verification: expresses that the sender is presumed still to believe in recent messages.

$$\frac{P \models \#(X), \; P \models Q \mid\!\sim X}{P \models Q \models X}$$

X should be in cleartext (so that it is a statement and can be believed). This rule is the only way of promoting a statement from 'once said' to 'believes'. How P came to believe in freshness is not part of this rule.

3. Jurisdiction:

$$\frac{P \models Q \Rightarrow X, \; P \models Q \models X}{P \models X}$$

4. Rules to do with sets of beliefs:

$$\frac{P \models X, \; P \models Y}{P \models (X, Y)} \qquad \frac{P \models (X, Y)}{P \models X} \qquad \frac{P \models Q \Rightarrow (X, Y)}{P \models Q \Rightarrow X}$$

5. Bidirectionality of keys:

$$\frac{P \models R \overset{K}{\leftrightarrow} R'}{P \models R' \overset{K}{\leftrightarrow} R} \qquad \frac{P \models Q \models R \overset{K}{\leftrightarrow} R'}{P \models Q \models R' \overset{K}{\leftrightarrow} R}$$

6. Seeing the whole of a formula, if you know the keys:

$$\frac{P \lhd (X, Y)}{P \lhd X} \qquad \frac{P \models Q \overset{K}{\leftrightarrow} P, \; P \lhd \{X\}_K}{P \lhd X}$$

7. Freshness extends:

$$\frac{P \mid\equiv \#(X)}{P \mid\equiv \#(X, Y)}$$

Given these postulates we may proceed as follows with the analysis of a protocol. Authentication protocols are usually expressed as a series of messages passed among the players, with the semantics of the messages left to the reader's imagination. Our notation can be used to express each protocol message in an idealized form as a formula, and we can see whether the postulates, together with assumptions made by the parties (which may differ from protocol to protocol) permit the deduction of beliefs by the parties which amount to the establishment of mutual authentication. To proceed further we must consider just what these beliefs should be.

6.3.3 The goal of authentication

It is not utterly obvious what the goal is and how it should be interpreted. The authors of this logic took authentication between A and B to be achieved if:

1. $A \mid\equiv A \overset{K}{\leftrightarrow} B$

2. $B \mid\equiv A \overset{K}{\leftrightarrow} B$

3. $A \mid\equiv B \mid\equiv A \overset{K}{\leftrightarrow} B$

4. $B \mid\equiv A \mid\equiv A \overset{K}{\leftrightarrow} B$

1 and 2 seem straightforward. They amount to saying that both partners believe that a certain key, the same key, is suitable for secure communication between them; suitability includes being new, rather than being re-used from a previous occasion, being secret, and (really a subset of secrecy) being competently manufactured, such as not being drawn from some small subset of the apparent key-space.

Argument may, however, arise from 3 and 4. They are requirements about each party's beliefs about the beliefs of the other, and turn out in practice to mean that each must have reason to believe that the other is present now. A protocol in which A asked an authentication server to supply it with a key for talking to B, and also to pass the key out of the blue sky to B with a note saying that it is for talking to A would not have met the latter two conditions though, in the absence of communication failure, it would have met the former two. The reason why there is room for argument is that the initiating principal has presumably engaged in authentication in order to communicate, and if it is indeed the case that one of them is not present then this fact will soon enough become apparent when the communication is attempted. An expression sometimes used in this context is that the final stages of authentication are piggy-backed on the early stages of communication. The authors followed did not take that view, preferring that the authentication protocol should have a clean end when all the requirements have been met.

It should be noted that this requirement is not the same as what logicians mean by common belief. That is a notion which has no place in an engineering subject, since it requires that A and B both believe that they both believe that they both believe ... that they both believe that K is suitable.

6.3.4 Informal groundwork

Before we embark on a worked example based on a published protocol it is worth reviewing in less formal terms some of the more detailed goals a good pro- tocol should attain. These seem mainly to concern authority and freshness.

The requirements for authority are that various crucial operations are done by the right agency. The leading one is creating a key, which is often done by an authentication server. We convince ourselves that the key comes from the server because it comes under cover of what we believe to be a shared secret between ourselves and the server; we accept such a key because we believe that the server has jurisdiction over statements that certain keys are suitable for certain com- munications — in short we believe it makes up keys properly.

Requirements for freshness have to do with protection against replay of mes- sages copied from the network. Any principal which could be confused by the use of illegitimate replays needs to have reason to believe that material on which it will act is fresh. The concept of freshness is introduced to abstract from the ways in which freshness may be mediated in concrete protocols. There are vari- ous ways in which this is done in practice, including:

> The use of challenge-response operations. A principal A requires to receive from B a response including (or including by implication) a nonce identifier just sent by A to B. Provided that this nonce has not been used before, and that it is not predictable, A assumes that the response is not a replay. Note that it is A that will make the judgement about freshness, and it was A's responsibility to use a sensible nonce.

> The use of time. If it is assumed that all principals have a reasonably com- patible view of what the time is, then A may assume that if a message that undoubtedly originated with B contains a time which is, in A's judgement, sufficiently close to the current time as perceived by A, then that message is not a replay, but fresh.

A point of some subtlety arises in connection with the use of time. B could in principle issue a large number of messages with time-stamps in the future, and with the time-stamps accompanying them in clear. An intruder could seek to replay one with a time-stamp near enough to the present to fool A. This may seem a little far-fetched (it is). It is however a suitable peg on which to hang the point that the participants in an authentication protocol are usually assumed to trust each other to go through the protocol honestly. Our picture should be one of honest principals striving to set up an authenticated channel between themselves in the face of an hostile world. None of what is said here sheds much light on what happens if a principal fails to meet the requirement. The most obvious mode of failure is to publish or otherwise to pass on what is meant to be the shared secret. A philosophical aside is appropriate here. It is no accident that the logic deals with belief but not knowledge. That something is a shared secret is fundamentally capable of being believed but not known.

6.3.5 The Needham and Schroeder protocol

Needham and Schroeder published their protocol in 1978 (Needham and Schroeder (1978)), and it forms a suitable example for the means of analysis. One could have taken a more recent one, but the advantage of using Needham and Schroeder is that the analysis shows how the authors were assuming something they did not realize, and makes it very clear why this assumption is necessary.

The concrete protocol as published is as follows, where A and B are the authenticating principals, K_{xy} is a key suitable for communication between X and Y, S is an authentication server with statically shared secrets with A and B, and N_w for various w are nonces.

1. $A \to S$ A, B, N_a
2. $S \to A$ $\{N_a, B, K_{ab}, \{K_{ab}, A\}_{K_{bs}}\}_{K_{as}}$
3. $A \to B$ $\{K_{ab}, A\}_{K_{bs}}$
4. $B \to A$ $\{N_b\}_{K_{ab}}$
5. $A \to B$ $\{N_b - 1\}_{K_{ab}}$

Only A deals directly with the server, which generates the conversation key K_{ab} and a certificate sealed with B's static key containing the conversation key and A's identity. This certificate is decrypted by B and then B carries out a challenge-response handshake with A, to assure itself that the certificate is not a replay. In the last message almost any non-identity function of N_b would do: it is just that message 5 must be different from message 4.

The idealized protocol is

1. $A \to S$ N_a
2. $S \to A$ $\{N_a, (A \overset{K_{ab}}{\longleftrightarrow} B), \#(A \overset{K_{ab}}{\longleftrightarrow} B), \{A \overset{K_{ab}}{\longleftrightarrow} B\}_{K_{bs}}\}_{K_{as}}$
3. $A \to B$ $\{A \overset{K_{ab}}{\longleftrightarrow} B\}_{K_{bs}}$
4. $B \to A$ $\{N_b, A \overset{K_{ab}}{\longleftrightarrow} B\}_{K_{ab}}$ signed B
5. $A \to B$ $\{N_b\, A \overset{K_{ab}}{\longleftrightarrow} B\}_{K_{ab}}$ signed A

The additional statements about K_{ab} in messages 2, 4, and 5 of the idealized protocol assure A that the key can be used as a nonce. It is legitimate to insert them because they are clearly believed. In order to start analysing the protocol we have to give some obvious assumptions:

$$A \mathrel{|\!\equiv} A \overset{K_{as}}{\leftrightarrow} S$$

$$S \mathrel{|\!\equiv} A \overset{K_{as}}{\leftrightarrow} S$$

$$B \mathrel{|\!\equiv} B \overset{K_{bs}}{\leftrightarrow} S$$

$$S \mathrel{|\!\equiv} B \overset{K_{bs}}{\leftrightarrow} S$$

$$S \mathrel{|\!\equiv} A \overset{K_{ab}}{\leftrightarrow} B$$

$$A \mathrel{|\!\equiv} (S \Rightarrow A \overset{K}{\leftrightarrow} B)$$

$$B \mathrel{|\!\equiv} (S \Rightarrow A \overset{K}{\leftrightarrow} B)$$

$$A \mathrel{|\!\equiv} (S \Rightarrow \#(A \overset{K}{\leftrightarrow} B))$$

$$A \mathrel{|\!\equiv} \#(N_a)$$

$$B \mathrel{|\!\equiv} \#(N_b)$$

$$S \mathrel{|\!\equiv} \#(A \overset{K_{ab}}{\leftrightarrow} B)$$

These are what is commonly called in US English boilerplate — the turgid exposition of the obvious which is an essential prerequisite for the use of formal methods. It would be tedious to attempt follow through the verification, which essentially consists of applying the message meaning rule to every received encrypted message, and making use of the rest of the postulates and the initial assumptions to reach the goal of mutual authentication stated earlier. The details of such verifications are best checked by machine.

There is another reason for not following through the detail of the verification: it does not work. At message 3, B can deduce by the message meaning rule that

$$S \mathrel{|\!\sim} A \overset{K_{ab}}{\leftrightarrow} B.$$

However, nothing enables this to be promoted to the form which would permit further deductions

$$S \mathrel{|\!\equiv} A \overset{K_{ab}}{\leftrightarrow} B,$$

and the desired goal can simply not be reached.

That there is a problem in this area was pointed out in 1981 by Denning and Sacco (1981), who observed that if an ill-wisher copied

$$\{K_{ab}, A\}_{K_{bs}}$$

from the wire, and, by unspecified means came to know K_{ab}, that is, to believe

$$A \stackrel{K_{ab}}{\longleftrightarrow} B,$$

then that ill-wisher could pretend to B that he was A indefinitely. The only way to make the deduction go through is to add an assumption on B's part which amounts to believing that no such thing has happened, namely:

$$B \models \#(A \stackrel{K_{ab}}{\longleftrightarrow} B).$$

If this assumption is added, then the end state is quickly reached by easy deductive steps.

It is pretty clear what was the matter. B never had the chance to offer a nonce to the server S, and therefore has no means of deducing freshness of the quantity that came from S. It is in fact easy to correct this problem by having the whole protocol start with B rather than A. This was pointed out in Needham and Schroeder (1987), which was published adjacent to an article Otway and Rees (1987) making a very similar suggestion. It indicates the need for a formalism such as the present one to observe that none of the people involved, nor the editor of the publication, noticed that the papers said essentially the same thing.

The logical approach sketched above has been used to study a number of protocols from the literature and has been extended to handle public-key encryption and the related topic of signature-functions.

6.4 Public-key systems

For completeness, some material is added here about the characteristic properties of applications of public-key systems. It will be recalled that in such systems, a principal has two keys, one of which is freely accessible to all and one of which is maintained secret; anything encrypted with one may be recovered by decryption with the other. We denote A's public and private keys by PK_a and SK_a respectively. Some obvious observations:

1. $\{M\}_{PK_a}$ is only comprehensible to A, but could have been made by anyone.

2. $\{M\}_{SK_a}$ must come from A, but is comprehensible to anyone.

These two, used alone, correspond to rather odd security requirements. The first is that of an anonymous caller to the police with information about the neighbourhood terrorists. The second is that of a royal proclamation. If we are concerned with directed communication from A to B we shall become involved with double encryption, of which there are two flavours:

3. $\{\{M\}_{PK_b}\}_{SK_a}$ and

4. $\{\{M\}_{SK_a}\}_{PK_b}$.

These both have the property that they could only have been made by A and that only B can recover M. They are however extremely different. The recipient of (4) can infer that A had seen M, because M is encrypted with something that only A knows. The recipient of (3) can infer no such thing; all that A has certainly seen is $\{M\}_{PK_b}$, which could have been made by anyone. With public-key systems, secrecy and signature go hand-in-hand, and there is room for debate as to which order to encourage. Note that in ordinary life a great many documents are signed by people who have not read them, though usually they could have done so had they wanted to. The logic of digital signature is subtle, and is beyond our current scope.

6.4.1 Authenticity of public keys

For public key systems to be useful it is necessary to be able to find out principals' public keys without difficulty. And with accuracy — consider example (1) above, where it is rather important that the public key is that of the police and not that of the terrorists. The usual recommendation is to have secure services available, not necessarily on a network, which will issue certificates to the effect that such-and-such a quantity is the public key of such-and-such a principal on such-and-such a date. The certificate itself is encrypted with the private key of the secure service, so that anyone who knows the public key of the service may read the certificate's contents. As long as this last key is really well-known, for example published in the newspaper, it is easy to be confident in the authenticity of an arbitrary principal's public key.

6.5 Concluding remarks

Because of the apparently paradoxical great difficulty of enforcing protection by physical separation in distributed systems, as against in centralized ones, encryption is used to achieve similar ends. It has been remarked that whenever anyone says, 'Oh, you solve that easily by encryption,' the speaker has not understood the problem; protection problems can indeed by solved by encryption but with a good deal of care, understanding, and attention to fine detail.

6.6 References

M. Burrows, M. Abadi, and R. M. Needham (1988). 'Authentication: A practical study in Belief and Action'. *Second Conference on Theoretical Aspects of Reasoning about Knowledge*, 1988.

D. E. Denning and G. M. Sacco (1981). 'Timestamps in key distribution protocols'. *Communications of the ACM* **24**(8): 533—536, Aug 1981.

W. Diffie and M. E. Hellman (1976). 'New Directions in Cryptography'. *IEEE Transactions on Information Theory* **IT-22**: 644—654, Nov. 1976.

National Bureau of Standards (1977). 'Data Encryption Standard'. *Federal Information Processing Standard Publication* **46**, Jan. 1977.

R. M. Needham and M. D. Schroeder (1978). 'Using Encryption for Authentication in Large Networks of Computers'. *Communications of the ACM* **21**(12): 993—999, December 1978.

R. M. Needham and M. D. Schroeder (1987). 'Authentication Revisited'. *ACM Operating System Review* **21**(1): 7, Jan. 1987.

D. Otway and O. Rees (1987). 'Efficient and Timely Mutual Authentication'. *ACM Operating System Review* **21**(1): 8—10, Jan. 1987.

R. L. Rivest, A. Shamir, and L. Adleman (1978). 'A Method for Obtaining Digital Signatures and Public Key Cryptosystems'. *Communications of the ACM* **21**(2): 120—126, February 1978.

V. L. Voydock and S. T. Kent (1983). 'Security mechanisms in high-level network protocols'. *ACM Computing Surveys* **15**(2): 135—171, June 1983.

D. J. Wheeler (1987). *Block Encryption*. Computer Laboratory Report 120, Cambridge University, 1987.

Chapter 7

Protection

S.J. Mullender

When people use a computer system, centralized or distributed, they have to trust the system to keep their data secure. Security in computer systems has many aspects: reliability, authenticity, privacy, integrity, and so on. In this chapter those aspects of security are under consideration that have to do with keeping data out of the wrong hands, that is, preventing unauthorized users from accessing data and resources illegitimately.

The mechanisms that prevent unauthorized access are referred to as *protection mechanisms*. We are thus using protection as a technical term which encompasses certain aspects of *security*. Security is a goal; protection is a set of mechanisms to achieve part of that goal.

7.1 Goals of protection

First and foremost, protection mechanisms prevent unauthorized users from accessing resources and data illegitimately. Protection mechanisms prevent users from stealing disk space, processor cycles, typesetter pages, etc. They prevent users from reading other people's files, modifying other people's data bases and disrupting other people's computations. Protection mechanisms are there to achieve what locks on houses and bicycles achieve in everyday life.

But protection mechanisms are also useful for other purposes. They can help to detect errors in programs; they can protect incompetent users against themselves; they can help prevent silly (but often expensive) mistakes; and they can even be used as tools in project management.

Different organizations require different levels of protection. The protection mechanisms that protect a university professor's file of student grades against modification by the students has to be of a different calibre from the one that protects information kept by the Kremlin from being seen by the CIA. Different kinds of information require different kinds of protection. The on-line manual pages do not have to be protected very much against unauthorized reading, but electronic mailboxes do.

Protection mechanisms are often only secure *in principle*. They are seldom secure *in practice*. The reason for this is that protection mechanisms are often not used properly or not used at all. Most protection problems are caused by human errors ranging from bugs in programs that should have been secure to users who just don't want to bother. These users, by the way, are often those who complain loudest when something does go wrong.

For these reasons, it is important that protection mechanisms are designed in such a way that it is obvious what they do and that they are easy to use. When it is easy to see what they do, they will be used correctly. When they are easy to use, they will be used more often. In addition, default protection should be maximum protection rather than minimum or no protection. When protection is too stringent, people will complain and then something can be done about it. If it is too lax, nobody will notice until it is too late.

7.2 Issues in protection

Before discussing any protection mechanisms, it is necessary to examine what kinds of *threats* protection mechanisms have to guard against. In this section, the areas for which protection mechanisms may be needed are investigated.

Protection mechanisms must deal with:

- *Secrecy*. Users must be able to keep data *secret*; that is, prevent other users from seeing it.

- *Privacy*. Users must be guaranteed that the information they give is used only for the purpose for which it was given.

- *Authenticity*. Data provided to a user must be *authentic*; that is, if some data purportedly comes from X, the user must be able to verify that it was indeed X who sent it.

- *Integrity*. Data stored in the system may not be corrupted by the system or by an unauthorized user.

A person or program trying to obtain illegitimate access to data or a resource is called an *intruder*. Intruders can use a variety of methods to obtain unauthorized access. They can (roughly) be classified as follows:

- *Browsing*. Intruders may attempt to read all the files in the system, read all the packets passing by on the network, read other processes' memory and so on without modifying any data. This is called *browsing*. Browsing is a favourite pastime for computer-science students in most universities; they consider it harmless, others don't.

- *Leaking.* An intruder may have an accomplice in the form of an otherwise legitimate user who *leaks* information to the intruder. Preventing this is very difficult and amounts to preventing communication between the accomplice and the intruder. The problem of making sure that a potential accomplice cannot leak any information to the outside world is called the *confinement problem* (Lampson (1973)).

- *Inferencing.* An intruder can try to obtain some item of information by putting two and two together. Stealing information by deriving an encryption key is an example of inferencing.

- *Masquerading.* An intruder may *masquerade* as an authorized user or program in order to gain access to a resource. A program masquerading as another is also known as a *Trojan horse.* Examples of Trojan horses are programs printing the login message on the screen in order to intercept users' passwords, editors that squirrel away a copy of the file being edited in the intruder's directory, programs that give the intruder superuser privileges which are left lying around in the hope that a superuser accidentally executes them, etc.

Naturally, the amount of effort put into the measures for preventing unauthorized access must be commensurate with the threat. Preventing industrial or military espionage requires very much more effort than preventing students from illegitimately sending electronic mail all over the world.

Military-style protection, for example, would be totally unsuitable for a research establishment. The protection mechanisms would get in the way of doing normal work. The point here is that protection mechanisms are inconvenient every now and then: they make the system slower, they require occasional detours, they require conscious thought. There is a trade-off between what the legitimate users are prepared to put up with and how much they care about the security of the system, and how much the intruder is prepared to invest in breaking the security system.

7.3 The access matrix

In order to model who may access what and how, we must introduce some terminology. Typically, we associate the rights to access certain objects and the absence of the right to access certain other objects with a human being. However, on occasion, it is also necessary to associate such rights with, say, a daemon or a server. Usually, rights to access objects are passed on from a user (or a server) to any processes executed by that user and from those processes to their offspring processes.

The term *domain* is used to indicate the set of things (made up of users, servers and processes) that may access certain objects in certain ways. So, for example, the right to write their home directory is usually part of all users' protection domain and is passed on to every program executed by those users. It is, however, not part (at least, not usually) of any other user's protection domain, so programs executed by other users do not inherit the right to write that directory.

The *objects* protected by the protection mechanism range from files and directories to processes, and even to protection domains. It is easy to see that protection domains need protection themselves by realizing that protection domains, just like other objects, can be created (for instance, by adding a new user to the system) and deleted and that it may be desirable to allow certain users or processes to *enter* other protection domains. In Unix, for instance, an operating system familiar to us all, the *suid* bit is used to indicate that a process can run in the protection domain of the owner of the binary of the process (rather than the protection domain of the user executing the program).

For every protection domain, a list can be made of all the objects accessible from the domain and the operations allowed on those objects. Similarly, for each object, a list can be made of all domains from which the object can be accessed and the operations allowed on the object from those domains. This information can be represented by a matrix, with a column for each object and a row for every domain. The matrix elements are sets of operations — sets of *rights* in this context — allowed from the domains on the object. This matrix is the *access matrix M*. The M_{ij}th element represents the set of rights that processes in domain i have on object j.

In a typical access matrix, most of the matrix elements will be empty sets (or, in the case of Unix, for example, most elements will have the same value (read access only)). Since there are typically hundreds of domains and tens of thousands of objects, storing an access matrix as such is not very efficient. For a distributed system, of course, the problem is even worse: storing the matrix (or something equivalent) in one place would cause an unacceptable bottleneck in the system. Obviously, the information in the access matrix must be split up.

There are two logical ways to split up the access matrix: by row or by column. When the access matrix is split up into columns, we get, per object, a list of domains and the set of operations allowed on the object from each domain. This is an *access control list* or ACL. When the access matrix is split up by row, we get, per domain, a list of objects and the operations allowed on each object. This is a *capability list*.

7.3.1 Access control lists

The simplest way of storing an ACL would be to store it as a list of {*domain, rights set*} pairs. Domains not in the list would be associated with the empty rights set. In practice, this approach is seldom taken. In most systems, as it turns out, it is not necessary to be able to express a different set of rights for each domain. It is often sufficient to classify domains and assign sets of rights to each class of domains. A few classes often suffice then.

In Unix, for instance, three classes of domain are associated with each object, *owner*, *group* and *others*. The *owner* class has only one domain in it, the object's owner's domain. Each domain belongs to one or more groups and each object is associated with one group. If a domain is in the group associated with the object, the rights in the *group* class apply. When neither *owner* or *group* rights apply, the *others* rights are used to determine what kind of access may be granted. Only the owner can change the rights. With executable objects, the *suid* bit can be set to make the program, when executed, enter the domain of the owner of the program.

The natural place to store an object's ACL is near the object. The best entity to check permissions when a client attempts an operation on an object is the server managing the object. In most traditional operating systems, the server is a part of the operating system. In distributed operating systems, servers often run on a different machine than their clients and only a few servers are part of the operating system itself.

Checking whether a client has permission to do an operation on an object requires knowing the client's domain (or domain class). In centralized systems, the operating system usually keeps track of each process' domain, so *authenticating* the client is easy. In a distributed system, knowing a process' domain may be very hard.

7.3.2 Capability lists

An entry in a capability list consists of the name of an object and a set of rights for operations on the object. Such an entry is called a *capability* (Dennis and Van Horn (1966)). To carry out an operation on an object, a process needs to have a capability for the object in its domain.

One would expect that capability lists are typically kept with the associated domain. Domains, however, can be rather abstract entities: domains do not carry out operations on objects; the processes in a domain do that.

In traditional capability systems, capability lists are often managed by the operating system kernel. For every operation on an object, the kernel checks whether the process has an appropriate capability. In a few others, capabilities are held by processes themselves. Cryptographic methods are then needed to prevent users from forging capabilities. See Section 7.5 for a discussion of an example of a distributed capability system that does this.

7.4 Trust in distributed systems

In traditional systems, protection mechanisms are enforced by the operating system. The hardware allows an operating system to run processes in such a way that they cannot interfere with each other and with the operating system itself. The operating system keeps track of the protection domain a process is in and checks permissions when a process accesses objects.

In distributed systems, however, this does not always work. Consider a distributed system where a network cable snakes through the building with a workstation in each office. If the system depends on the security of the operating system kernel for protection, breaking into the system is very easy: Workstation almost invariably have a reboot button and the option of bootstrapping themselves from floppy disk. A malicious user only needs to prepare a version of the operating system that circumvents the protection mechanisms to break the security of the system.

One would think that it would be possible, at least in principle, to build a secure distributed operating system that depends on the security of the operating system kernel in each of the machines. The workstations should be constructed so they will only boot from the network (where they will receive the official version of the operating system kernel from a trusted bootstrapping server). The only way to break the system's security then would be to meddle with the hardware itself (for example, replace EPROMs).

But even this approach is fraught with danger. Our malicious user could temporarily disconnect the workstation from the network, connect to another network with a private version of the bootstrapping server and load a malicious kernel. The machine could then be reconnected to the normal network to steal all sorts of secrets. Simpler still, the malicious user can just connect a different machine altogether; one without a secure operating system kernel.

The moral is that it is very easy to obtain unprotected access to a network. Most network interfaces even obligingly have a mode in which they will receive *every* packet on the network, even packets not addressed to the interface (on Ethernet, this is aptly named *promiscuous mode*).

Given this situation, it must be obvious that network packets should be encrypted if any degree of privacy is desirable in a distributed system. A client must *prove* its identity to an object's server so the server can derive its access rights. This too must be done by cryptographic means. An intruder could otherwise replay or reconstruct the proof and impersonate an authentic client.

There is no way that one can avoid trusting certain services in a computer system. One certainly has to trust one's workstation's operating system kernel. If that were not to be trusted, it could give away every bit of information used on the workstation to an intruder. If one has to trust the kernel one runs on a workstation, one also has to trust the bootstrapping mechanism by which the code is loaded. If the machine is loaded from a local disk, all is relatively okay, although it is still important to see if there are ways for an intruder to gain access to the kernel binary. If the machine bootstraps over the network, danger lurks everywhere. Very few, if any, bootstrapping protocols have any encryption in them which makes it relatively easy for an intruder to offer an untrustworthy kernel image to a workstation. Bootstrapping is definitely an area where all distributed systems today have security flaws.

Trust must also be placed in the services that one uses. A file server, for instance, must be trusted not to give away the contents of a file to unauthorized users. Conceptually, of course, users could encrypt their files before offering them to the file server for storage, but even then the file server must still be trusted to store the bits of the file reliably and return the same bits later when the file is read. Trust in services is unavoidable.

But trusting services should not be confused with trusting communication with services. One way for an intruder to break into a system is to pose as a trusted service and hope that an unsuspecting user will communicate with it rather than with the real thing. There must be mutual authentication between client and server; both must be sure of the other's identity before serious exchanges of confidential information can commence.

But how can a client set up communication with a server and make sure that the process that purports to be the server is really the right one? As Roger Needham discusses in Chapter 6, client and server must *share a secret* that no potential intruder knows. Using the secret, a secure communication channel can be set up using encryption.

What if no shared secret exists (yet)? What if client and server have never communicated before? At first glance, it would seem that with a public-key cryptographic system the problem is solved: The client encrypts messages with the client's private key and with the server's public key. The server subsequently decrypts them with the complementary keys. This leads us straight to the heart of the *key distribution problem*:

How can a client know which is the server's public key? The server can publish the public key, but so can an intruder. Both server and intruder will claim that theirs is the correct public key for the server and there is no way to decide which one is right. A third party is needed, trusted by clients and servers, which provides the appropriate keys.

Once we realize that we need a trusted *authentication server* anyway, it is easy to see that there is little point in using public key encryption (which is computationally very expensive) to prevent intruders from eavesdropping on client/server communication. The authentication server can pass on or create a conventional key for use by client and server for a session. Public key may be useful for the initial contact between a process and the authentication server, though. Then the authentication server's public key can be used to communicate with the authentication server in order to register with the system.

7.5 Protection in Amoeba†

The use of capabilities as a conceptual base for distributed systems has been minimal to date, a few exceptions being the Eden system (Almes *et al.* (1985)), LINCS (Donnelley (1981)), and ACCENT (Rashid and Robertson (1981)). Our scheme also uses a distributed capability mechanism, but it differs from each of these in significant ways, which we will describe after discussing our proposal.

† Part of the material in this section was derived from Tanenbaum, Mullender, and van Renesse (1986).

This section describes a scheme in which user processes manipulate capabilities directly in their own address spaces. Except for some very special parts of it, the kernel does not even know that capabilities are in use. To prevent users from forging new capabilities or tampering with existing ones, capabilities are protected cryptographically. This cryptographic protection scheme will first be described in some detail, followed by a discussion of how these capabilities are used in the Amoeba distributed operating system.

7.5.1 Background on Amoeba

Amoeba is an object-based distributed operating system. Its semantic model is having client processes perform operations on objects managed by server processes. Objects are specified by capabilities. Operations are carried out by having processes exchange messages, generally in the form of a request from a client followed later by a reply from a server. The standard message format provides a place for one capability in the header, typically for the object being operated on, but users are free to put other capabilities in the data field as required. The header also contains room for the operation code and some parameters.

After making a request, a client blocks until the reply comes in, so the approach can be regarded as a simple remote procedure call mechanism (Birrell and Nelson (1984); Spector (1982)). The system does not use 'connections' or virtual circuits or any other long-lived communication structures.

7.5.2 Ports

Every server has one or more *ports* to which client processes can send messages to contact the service (the server process). Ports consist of large numbers, typically 64 bits, which are known only to the server processes that comprise the service, and to the server's clients. For a public service, such as the file system, the port will generally be made known to all users. The ports used by an ordinary user process will, in general, be kept secret. Knowledge of a port is taken by the system as *prima facie* evidence that the sender has a right to communicate with the service. Of course, the service is not required to carry out work for clients just because they know the port, for example, the file server will refuse to read or write files for clients lacking appropriate file capabilities. Thus two levels of protection are used here: ports for protecting access to servers, and capabilities for protecting access to individual objects. These two mechanisms are related, as will be shown later.

Although the port mechanism provides a convenient way to provide partial authentication of clients ('if you know the port, you may at least talk to the service'), it does not deal with the authentication of servers. How does one ensure that malicious users do not listen on the file server's port, and try to impersonate the file server to the rest of the system?

One approach is to have all ports manipulated by kernels that are presumed to be trustworthy and are supposed to know who may listen on which port. As mentioned above, we reject this strategy because on some machines, such as personal computers, users may be able to tamper with the operating system kernel, and also because we believe that by making the kernel as small as possible, we can enhance the reliability of the system as a whole. Instead, we have chosen a different solution that can be implemented in either hardware or software.

In the hardware solution, we need to place a small interface box, which we call an F-box (Function-box) between each processor module and the network. The most logical place to put it is on the VLSI chip that is used to interface to the network. Alternatively, it can be put on a small printed circuit board inside the wall socket through which personal computers attach to the network. In those cases where the processors have user mode and kernel mode and the operating systems can be trusted, it could be put into the operating system. In the software solution, we build the F-box out of cryptographic algorithms, giving the same functional effect as the hardware F-box. In any event, we assume that, somehow or other, all messages entering and leaving every processor undergo a simple transformation that users cannot bypass.

The transformation works like this. Each port is really a pair of ports, P, and G, related by: $P = F(G)$, where F is a (publicly-known) one-way function (Evans, Kantrowitz, and Weiss (1974); Purdy (1974); Wilkes (1968)) performed by the F-box. The one-way function has the property that given G it is a straightforward computation to find P, but that given P, finding G is not feasible.

Using the one-way F-box, the server authentication can be handled in a simple way, as illustrated in Figure 7.1. Each server chooses a get-port, G, and computes the corresponding put-port, P. The get-port is kept secret; the put-port is distributed to potential clients or, in the case of public servers, is published. When the server is ready to accept client requests, it does a $get(G)$. The F-box then computes $P = F(G)$ and waits for messages containing P to arrive. When one arrives, it is given to the process that did $get(G)$. To send a message

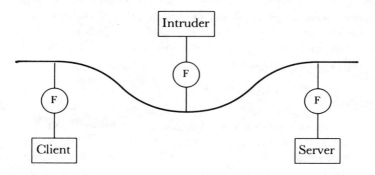

Figure 7.1 Clients, servers, intruders, and F-boxes.

to the server, the client merely does $put(P)$, which sends a message containing P in a header field to the server. The F-box on the sender's side does not perform any transformation on the P field of the outgoing message.

Now let us consider the system from an intruder's point of view. To impersonate a server, the intruder must do $get(G)$. However, G is a well-kept secret, and is never transmitted on the network. Since we have assumed that G cannot be deduced from P (the one-way property of F) and that the F-box cannot be circumvented, the intruder cannot intercept messages not intended for him. An intruder doing $get(P)$ will simply cause his F-box to listen to the (useless) port $F(P)$. Replies from the server to the client are protected the same way, only with the client picking a get-port for the reply, say, G', and including $P' = F(G')$ in the request message.

The presence of the F-box makes it easy to implement digital signatures for further authentication still, if that is desired. To do so, each client chooses a random signature, S, and publishes $F(S)$. The F-box must be designed to work as follows. Each message presented to the F-box for transmission contains three special header fields: destination (P), reply (G'), and signature (S). The F-box applies the one-way function to the second and third of these, transmitting the three ports as: P, $F(G')$, and $F(S)$, respectively. The first is used by the receiver's F-box to admit only those messages for which the corresponding get has been done, the second is used as the put-port for the reply, and the third can be used to authenticate the sender, since only the true owner of the signature will know what number to put in the third field to insure that the publicly-known $F(S)$ comes out.

It is important to note that the F-box arrangement merely provides a simple *mechanism* for implementing security and protection, but gives operating system designers considerable latitude for choosing various *policies*. The mechanism is sufficiently flexible and general that it should be possible to put it into hardware without precluding many as-yet-unthought-of operating systems to be designed in the future. In effect, it is a protected associative addressing scheme. The associative addressing can be simulated in software when the kernels are trusted by having each one maintain a cache of (port, machine-number) pairs. If a port is not in the cache, it can be found by broadcasting a *locate* message. How this can be carried out efficiently, even in a network without broadcasting, is discussed in Mullender and Vitanyi (1988), along with many of the implications of location-independent addressing, process migration, etc.

7.5.3 Capabilities

In any object-based system, a mechanism is needed to keep track of which processes may access which objects and in what way. The normal way is to associate a capability with each object, with bits in the capability indicating which operations the holder of the capability may perform. In a distributed system this mechanism should itself be distributed, that is, not centralized in a single monolithic 'capability manager'. In our proposed scheme, each object is

64 bits	32 bits	32 bits	64 bits
Port	Object	Rights	Check

Figure 7.2 A Capability

gle monolithic 'capability manager'. In our proposed scheme, each object is managed by some server, which itself is a user (as opposed to kernel) process, and which understands the capabilities for its objects.

A capability typically consists of four fields as illustrated in Figure 7.2.

1.   The *put-port* of the server that manages the object,

2.   An *object number*, meaningful only to the server managing the object,

3.   A *rights field*, containing a 1 bit for each permitted operation,

4.   A *check field*, for protecting each object.

The basic model of how capabilities are used and protected can be illustrated by a simple example. A client wishes to create a file using the file server, write some data into the file, and then give another client permission to read (but not modify) the file just written. To start with, the client sends a message to the file server's put-port specifying that a file is to be created. The request might contain a file name, account capability, etc. The server then picks a random number, stores this number in its object table, and inserts it into the newly-formed object capability. The reply will contain this capability for the newly created (empty) file.

To write the file, the client would send a succession of data messages, each containing the capability and some data. When each *write* request arrived at the file server process, the server would use the *object* field contained in the capability as an index into its file tables to locate the object. For a Unix-like file server, the object number would be the i-number, which could be used to locate the i-node.

Several object protection systems are possible using this framework. In the simplest one, the server merely compares the random number in the file table (put there by the server when the object was created) to the one contained in the capability. If they agree, the capability is assumed to be genuine, and all operations on the file are allowed. This system is easy to implement, but does not distinguish between *read*, *write*, *delete*, and any other operations that may be performed on objects. However, the basic idea can easily be modified to provide that distinction. We will now describe three different algorithms for protecting the access rights.

In the first version, when a file (object) is created, the random number chosen and stored in the file table is used as an encryption/decryption key. The capability is built up by taking the *rights* field, which is initially all 1s to indicate that all operations are legal, and the *check* field (64 bits, for instance), which contains a known constant, say, 0, and treating them as a single number. This number is then encrypted by the key just stored in the file table, and the result put into the newly minted capability in the combined *rights-check* field.

When the capability is returned for use, the server uses the *object* field (not encrypted) to find the file table and hence the encryption/decryption key. If the result of decrypting the capability leads to the known constant in the *check* field, the capability is almost assuredly valid, and the *rights* field can be believed. Clearly, an encryption function that mixes the bits thoroughly is required to ensure that tampering with the *rights* field also affects the known constant. X-ORing a constant with the concatenated *rights* and *check* fields will not do.

A second algorithm for protecting the *rights* field makes use of one-way functions, similar to the way ports are protected. When a server is asked to create a new object, it generates a random number, as usual. The *rights* field is then X-ORed with the random number and then used as the argument of the one-way function, F, yielding a value that is put into the *check* field of the capability. Symbolically,

$$\textit{check field} = F(\text{random-number XOR } \textit{rights} \text{ bits}).$$

The *rights* field is included in the capability itself in plaintext. When a capability arrives at the server, it finds the original random number from its internal tables and XORs the plaintext *rights* field with it, passing this result through F. If the result agrees with the *check* field in the capability, the capability is considered valid. Although a user can tamper with the plaintext *rights* field, such tampering will result in the server ultimately rejecting the capability.

When either of these protection systems are used, the owner of an object can easily give an exact copy of its capability to another process by just sending it the bit pattern, but to pass, say, read-only access, is slightly harder. To accomplish this task, the process must send the capability back to the server along with a bit mask and a request to fabricate a new capability with fewer rights.

The organization of capabilities and objects discussed above has the interesting property that although no central record is kept of who has which capabilities, it is easy to revoke existing capabilities. All that the owner of an object need do is ask the server to change the random number stored in its internal table and return a new capability. Obviously this operation must be protected with a bit in the *rights* field, but, if it succeeds, all existing capabilities for that object are instantly invalidated.

7.5.4 Protection with software F-boxes

Earlier it was said that protection could also be achieved in software (that is, without F-boxes). It is slightly more complicated, since it uses both conventional and public-key encryption (Diffie and Hellman (1976)), but it is still quite usable.

The method makes use of a trusted *key server*, with which all clients and servers must register before they can start mutually authenticated communication.

When registering with the key server, a communication key is established that only the client or server and the key server know. Clients and servers can use that key to exchange messages with the key server. The essence of the method is that, when a client wishes to talk to a server, it asks the key server to prepare an encrypted message which only the server can decrypt. The client can then send that message to the server, trusting that, if an appropriate response comes, it can only have come from the authenticated server. The server uses the same method to authenticate the client (if this is necessary; after all, Amoeba is a capability-based system, so many servers do not need to know the identity of their clients; they just need a capability for the object that the client wishes to access as proof of the right of that client to do so).

The key server
In this protection model we assume the presence of a *key server* that yields appropriate keys when given a port. The key server stores triples consisting of

get port (G), put port (P), encryption key (K)

The indices ks, c and s are used to indicate that ports or keys belong to key server, client or server. The index x indicates either client or server.

All first requests to the key server are encrypted with the key server's public key E_{ks} and contain a conventional key K_x for the encryption of the reply and also for any future key server requests. All conventional keys may be cached and re-used for the communication between the processes for which the key was established. When a party loses a key, a new key can be established through the protocols described here.

The key server recognizes three requests: *register port*, *get key* and *wrap key*. A description of each of the calls follows.

- *Register port*
  To key server: [*Register port*, $\{G_x, K_x\}_{E_{ks}}$]
  The message is encrypted with the key server's public key; only the key server can decrypt it with its private key. It contains the requestor's *get port* and a conventional key K_x. The key server computes the put port, P_x, stores the triple (G_x, P_x, K_x) and returns
  Reply: [*Port registered*, $\{P_x\}_{K_x}$]

- *Get key*
  To key server: [*Get key*, $\{G_x, K'_x\}_{E_{ks}}$]
  Get key is used by client and server processes that do not know the key associated with their port. Just reregistering would not work if there are multiple client or server processes. The request has two parameters, the requestor's *get port* to prove to the key server the right to obtain the key and a conventional key, K'_x, for the encryption of the reply. The key server looks up the triple (G_x, P_x, K_x) and returns
  Reply: [*Got key*, $\{P_x, K_x\}_{K'_x}$]

- *Wrap key*
  To key server: $[Wrap\ key,\ \{G_x,\ P_y, K'_x\}_{K_v}]$
  The request has three parameters, the get port of the requesting process, the put port of the process with which communication must be established and a conventional key, K'_x which must be shared with the other process. The key server looks up the triple $(G_y,\ P_y,\ K_y)$ and returns
  Reply: $[Wrapped\ key,\ \{\{P_x,\ K'_x\}_{K_v}\}_{K_v}]$

Establishing communication

Now suppose a client c wishes to establish communication with a server s. We assume that client and server have already registered with the key server, so the key server holds the two triples $(G_c,\ P_c,\ K_c)$ and $(G_s,\ P_s,\ K_s)$. The client knows its own get and put ports G_c and P_c, the key with which it communicates with the key server K_c and the put port of the server P_s. The server knows its ports G_s and P_s, and its key K_s but doesn't have to know anything about the client.

Establishing communication goes as follows. The client generates a session key K_1 and sends a *wrap key* request to the key server, containing

$$[Wrap\ key,\ \{G_c,\ P_s, K_1\}_{K_c}]$$

The server returns

$$[Wrapped\ key,\ \{\{P_c,\ K_1\}_{K_s}\}_{K_c}]$$

The client now has the session key K_1 and its identity represented by P_c, encrypted with the server's key in its possession. It sends this to the server in a request to establish communication which may be left otherwise unencrypted.

The server, after receiving the message, knows that the message must have been originally made by the key server. After all, only the key server is capable of encrypting anything with K_s. Since the server trusts the key server, it also trusts that the client must have proved its identity to the key server with its get port G_c. The key K_1, therefore, is only known by that client (and the key server). The server then generates its own key K_2 and asks the key server to wrap that up by sending

$$[Wrap\ key,\ \{G_s,\ P_c, K_2\}_{K_s}]$$

The server returns

$$[Wrapped\ key,\ \{\{P_s,\ K_2\}_{K_c}\}_{K_s}]$$

and sends the part encrypted with K_c back to the client.

Client and server now both know K_1 and K_2. The two keys are XOR-ed to form a session key $K_{c,s} = K_1 \oplus K_2$. All subsequent requests and replies are encrypted with this key. If one of the parties loses the session key, the parties can re-authenticate using the above protocol.

Why don't client and server just use K_1? After all, it is in the interest of the client to come up with a good key and not to give the key away to an intruder.

Imagine the following scenario: a good guy tells his bank server to transfer some money to the bad guy's account. The bad guy records all the message on the network and plays back to the bank server the message communicating K_1 (which is still encrypted with K_s) and the message requesting the funds transfer (which is still encrypted with K_1). This way, the transfer will occur twice. The bad guy can't decrypt any of the messages and can't make up any of his own, but he can certainly cause some damage.

By having the server return K_2, this is prevented (the server never uses the same key twice, of course). In effect, the server's message to the client is used to guarantee the *freshness* of the session key $K_{c,s}$.

7.5.5 Discussion

In this chapter it has been shown how ports and capabilities can be managed in a protected way in a distributed operating system. By moving the entire capability management out of the kernel, we can provide a minimal kernel, and yet have a powerful and general conceptual basis for naming and protection throughout the system. A number of examples of how capabilities are used in Amoeba were presented as examples.

The Eden (Almes *et al.* (1985)) and ACCENT (Rashid and Robertson (1981)) systems also use capability-like mechanisms for protection, but in both cases, the ultimate responsibility for managing the capabilities rests with the kernel. In Eden, users may manage capabilities directly, but the kernel maintains copies, to enable it to verify each one before it is used. We maintain that moving all of the capability management out of the kernel is a step in the right direction. Just as file servers are now rarely part of the kernel of distributed systems, capability management should not be either. The smaller and simpler the kernel, the easier it is to write, debug, and maintain. Furthermore, if the system consists of a building full of rooms with wall sockets into which any user can plug any machine, protection based on trusted kernels managing capabilities becomes impossible. A malicious user could modify his kernel to subvert the capability checking and thereby bypass the protection scheme.

In Donnelley (1981), a description is given of work being done at Lawrence Livermore Laboratory is given. Two schemes are described, one using a password in each capability, and one using public key cryptography. Although these schemes are similar to ours in some ways, they do not provide a way to protect individual rights bits to allow one capability to read an object and another to write it. Furthermore, our proposal addresses the problem of how to prevent users from impersonating servers or reading network traffic not intended for them. Both the F-boxes and the matrix method described above can be used to fight wire tapping.

7.6 References

G. T. Almes, A. P. Black, E. D. Lazowska, and J. D. Noe (1985). 'The Eden System: A Technical Review'. *IEEE Transactions on Software Engineering* **SE-11**: 43—59, Jan. 1985.

A. D. Birrell and B. J. Nelson (1984). 'Implementing Remote Procedure Calls'. *ACM Transactions on Computer Systems* **2** (1): 39—59, February 1984.

J. B. Dennis and E. C. Van Horn (1966). 'Programming Semantics for Multi-programmed Computations'. *Communications of the ACM* **9** (3): 143—155, 1966.

W. Diffie and M. E. Hellman (1976). 'New Directions in Cryptography'. *IEEE Transactions on Information Theory* **IT-22**: 644—654, Nov. 1976.

J. E. Donnelley (1981). 'Managing Domains in a Network Operating System'. *Proceedings On-Line Conf. on Local Networks and Distributed Office Systems*: 345—361, Newcastle, GB, May 1981.

A. Evans, W. Kantrowitz, and E. Weiss (1974). 'A User Authentication Scheme Not Requiring Secrecy in the Computer'. *Communications of the ACM* **17** (8): 437—442, August 1974.

B. W. Lampson (1973). 'A Note on the Confinement Problem'. *Communications of the ACM* **6** (10): 613—615, October 1973.

S. J. Mullender and P. M. B. Vitanyi (1988). 'Distributed Match-Making'. *Algorithmica* **3**: 367—391, 1988.

G. B. Purdy (1974). 'A High Security Log-in Procedure'. *Communications of the ACM* **17** (8): 442—445, August 1974.

R. F. Rashid and G. Robertson (1981). 'Accent: A Communication Oriented Network Operating System Kernel'. *Proceedings Eighth Symposium on Operating System Principles*: 64—75, 1981.

A. Z. Spector (1982). 'Performing Remote Operations Efficiently on a Local Computer Network'. *Communications of the ACM* **25** (4): 246—260, April 1982.

A. S. Tanenbaum, S. J. Mullender, and R. van Renesse (1986). 'Using Sparse Capabilities in a Distributed Operating System'. *Proc. of the 6th Int. Conf. on Distributed Computing Systems*: 558—563, Amsterdam, May 1986.

M. V. Wilkes (1968). *Time-Sharing Computer Systems*. American Elsevier, New York, 1968.

Chapter 8

Accounting and Resource Control

S.J. Mullender

A computer system provides a set of services to its users: execution of programs, storage of files, printing listings, typesetting of books about distributed systems, and so on. Each of these services makes demands on the system's resources: computer time, disk space, paper, film, etc. This chapter deals with the registration of the use of services, and how this can be controlled in a distributed environment.

Accounting is the registration of the use of services. Such registration is needed, not only in commercial computer systems for billing clients for services rendered, but also in non-commercial systems for dividing available resources evenly over users competing for them.

Resource control is the mechanism for enforcing resource management policies. Generally, a client (which can be a human user, a process, or a service) is not allowed an unlimited supply of any resource. Some resources are expensive (phototypesetter pages), most are available only in limited supply (disk blocks). Policies for resource management dictate when and how much a client may use of a resource. Resource control mechanisms realize these policies.

Resource control is really a special area of what we might call *service control*: in a distributed operating system all resources are made available through services; and services not only define the set of operations on the resource, but also the rules for accessing the resource. The traditional operating system view of resource accounting is limited to only a few resources: computer time, paper used, tapes mounted, but not the use of the expert knowledge that might be embedded in a particular program. The more general view of building mechanisms to account for the use of services, rather than resources, is obviously preferable.

Accounting and service control are closely related. Service control is not possible without accounting mechanisms; therefore, accounting mechanisms must be designed with regard to both existing resource-management policies and desirable, but not yet existing service-management policies. Both accounting and service control mechanisms must be designed with great flexibility to allow them to be used for carrying out a variety of existing policies, but also for many as yet unthought of policies of the future.

8.1 Accounting and service control

In this section we show the differences between accounting and resource control mechanisms used in traditional centralized operating systems, and those necessary for open distributed operating systems as we see them.

8.1.1 Closed centralized systems

Until a few years ago, a typical computer centre had one or two huge computers with many peripherals attached to them. The computer was a very expensive machine, and everything was oriented towards using it as efficiently as possible. This way of thinking is clearly reflected in the accounting mechanisms used by most computer centres: the unit of accounting is a 'system second'. As the name suggests, a system second indicates one second of CPU time, although it is not solely used as a unit of CPU time consumed, it is also used to account for I/O done, as a measure for printed pages, for the use of tape drives, etc.

Resource control policies consist mostly of giving users a *budget*, an amount of system time with which a user buys CPU seconds, disk space, and so on. Periodically, an amount can be added to the budget, the amount often based on past use and estimated future needs. Additionally, a maximum limit will be set for each type of resource, independent of the current budget: so, time limits will be set on processes, quotas on disk space, so many pages of output, etc.

More instructive than summing up what traditional accounting mechanisms can do is, perhaps, to look at some of the things traditional accounting mechanisms do not do. There is no *software accounting*, accounting of who uses how much of which software. In the past this was not necessary. The programs used by clients of the computer centre would either be owned by the computer centre or by the clients themselves. The computer centre would pay for the development cost of the software, or buy the software out of the system seconds income. Software was cheap compared to hardware in the early days of computing, and this is reflected in the accounting and resource control mechanisms of many computer centres to this day.

Another useful feature lacking in the accounting mechanisms of traditional systems is a mechanism that one user of the system can use for accounting services rendered to another user. The traditional view has always been of one producer of service, 'the system', and many consumers, 'the users'.

8.1.2 Open distributed systems

There are important differences between traditional closed centralized systems and modern open distributed systems that affect the mechanisms needed for accounting and resource control. Whereas in traditional systems accounting was primarily done to register consumption of *resources*, in modern open systems it is done to register the consumption of *services*. The distinction is arguable, perhaps, but it illustrates a change of view of operating systems, away from just disk blocks, CPU seconds and phototypesetter pages, towards an integrated view of services in a much wider sense of the word. A service is not just the provision of disk space or computing power, but it is these things, combined with the research effort, the development, the maintenance of the service.

To illustrate how this integrated view can lead to fairer accounting policies, consider a computer centre that provides two compilers for its users, a fast one which produces good code, and a slow one which produces poor quality code. Since accounting and billing are usually based on computer time consumed, using the bad compiler will cost the user more than using the good one. Perhaps this is one of the reasons that computer centres usually provide such primitive service to their clients. It is obvious that accounting policies should be based on both quantity and quality of the service used, rather than just quantity of certain resources consumed.

Another development in open distributed systems is that services are no longer exclusively provided by 'the system'. The notion of one central authority serving many users no longer applies in distributed systems, consisting of a mixture of collectively owned and privately owned processors. But even when 'the system' as a whole is owned by one administration, it may still be desirable to allow ordinary users to provide services in return for financial gain or other services.

A third major change is in the structure of services. In traditional systems accounting was done at one level only, basic resources, such as disk blocks and CPU seconds. Modern, service-oriented systems have a hierarchy of services. One service makes use of other services in order to function. The accounting mechanisms must provide the tools for accounting in hierarchies of services.

8.1.3 Accounting

Accounting is the registration of service consumption by clients. The problem is to determine *how much* of a service each client uses. There are several aspects to this problem. First, the amount of mutual trust needed between service producer and service consumer: a service might claim it gave service to a client, which actually received none. Second, the way in which service consumption is measured: is compiling a ten-line program half as cheap as compiling a twenty line program? Third, the relation between different services: how does file service compare to phototypesetter service?

An important aspect in solving these problems is the relationship between the security required and mutual trust needed on the one hand, and the cost in effort and complexity of realizing such security on the other. At one end of the spectrum, one can imagine a system where clients are trusted to register their resource consumption themselves; a system, thus, that works only through a high degree of mutual trust. At the other end of the spectrum, a system can be imagined where there is no trust between clients and servers whatsoever. Clients and servers negotiate contracts, perhaps, establishing a mutually verifiable computation of cost, making transaction logs adorned with digital signatures for examination by an impartial referee, in case of dispute. In most cases, neither approach is acceptable; the first because it assumes more honesty on the part of clients than can reasonably be expected; the second because its realization is far too costly in terms of complexity and speed. A reasonable middle course has to be found, accepted as trustworthy enough for clients and servers to use, and acceptable in cost.

In traditional accounting mechanisms, all service is provided by the 'system', including accounting. Clients must thus trust the 'system' completely, since it both provides the service and does the accounting. In a distributed system, with many users providing service to others this strategy is not possible.

In an open system, where every user may decide to set up service for other users, an 'open market' of services is likely to arise. Services will compete in quality and cost, which leads to improved and cheaper service. In such an open market, service providers set the price of their product.

We have opted for an accounting mechanism where the service computes the cost of the operations it carries out on behalf of its clients. The reason for this is twofold. First, the provider of the service (a human being, or an organization) decides on the cost of the service: 'My files cost such-and-such per block, take it or leave it.' Second, the service is in the most practical position to carry out the computation of costs. This implies that clients have to trust services to 'keep their word', they have to trust services to compute any costs according to the rules, which should probably be published in advance.

Because, in an open system, clients can choose which service carries out their work, it can be expected that clients will choose the service they trust to do the work properly and securely. A client, using file server X, trusts X not to reveal any files to other clients, for example. We therefore believe that it is acceptable that clients have to trust the services they use to some degree. If possible, however, clients should only have to have limited faith in the honesty of a service, that is, clients should not be forced to entrust their whole budget to a service; it would be too easy for a malicious user to set up a service to rob one or two clients of their budget. The accounting mechanisms must make it possible that clients entrust a limited amount to the service, an amount that covers the cost of the service exactly. A malicious service can still cheat in this set-up, but only by collecting the price of one unit of service without carrying it out. A client, robbed in this way, will never use any of the services offered by that user again, so the malicious user's gain will be negligible compared to the loss of trust of its clients.

Disk blocks cannot be compared to CPU seconds. Although the consumption of both is often expressed in the same unit, and must sometimes be expressed in money, we believe that the different nature of different resources and services requires a possibility to account for them in different ways, using different units and combinations of units. This allows much more freedom for resource management services to control access to different types of services independently.

8.1.4 Resource control

Resource control mechanisms — or, perhaps, *service* control mechanisms — have the task of adjusting clients' and services' budgets as services are provided, and of enforcing policies for fair distribution of resources and services in limited supply. These mechanisms should be general enough to be applicable to a wide class of services and resource management policies.

Records of service consumption must be kept in order to carry out any resource control and accounting. As stated in the previous section, a service provides the information about services consumed by its clients. In return, resource control mechanisms must provide services with information about clients' *'creditworthiness'* — whether clients have a right to receive more service.

In principle, before carrying out a request, a service must check if the client is credit-worthy, that is, whether the client has any budget left or used up his fair share of service already. After carrying out the request, a service must register the consumption of service with a bookkeeping service. If the service-control service must be consulted before each request and informed after each request, network traffic will triplicate, and simple transactions will take more than three times longer. Clearly, this is unacceptable. Caching strategies are required with which services can avoid having to consult an accounting service for every transaction.

8.1.5 The triangular relationship of client, service and bank

When people go shopping, they make transactions: goods are received or a service is rendered in return for money. These transactions between people and shops (clients and services) nearly always take place without the need of a mutually trusted third party. One of the reasons for this is that shopkeepers are able to trust that the money they receive is genuine. Money cannot easily be forged, so a person can only spend it once.

In transactions between computers, where the equivalent of money must be represented electronically, copying money is very easy to do. Electronic transactions must therefore be handled differently. If money is represented by an (authenticated) bit pattern, nothing prevents a client from giving it to a number of different services in payment for services rendered (or to be rendered). Money would have no value as it could be copied without limit. Even sequence numbers on bank notes would not help: on each payment, the recipient would have to check whether the received money had already been spent somewhere else.

Instead of electronic money, electronic cheques could be used in payment. However, the use of these suffers from the same drawback as using electronic bank notes: the service must always check with the bank whether the cheque is good. In the Netherlands, and in many other countries as well, a guaranteed cheque exists. Banks have agreed to honour these cheques up to a maximum amount whether or not there is any money in the account to meet it. By limiting the number of blank cheques in possession of an account holder, the banks limit their risk. Again, this system fails if clients can copy cheques at will: the risk to the banks will become too great.

The concepts of bank notes and of cheques can be combined to yield a better method of payment. A bank can hand out numbered bank notes payable to one service only. When a client presents such a bank note to the correct service, the service checks if it has not received a note with that number on it before; if this is indeed not the case, the note is genuine and it can be put in the bank at a later time. To prevent forgery, such notes could consist of the text *"This is bank note number thingumajig, with a value of thingumabob, intended for service what's-its-name"* signed by the bank server; that is, encrypted with the bank server's secret key.

This method does not require a client or a server to check with the bank on every transaction: a client can order a large number of bank notes at once, and a server can collect a large number of them before going to the bank. The method does require that the server keep a list of received bank note numbers; and, unless measures are taken, this list can become very long indeed. To restrict the size of the list, it is possible to require clients to hand over bank notes in order of increasing serial numbers. Two disadvantages remain, however, the least of which is that the amounts on the bank notes are fixed, so it is possible that quite a few bank notes must change hands to pay for one transaction; it is even possible that services must give *change*. The most important disadvantage is that the public key encryption required — to protect bank notes from forgery and to allow services to inspect the authenticity of received bank notes — makes bank notes inconveniently large (on the order of a thousand bytes) and therefore not very useful in most applications.

In the next sections we shall examine a bank server structure that does not have these drawbacks. The basic idea is for clients to deposit a sufficient amount in the service's account before requesting it to work. Naturally, the service must know which client deposits which amount, and later, when the client makes a request, it should be able to tell the request came from the same client that deposited the money. One method is to have each client pass some sort of identifying capability along with each request and each deposit, but the Amoeba distributed system has a signature mechanism that is ideal for just this purpose: When a client deposits money for a server at the bank, it provides a signature. The money received will then be labelled with that signature. When the client later makes a transaction with a service, it again includes its signature with the request. The service can then tell it is the same client that made the deposit.

8.2 Bank service

The Amoeba bank service manages accounting information in a way that resembles the way a bank handles money. Different accounting units (units representing disk blocks, CPU seconds) are represented by *virtual money* in different *currencies*, analogous to real money. Clients and services maintain *accounts* between which amounts of virtual money can be transferred.

8.2.1 Bank accounts

The objects, managed by the bank service are *bank accounts*. There are two types, *private* and *business*. Both types of account can contain virtual money, and various requests are available to transfer virtual money from one account to another.

Bank accounts are protected by capabilities. There are rights that control withdrawal from an account, examination of an account, deposits into an account, etc. Services must know the identity of their clients in order to do their accounting. Digital signatures are used for client authentication.

Private accounts are very like regular bank accounts: after an account is created, virtual money can be deposited into it and withdrawn from it. Usually a private account is manipulated solely by its owner, but business accounts are different. In contrast to private accounts, whose contents can be thought of as a an amount of virtual money, a business account can be thought of as many amounts of virtual money, one for — or rather, from — each client that deposited virtual money into the account. With bank accounts in the real world, the holder is notified *who* deposits into it; with our business accounts this is not necessary because deposited virtual money is automatically tagged with its source. The owner of a business account must specify a source when manipulating the account; otherwise, business accounts are little different from private accounts.

Business accounts are especially intended for services. Before a client can use a service that requires payment in the form of virtual money, a deposit must be made into the service's business account. Then requests can be sent to the service. The service, before carrying out a request, makes sure there is enough in its business account to pay for the request, then carries out the request, and finally transfers the cost of the request from the business account to a private account.

Although, in principle, the bank service is used as just described, it is rather inefficient when used exactly in this way. However, the design of the bank service allows some simple optimizations that make it quite efficient. When a client deposits into a service's business account, the amount will usually be sufficient to pay for a large number of requests — enough for a whole day's file service, for instance. The service, before honouring the first request, must examine the account, but once the amount in it is known, the service may carry out requests until that amount is consumed without further examining it; the client cannot secretly withdraw from the account behind the service's back, because the virtual money is already in the service's business account. The service can adjust its business account periodically; it is not necessary to make a transfer from the business account to a private account after each request.

Client crashes do not affect the bank service mechanisms at all. Server crashes do have consequences, if a server crashes after a request has been carried out, but before the business account has been adjusted. Server crashes are infrequent, however, and the damage is limited to the cost of a few transactions. The frequency with which services adjust their business accounts must be low to reduce network traffic, but an order of magnitude higher than the frequency of server crashes.

8.2.2 Capabilities and signatures

Accounts are protected by capabilities and authentication is done through the use of signatures. In this section we shall describe how capabilities and signatures are used for protection.

When a client creates a private account, two capabilities are returned, an *owner* capability with all rights on, and a *deposit* capability with only the right to deposit into the account. The client keeps the owner capability to himself, of course, but the deposit capability is usually given away to the service providing the virtual money (a system manager, for instance).

When a business account is created, the bank server also returns two capabilities, an *owner* capability, and a *client* capability. The owner capability is kept carefully secret, but the client capability is published to the service's potential clients. This capability allows a client to deposit into the business account, and to read the balance of its own deposits into it. Once deposited, a client capability gives no right to withdraw from a business account.

Before explaining how *signatures* are used to authenticate clients, it is perhaps useful to quickly recall the signature mechanism presented in Chapter 7 (Section 7.5), since it is used to provide authentication of requests sent to a service. A packet may contain a signature, a bit string that can be used as proof of the identity of the sender. A process, wishing to send a signed packet, puts his signature, S, in the signature field of the packet. Before the packet arrives, the F-boxes replace S by $F(X)$, where F is a one-way cipher. S can be viewed as a capability for producing $F(S)$. The mechanism is used as a means of proving 'This message comes from the same source as a previous one.'

Before depositing into a service's business account, a client chooses a signature, S, for identification. $F(S)$ is included in the request to the bank server to transfer an amount from its private account into the business account. This request contains two capabilities, a capability with a *withdraw* right for the client's private account and a capability with the *deposit* right for the service's business account; furthermore, the request contains $F(S)$ for identification in later requests to the service. The bank server, receiving this request, withdraws the amount from the client's account, and deposits it into the business account, tagged with $F(S)$.

Subsequently, the client sends requests to the service, each of which contains signature S in the signature field. Before the service receives the request, an F-box has converted S to $F(S)$. When a service receives the first request from a client, it sends a request to the bank server to read the balance of its business account tagged with $F(S)$. This request contains a capability for the business account with the *inspect* right and $F(S)$. If the amount read is sufficient, the request is carried out and an appropriate amount is transferred from the business account to a private account.

8.2.3 Maintenance of a cache

Each service can maintain a cache, an entry consisting of a triple (s, b, c) of a client's signature, a balance, and the amount of service consumed. When a request is received, the cache is searched for an entry with the correct signature. If an entry is found, and the balance, b, is sufficient, the request is carried out, and the cost of the request is subtracted from b and added to c. If there is no entry for that client in the cache, a request is sent to the bank server to read the client's account. Then an entry is made with b set to the client's balance and c set to zero.

Periodically, the cache is examined, and for all cache entries with non-zero c, a request is sent to the bank server to transfer an amount c, tagged with s in its business account to a private account. The bank server returns the new balance (which is b or a larger amount, if the client deposited in the mean time) that the service uses to update the cache.

If, upon reception of a request, a service finds insufficient funds in its cache, it first updates the cache as described above to see if the client has made a deposit in the mean time. If the amount there is also insufficient, the request is not carried out, and a reply is sent instead, requesting more funds.

8.2.4 Currencies

In a previous section the problem of comparing different kinds of service was broached. If only one accounting unit is used, it is difficult to exercise precise control over a number of different resources and services. What to do, for instance, if there is an ample supply of CPU cycles, but disk blocks are in scarce supply? Clearly, accounting mechanisms can be made more versatile if different units of accounting can be used for different kinds of resources.

Different units of accounting are represented by virtual money in different *currencies*. It is thus possible, for instance, to do accounting of disk blocks in *virtual guilders*, accounting of compilations in *virtual dinars*, and accounting of CPU seconds in *virtual yen*. New currencies can be created and removed dynamically, and conversion between currencies is possible. There is also the possibility of *minting* more virtual money in some currency, if that is useful.

Different currencies are applied in different ways to obtain different types of accounting. This is illustrated by two simple examples. Suppose, the manager of a computer centre wants to set a maximum to the number of disk blocks that each user may occupy at any moment. This is implemented by creating a currency — say, *virtual roubles* — that represents disk blocks. When a user enters the system, he or she receives an amount of *virtual roubles*. When a disk block is allocated, an amount must be paid; when a block is released, the amount is returned. Suppose now that our manager wants to set a maximum number of CPU seconds per week that each user may consume. This is done by creating a currency — say, *virtual dollars* — that is used to pay each user a weekly salary to buy CPU seconds with. Several policies may be adapted for allowing users to take *virtual dollars* saved up into the next week, by making the salary depend on the amount left over at the end of the week.

These examples serve to illustrate that the provider of some services will wish to create a virtual currency to control the use of that service. For this reason, it is the providers of the services in the system and not the bank service who decide to create new currencies and the amounts to be minted. Naturally, the bank server itself — being a provider of a service also — may create some currency that controls the creation of other currencies, for instance, to prevent any one user from creating too many currencies.

Services can ask to be paid in combinations of currencies. A phototypesetter service, for instance, may adopt the policy to demand payment in real money (represented by some virtual currency) to cover the cost of photographic material (paper, developer), in addition to payment in another virtual currency that prevents a (rich) user from occupying the phototypesetter too long at a time.

8.2.5 Bank server requests

The commands to the bank server can be divided into two categories: those that manage accounts, and those that manage currencies. Not all requests will be discussed here, but a subset that amply illustrates how the bank service is used. Before the bank service requests are described in detail, however, a few remarks on notation are necessary. Some requests, such as the request to transfer an amount from one account to another, operate on two objects. In these cases, one object (the account from which the withdrawal is made) will be the *primary* object, that is, the object indicated by the capability of the request, while the second object will be the *secondary* object, that is, the object whose capability is contained in the request's data. In the notation used, the first parameter of each request is special; it indicates the *capability* field of the request. Although the bank service does require signatures in some of its requests, the *signature* field is not needed in requests to the bank service; only *public signatures* have to be sent to it. Note that this allows the bank service to use its own accounting mechanisms on its clients. When a capability refers to an object, and no confusion results, the same names will be used for the capability of the object and the name of the object.

CreateBusinessAccount(*BankService*);
returns: *OwnerCapability* , *DepositCapability*

The *BankService* capability in this request is the public capability that allows all clients of the bank service to create new objects. The bank service will create an empty business account and return two capabilities for it, an owner capability and a capability to give to clients to deposit into the account.

CreatePrivateAccount(*BankService*);
returns: *OwnerCapability* , *DepositCapability*

This request creates an empty private account and, like the *CreateBusinessAccount* request, returns two capabilities for it.

Transfer(*FromAccount, FromSignature* , *ToAccount* , *ToSignature* , *Amount*);
returns: Balance of *FromAccount*

This request is used to transfer amounts from one account to another (both can be business or private). The signature parameters are only needed for transfers from and to business accounts; for private accounts, the signatures can be dummy parameters. Note, that the signatures need not be in the request's *signature* field, the public signature suffices. *Amount* represents a list of virtual currencies and amounts.

Inspect(*Account, signature*);
returns: Balance of *Account*

The bank server inspects the account indicated by *Account* , and returns its balance. If it is a business account, *signature* can be used to tell the bank server to consider only the balance of the account, deposited under that signature.

RemoveAccount(*Account*);
returns: Acknowledgement

The bank server removes the account (business or private) after making sure it is empty. If this is not the case, the request fails.

CreateCurrency(*BankServer, Account* , *Amount*);
returns: *MintCapability* , *Name*

A new currency is generated, of which *Amount* is minted and put in *Account* . A capability for controlling the currency is returned, plus a small integer which functions as the name of the new currency.

Mint(*MintCapability, Account* , *Amount*);
returns: Acknowledgement

Amount is minted of the currency to which *MintCapability* refers; it is deposited into *Account* .

RemoveCurrency(*MintCapability*);
returns: Acknowledgement

A currency is removed. All amounts of the currency in all accounts are deleted.

8.3 Accounting policies

The bank service mechanisms, presented in the previous section, can only be useful if they serve an efficient implementation of a wide variety of accounting policies. In this section some of the existing accounting policies will be reviewed, and it will be shown how they can be realized.

8.3.1 Payment for services

An important application of accounting is in computing the cost of services consumed. This is not only useful in commercial computer centres that must bill their clients in accordance with their service consumption, but also for educational institutes, where it is useful, for example, to charge students for excessive use of expensive resources, such as line printer paper or phototypesetter pages.

Accounting for the cost of services is one of the simplest applications of bank service. In principle, each user (periodically) receives an amount in some currency, representing a *budget* or *salary*. This currency is used to pay for services consumed, as described earlier. At any time, the difference between the sum given to the user and the amount left over in the user's account represents the amount consumed.

For accounting purposes, a service is considered to *let* its resources to clients and carry out operations for clients. In principle, charges can be levied on the operations, and hire on the consumption of resources. The charge on execution of requests is a function of the cost of carrying them out, the hire of resources is a function of the type, amount and time the resource is consumed.

A file server, for instance, stores files and carries out operations on them. It can charge an amount for each operation carried out, plus an additional sum per day for the consumed file space. Several policies can be adopted when clients have insufficient funds to pay for file service. It can start to refuse to carry out operations for its clients, it can also make client files inaccessible until sufficient budget is once again available, and, in extreme cases, it can altogether remove unpaid-for client files.

The charges levied on execution of requests are collected after each request. Charges on resource hire can be collected in several ways. They can be collected when the resource is returned, but this may result in clients keeping a resource past the point where their budget runs out. The charges can be collected periodically — say, every hour, or minute, depending on the resource. But they can also be collected whenever a client requests an operation on the resource; charges are collected then, anyway.

8.3.2 Quota, budgets and salaries

To prevent a user from using too much of a resource at once, *quota* are usually established. A *quota* is a maximum amount or maximum number that a user may consume of a resource. Examples of quota are n disk blocks, m magnetic tapes, p CPU seconds per day, q line printer pages per week. Quota can be separated into two kinds: *absolute* and *per unit of time*. Absolute quota are used for *reallocable* resources, resources that a client uses for some time, and then gives back so they can be used by another. Quota per unit of time are used for *allocate-once* resources, resources that a client uses up and can not be returned to be used by another. Disk blocks and magnetic tapes are examples of reallocable resources, CPU seconds and phototypesetter pages are examples of allocate-once resources.

Quota for reallocable resources are simple to implement. Every user, when given access to the system receives a *budget*, an amount of virtual currency representing maxima on resources that may be used. Whenever the user requests more resources, they must be paid for from the budget. Whenever the user returns resources, the payment is returned.

When more of a resource becomes available, or fewer users have to share the resource, budgets may be increased; when more users have to share a resource, or the resource becomes scarcer, budgets must be decreased. It is a simple matter to increase users' budgets, but it is harder to decrease them: the complete budget may already have been invested, so there may not be enough budget left to take away. One way to decrease budgets is to *devalue* the currency representing the resource, that is, make the resource more expensive. However, this will favour users that obtained their resources at the old price, and they will not be willing to return any of their resources, because they will not be able to obtain the same amount later. In most cases, it is not possible to take away resources from users by pure mechanical means, anyway: when more users have to share the same disk space, for instance, the old users must make room for the new; however, the old users will have valuable information stored in their disk space, and the 'system' cannot just take away some of the old users' disk blocks.

For allocate-once resources a slightly different approach can be used, based on *salaries*. Every user receives an hourly, daily, monthly (or whatever is appropriate) salary with which to pay for consumption of allocate-once resources. The salary can be independent of the amount left over in the users' accounts, which makes it possible for users to save up for future use. The salary can also be made dependent on the left-over amount, to restrict saving, or to prevent it altogether.

Often, it will be useful to combine budgets and salaries. For instance, a user could be given a budget to restrict the number of tape drives used simultaneously, and a salary to restrict the time the tape drives are allocated.

PART IV
Data Storage

The subject of data storage in distributed systems encompasses distributed file systems and distributed database systems. In Chapter 9, Satyanarayanan describes his own Andrew file system after giving an overview of issues in distributed file system design and current work in the area. The Andrew project, and its successor, the Coda project, are among the most ambitious projects in terms of expected size of the eventual running system.

The authors of this book felt that one or two chapters on distributed databases would hardly do the subject justice. The reader is better served by finding a book devoted exclusively to distributed database systems, such as Ceri and Pelagatti's *Distributed Databases — Principles and Systems* (1984), Published by McGraw-Hill (ISBN 0-07-010829-3).

Chapter 9

Distributed File Systems

M. Satyanarayanan

9.1 Introduction

As in other domains of human activity, *sharing of information* is pervasive in distributed systems. Each user in a distributed system is potentially a creator as well as a consumer of data. A user may wish to make his actions contingent upon information from a remote site, or may wish to update remote information. Sometimes the physical movement of a user may require his data to be accessible elsewhere. In both scenarios, ease of data sharing considerably enhances the value of a distributed system to its community of users. The technical challenge is to support this sharing in a secure, reliable, efficient and usable manner that is independent of the size and complexity of the distributed system.

Distributed file systems constitute the primary class of mechanisms that have been evolved to support data sharing. The goal of this paper is to provide an understanding of the current state of the art in this area. The first part of the discussion, Section 9.2 is a general treatment of basic issues. Section 9.3 then presents an in-depth case study of *Andrew,* a contemporary distributed file system. Many implementation and design details emerge in the course of this case study. Finally, Section 9.4 concludes the paper with an examination of current research in distributed file systems.

9.2 Fundamentals

Our study of distributed file systems begins with a taxonomy of design issues. Section 9.2.1 describes these issues and their relationship to models of computing. Section 9.2.2 contrasts file systems with databases, the other major class of mechanisms for sharing data. Section 9.2.3 then summarizes the results of a number of empirical studies of file systems and, finally, Section 9.2.4 traces the history and evolution of distributed file systems, focusing on the major distributed file systems that have been built to date.

9.2.1 Taxonomy

Permanent storage is a fundamental abstraction in computing. It consists of a named set of objects that come into existence by explicit creation, are immune to temporary failures of the system, and persist until explicitly destroyed. The naming structure, the characteristics of the objects, and the set of operations associated with them characterize a specific refinement of the basic abstraction. A file system is one such refinement.

From the perspective of file system design, computing models can be classified into four levels. The set of design issues at any level subsumes those at lower levels. A file system for a higher level will have to be more sophisticated than one that is adequate for a lower level.

In the simplest model, exemplified by IBM MS-DOS (IBM (1983)) and Apple Macintosh (Apple Computer, Inc (1985)), one user at a single site performs computations via a single process. A file system for this model must address four key issues:

- *Naming*
  How does the user name files? Is the name space flat, as in early file systems, or hierarchically organized, as in Unix (Ritchie and Thompson (1974))? Must the name space be tree-structured, or can it contain cycles? How long can file names be? Do file names contain implicit structure, such as a file extension, that is of semantic significance? Can multiple versions of a file exist?

- *Programming interface*
  How do applications access the file system? Two broad strategies are possible, along with numerous refinements of each. One approach is to map files into the address space of a process and to access their contents as virtual memory. This strategy was first incorporated in Multics (Organick (1972)). The alternative approach, exemplified by Unix, is for the operating system to export an interface with a set of file operations. In some systems the set of primitive file operations may include support for *atomic transactions* (Lampson (1981)), whereby a series of modifications to one or more files is not permanently visible unless the user *commits* these modifications.

- *Physical storage*
  How is the file system abstraction mapped onto physical storage media? Is the programming interface independent of storage media? Performance considerations usually dictate large block transfers to and from the media. However smaller block sizes reduce fragmentation. How are these conflicting requirements balanced? A good discussion of these issues may be found in the description of the Unix 4.2BSD file system (McKusick *et al.* (1984)).

- *Integrity*
  How are files kept consistent across power, hardware, media and software failures? This problem is of particular importance when a file system uses volatile memory as a write-back cache to achieve high performance. Recovering from failures may then require tools such as *fsck* in Unix (McKusick and Kowalski (1986)) to repair structural inconsistencies. Even if write-back is not used, file backup and restore utilities are necessary to protect against media failure and user errors.

The next level in this taxonomy involves a single user computing with multiple processes at one site. The OS/2 operating system (Letwin (1988)) is an example of such a model. *Concurrency control* now becomes a relevant issue, with the file system having to support the specification and enforcement of synchronization policies. A number of questions arise in this context. What should be the granularity at which synchronization is supported: entire files, individual bytes of a file, or some intermediate unit such as a logical page or a disk block? What locking modes are supported and what are the legal combinations of locks that can coexist? *Serializability* is a useful notion, particularly when atomic transactions are supported. An execution instance of interleaved transactions is serializable if some sequential execution order of those transactions would yield the same effect. How is serializability realized in the implementation? *Deadlocks* are a potential outcome of interleaved executions of processes. How are deadlocks detected or avoided? Concurrency control continues to be a fertile area of theoretical and experimental research. The survey by Bernstein and Goodman (1981) treats this material in depth.

The classical timesharing model constitutes the next level of the taxonomy. At this level there are multiple users sharing data and resources on a single computer. *Security* now becomes relevant and many protection questions arise. How are users identified and authenticated? Can users be aggregated into groups? Does one use a capability model as in Hydra (Wulf, Levin, and Harbison (1981)), or an access-list model as in Multics (Saltzer (1974))? At what granularity can protection policies be expressed? What are the privileges that can be granted? How do these privileges map on to individual file operations? Is revocation possible?

The highest level of the taxonomy involves many users physically dispersed in a network of timesharing computers. In this view, a distributed file system is merely a distributed implementation of the multi-user, single-site file system abstraction. The challenge is in realizing this abstraction in an *efficient* and *robust* manner. Some aspects of the system, such as user authentication, may require fundamentally different techniques. Other aspects, such as concurrency control and support for atomic transactions, may involve major modifications to single-site techniques.

One issue unique to distributed file systems, is the location of files. The simplest approach is to embed location information in file names. Constructs such as '*/../machine/localpath*' (as in Unix United (Brownbridge, Marshall, and

Randell (1982))), '/server/localpath' (as in Cedar (Schroeder, Gifford, and Needham (1985))), and 'machine::device:localpath' (as in Vax/VMS (December (1985))) are examples of this approach. Unfortunately, the embedding of physical information in a logical name space has negative consequences. Firstly, users have to remember machine names to access data. Although feasible in a small environment, this becomes increasingly difficult as the system grows in size. Secondly, it is inconvenient to move files between sites. Changing the location of a file also changes its name, which means that file names embedded in application programs and in the minds of users are invalidated. A better approach is to use true *location transparency*, where the name of a file is devoid of location information. File movement then becomes an operation that is totally transparent to users because an explicit file location mechanism maps names to storage sites during normal file system operation.

Another fundamental issue in a distributed environment is *availability*. Since the site where the data is being used can be different from its storage site, failure modes are substantially more complex than in a single-site environment.

Replication, the basic technique used to achieve high availability, introduces complications of its own. Since multiple copies of a file are present, changes have to be propagated to all the replicas. Such propagation has to be done in a consistent and efficient manner.

9.2.2 Databases

A *database* is another refinement of the permanent storage abstraction. How does one classify a storage repository as a file system or a database? This can sometimes be a difficult problem. There are distributed file systems such as Alpine (Brown, Kolling, and Taft (1985)) and Locus (Walker *et al.* (1983)) that provide operations typically associated with databases. Single-site file systems from vendors, such as DEC VMS (December (1986)) and IBM MVS (IBM (1987a)), provide support for databases to be built on top of them. There are also database systems such as Ingres (Stonebraker *et al.* (1976)) and Informix (Informix (1986)) that reside on Unix, whose storage repository is clearly a file system.

Thus *functionality* is not an adequate basis for distinguishing file systems from databases. A more sound criterion is the *storage model* presented to application programs and users. A file system views the data in a file as an uninterpreted byte sequence† A database, in contrast, encapsulates substantial information about the types and logical relationships of data items stored in it. Since the data is typed, the database can enforce constraints on values. The details of the storage model depend on whether the database is relational, network, or hierarchical. In all cases, however, a database embodies substantially greater knowledge of the data stored in it than a file system.

---

† Certain file systems such as IBM MVS allow the user to specify data organization. However this pertains to the physical layout of the data, not to its value or logical structure.

Another fundamental distinction between file systems and databases is in the area of naming. A file system provides access to a file *by name*. A database, on the other hand, allows *associative access*. Data items can be accessed and modified in a database based on user-specified predicates.

Neither the difference in storage model nor in naming makes it a priori more difficult to build distributed databases than file systems. However, the circumstances that lead to the use of a database are often precisely those that make distribution of data difficult. The use of databases is most common in applications where data has to be concurrently shared for reading and writing by a large number of users. These applications usually demand strict consistency of data as well as atomicity of groups of operations. Although the total quantity of data in the database may be large, the granularity of access and update is usually quite fine. It is this combination of application characteristics that makes the implementation of distributed databases substantially harder than the implementation of distributed file systems.

Distributing a database is particularly difficult at large scale. Whereas distributed databases typically span less than ten nodes today, distributed file systems spanning tens of nodes are common place. Larger distributed file systems, such as Andrew, already encompass over 500 nodes and growth to thousands of nodes is anticipated. Providing full database functionality at such large scale is an unexplored problem at the present time. As mentioned earlier in this section, single-site databases have often been built on top of a file system. This practice needs to be reconsidered in a distributed environment. The need to support databases seriously constrains the design of a distributed file system, affecting both its scalability and performance. Decoupling database implementation from file system implementation may prove to be wise in a large distributed environment. This issue is discussed further in Section 9.4.3.

9.2.3 Properties of files

The behaviour of a file system is strongly influenced by the characteristics of the files stored in it. Both functionality and performance are negatively affected if the design of a file system is inconsistent with its usage. Knowledge of file properties can be exploited in the design and configuration of file systems. For example, file sizes and request rates by users determine hardware parameters such as minimum disk capacity and performance. The size distribution of files also determines optimal storage block size, since this has to be a trade off between efficiency and internal fragmentation. Architectural decisions such as the use of caching or read ahead, as well as policy decisions such as cache management and file migration algorithms are other instances where empirical knowledge of file properties is valuable.

Empirical observations of real systems involve many practical difficulties. Instrumentation of file systems usually requires modifications to the operating system. The technique used for instrumentation should not affect system performance significantly. The total volume of data generated is usually large, and needs to be stored and processed efficiently.

In addition to the difficulty of collecting data, there are two fundamental concerns about its interpretation. Generality is one of these concerns. How specific are the observations to the system being observed? Data of widespread applicability is obviously of most value. Fortunately, independent investigators have obtained similar results on a variety of systems. Although these studies differ in their details, there is substantial overlap in the set of issues they investigate. More importantly, there are no serious contradictions. The systems examined include IBM MVS (Revelle (1975); Smith (1981); Stritter (1977)), DEC PDP-10 (Satyanarayanan (1981); Satyanarayanan (1984a)), and Unix (Floyd (1986a); Floyd (1986b); Majumdar and Bunt (1986); Ousterhout et al. (1985)). There is thus confidence in the robustness of these results.

The second concern relates to the interdependency of design and empirical observations. Are the observed properties an artifact of existing system design or are they intrinsic? Little is known about the influence of system design on file properties, although the existence of such influence is undeniable. For example, in a design that uses whole-file transfer, such as Andrew, there is substantial disincentive to the creation of very large files. In the long run this may affect the observed file size distribution. It is therefore important to revalidate our understanding of file properties as new systems are built and existing systems mature.

Studies of file systems fall into two broad categories. Early studies (Revelle (1975); Satyanarayanan (1981); Smith (1981); Stritter (1977)) were based on *static* analysis, using one or more snapshots of a file system. The data from these studies is unweighted. Later studies (Floyd (1986a); Floyd (1986b); Majumdar and Bunt (1986); Ousterhout et al. (1985); Satyanarayanan (1984a)) are based on *dynamic* analysis, using continuous monitoring of a file system. These data are weighted by file usage. Data for files which are not accessed during the period of observation are not included in the latter studies. Taken together, these studies shed light on a number of questions that are important in the design and implementation of distributed file systems:

- What is the size distribution of files?

- What are the relative and absolute frequencies of different file operations?

- How often does the data in a file change?

- How often do users share files for reading and for writing?

- Does the type of a file substantially influence its properties?

The most consistent observation in all the studies is the skewing of file sizes toward the low end. In other words, most files are small, typically in the neighbourhood of 10 kilobytes. Another common observation is that read operations on files are much more frequent than write operations. Random accessing of a file is rare, even in an operating system such as Unix which provides good support for it. A typical application program reads an entire file into its address space sequentially and then performs nonsequential processing on the in-memory data. A related observation is that a file is usually read in its entirety once it has been opened.

Averaged over all the files in a system, data appears to be highly mutable. The *functional lifetime* of a file, defined as the time interval between the most recent read and the most recent write, is skewed toward the low end. In other words, data in files tends to be frequently overwritten. Although the mean functional lifetime is small, the tail of the distribution is long, indicating the existence of files with long-lived data.

Most files are read and written by one user. When users share a file, it is usually the case that only one of them modifies it. Fine granularity read-write sharing of files is rare. It is important to emphasize that these are observations derived from research or academic environments. Environments that make extensive use of databases may show substantially greater write-sharing of data.

File references show substantial locality of reference. If a file is referenced there is a high probability it will be referenced again in the near future. Over short periods of time the set of referenced files is a very small subset of all files.

These observations apply to the file population as a whole. If one were to focus on files of a specific type their properties may differ significantly. For example, system programs tend to be stable and rarely modified. Consequently the average functional lifetime of system programs is much larger than the average over all files. Temporary files on the other hand show substantially shorter lifetimes. More fine-grained classification of files is also possible, as demonstrated by some of the investigations mentioned earlier (Floyd (1986a); Floyd (1986b); Satyanarayanan (1981)).

9.2.4 Evolution

The earliest model of remote file access involved user-initiated file transfers between a client machine and a dedicated file server with large amounts of disk storage. The correspondence between local file names and remote file names was maintained by users. The distinction between local and remote files was visible to users, since local file operations could not be applied to remote files. Although this model is no longer viewed as a distributed file system, it did serve as the primary model of data sharing in the early days of distributed computing. Examples of this approach are IFS for the Alto personal computers (Thacker *et al.* (1981)) and the Datanet file repository on the Arpanet (Marill and Stern (1975)).

A major step in the evolution of distributed file systems was the recognition that access to remote files could be made to resemble access to local files. This property, called *network transparency*, implies that any operation that can be performed on a local file can also be performed on a remote file. The extent to which an actual implementation meets this ideal is one measure of quality. Unix United (Brownbridge, Marshall, and Randell (1982)) and Cocanet (Rowe and Birman (1982)) are two early examples of systems that provided network transparency. In both cases the name of the remote site was a prefix of a remote file name.

A number of experimental file systems were built in the decade from 1975 to 1985. Each of these systems concentrated on a specific subset of the issues discussed in Section 9.2.1. Much research interest was focused on providing efficient support for atomic transactions and concurrency control on remote files. Felix (Fridrich and Older (1981)), XDFS (Mitchell and Dion (1982)), Alpine (Brown, Kolling, and Taft (1985)), and Swallow (Svobodova (1981)) are examples of such systems. The survey by Svobodova (Svobodova (1984)) contains an excellent comparative discussion of these and other similar efforts.

The Cambridge file system (Birrell and Needham (1980)) and the CMU-CFS file system (Accetta *et al.* (1980)) examined how the naming structure of a distributed file system could be separated from its function as a permanent storage repository. The latter also addressed access control, caching, and transparent file migration on to archival media. Cedar (Schroeder, Gifford, and Needham (1985)), the first file system to demonstrate the viability of caching entire files, contained a number of design decisions motivated by its intended application as a base for program development. The Amoeba file system (Mullender and Tanenbaum (1985); Mullender and Tanenbaum (1986)) examined optimistic concurrency control techniques and the use of capabilities for protection.

Locus (Popek *et al.* (1981); Walker *et al.* (1983)) was a landmark system in two important ways. First, it identified location transparency as an important design criterion. Second it proposed replication, along with a mechanism for detecting inconsistency, to achieve high availability. Locus also provided support for atomic transactions on files and generalized the notion of transparent remote access to all aspects of the operating system. *Weighted voting*, an alternative way of using replication for data availability, was demonstrated in Violet (Gifford (1979a); Gifford (1979b)).

The rapid decline of CPU and memory costs *vis a vis* disk storage motivated research on workstations without local disks or other permanent storage media. In such a system, a *disk server* exports a low-level interface that emulates local disk operations. Diskless operation has been successfully demonstrated in systems such as V (Cheriton and Zwaenepoel (1983)), RVD (IBM (1987b)) and Sun NFS (SUN (1986)). Whether a workstation uses a local or remote disk is, in theory, orthogonal to the design of a distributed file system. But the consequences of remote disk access on performance, availability and security are sufficiently important that it has to be viewed as a fundamental design constraint.

The Andrew file system, described in depth in Section 9.3, addresses issues of performance, security and operability in the context of a large distributed environment. Both Andrew and the Sprite file system (Nelson, Welch, and Ousterhout (1988)) exploit caching as the primary mechanism to achieve high performance. Andrew caches on local disks, while Sprite uses large main memory caches on clients.

Distributed file systems have now emerged from the realm of experimental prototypes to production quality implementations. Vendor-supported systems such as NFS from Sun Microsystems, RFS from AT&T (Rifkin *et al.* (1986)), and Domain from Apollo (Leach *et al.* (1985)) are now in extensive use. Andrew, available from IBM, is now beginning to be used at sites other than CMU. There is no doubt that distributed file systems will continue to play an important role in the future and will form an indispensable component of distributed systems. However, as discussed in Section 9.4, the process of evolution is far from complete.

9.3 Case study

Andrew is a distributed computing environment that has been under development at Carnegie Mellon University (CMU) since 1983. A unique characteristic of Andrew is its expected final size. It is anticipated that each individual at CMU will eventually possess a workstation, thus implying an eventual scale of 5000 to 10 000 nodes. In mid-1987, there were about 400 workstations and 16 file servers with about 6000 Mbytes of shared data in regular use by over 1000 users.

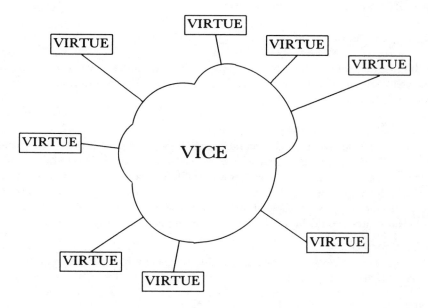

Figure 9.1 Vice and Virtue. The amoeba-like structure in the centre is a collection of networks and servers that constitute Vice. Virtue is typically a workstation, but can also be a mainframe.

Andrew combines a sophisticated user interface feasible only in personal computing with the data-sharing simplicity of timesharing. This synthesis is achieved by close cooperation between two kinds of components, *Vice* and *Virtue*, shown in Figure 9.1. A Virtue workstation provides the power and capability of a dedicated personal computer, while Vice provides support for the timesharing abstraction.

Although Vice is shown as a single logical entity in Figure 9.1, it is actually composed of a collection of servers and a complex local area network. This network spans the entire CMU campus and is composed primarily of Ethernet and IBM Token Ring segments (with a few optic fiber and Appletalk limbs) interconnected via active elements called *Routers*. Figure 9.2 shows the details of this network. Each Virtue workstation runs the Unix 4.3BSD operating system,† and is thus an autonomous computational node. A distributed file system that spans all workstations is the primary data-sharing mechanism in Andrew.

The goals and directions of the Andrew project have been described by Morris *et al.* (1986). The file system has been discussed extensively in papers focusing on architecture (Satyanarayanan *et al.* (1985)), performance (Howard *et al.* (1988)), security (Satyanarayanan (1987)), and the influence of scale (Satyanarayanan (1988a)). Publications are also available on other components of Andrew such as the user interface (Palay *et al.* (1988)) and the message system (Borenstein *et al.* (1988)). A retrospective on the high-level design decisions in Andrew is presented by Morris (1988).

9.3.1 Goals

The high-level goal of the Andrew file system is to emulate a giant timesharing file system spanning the entire CMU campus. More specific goals are as follows:

● *Location transparency*
  There should be a single name space for all shared files in the system. Given the size of the system, it is unacceptable to require users to remember details such as the current location of a file or the site where it was created. Consequently, the naming scheme should not incorporate any information about the location of files. Further, the resolution of file names to network storage sites should be performed by the file system.

● *User mobility*
  Users should be able to access any file in the shared name space from any workstation. The performance characteristics of the system should not discourage users from accessing their files from workstations other than the one at which they usually work.

† Unix is a trademark of AT&T. In the rest of this chapter the term 'Unix' will refer to the 4.3BSD version.

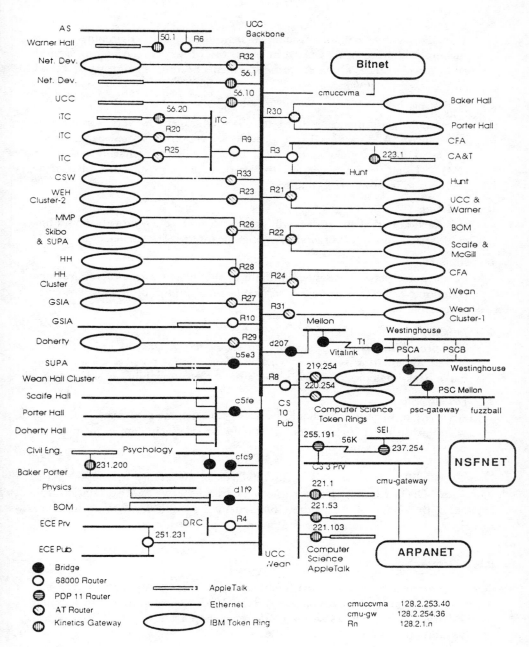

Figure 9.2 Carnegie Mellon Internet, August 25 1987.

- *Security*
  The file system cannot assume a benevolent user environment. To encourage sharing of files between users, the protection mechanism should allow a wide range of policies to be specified. Security should not be based on the integrity of workstations.

- *Performance*
  Acceptable performance is hard to quantify, except in very specific circumstances. Andrew's goal is to provide a level of file system performance that is at least as good as that of a lightly-loaded timesharing system at CMU. Users should never feel the need to make explicit file placement decisions to improve performance.

- *Scalability*
  It is inevitable that the system will grow with time. Such growth should not cause serious disruption of service, nor significant loss of performance to users.

- *Availability*
  Single point network or machine failures should not affect the entire user community. Temporary loss of service to small groups of users is, however, acceptable.

- *Integrity*
  The probability of loss of stored data should be at least as low as on the current timesharing systems at CMU. Users should not feel compelled to make back-up copies of their files because of the unreliability of the system.

- *Heterogeneity*
  A variety of workstations should be able to participate in the sharing of files via the distributed file system. It should be relatively simple to integrate new types of workstation.

Noticeably absent from the above list of goals is the ability to support large databases. Given existing local area network transfer rates and workstation disk capacities, the design of the Andrew file system is suitable for files up to a few megabytes in size. Database access requires a separate mechanism.

9.3.2 Design

The core of the Andrew file system architecture is described in this section, while its implementation and evolution are discussed in the next section. In focusing on the basic aspects, this discussion omits many important areas. Two of these, security and operability, are discussed later.

Naming

From the point of view of application programs on workstations, the space of file names is partitioned into two subspaces: *local* and *shared*. Figure 9.3 illustrates

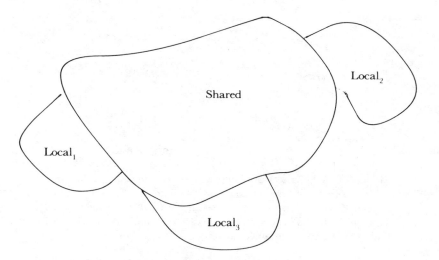

Figure 9.3 Shared and local name spaces. This is a Venn diagram depicting local and shared name spaces. *Local*₁, *Local*₂, and *Local*₃ correspond to files in the local file systems of three different workstations. *Shared* corresponds to the shared set of files in the system, and is identical for all the workstations.

this partitioning. The shared name space is identical on all workstations and though distributed across multiple file servers, appears totally homogeneous to application programs. Since file names do not contain the identity of servers there is no means by which an application program can determine which file server is storing a particular file. The local name space is small, distinct for each workstation, and contains files that are either essential for workstation initialization or are temporary files such those containing intermediate output from compiler phases. In practice, almost all files accessed by users are in the shared name space. Consequently users can move at will from one workstation to another and continue to see a consistent image of their files.

Both the local and shared name spaces are hierarchically structured, and are similar to a timesharing Unix file system. In Unix terminology, the local name space is the *root file system* of a workstation and the shared name space is *mounted* on the node '/cmu' during workstation initialization. Figure 9.4 depicts this situation. Since all shared file names generated on the workstation have '/cmu' as a prefix of their path name, it is trivial to disambiguate between local and shared files.

Unix expects to find system files in its local name space. However, through the use of symbolic links, the vast majority of system files can be placed in the shared name space. For example, on a SUN workstation, the local directory */usr/local/bin* is a symbolic link to the remote directory */cmu/unix/sun/usr/local/bin*; on a VAX, */usr/local/bin* is a symbolic link to */cmu/unix/vax/usr/*

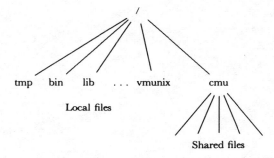

Figure 9.4 A Unix workstation's view of the file system. The files in the '/cmu' subtree are common to all the workstations in the system. Certain directories and files in the local name space, such as '/bin' and '/lib', are symbolic links into '/cmu'. All other local files are inaccessible to other workstations.

local/bin. In this way, accesses to most common system files are automatically translated to remote accesses. This greatly reduces the amount of disk space required locally, and simplifies the distribution of new releases of system software. As indicated in the example, symbolic links are also of value in supporting diversity in workstation hardware.

Intercept and caching

Entire files are cached on demand at workstations. When an application program makes a system call to open a file, the request is first examined by the workstation operating system to determine whether the file is local or shared. In the former case, the open request is satisfied exactly as it would be in a stand-alone system. For a shared file, the request is relayed to a local process, Venus, running on behalf of the file system. Venus manages the local cache and the communication with the remote file server. For an open request for a shared file, Venus checks the cache for the presence of a valid copy. If such a copy exists, the open request is treated as a local file open request to the cached copy. If the file is not present in the cache, or if the copy is not current, a fresh copy is fetched from the appropriate file server. All these actions are transparent to application programs: they merely perform a normal file open.

After a file is opened, individual read and write operations on a shared file are directed to the cached copy: no network traffic is generated on account of such requests. On a close request, the cached copy is first closed as a local file; if it has been modified, the updated copy is then transmitted to the appropriate file server. The cache thus behaves as a write-through cache on closes.

The caching mechanism allows complete mobility of users with minimum performance penalty. If a user places all his files in the shared name space (the default), his workstation becomes 'personal' only in the sense that it is owned by him. The user can move to any other workstation attached to Vice and use it exactly as he would use his own workstation. The only observable difference would be an initial performance degradation as the cache on the new workstation is filled with that user's working set of files.

Locality of file references by typical users makes caching attractive. The caching of entire files has a number of benefits:

- A whole-file transfer approach contacts servers only on opens and closes. Read and write operations, which are far more numerous, are transparent to servers and cause no network traffic.

- Most files in a Unix environment are read in their entirety. Whole-file transfer exploits this property by allowing the use of efficient bulk data transfer protocols.

- Disk caches retain their entries across reboots, a surprisingly frequent event in workstation environments. Since few of the files accessed by a typical user are likely to be modified elsewhere in the system, the amount of data fetched after a reboot is usually small.

- Finally, caching of entire files simplifies cache management. Venus only has to keep track of the files in its cache, not of their individual pages.

This approach does have its drawbacks, however. Although diskless operation is possible, workstations require local disks for acceptable performance. Files which are larger than the local disk cache cannot be accessed at all. Strict emulation of Unix concurrent read and write semantics across workstations is impossible, since reads and writes are not intercepted. Building a distributed database using such a file system is difficult, if not impossible. Fortunately these drawbacks have not proved to be serious in practice.

Data location and replication

Each server in Vice runs a file server process that supports operations such as storing and retrieving files in response to requests from Venii on workstations. The hierarchical file name space is partitioned into disjoint subtrees, and each such subtree is served by a single server, called its *custodian*. Storage for a file, as well as the servicing of requests for it, are the responsibility of the corresponding custodian. Changing the custodian of a subtree is a relatively heavyweight operation: the design is predicated on the assumption that such changes do not occur on a minute-to-minute basis.

Certain subtrees that contain frequently read, but rarely modified files, may have read-only replicas at other servers. Such read-only copies are created by a process called *cloning*, initiated by system administrators. Read-only copies are typically created for system files, in order to enhance availability and to distribute the server load evenly.

Each server contains a copy of a fully replicated location database that may be queried by Venii to ascertain the custodian of any file. The size of this replicated database is relatively small because custodianship is on a subtree basis: if all files in a subtree have the same custodian, there need only be an entry for the root. The location database changes relatively slowly for two reasons. First, most file creation and deletion activity occurs at depths of the naming tree far below that at which the assignment of custodians is done. Second, reassignment of custodians is infrequent and is initiated via administrative procedures. Consequently, a specialized propagation mechanism that lazily updates custodianship information at all servers is feasible.

9.3.3 Implementation

An initial prototype of the Andrew file system was built to validate its basic architecture. This prototype was made available to a user community of about 400 users with access to about 100 workstations. In the light of experience, the original architecture was refined and a completely new implementation built. The presentation in this section is organized chronologically. First, the prototype implementation is described; then the experience with the prototype is discussed. Finally, the revised implementation is described.

Prototype implementation

In the prototype, Venus on a client workstation would rendezvous with a process listening at a well-known network address on a server. This process then created a dedicated process to deal with all future requests from the client. The dedicated process persisted until its client terminated the network connection. In steady state a server typically operated with as many processes as there were clients who had ever contacted it. Since Unix does not allow sharing of address spaces between processes, all communication and manipulation of data structures between server processes took place via files in the underlying file system. User-level file locking was implemented by a dedicated lock server process which serialized requests from the separate server processes and maintained a lock table in its address space.

Data and associated Vice status information were stored in separate files. Each server contained a directory hierarchy mirroring the structure of the Vice files stored on it. Vice file status information, such as an access list, was stored in shadow directories called *.admin* directories. The directory hierarchy contained *stub* directories to represent portions of the Vice name space that were located on other servers. The location database that maps files to servers was thus embedded in the file tree. If a file were not on a server, the search for its name would end in a stub directory which identified the server containing that file. Below the top levels of the Vice name tree, files in the same subtree were likely to be located on the same server. Hence clients cached pathname-prefix information and used this as the basis of a heuristic to direct file requests to appropriate servers.

The Vice-Venus interface named files by their full path name. There was no notion of a low-level name, such as the *inode* in Unix. A rudimentary form of read-only replication, restricted to the topmost levels of the Vice name tree, was present. Each replicated directory had a single server site to which all updates were directed. An asynchronous slow-propagation mechanism reflected changes made at this site to the read-only replicas at all other sites.

All cached copies of files were considered suspect by Venus. Before using a cached file, Venus would verify its timestamp with that on the server responsible for the file. Each open of a file thus resulted in at least one interaction with a server, even if the file were already in the cache and up to date.

Prototype experience

Experience with the prototype put to rest a key concern: namely, the successful emulation of Unix file system semantics using caching and whole-file transfer. Most application programs were able to use Vice files without recompilation or relinking. There were, however, some areas of incompatibility with standard Unix semantics.

Although access to remote files was slower than to local files, the overall performance was substantially better than that of a loaded timesharing file system. Performance was usually acceptable up to about 20 active users per server.

The prototype was difficult to operate and maintain. The use of a dedicated process per client on each server caused critical resource limits to be exceeded on a number of occasions. It also resulted in excessive context switching overhead and in high virtual memory paging demands. However, it did have the virtue of simplicity and resulted in a relatively robust system because the failure of an individual server process affected only one client. The remote procedure call package was built on top of a reliable byte-stream abstraction provided by the kernel. While this simplified the system's implementation, it frequently caused network-related resources in the kernel to be exceeded. The embedding of the file location database in stub directories in the Vice name tree made it difficult to move user directories between servers. The absence of enforceable disk storage quotas on individual users exacerbated this problem.

Revised implementation

The revised implementation embodies a number of changes made to improve performance. These changes are in four distinct areas:

- Cache management

- Name resolution

- Communication and server process structure

- Low-level storage representation

Caching, the key to Andrew's ability to scale well, is further exploited in the redesign. Venus now caches the contents of directories and symbolic links in addition to files. A significant point of departure from the prototype is the manner in which cache entries are kept consistent. Rather than checking with a server on each open, Venus now assumes that cache entries are valid unless otherwise notified. When a workstation caches a file or directory, the server promises to notify it before allowing a modification by any other workstation. This promise, called a *callback*, dramatically reduces the number of cache validation requests received by servers. A small amount of cache validation traffic is still present, usually to replace callbacks lost on account of machine or network failures. When a workstation is rebooted, Venus considers all cached files and directories suspect and generates a cache validation request for the first use of each such entry.

To reduce server CPU overhead, and to provide a better emulation of Unix semantics, the translation of Vice path names to file identifiers is now performed by Venus. Each Vice file or directory is now identified by a unique fixed-length file identifier called *fid*. An entry in a directory maps a component of a path name to a fid. A fid is 96 bits long and has 3 components: a 32-bit *volume number*, a 32-bit *vnode number* and a 32-bit *uniquifier*. Servers are presented with fids and are, in fact, unaware of path names.

A volume resembles a logical disk pack and identifies a set of files located on one server. Custodianship information is contained in a *volume location database* replicated on each server. This is a slowly changing database that allows every server to identify the location of every volume in the system. It is the aggregation of files into volumes that makes it possible to keep the location database to a manageable size. More detailed information on volumes is presented in Section 9.3.7.

To reduce context switching and paging overheads, and to allow caching of critical shared information in virtual memory, the revised implementation uses a single Unix process per server. A user-level mechanism supports multiple nonpreemptive *lightweight processes* (LWPs) within one Unix server process. An LWP is bound to a particular client only for the duration of a single server operation. A client thus has long-term state on a server, but not a corresponding thread of control associated with it. Since Venus also uses the LWP mechanism, it can act concurrently on remote file access requests from multiple user processes on its workstation.

As in the prototype, clients and servers communicate via a remote procedure call mechanism. Unlike the prototype, however, this implementation is entirely outside the kernel and is capable of supporting many hundreds or thousands of clients per server. It is integrated with the LWP mechanism, thus allowing the server to continue servicing client requests unless all its LWPs are blocked on network events. The RPC mechanism runs on a variety of workstations, provides exactly-once semantics in the absence of failures, supports whole-file transfer using an optimized bulk transfer protocol, and provides secure, authenticated communication between workstations and servers.

As in the prototype, servers use Unix files to hold Vice data. To eliminate the overhead of path-name translation, servers now name these files by their low-level Unix identifiers. This involves modification to the Unix kernel, since the low-level identifiers are not visible to user-level processes. For efficiency Venus also uses this mechanism to access its cache files.

9.3.4 Performance

This section discusses three specific questions relating to the performance of distributed file systems. The discussion centres on Andrew, although other distributed file systems are considered where appropriate. The questions addressed by the next three sections are:

- What is the penalty for accessing remote files instead of local files?

- How important is caching, and how critical is the technique used for maintaining cache consistency?

- What is the overall performance of Andrew in relation to other designs?

These questions have been investigated in Andrew using a benchmark. Details of this benchmark may be found in the paper by Howard *et al.* (1988), which examines the performance of Andrew in depth. The same benchmark is also used in the performance analysis of the Sprite file system reported by Nelson, Welch, and Ousterhout (1988).

Local versus remote

A key concern in early designs of distributed file systems was whether the cost of remote file access would prove prohibitive. Extensive experience now indicates that this need not be the case. Data from a variety of systems shows that under favourable circumstances, the degradation due to remote access is typically between 10 and 20 per cent. Andrew, for instance, shows a 19 per cent slowdown when running a benchmark on remote files. On the same benchmark, Sprite suffers a 12 per cent degradation. Popek *et al.* (1981) report that Locus suffers 13 per cent degradation when reading long files sequentially. In the V system, Cheriton and Zwaenepoel (1983) indicate a 18 per cent degradation in page-level access to files.

It is important to emphasize that the numbers reported in the previous paragraph were obtained under a different experimental conditions, using different performance metrics. Interpretation and comparison of these numbers should only be done with caution. Nonetheless, these independent observations provide substantial evidence that the cost of remote access can be kept under 20 per cent when the load is low.

Caching

Caching is an extremely important mechanism for achieving good performance in a distributed file system. In Andrew, caching is so fundamental that it is an inseparable part of the architecture. It is not possible to conduct experiments with caching turned off. Thus there are no performance figures to quantify the contribution due to caching.

Sprite, however, is capable of being run with caching disabled. Nelson, Welch, and Ousterhout (1988) report extensively on the effect of caching in Sprite. They state that client caching reduces server utilization by more than a factor of 2, and network utilization by a factor of 10. Scalability is also improved dramatically. Without client caching, a load of 7 clients per server causes a 150 per cent degradation in performance. With caching, the degradation is only 30 per cent.

The technique used for maintaining cache consistency can make a substantial difference in performance. The obvious approach, used in the Andrew prototype, is to check the validity of a cached file on each operation. Since Andrew caches entire files, this check is made whenever a file is opened. Measurements of the prototype indicated that over 65 per cent of the requests to a server were cache validation requests. Since write sharing is relatively rare in a distributed file system, virtually all of these validation requests were superfluous.

In the revised Andrew implementation, clients are no longer responsible for cache validity. Rather, it is the server that informs all clients with cached copies of a file when that file is modified. This change, together with the others described in Section 9.3.3, improves the scalability of Andrew dramatically. With the prototype, increasing the number of clients simultaneously using the server from 1 to 10 caused the total running time of the benchmark to increase by over 300 per cent. In the revised implementation, increasing the number of clients from 1 to 20 increased the running time by less than 100 per cent. Although this improvement is the net result of a number of different changes, the reduction in the number of server requests and utilization point to the importance of callback.

Nelson, Welch, and Ousterhout (1988), however, come to a different conclusion regarding the value of callback. Using the same benchmark, they conclude on the basis of simulations that Sprite's performance would only be improved by a few per cent if they used callback. They attribute their contradictory conclusion to the fact that Sprite is implemented in the kernel whereas Andrew is implemented entirely as user processes. They conjecture that the performance benefits of callback would be substantially reduced if Andrew were implemented in the kernel.

Overall scalability

Since the design choices of Andrew are all biased toward scalability, it is appropriate to evaluate their net effect in relation to alternative distributed file system designs. Howard *et al.* (1988) present details of experiments comparing Andrew with the Sun Microsystems NFS file system (SUN (1986)). These experiments were performed on identical hardware configurations, simplifying the interpretation of results.

NFS shows an increase of 150 per cent in total benchmark running time when the number of clients per server is increased from 1 to 18. Andrew shows an increase of

49 per cent with a cold cache, and an increase of 23 per cent with a warm cache. At 18 clients, NFS server CPU utilization is 100 per cent, while Andrew server utilization is about 40 per cent. The corresponding server disk utilization is over 95 per cent in the case of NFS, while it is only about 25 per cent for Andrew.

These results are particularly relevant since NFS is a mature, highly-tuned, kernel implementation supported by a major vendor and widely perceived as a *de facto* standard by the Unix community. While the Andrew implementation used in this comparison was well-tuned, it was entirely outside the Unix kernel. Substantial performance improvement can be anticipated if Andrew is moved into the kernel.

Nelson, Welch, and Ousterhout (1988) compare Andrew and Sprite using the benchmark mentioned earlier. The comparison shows that Sprite is about 30 per cent better in absolute performance, but does not scale as well as Andrew. Each additional client contributes 5.4 per cent server CPU utilization in Sprite while it only contributes 2.4 per cent in Andrew. Thus Andrew compares favourably in scalability to both NFS and Sprite.

9.3.5 Security

Since Andrew is a large-scale system, the casual attitude towards security typical of closely-knit distributed environments is no longer viable. The relative anonymity of users in a large system requires security to be maintained by enforcement rather than by the good will of the user community. Most distributed systems present a facade of security by using simple extensions of the mechanisms used in a timesharing environment.

For example, network traffic between clients and servers is sent in the clear, thereby allowing a malicious individual to eavesdrop. Authentication is often implemented by sending a password in the clear to the server, which then validates it. Besides the obvious danger of sending passwords in the clear, this also has the drawback that the client is not certain of the identity of the server. The design of Andrew pays serious attention to these and related security issues, while ensuring that the mechanisms for security do not inhibit legitimate use of the system (Satyanarayanan (1987)).

A fundamental assumption pertains to the question of who enforces security in Andrew. Rather than trusting thousands of workstations, security in Andrew is based on the integrity of the much smaller number of Vice servers. These servers are located in physically secure rooms, are accessible only to trusted operators, and run software that is above suspicion. No user software is ever run on servers. Workstations may be owned privately or located in public areas. Andrew assumes that owners may modify both the hardware and software on their workstations in arbitrary ways. The network underlying Andrew has segments in every building at CMU, including student dormitories. It is impossible to guarantee the physical integrity of this network. Consequently Andrew security is not based on the integrity of the network wiring or routers. Rather, end-to-end mechanisms based on encryption are used.

Protection domain

In Andrew, the protection domain is composed of *users* and *groups*. A user is an entity, usually a human, that can authenticate itself to Vice, be held responsible for its actions, and be charged for resource consumption. A group is a set of other groups and users, associated with a user called its *owner*.

A group named 'System:Administrators' is distinguished. Membership in this group endows special administrative privileges, including unrestricted access to any file in the system. The use of a group 'System:Administrators' rather than a pseudo-user (such as 'root' in Unix systems) has the advantage that the actual identity of the user exercising special privileges is available for use in audit trails. This is particularly important in view of the scale of Andrew. Another advantage is that revocation of special privileges can be done by modifying group membership rather than by changing a password and communicating it securely to the users who are administrators.

Membership in a group is inherited. The privileges that a user has at any time are the cumulative privileges of all the groups he belongs to, either directly or indirectly. New additions to a group, *G*, automatically acquire all privileges granted to the groups to which *G* belongs. Conversely, when a user is deleted, it is only necessary to remove him from those groups in which he is explicitly named as a member. Inheritance of membership conceptually simplifies the maintenance and administration of the protection domain. The scale of Andrew makes this an important advantage. Hierarchical group structures have also been shown to be useful in Grapevine (Birrell *et al.* (1982)).

A common practice in many timesharing and distributed systems is to create a single entry in the protection domain to stand for a collection of users. Such a collective entry, often referred to as a 'group account' or a 'project account', may be used for a variety of reasons. It may be the case that excessive administrative overheads are involved in adding new users. Sometimes the identities of all collaborating users may not be known a priori. A rigid protection mechanism may make it simpler to allow appropriate access to a single pseudo-user than to a number of users.

The use of collective entries is detrimental to security in a large environment like Andrew. Such entries exacerbate the already difficult problem of accountability in a large distributed system. In Andrew, the hierarchical organization of the protection domain and the use of an access list mechanism for file protection makes specification of protection policies particularly simple. This reduces the motivation for collective entries.

Authentication

Authentication is the indisputable establishment of identities between two mutually suspicious parties in the face of adversaries with malicious intent. In Andrew, the two suspicious parties are a user at a Virtue workstation and a Vice server, while the adversaries are eavesdroppers on the network or modified network hardware that alters the data being transmitted.

The RPC mechanism used in Andrew provides support for secure, authenticated communication between mutually suspicious parties. To establish a connection between parties to ensure this, a three-phase handshake takes place between client and server. The client supplies a variable-length identifier and an encryption key for the handshake. The server provides a key look-up procedure and a procedure to be invoked on authentication failure. The latter allows the server to record and possibly notify an administrator of suspicious authentication failures. At the end of a successful authentication handshake, the server is assured that the client possesses the correct key, while the client is assured that the server is capable of looking up his key. The use of randomized information in the handshake guards against replays by adversaries.

Andrew uses a two-step authentication scheme that is closely integrated into the RPC mechanism. When a user logs in to a workstation, the password he types in is used as the key to establish a secure RPC connection to an authentication server. A pair of *authentication tokens* is then obtained for the user on this secure connection. These tokens are passed to Venus and are saved by it to establish secure RPC connections on behalf of the user to file servers.

The level of indirection provided by tokens yields transparency and robustness. These criteria are important from the point of view of usability as well as scalability. Venus is able to establish secure connections to file servers without users having to supply their passwords each time a server is contacted. Passwords do not have to be stored in the clear on workstations. Since tokens expire after a finite time (typically 24 hours) there is a limit on how long lost tokens can cause damage. Finally, system programs other than Venus can use the tokens to authenticate themselves to Vice without user intervention.

The authentication server runs on a trusted Vice machine. For robustness, there are multiple instances of the authentication server. These are slaves and respond only to queries. Only one server, the master, accepts updates. Changes are propagated to slaves by the master. Server performance is considerably improved by maintaining a write-through cache copy of the entire database in the server's virtual memory. A modification to the database immediately overwrites cached information. The copy on disk is not, however, overwritten. Rather, the change is appended to an audit trail maintained in the authentication database. This improves accountability in a system administered by multiple individuals.

File system protection

As the guardian of shared information in Andrew, Vice enforces the protection policies specified by users. The scale, character and periodic change in the composition of the user community in a university necessitate a protection mechanism that is simple to use yet allows complex policies to be expressed. A further consequence of these factors is that revocation of access privileges is an important and common operation.

Andrew uses an *access list* mechanism for protection. The total rights specified for a user are the union of all the rights collectively specified for him and for all the groups of which he is a direct or indirect member. In conjunction with the ability to specify groups hierarchically, accumulation of rights allows the large and diverse user community served by Andrew to specify flexible protection policies.

An access list can specify *negative rights*. An entry in a negative rights list indicates *denial* of the specified rights, with denial overriding possession in cases of conflict. Negative rights are primarily a means of rapidly and selectively revoking access to sensitive objects. Although such revocation is more properly done by changes to the protection domain, the changes may take time to propagate in a large distributed system. Negative rights can reduce the window of vulnerability, since changes to access lists are effective immediately. They effectively decouple the problems of rapid revocation and propagation of information in a large distributed system.

Vice associates an access list with each directory. The access list applies to all files in the directory, thus giving them uniform protection status. The primary reason for this design decision is conceptual simplicity. Users have, at all times, a rough mental picture of the protection state of the files they access. In a large system, the reduction in state obtained by associating protection with directories rather than files is considerable.

In Unix, a file has 9 *mode bits* associated with it. These mode bits are, in effect, a three-entry access list specifying whether or not the owner of the file, a single specific group of users, and everyone else can read, write or execute the file. Venus provides a close emulation of Unix protection semantics. The Vice access list check described in the previous paragraph performs the real enforcement of protection. In addition, the three owner bits of the file mode indicate readability, writability or executability. These bits, which now indicate what can be done to the file rather than who can do it, are set and examined by Venus but ignored by Vice. The combination of access lists on directories and mode bits on files has proved to be an excellent compromise between providing protection at fine granularity, retaining conceptual simplicity and retaining Unix compatibility.

9.3.6 Design principles

A few simple principles underlie the design of the Andrew file system. The rest of this section discusses these principles and points out instances of their application.

- *Workstations have the cycles to burn.*

  Whenever there is a choice between performing an operation on a workstation and performing it on a central resource, it is preferable to choose the workstation. This will enhance the scalability of the design, since it lessens the need to increase central resources as workstations are added.

  Vice requires that each workstation contacts the appropriate custodian for a file before operating on it. Client requests cannot be forwarded from one server to another. This design decision is motivated by the observation that it is preferable to place the burden of locating and communicating with custodians on workstations rather than servers.

The traversal of path names by workstations rather than servers in the revised implementation is another instance of the application of this principle.

- *Localize if possible*

If possible, use a nearby resource rather than a distant one. This has the obvious advantage of improved performance and the additional benefit that each part of the distributed system is less susceptible to events such as overloading in other parts. Potentially in conflict with this principle is the goal of user mobility, which requires data to be easily locatable. A successful design has to balance these two considerations.

The decision to transfer entire files rather than individual pages is an application of this principle. Read and write operations are much more frequent than opens and closes. Contacting Vice only on opens and closes reduces usage of remote resources.

The replication of read-only subtrees enables system programs to be fetched from the nearest replica rather than its custodian. Caching also exploits locality, but is discussed separately because it is so fundamental to the design.

- *Exploit class-specific file properties.*

As mentioned in Section 9.2.3, files can often be grouped into a small number of easily identifiable classes that reflect their access and modification patterns. For example, files containing the binaries of system programs are frequently read but rarely written. On the other hand, temporary files containing intermediate output of compiler phases are read at most once after they are written. These class-specific properties provide an opportunity for independent optimization, and hence improved performance, in a distributed file system design.

The fact that system binaries are treated as replicated, read-only files is a case where this principle is being used. The principle can be exploited further by allowing a subset of the system binaries to be placed in the local file systems of individual workstations. Since such files change infrequently, explicit installation of new versions of these files by users is acceptable. The storage of temporary files in the local, rather than shared, name space of a workstation is another instance of a file-specific design decision.

- *Cache whenever possible.*

Both the scale of the system and the need for user mobility motivate this principle. Caching reduces contention on centralized resources. In addition, it transparently makes data available wherever it is being currently used.

Venus caches files and status information about them. It also caches information about the custodianship of files. The move to a single-process server structure in the revised implementation was partly to allow servers to cache critical shared data structures.

● *Avoid frequent, system-wide rapid change.*
The more distributed a system is, the more difficult it is to update distributed or replicated data structures in a consistent manner. Both performance and availability are compromised if such changes are frequent. Conversely, the scalability of a design is enhanced if it rarely requires global data to be consistently updated.

The replicated custodian database in Vice changes slowly. Caching by Venus, rather than custodianship changes in Vice, is used to deal with rapid movement of users.

Another instance of the application of this principle is the use of negative rights. Vice provides rapid revocation by modifications to an access list at a single site rather than by changes to a replicated protection database.

● *Trust the fewest possible entities.*
A system whose security depends on the integrity of the fewest possible entities is more likely to remain secure as it grows.

Rather than trusting thousands of workstations, security in Andrew is predicated on the integrity of the much smaller number of Vice servers. The administrators of Vice need only ensure the physical security of these servers and the software they run. Responsibility for workstation integrity is delegated to the owner of each workstation. Further, Andrew relies on end-to-end encryption rather than physical link security.

9.3.7 Issues concerning large systems

The scale of a distributed system is a fundamental influence on its design. Mechanisms which are acceptable in small distributed systems often fail to be adequate in the context of a larger system. Scale is thus a primary factor that guides the design and implementation of large distributed systems. The next three sections discuss specific aspects of large distributed systems in the context of Andrew. The first section describes a mechanism designed to simplify system operation, the second points out the significance of network topology, and the last section emphasizes the importance of recognizing heterogeneity as an inevitable consequence of growth.

Operability

As the scale of a system grows, issues of *operability* assume major significance. It is important that the system is easy for a small staff to run and monitor. Regular operational procedures should cause minimal inconvenience to users. Andrew uses a data structuring primitive called a *volume* (Sidebotham (1986)) to address these issues.

A volume is a collection of files forming a partial subtree of the Vice name space and having the same custodian. Volumes are glued together at *mount points* to form the complete name space. A mount point is a leaf node of a volume that specifies the name of another volume whose root directory is attached at that node. Mount points are not visible in path names; Venus transparently recognizes and crosses mount points during name resolution. The mount mechanism in Vice is thus conceptually similar to the standard Unix mount mechanism. Volume-to-server mapping information is maintained in the volume location database replicated at all servers.

A volume resides within a single disk partition on a server, and may grow or shrink in size. Volume sizes are usually small enough to allow many volumes per partition. Typically a separate volume is allocated for each user. Disk storage quotas are implemented on a per-volume basis. Such an enforcement mechanism has proved more successful than voluntary compliance in a large and diverse community of users. The maximum size of a volume is specified when it is created, but system administrators can change easily change this later. The responsibility for managing space within a volume is left to its owner. The owner is accountable for all the data stored in his volume, even if other users have access rights to create files in some of his directories.

Since a volume is a logical rather than physical storage entity it is possible to perform a number of operations on it without taking a server off line. Redistribution of volumes between servers or between disk partitions on a single server are examples of such operations. When a volume is moved the volume location database is updated. The update does not have to be synchronous at all servers since temporary forwarding information is left with the original server after a move. It is thus always possible for a workstation to identify the server responsible for a volume. A volume may be used, even for update, while it is being moved.

The actual movement is accomplished by creating a frozen copy-on-write snapshot of the volume called a *clone*, constructing a machine-independent representation of the clone, shipping it to the new site, and regenerating the volume at the remote site. During this process the volume may be updated at the original site. If the volume does change, the procedure is repeated with an incremental clone, shipping only those files that have changed. Finally the volume is briefly disabled, the last incremental changes shipped, the volume made available at the new site, and requests directed there. The volume move operation is atomic — if either server crashes the operation is aborted.

Read-only replication of volumes containing system binaries improves availability, serviceability and performance. Any one of a collection of servers with identical sets of read-only volumes (and no read-write volumes) can be introduced or withdrawn from service with virtually no impact on users. The locations of read-only replicas of a volume are specified in the volume location database. Access of read-only files is particularly efficient since no callbacks are needed. The movement mechanism guarantees mutual consistency of files within a volume at all replication sites. However, there may be some period of time during which certain replication sites have an old copy of the volume while others have the new copy. Read-only volumes are also valuable in system administration since they form the basis of an orderly release process for system software. It is easy to back out a new release in the event of an unanticipated problem with it.

Volumes form the basis of the backup and restoration mechanism in Andrew. To backup a volume, a read-only clone is first made, thus creating a frozen snapshot of those files. Since cloning is an efficient operation, users rarely notice any loss of access to that volume. An asynchronous mechanism then transfers this clone to a staging machine from where it is dumped to tape. The staging software is not aware of the internal structure of volumes but merely dumps and restores them in their entirety. Volumes can be restored to any server, since there is no server-specific information embedded in a volume.

Experience has shown that a large fraction of file restore requests arise from accidental deletion by users. To handle this common special case, the cloned read-only backup volume of each user's files is made available as a read-only subtree in that user's home directory. Restoration of files within a 24-hour period can thus be performed by users themselves using normal file operations. Since cloning uses copy-on-write to conserve disk storage, this convenient backup strategy is achieved at modest expense.

Network topology

As a distributed system grows in scale, the topology of the underlying network becomes an increasingly important contributor to performance and operability. Whereas a small-scale network typically consists of a simple single-segment Ethernet cable, a large network is substantially more complex in its topology. For example, the network at CMU is composed of a shared *backbone* to which a number of semi-independent *subnets* are attached via devices called *routers* that perform packet switching. Multiple backbones may be added for enhanced reliability and performance.

A variety of factors account for this complex topology. First, electrical considerations limit the lengths of individual local area network (LAN) segments and the density of machines on them. Second, maintenance and fault isolation are simplified if a LAN is decomposable. Third, administrative functions such as the assignment of unique host addresses can be decentralized if a LAN can be partitioned. These considerations will increase in importance as distributed systems become more pervasive.

Distributed systems such as the Andrew file system mask underlying network complexity. Neither users nor application programs pay attention to the details of the network traffic they generate. Unfortunately, performance inhomogeneities cannot be hidden even when a network is rendered functionally homogeneous. Routers, which introduce load-dependent transmission delays, are the primary source of performance inhomogeneity. Uneven loading of subnets is a secondary cause. Ignoring the effects of network topology can result in less than optimal use of a network by a distributed system. Nonuniform performance is already observed by users of Andrew. Further growth will exacerbate the problem.

The interaction between network topology and distributed system performance is still poorly understood. A preliminary effort, described by Lorence and Satyanarayanan (1988) introduces the notion of *network locality*. The property whereby a small fraction of many possible host pairs account for most end-to-end network traffic is defined as *logical network locality*. It is influenced by the behaviour of users and application programs and by the design of distributed systems. *Physical network locality*, on the other hand, is defined as the property whereby most network traffic traverses as few routers as possible, preferably none. It is influenced by logical network locality, network topology, and the placement of hosts. Since physical locality minimizes network delays, an optimal mapping of a distributed system on to a network will exhibit the highest possible physical locality.

Even a simple distributed system architecture can result in relatively complex network traffic patterns. Andrew is a good example of this. First, it is indeterminate which one of a number of system volume replicas gets used by a workstation. Second, since the files of a user are typically located on one server, this server is likely to participate in most of the traffic with the user's workstation. However, when a user at a public workstation logs out and a new user starts work, most of the workstation references will be to the file server that stores the files of the new user. Even users who have workstations dedicated to them may localize their references to different servers as they proceed with different aspects of their computing activities. Third, when a file is modified, all workstations with currently valid cache copies are notified by the server responsible for that file. Although write-sharing is rare for private files, it is common for shared writable directories such as bulletin boards. The effect of this aspect of the design on locality is an open question. The presence of PCServers, discussed in the next section further complicates traffic patterns. Thus the logical simplicity of the Andrew file system at the user level does not carry over to the next level of detail. Although the existence of locality is undeniable, it is impossible to characterize this locality without observation and measurement.

Network locality is not specific to Andrew. Even in a network used only for terminal emulation and user-initiated file transfers, there will be locality arising from the fact that users deal with a small number of hosts at a time, typically one. In general, if we define a logical *connection* as a source-destination pair, only a subset of possible connections will contribute significantly to traffic at any given time. How small this subset is, and how rapidly its membership changes are measures that characterize the locality of a network.

A complete understanding of a distributed system requires data on its short, medium and long-term locality. This information can be used in tuning a distributed system for optimal performance. Information about logical network locality can be used to improve physical network locality by modifications to topology, placement of hosts, and design of distributed system software.

Heterogeneity

As a distributed system grows over time it tends to grow more heterogeneous. This is true even if the original intent of the designers was to build a homogeneous system. Andrew, for instance, was initially seen as having a single type of workstation, running one operating system, with the network constructed of a single type of physical media. In its present form, however, Andrew is far from being completely homogeneous. This is partly due to the fact that Andrew was built in a university environment, where administrative control is decentralized, but certain aspects of its evolution are typical of any distributed system that grows significantly over time

The first reason for heterogeneity is that a distributed system becomes an increasingly valuable resource as it grows in size and stores larger amounts of shared data. There is then considerable incentive and pressure to allow users who are currently outside the scope of the system to participate in the use of its resources. These new members of the system are likely to have hardware and software that are different from the standard in the distributed system.

A second source of heterogeneity is the improvement in performance and decrease in cost of hardware over time. This makes it likely that the most effective hardware configurations will change over the period of growth of the system. Diversity is inevitable, unless one is willing to forego a priori all such improvements, or is willing to bear the cost of total replacement of existing equipment at each stage of enhancement. In Andrew, workstations span a variety of types such as Sun2s, Sun3s, DEC MicroVaxes and IBM RTs.

A third reason for heterogeneity is the need to use existing hardware that is not identical. This is almost always for cost considerations and is likely to be particularly true for network hardware. A substantial part of the cost of implementing a network is the labour involved in laying the cables. There is considerable cost benefit in growing a network by using an existing network rather than by creating a new network to enforce homogeneity. The complexity of the campus network at CMU, as shown in Figure 9.2, is partly due to this reason.

Andrew addresses heterogeneity in a number of different ways. By using a widely supported version of the Unix operating system, and by implementing most of Andrew outside the kernel, the process of porting Andrew to new workstations is simplified. By using the DARPA IP/UDP network protocols as standard, and by building a highly portable RPC package on top of them, it has been possible for Andrew software to ignore diversity in network media. The extensive use of symbolic links to structure the local name space of workstations addresses the issue of heterogeneity in workstations, as mentioned in Section 9.3.2.

Functional specialization is a valuable technique in dealing with heterogeneity. Such a technique is used in Andrew for supporting personal computers (PCs) such as the IBM PC and the Apple Macintosh. These machines differ from fully-fledged Andrew workstations in that they do not run Unix, they typically possess limited amounts of memory, and they often do not possess a local disk. Caching of whole files is not a viable design strategy for such machines. Rather, PCs access Vice via a mechanism called *PCServer* (Raper (1986)).

PCServer runs on an Andrew workstation and makes its file system appear to be a transparent extension of the file systems of a number of PCs. Since Vice files are transparently accessible from the workstation, they are also transparently accessible from the PC. The workstation thus acts as a surrogate for Vice. The protocol between PCServer and its clients is tuned to the capabilities of a PC. From the point of view of Venus, it appears as if the PC user had actually logged in at the workstation running PCServer. The decoupling provided by PCServer allows the Andrew file system to exploit techniques essential to good performance at large scale, without distorting its design to accommodate machines with limited hardware capability (Satyanarayanan (1984b)).

Designs that ignore heterogeneity often have hidden assumptions pertaining to scalability. For example, Sun NFS uses large logical packet sizes and depends on low-level packet fragmentation on Ethernet to achieve performance in its network protocols. This works well on a single Ethernet cable, but performs poorly in a complex network because of limitations of the routing elements. As another example, the V system depends on multicast support in the network media and interfaces to support parallel communication. While this functionality is available on Ethernet, it is not necessarily available on all segments of a large heterogeneous network. Both these examples describe situations where the technical decisions are defensible in the context in which they were made, but which render growth difficult.

Although the details of the evolution of distributed systems may vary, the underlying causes of heterogeneity discussed here are pervasive. Recognizing this at the outset is likely to produce a design that is better able to cope with growth.

9.4 Future directions

Where is the horizon today with regard to the sharing of data in distributed systems? Three unsolved problems stand out as being of vital importance and urgency. The first problem is availability. The second is further scaling, particularly over large geographic areas and the third pertains to database access in large distributed systems. Each of these issues is briefly addressed in the following sections.

9.4.1 Availability

As reliance on distributed file systems increases, the problem of availability becomes more acute. Today, a single server crash or network partition can seriously inconvenience many users in Andrew. How does one build a distributed file system that encompasses many hundreds or thousands of workstations yet is resilient to failures? *Coda*, a current research project at Carnegie Mellon, addresses this question. Its goal is to provide the highest degree of availability in the face of all realistic failures, without significant loss of usability or performance.

Like Andrew, Coda distinguishes clients from servers and uses caching of entire files as its remote access mechanism. Whole-file transfer simplifies the handling of failures since a file can never be internally inconsistent. Coda masks server failures and network partitions to the fullest extent possible. Failures during a file operation are totally transparent at the user level unless the operation requires data that is neither cached locally nor present at any accessible server.

As in Andrew, files are aggregated into volumes. Coda replicates data at the volume level. When a file is fetched, the actual data is transferred from only one server. However, the other available servers are queried to verify that the copy of the file being fetched is indeed the most recent. After modification, the file is stored at all the server replication sites that are currently accessible. To achieve good performance, Coda uses a parallel RPC mechanism (Satyanarayanan and Siegel (1988)) with extensions to use multicast when available. Files can be transmitted in parallel using this mechanism.

Consistency, availability and performance tend to be mutually contradictory goals in a distributed system. For those few files which must remain consistent at all times, the initial version of Coda will not provide replication. For all other files, Coda's strategy is to provide the highest availability at the best performance. The most recent copy that is physically accessible is always used to satisfy a file request. Coda's view is that inconsistency is tolerable if it is rare, occurs only under conditions of failure, is always detected, and is allowed to propagate as little as possible. It is the relative infrequency of simultaneous write-sharing of files by multiple users (a property mentioned in Section 9.2.3) that makes this a viable strategy.

The implementation of Coda involves the development of network protocols, failure recovery mechanisms, mechanisms for detecting inconsistency, and support for fully partitioned operation. It also involves the development of tools to help users resolve inconsistencies. In a limited number of cases, Coda may itself be able to repair inconsistencies. As in Locus, inconsistency is detected by the use of *version vectors*. The version vector associated with a file indicates the number of updates that were performed at each replication site in order to arrive at that copy of the file. Coda uses atomic transactions at servers to ensure that the version vector and data of a file are mutually consistent at all times. The Coda implementation uses Camelot (Spector *et al.* (1987)) for transaction support. Camelot, in turn, uses Mach (Accetta *et al.* (1986)) for operating system support.

High availability is also a key concern of a distributed file system being built at Digital Equipment Corporation's System Research Center. Although this design also uses replication, its strategy is substantially different from that of Coda. At any time, exactly one of the servers that holds a file is its *primary* site. Clients interact only with the primary site, which assumes the responsibility of propagating changes to the other replication sites. In case of partition, file updates are allowed only in the partition containing a majority of the replication sites. When the primary site is down, a new primary site is elected.

9.4.2 Further scaling

Distributed systems continue to grow in scale and complexity, with no obvious limits in sight. The presence of a scalable location-transparent distributed file system such as Andrew is a major asset in such a computing environment. Users appreciate the conceptual simplification that such a system provides. System administrators and operational staff, on the other hand, appreciate the ability to focus their efforts on the relatively small number of servers rather than the much larger number of clients. The existence of specific clients need not even be known to them!

One problem that becomes apparent at large scale is the need for *decentralization*. The ability to delegate administrative responsibility along lines that parallel institutional boundaries is critical for smooth and efficient operation. The ideal model of decentralization is one in which users perceive the system as monolithic even when their accesses span servers in many administrative domains. In practice, of course, most accesses from a client are likely to be directed to a server in the same administrative domain.

Andrew has recently been extended to allow decentralized operation. A cooperating group of *cells* adhering to a standardized set of protocols and naming conventions (Zayas and Everhart (1988)) can jointly provide the image of a single file name space. This mechanism is reminiscent of the gluing together of file systems provided by Unix United (Brownbridge, Marshall, and Randell (1982)), except that it provides a location transparent name space, greater emphasis on security, and substantially higher performance because of caching. Cross-cell authentication and translation of user identities in different administrative domains are important problems that have to be solved in implementing this model.

Another dimension to scaling is the extension of the distributed file system paradigm over wide geographic areas. Virtually all distributed file systems today are designed with local area networks in mind. Can such designs be extended over networks such as the Arpanet, where latencies are much longer and network congestion a more serious problem? An effort is currently under way to modify the Andrew network protocols to operate over wide-area networks. With its emphasis on caching and minimization of client-server interactions, the design of Andrew seems ideally suited for such extension.

As distributed systems grow larger it becomes increasingly difficult to identify causes of malfunction. Debugging of large distributed systems with the primitive tools currently available is time-consuming and sometimes unsuccessful. Although this is not an area of intense research at the present time, its importance will be increasingly felt in the future.

Finally, a question that arises at very large scale is whether a single hierarchically organized name space is indeed the most appropriate model for sharing data. This paradigm, originally invented for timesharing systems of tens or hundreds of users, has been successfully extended to distributed file systems of a thousand or so nodes. Will it be the best model when there two orders of magnitude or more nodes? Pathnames become longer and it becomes increasingly difficult to search for files whose name is not precisely known. The Quicksilver file system (Cabrera and Wyllie (1987)), currently under development at the IBM Almaden Research Center, addresses this issue. Its approach is to provide mechanisms for a user to customize his name space. Since the customization is location-transparent the user retains his context when he moves to any other node in the system.

9.4.3 Database access

Databases are an important alternative to file systems for storing, retrieving and sharing data. As discussed in Section 9.2.2, the fundamental differences between databases and file systems lie in their data models and naming structures. But it is the emphasis on concurrency control, atomicity and fine-granularity data access that makes it more difficult to build a distributed database system than a distributed file system. Not surprisingly, distributed databases today are much smaller in scale than distributed file systems. How can database access be provided in a distributed system consisting of hundreds or thousands of nodes?

In its most general form the problem seems hopelessly difficult. Conceptually, a database is a focal point for enforcing concurrency control and atomicity properties. If the control structures to enforce these properties are physically distributed, the resulting network protocols have to be substantially more complex. The feasibility of fully distributing data and control at small scale has been demonstrated by systems such as R* (Lindsay *et al.* (1984)). But this approach does not scale trivially to larger distributed systems.

A less ambitious approach attempts to provide *distributed access* to data on a single large database server. Although the data itself is located at a single site, transparent access to this data is possible from many sites. In this model the database requirements of a large distributed system are met by a small number of powerful database servers each exporting a standardized network interface to a very large collection of clients.

It is important to emphasize that this solution is of lower functionality than a fully distributed database. For example, it is not possible to have queries that span multiple servers except in those cases where the client performs query decomposition and merging of results from individual servers. There is no obvious way to provide concurrency control and atomicity on data spread across multiple servers, although these properties are available on data located entirely on one server.

The merit of this approach is that it is substantially simpler to implement, is likely to be more scalable, and may meet the database requirements of a significant number of distributed applications. Such a system, *Scylla*, has been demonstrated at CMU by integrating an off-the-shelf relational database system, Informix, with the RPC2 remote procedure call package (Satyanarayanan (1988b)). Current work on this system investigates the use of caching by clients and the development of a common high-level protocol to allow clients to access a heterogeneous collection of database servers.

It is also possible that the two approaches could be combined. A small number of powerful database servers could be tightly coupled to provide a fully distributed database and support a much larger number of clients. Since the number of servers is small, the distributed data management problem remains solvable. At the same time, the database can be accessed from all the sites in the system. An important question in this model is whether caching can be exploited at the clients to improve performance.

9.4.4 Conclusion

Since the earliest days of distributed computing, file systems have been the most important and widely used form of shared permanent storage. The continuing interest in distributed file systems bears testimony to the robustness of this model of data sharing. We understand how to implement distributed file systems that span a few hundred to a few thousand nodes. As mentioned in the preceding sections, many challenges face us in scaling distributed file systems beyond this. Only experimentation and experience will reveal whether this paradigm can be efficiently implemented in distributed systems of 10 000 or more nodes. Whether users will find this a usable paradigm at such a large scale is another question and one that cannot be meaningfully addressed in the abstract. The large distributed systems of the next decade will provide us with an opportunity to explore these issues.

9.5 References

M. Accetta, G. Robertson, M. Satyanarayanan, and M. Thompson (1980). *The Design of a Network-based Central File System.* CMU-CS-80-134, Department of Computer Science, Carnegie Mellon University, 1980.

M. Accetta, R. Baron, W. Bolosky, D. Golub, R. Rashid, A. Tevanian, and M. Young (1986). 'Mach: A New Kernel Foundation for UNIX Development'. *Proceedings of the Summer Usenix Conference*, Atlanta, GA, July 1986.

Apple Computer, Inc (1985). *Inside Macintosh.* Addison Wesley, Reading, MA, 1985.

P. A. Bernstein and N. Goodman (1981). 'Concurrency Control in Distributed Database Systems'. *ACM Computing Surveys* 13 (2): 185—221, June 1981.

A. D. Birrell and R. M. Needham (1980). 'A Universal File Server'. *IEEE Transactions on Software Engineering* SE-6: 450—453, Sept. 1980.

A. D. Birrell, R. Levin, R. M. Needham, and M. Schroeder (1982). 'Grapevine: An Exercise in Distributed Computing'. *Communications of the ACM* **25**: 260—274, April 1982.

N. Borenstein, C. Everhart, J. Rosenberg, and A. Stoller (1988). 'A Multimedia Message System for Andrew'. *Usenix Conference Proceedings*, 1988.

M. R. Brown, K. N. Kolling, and E. A. Taft (1985). 'The Alpine File System'. *ACM Transactions on Computer Systems* **3**: 261—293, Nov. 1985.

D. R. Brownbridge, L. F. Marshall, and B. Randell (1982). 'The Newcastle Connection'. *Software Practice and Experience* **12**: 1147—1162, Dec. 1982.

L. F. Cabrera and J. Wyllie (1987). *QuickSilver Distributed File Services: An Architecture for Horizontal Growth.* RJ5578, Computer Science Department, IBM Almaden Research Center, 1987.

D. R. Cheriton and W. Zwaenepoel (1983). 'The Distributed V Kernel and its Performance for Diskless Workstations'. *Proceedings Ninth Symposium on Operating System Principles*: 128—140, New York, October 1983.

December (1985). *VMS System Software Handbook.* Digital Equipment Corporation, Maynard, Mass, 1985.

December (1986). *VAX Record Management Services Reference Manual.* AA-Z503B-TE, Digital Equipment Corporation, 1986.

R. Floyd (1986a). *Directory Reference Patterns in a Unix Environment.* Department of Computer Science, University of Rochester, 1986.

R. Floyd (1986b). *Short-Term File Reference Patterns in a Unix Environment.* Technical Report-177, Department of Computer Science, University of Rochester, 1986.

M. Fridrich and W. Older (1981). 'The FELIX File Server'. *Proceedings of the Eighth Symposium on Operating System Principles*: 37—44, 1981.

D. K. Gifford (1979a). *Violet, an Experimental Decentralized System.* CSL-79-12, Xerox Corporation, Palo Alto Research Center, 1979.

D. K. Gifford (1979b). 'Weighted Voting for Replicated Data'. *Proceedings of the Seventh Symposium on Operating System Principles*: 150—162, December 1979.

J. H. Howard, M. J. Kazar, S. G. Menees, D. A. Nichols, M. Satyanarayanan, R. N. Sidebotham, and M. J. West (1988). 'Scale and Performance in a Distributed File System'. *ACM Transactions on Computer Systems* **6**(1), 1988.

IBM (1983). *Disk Operating System, Version 2.1.* 1502343, IBM Corporation, 1983.

IBM (1987a). *Access Method Services, OS/VS2.* GC26-3841, IBM Corporation, 1987.

IBM (1987b). 'The Remote Virtual Disk Subsystem'. In *Academic Operating System*, Volume III. IBM Corporation, Palo Alto, CA, 1987.

Informix (1986). *Informix-SQL Relational Database Management System User Guide*. Informix Software, Inc, 1986.

B. Lampson (1981). 'Atomic transactions'. In Goos and Hartmanis (Ed.), *Distributed Systems — Architecture and Implementation*, Volume 105, pages 246—265. Springer-Verlag Lecture Notes in Computer Science, Berlin, 1981.

P. J. Leach, P. H. Levine, J. A. Hamilton, and B. L. Stumpf (1985). 'The File System of an Integrated Local Network'. *Proceedings of the ACM Computer Science Conference*, 1985.

G. Letwin (1988). *Inside OS/2*. Microsoft Press, 1988.

B. G. Lindsay, L. M. Haas, C. Mohan, P. F. Wilms, and R. A. Yost (1984). 'Computation and Communication in R*: A Distributed Database Manager'. *ACM Transactions on Computer Systems* **2** (1): 24—38, February 1984.

M. Lorence and M. Satyanarayanan (1988). 'IPWatch: A Tool for Monitoring Network Locality'. *Proceedings of the 4th International Conference on Modelling Techniques and Tools for Computer Performance Evaluation*, 1988. (Also available as Tech. Rept.CMU-ITC-067, Information Technology Center, Carnegie Mellon University.)

S. Majumdar and R. B. Bunt (1986). 'Measurement and Analysis of Locality Phases in File Referencing Behaviour'. *Proceedings of Performance '86 and ACM Sigmetrics*, 1986.

T. Marill and D. Stern (1975). 'The Datacomputer — A Network Data Utility'. *Proceedings of AFIPS National Computer Conference 44*, 1975.

M. K. McKusick, W. N. Joy, S. J. Leffler, and R. S. Fabry (1984). 'A Fast File System for Unix'. *ACM Transactions on Computer Systems* **2** (3), 1984.

M. K. McKusick and T. J. Kowalski (1986). 'Fsck — The Unix File System Check Program'. In *Unix System Manager's Manual, 4.3 Berkeley Software Distribution*. University of California, Berkeley, 1986.

J. G. Mitchell and J. Dion (1982). 'A Comparison of Two Network-based File Servers'. *Communications of the ACM* **25** (4): 233—245, April 1982.

J. H. Morris, M. Satyanarayanan, M. H. Conner, J. H. Howard, D. S. Rosenthal, and F. D. Smith (1986). 'Andrew: A Distributed Personal Computing Environment'. *Communications of the ACM* **29** (3), 1986.

J. H. Morris (1988). ''Make or Take' Decisions in Andrew'. *Usenix Conference Proceedings*, 1988.

S. J. Mullender and A. S. Tanenbaum (1985). 'A Distributed File Service Based on Optimistic Concurrency Control'. *Proceedings of the 10th Symposium on Operating Systems Principles*: 51—62, Orcas Island, WA, December 1985.

S. J. Mullender and A. S. Tanenbaum (1986). 'The Design of a Capability-Based Distributed Operating System'. *The Computer Journal* **29**(4): 289—300, 1986.

M. N. Nelson, B. B. Welch, and J. K. Ousterhout (1988). 'Caching in the Sprite Network File System'. *ACM Transactions on Computer Systems* **6**(1), 1988.

E. I. Organick (1972). *The Multics System: An Examination of its Structure.* MIT Press, Cambridge, MA, 1972.

J. Ousterhout, H. Da Costa, D. Harrison, J. Kunze, M. Kupfer, and J. Thompson (1985). 'A Trace-Driven Analysis of the Unix 4.2 BSD File System'. *Proceedings of the Tenth Symposium on Operating System Principles*, 1985.

A. J. Palay, W. J. Hansen, M. L. Kazar, M. Sherman, M. G. Wadlow, T. P. Neuendorffer, Z. Stern, M. Bader, and T. Peters (1988). 'The Andrew Toolkit — An Overview'. *Usenix Conference Proceedings*, 1988.

G. Popek, B. Walker, J. Chow, D. Edwards, C. Kline, G. Rudisin, and G. Thiel (1981). 'LOCUS, A Network Transparent, High Reliability Distributed System'. *Proceedings of the Eighth Symposium on Operating System Principles*, 1981.

L. K. Raper (1986). *The CMU PC Server Project.* CMU-ITC-051, Information Technology Center, Carnegie Mellon University, 1986.

R. Revelle (1975). *An Empirical Study of File Reference Patterns.* RJ 1557, IBM Research Division, 1975.

A. P. Rifkin, M. P. Forbes, R. L. Hamilton, M. Sabrio, S. Shah, and K. Yueh (1986). 'RFS Architectural Overview'. *Usenix Conference Proceedings, Atlanta, Georgia*, 1986.

D. M. Ritchie and K. Thompson (1974). 'The Unix Time Sharing System'. *Communications of the ACM* **17**(7), 1974.

L. A. Rowe and K. P. Birman (1982). 'A Local Network Based on the Unix Operating System'. *IEEE Transactions on Software Engineering* **SE-8**(2), 1982.

SUN (1986). *Networking on the SUN Workstation.* 800-1324-03, Sun Microsystems, Inc, Mountain View, California, 1986.

J. H. Saltzer (1974). 'Protection and the Control of Information Sharing in Multics'. *Communications of the ACM* **17**(7), 1974.

M. Satyanarayanan (1981). 'A Study of File Sizes and Functional Lifetimes'. *Proceedings of the Eighth Symposium on Operating System Principles*, 1981.

M. Satyanarayanan (1984a). 'A Synthetic Driver for File System Simulations'. *Proceedings of the International Conference on Modelling Techniques and Tools for Performance Analysis, Paris*, 1984.

M. Satyanarayanan (1984b). *Supporting IBM PCs in a Vice/Virtue Environment*. CMU-ITC-002, Information Technology Center, Carnegie Mellon University, 1984.

M. Satyanarayanan, J. H. Howard, D. N. Nichols, R. N. Sidebotham, A. Z. Spector, and M. J. West (1985). 'The ITC Distributed File System: Principles and Design'. *Proceedings of the Tenth Symposium on Operating System Principles*, 1985.

M. Satyanarayanan (1987). *Integrating Security in a Large Distributed Environment*. CMU-CS-87-179, Department of Computer Science, Carnegie Mellon University, 1987.

M. Satyanarayanan (1988a). 'On the Influence of Scale in a Distributed System'. *Proceedings of the Tenth International Conference on Software Engineering*, 1988.

M. Satyanarayanan (1988b). *RPC2 User Manual*. CMU-ITC-84-038, Department of Computer Science, Carnegie Mellon University, 1988.

M. Satyanarayanan and E. H. Siegel (1988). 'Parallel Communication in a Large Distributed Environment'. *IEEE Transactions on Computers*, 1988. (accepted for publication.)

M. Schroeder, D. Gifford, and R. Needham (1985). 'A Caching File System for a Programmer's Workstation'. *Proceedings Tenth Symposium on Operating System Principles*: 25—34, 1985.

R. N. Sidebotham (1986). 'Volumes: The Andrew File System Data Structuring Primitive'. *European Unix User Group Conference Proceedings*, 1986. (Also available as Technical Report CMU-ITC-053, Information Technology Center, Carnegie Mellon University.)

A. J. Smith (1981). 'Analysis of Long Term File Reference Patterns for Application to File Migration Algorithms'. *IEEE Transactions on Software Engineering* 7(4), 1981.

A. S. Spector, D. Thompson, R. F. Pausch, J. L. Eppinger, D. Duchamp, R. Draves, D. S. Daniels, and J. J. Bloch (1987). *Camelot: A Distributed Transaction Facility for Mach and the Internet*. CMU-CS-87-129, Department of Computer Science, Carnegie Mellon University, 1987.

M. Stonebraker, E. Wong, P. Kreps, and G. Held (1976). 'The Design and Implementation of INGRES'. *ACM Transactions on Database Systems* 1(3), 1976.

E. P. Stritter (1977). *File Migration*. Ph.D. Thesis, Stanford University, 1977.

L. Svobodova (1981). 'A Reliable Object-Oriented Data Repository for a Distributed Computer System'. *Proceedings Eighth Symposium on Operating System*

Principles: 47—58, 1981.

L. Svobodova (1984). 'File Servers for Network-Based Distributed Systems'. *ACM Computing Surveys* **16** (4), 1984.

C. P. Thacker, E. M. McCreight, B. W. Lampson, R. F. Sproull, and D. R. Boggs (1981). 'Alto: A Personal Computer'. In D. P. Siewiorek, C. G. Bell, and A. Newell (Eds.), *Computer structures: Principles and Examples*. McGraw-Hill, New York, NY, 1981.

B. Walker, G. Popek, R. English, C. Kline, and G. Thiel (1983). 'The LOCUS Distributed Operating System'. *Proceedings Ninth Symposium on Operating System Principles*: 49—70, 1983.

W. A. Wulf, R. Levin, and S. P. Harbison (1981). *Hydra/C.mmp: An Experimental Computer System*. McGraw-Hill, New York, NY, 1981.

E. R. Zayas and C. F. Everhart (1988). *Design and Specification of the Cellular Andrew Environment*. CMU-ITC-070, Information Technology Center, Carnegie Mellon University, 1988.

PART V

Transactions

One of the most basic ingredients of a fault-tolerant system is a *transaction mechanism*. A transaction brackets a number of operations in such a way that either all of them happen or — in the case of a failure — none of them do. Transactions make crash recovery much easier, because a transaction can only end in two states: transaction carried out completely, or transaction failed completely.

In Chapter 10, Spector gives an introduction to transaction-processing techniques in distributed systems. The Camelot system he developed at Carnegie Mellon University serves as an example. How to use transactions is the subject of Chapter 11. In this chapter, Weihl uses a mail system as an illustration of an application using transactions for fault tolerance. Chapter 12 gives the theoretical background of nested transactions.

Chapter 10

Distributed Transaction Processing Facilities

A. Z. Spector

This chapter defines the transaction concept and motivates its use in distributed systems. The chapter then goes on to survey some of the key techniques used to implement transaction processing facilities. To provide more concreteness, the chapter concludes with a description of the Camelot distributed transaction processing facility.

10.1 Introduction

Distributed transactions are an important programming paradigm for simplifying the construction of reliable and available distributed applications, particularly applications that require concurrent access to shared, mutable data.

In this chapter, a transaction is defined a collection of operations bracketed by two markers: `Begin_Transaction` and `End_Transaction`. Transactions provide three properties that reduce the attention a programmer must pay to concurrency and failures (Gray (1980); Spector and Schwarz (1983)):

1. **Failure atomicity.** Failure atomicity ensures that if a transaction's work is interrupted by a failure, any partially completed results will be undone. A programmer or user can then attempt the work again by reissuing the same

The research described in this chapter was sponsored by IBM and the Defense Advanced Research Projects Agency (DOD), ARPA Order No. 4864 (Amendment 20), under contract F33615-87-C-1499 monitored by the Avionics Laboratory, Air Force Wright Aeronautical Laboratories, Wright-Patterson AFB.

The views and conclusions contained in this document are those of the authors and should not be interpreted as representing the official policies, either expressed or implied, of any of the sponsoring agencies or the United States government.

or a similar transaction. Sometimes, failure atomicity is referred to just as atomicity. A programmer may choose to *abort* a transaction at any time which will cause all partial computations to be undone.

2. **Permanence.** If a transaction completes successfully, the results of its operations will never be lost, except in the event of catastrophes. Systems can be designed to reduce the risk of catastrophes to any desired probability. Sometimes, permanence is referred to as *durability.*

3. **Serializability.** Transactions are allowed to execute concurrently, but the results will be the same as if the transactions executed serially. Serializability ensures that concurrently executing transactions cannot observe inconsistencies. Programmers are therefore free to cause temporary inconsistencies during the execution of a transaction knowing that their partial modifications will never be visible. Serializability is sometimes also called *isolation.*

The serializability property can be relaxed so as to provide weaker, but still useful, consistency guarantees. For example, there may be multiple transactions interleaving enqueuing operations on the same queue; this queue is variously called a *weak queue* or a *semi-queue* (Schwarz and Spector (1984); Weihl and Liskov (1983)).

A transaction that performs operations on objects scattered across a distributed system is said to be a *distributed transaction.* The distribution of objects on multiple processing nodes permits increased performance and system availability due to parallelism and the storage of multiple copies of data. For example, the use of replicated objects can permit access to data despite the failure of some of the nodes on which those data reside. As in centralized systems, transactions control the effects of parallelism and failures, thereby making it easier to maintain invariants on shared data.

Consider a unanimous-update replication scheme (Alsberg and Day (1976)), in which updates must be done to all copies of an object. As long as reads and updates are always done within the scope of a transaction, a programmer can be sure that all copies will always appear to have the same value. In the syntax of the Camelot library (Eppinger, Mummert, and Spector (1989)), the following code will update two copies of a replicated object.

```
Begin_Transaction
    Server_Call("Replica1", update(ARGS, object, newValue));
    Server_Call("Replica2", update(ARGS, object, newValue));
End_Transaction(status)
if (status == 0)
    printf("Update completed.0)
else if (status == Server_Call_Timeout)
    ...
```

The transaction processing systems will ensure that either both updates are done, or that neither update is done, regardless of client or server machine crashes, and regardless of other clients attempting to update the object.

IBM Almaden's R* and Quicksilver, MIT's Argus, Carnegie Mellon's Camelot, AT&T's Tuxedo, and Tandem's NonStop SQL (Eppinger and Spector (1989); Haskin *et al.* (1988); Lindsay *et al.* (1984); Liskov and Scheifler (1983); Tandem *et al.* (1987); Tuxedo (1988)) are six of many systems that support distributed transactions.

To better support parallelism and limit the effects of failures, transactions can be *nested* (Moss (1981); Reed (1978)):

- An outermost (or *top-level*) transaction can initiate multiple nested transactions that can execute in parallel with each other. Nested transactions may in turn spawn other nested transactions. In the model described here, a parent suspends its operation until all of its children commit or abort.

- A nested transaction may obtain locks that are held by an ancestor, though not a sibling. (This is sensible since an ancestor is suspended while its children operate.)

- When a transaction commits, all of its locks, including those that it inherited are returned to, and then held by, its parent. Hence, all locks are held until the outermost parent commits or aborts, at which time they are dropped. Correspondingly, the effects of a nested transaction are made permanent only when its top-level transaction commits.

- If a failure occurs that causes a nested transaction to abort before it reaches the end of its work, all of its work is undone, all locks that it acquired are either dropped or returned to its parent, and its parent is notified. The parent may then choose to continue processing or itself abort.

Nested transactions permit a transaction to spawn children that can run in parallel. That is to say, all children are synchronized so that the parent transaction still exhibits serializability. Nested transactions also are permitted to abort without causing the loss of the entire parent transaction's work. This can permit parent transactions to tolerate failures.

Broadly speaking, transaction processing techniques make a valuable addition to a distributed systems programming environment. When coupled with RPC, authentication and protection techniques, linguistic support, etc., transactional semantics provide a rich base for constructing reliable programs. As of the date of this paper, transaction processing techniques are acknowledged to be a key technology for reliable commercial systems. Additionally, many computer scientists believe that transaction processing techniques will prove to be widely applicable to the design of many types of distributed systems. This conjecture will only be proven as general purpose distributed transaction processing facilities are perfected and made widely available.

10.2 The design of a transaction processing facility

This section addresses the issues of implementing distributed transactions. To provide a more concrete explanation, the implementation will be discussed in terms of the client/server model introduced in Section 10.2.1 and in terms of a layered operating system model presented in Section 10.2.2. Failure and concurrency issues will be considered separately in Sections 10.2.3 and 10.2.4, respectively.

10.2.1 The client/server model

For reasons of security, abstraction, and maintenance, data objects are encapsulated in protected subsystems or servers. There are several models for accessing these objects including protected procedure calls (Saltzer (1974)), capabilities (Fabry (1974)), and the client/server model (Watson (1981)). The principles described in this paper apply to all of these models, but the client/server model will be emphasized.

In the client/server model, servers manage recoverable data objects. A server defines operations that are exported to clients. Clients invoke these operations to manipulate the data managed by a server. Operations are invoked by using an RPC interface (Birrell and Nelson (1984)). Servers that manage recoverable data objects and allow clients to manipulate them transactionally are variously called *data servers* in TABS (Spector *et al.* (1985)) and Camelot (Eppinger and Spector (1989)), *guardians* in Argus (Liskov *et al.* (1987)), and *resource managers* in System R (Astrahan *et al.* (1976)) and R* (Lindsay *et al.* (1984)). Servers can, in turn, be clients of other servers. Top-level clients that export no abstractions are called *applications* here.

Some programming languages, such as Argus (Liskov *et al.* (1987)) and Avalon (Herlihy and Wing (1987)) and language extension packages such as the one provided with Camelot (Bloch (1989)) provide support for transaction processing. Statements such as `Begin_Transaction` and `End_Transaction` group operations into transactions. Typically, an application will begin a transaction, execute one or more remote procedure calls to various servers, and end the transaction. The remote procedure calls will execute on behalf of the transaction.

A client may execute a remote procedure call to invoke operations on a server that is on the same node as the client. Most remote procedure call systems transparently extend across a network. Consequently, the client need not know when a remote procedure call goes across the network nor need he know when a transaction becomes distributed. Remote procedure calls allow clients to invoke operations on servers executing on the same or different nodes.

Logically, servers are structured as an infinite loop. The server simply receives requests from clients to invoke operations on behalf of transactions. To implement the operations it exports, a server can invoke remote procedure calls to other servers or it can read/update its own data. For example, a transactional file system might be implemented by storing all the files in storage managed by the server, or by using several other servers on different nodes to provide high availability. Physically, a server may have many threads of control each capable of simultaneously handling requests from clients.

Transactionally updating storage is complicated because of the failures that must be tolerated. Section 10.2.3 discusses these failures and presents an overview of how transaction systems recover from them. For a detailed discussion of techniques servers can use to update storage transactionally, see Eppinger (1989).

10.2.2 System model

Transaction support is provided for applications and data servers. This support can be implemented in the operating system, in several servers (or layers) outside the operating system in libraries that execute in each application and data server, or using a combination of these techniques. Regardless of where transaction support is provided, this section simply considers it as residing in a single logical layer that is located between the hardware and the applications/data servers, and those that are not, are given.

Among its primary functions, the transaction support layer helps data servers and applications cope with failures that are not masked by hardware devices or their low-level driver software. Three devices are considered: communications, processor, and storage. Below, descriptions of the types of failure that are masked by the device/driver layers.

Most communication failures are masked. Data are sent over communications lines in messages. It is expected that messages may be corrupted, duplicated, reordered, and lost. The device driver uses checksums to detect corrupted messages and sequence numbers to detect duplicate, reordered, and lost messages. Corrupted, duplicated, and reordered messages are thrown away; missing messages are re-sent. On many networks, messages will be duplicated, reordered, and lost every few seconds. There is an extremely small chance that the checksums and sequence numbers will not detect bogus messages; this is a nonrecoverable error. If the network is partitioned, communications among nodes may be lost. Partitions are not masked: messages will not get through. It is difficult to distinguish a network partition from other cases, such as a slow node, a lock wait, or a deadlock.

Processor failures are recoverable, but they must be detected and the processor must raise an exception or halt. Such processors are called 'fail-fast' (Gray (1979)). For example, if the floating point processor is bad, the central processor must detect this and complain or halt. The processors cannot make up a number and continue. If power is lost, processors should halt without executing random instructions. In summary, fail-fast processors do not mask errors, but rather, by halting rather than corrupting data, they permit restart and recovery.

Storage failures are typically not masked. Failures are detected by parity bits or checksums. Storage is divided into three classes:

1. **Volatile storage** is where portions of objects reside when they are being accessed. The contents of volatile storage are lost if the system crashes or if power is lost. If an error is encountered with some part of volatile storage the processor should complain and halt. Volatile storage is typically dynamic RAM.

2. **Non-volatile storage** is where objects reside when they have not been accessed recently. The contents of non-volatile storage are lost less frequently than those of volatile storage, and always in a detectable way. If some pages of non-volatile storage are lost or damaged, the I/O call to the device/driver layer will return an error. Magnetic disks are usually used for non-volatile storage.

3. **Stable storage** is assumed to retain information despite system crashes and power problems. Stable storage is frequently implemented by writing duplicate, failure-independent copies on non-volatile storage. If data stored in one copy is damaged, the other copy can still be used.

10.2.3 Expected failures

Six of the major functions needed to implement transactions are as follows:

- **Transaction management** responsible for reaching consensus among a transaction's participants as to whether the transaction commits or aborts.

- **Recovery management** responsible for restoring the state after a failure, *i.e.,* undoing the effects of incomplete and aborted transactions and redoing the effects of committed transactions.

- **Buffer management** responsible for moving data between volatile and non-volatile storage.

- **Log management** responsible for the log.

- **Lock management** responsible for concurrency control.

- **Communications management** responsible for transparently extending communications across the network and notifying transaction management when transactions become distributed.

For reasons of node autonomy, it makes sense to have each component on each node.

In typical implementations, there is much cooperation among these components. The recovery and locking components look to the transaction management component to learn whether a transaction has committed, aborted, or is still active. Recovery, buffer, and transaction components all use the log component to read and write records to stable storage. The transaction, recovery, buffer, and log components all deal with the problem of failure. The next two sections describe the techniques nodes use to recover from failures locally and the protocols that participating nodes use to achieve consensus about whether a distributed transaction commits. Lock management deals with concurrency and is discussed in Section 10.2.4.

Recovery techniques

A transaction management component is responsible for reaching consensus about whether a transaction commits or aborts. The recovery component looks only to the transaction management component to learn whether a transaction has committed, aborted, or is still active.

To fulfill failure atomicity and permanence requirements in spite of the failures enumerated above, transaction systems provide recovery support. Recovery is supported for transaction failure, server failure, node failure, and media failure.

- *Transaction failure* is when one of the servers participating in a transaction decides to abort the transaction. All of the transaction's effects at all of the participating servers must be undone. In case of a communications failure, the system can abort transactions whose messages cannot get through.

- *Server failure* is when a data server crashes due to an unanticipated condition such as a shortage of resources or a transient software error. All of the active transactions in which the server is participating are aborted. When the server restarts, the effects of all aborted transactions will be undone, and the effects of all committed transactions will be preserved.

- *Node failure* is when a processor crashes due to a hardware error or a software failure such as the kernel running out of resources. All of the active transactions in which the node is participating are aborted. When the node restarts, the effects of all aborted transactions will be undone, and the effects of all committed transactions will be preserved. This is logically the same as all of the servers on a node crashing, except that the node's transaction facility also crashes.

- *Media failure* occurs when some of a node's non-volatile storage is damaged. The contents of this storage must be restored.

There are several techniques for locally implementing failure atomicity and permanence, including intentions lists (Lampson (1981)), shadow paging (Gray *et al.* (1981)), and write-ahead logging (Peterson and Strickland (1983); Schwarz (1984)). Hybrid approaches have also been used (Gray *et al.* (1981)).

An intentions list can be used to guarantee failure atomicity and permanence. This is done in order as follows:

1. All the changes that a transaction wants to make to data objects are stored in a list.

2. That list is written out to non-volatile storage.

3. It is determined from the transaction manager if the transaction committed or not.

4. If the transaction did commit, change the objects in non-volatile storage.

5. Then delete the list.

The list must be carefully written to non-volatile storage so it can be recognized that the list is complete. By deferring updates to objects until the transaction is committed, the transaction is aborted simply by deleting the list. In case of node or server failure, the system restarts and the list is consulted and the following cases may occur:

●   If there is no list, the transaction (if any) is aborted.

●   If the list is incomplete, the node crashed while writing it; the transaction is aborted and the list deleted.

●   If the list is complete, the node crashed while making the real updates to objects in non-volatile storage; the system makes the updates described in the list and then deletes the list.

Shadow paging is another way to provide failure atomicity and permanence. Non-volatile storage is organized as a tree (*e.g.*, by logical address or as a hierarchical file system). The transaction makes changes to vertices of the tree by writing new vertices in unused locations in non-volatile storage. Changes are incorporated into the tree by writing new versions of parent vertices in unused locations. Changes to ancestor vertices continue until the least common ancestor vertex of all the changed vertices is changed. This vertex is then updated in place after consulting the transaction manager. This last update is called an *atomic pointer swap*. In the event of node or server failure, the system restarts. A transaction that has not yet done the atomic pointer swap is aborted. A transaction that has done the atomic pointer swap is committed.

A *write-ahead log* is similar to an intentions list with many optimizations. Write-ahead logging uses an append-only *log*, structured as a sequence of variable-length records. The log is maintained in non-volatile or stable storage. Updates to a data object are made by modifying a copy of the object cached in volatile storage and by spooling one or more records to the log. These records contain an undo component that permits the effects of aborted transactions to be undone, and a redo component that permits the effects of committed transactions to be redone. Special care must be taken when copying a modified object's pages back to non-volatile storage; the pages cannot be copied back to non-volatile storage until all spooled log records pertaining to those pages have been written to the log. When a cached page is copied back to non-volatile storage, it is copied back to the page from which it was previously read.

In addition to records describing changes to non-volatile storage, records indicating that transactions commit and abort are spooled to the log. To commit a transaction, the spooled log records describing all changes made by the transaction and a commit record for the transaction are written to the log. When the system restarts after a crash, the log is consulted. Modifications made by transactions for which no commit record exists are undone. Modifications made by committed transactions are redone.

Intentions lists and shadow paging are simple ways to provide failure atomicity and permanence. Write-ahead logging is more complicated, but provides several performance advantages.

- Write-ahead logging, like intentions list techniques, does not scatter data all over non-volatile storage. Applications that access data sequentially get a significant performance improvement. Special indices to keep track of non-volatile storage are not needed. Furthermore, write-ahead logging only minimally influences the I/O strategy used to move data to/from the buffer pool.

- A write-ahead log allows multiple transactions to execute simultaneously using the same log.

- Write-ahead logging allows changes to non-volatile storage to be buffered. This allows updates to non-volatile storage to be grouped together and performed as one. This substantially reduces the cost of stable state transitions.

- System restart using a write-ahead log can be done with as little as one scan of the log. Optimizations to the recovery process can be applied without sacrificing forward processing performance. In particular, these optimizations reduce the amount of the log that is scanned at system restart. See Schwarz (1984).

- Transaction commitment protocols are frequently implemented by using a log. If the recovery algorithm is also log-based, distributed transactions can be made very efficient by sharing a common log.

For these reasons, the rest of this paper will assume that write-ahead logging is the method being used for guaranteeing failure atomicity and permanence.

Generally, there are two ways of describing updates in log records: physically and logically. When physical logging is used, log records contain the after (or before and after) images of the bytes being modified. This type of logging is called new-value or old-value/new-value logging. Logical or operation logging allows a description of the change to be written into the log. This description can be very compact. The description may describe how to redo the change, or how to redo and undo the change. The choice of which values to write in the log can affect the paging strategy. New-value logging requires that modified pages need not be written back to non-volatile storage until after the transaction commits. It would appear that a hybrid approach using both physical and logical logging has the best properties.

To reduce the amount of time it takes to process the log after a node or server failure, additional records are written to the log. Fetch records indicate when a page is first modified (since its last write). End-write records indicate when a page is successfully written back to non-volatile storage. Checkpoint records contain a list of active transactions and a list of cached (or active) pages. These additional records contain enough summary information to allow the recovery scan of the log to terminate early.

A separate log can be maintained for each server on a node, but if the appropriate interface is provided, a common log can be used by all servers on the same node. The performance improvement is potentially very great. All the log records spooled by servers on the node can be written to the log together, thus reducing the number of expensive log writes. It will also be seen in the next section that there are several commit protocol optimizations that can be used when there is a common log.

As mentioned above, write-ahead logging allows changes to non-volatile storage to be buffered. This allows expensive updates to non-volatile storage to be grouped together and amortized. All accesses to non-volatile storage are done via volatile primary memory. By caching pages of non-volatile storage in volatile storage, non-volatile reads and writes can be reduced. The pages used in the volatile cache are called the buffer pool. The buffer pool is managed by the buffer manager or the page manager.

Transaction processing systems use stable storage for an append-only log that describes modifications to recoverable storage. As described above, it is possible for non-volatile pages to fail spontaneously. In this case, media recovery is run. The log can be used to recover these pages; all changes (since the page was initialized) have been recorded in the log. However, processing the entire log can take a long time. Further, we cannot permit the log to have unlimited growth. Therefore, in order to speed up media recovery and to reduce the size of the log, *log reclamation* is performed at regular intervals.

To reclaim the log, the system first makes a copy of the non-volatile storage used to store recoverable data. If the system is running while the copy is taken, the copy may not be consistent with any one point in the log (because the pages copied earlier may be missing updates made while other pages were copied later). The backup copy is made consistent with the end of the log by using the log to make the missing changes to the backup copy. Finally, the system scans backwards through the log, examining the checkpoint records to determine where to truncate the log.

Transaction commitment protocols

Because many nodes may participate in a transaction, there needs to be a protocol to achieve consensus among the participants as to whether a transaction commits or not. This section describes the two-phase distributed transaction commitment protocol and optimizations for node-local and server-local special cases. Other commit protocols exist — for details see Duchamp (1988) or Skeen (1982).

Any participant should be able to abort a transaction at any time. This helps the participants to control access to their resources. For example, many concurrency control techniques lock out access to objects being accessed by an active transaction. If a transaction is blocking access to objects for a long period of time, the participant may want to abort the transaction to allow other transactions to access the objects (see Section 10.2.4). Unfortunately, all commitment protocols have a window of vulnerability, in which participants may not be able to unilaterally abort the transaction.

The most common commit protocol, the two-phase commitment protocol, is general and inexpensive. The window of time during which participants are not allowed to abort the transaction is also small. The two-phase commitment protocol is run after all of the transaction's updates have been (tentatively) done. At this point one of the participants is appointed to be the coordinator. The coordinator is frequently the participant who began the transaction or a participant on a reliable node, such as a central server.

The two-phase commitment protocol has two message-passing phases, hence its name. Figure 10.1 shows the protocol. In the first phase, the coordinator asks each of the other participants, called subordinates, if they are willing to prepare. If any subordinate replies negatively, the transaction is aborted. By answering positively, the subordinate gives up its right to abort the transaction. The subordinate must be prepared to commit or abort the transaction as specified by the coordinator. In a write-ahead log based recovery scheme, this preparation means forcing out the proper records to the log so that if a node or server fails, the subordinate will be able to commit or abort the transaction at restart.

If all the subordinates respond affirmatively, the coordinator forces out a commit record. After the coordinator forces its log, it notifies each of the subordinates of the decision to commit the transaction. Each subordinate must respond to the commit message so that the coordinating node can purge its data structures of the information about this transaction.

If any of the messages are lost, after a suitable time, the coordinator will resend its last message to the subordinate. If any subordinate crashes before its Yes reply is received, the transaction will be aborted. If the coordinator crashes before it forces its log, this will also cause the transaction to be aborted. If the coordinator's log is successfully forced, the transaction will be committed.

The biggest problem with the two-phase commitment protocol is that the coordinator might crash while the subordinates are prepared. This means that subordinates will not be allowed to abort an active transaction, potentially for a long period of time. While this is a rare circumstance, it may happen and it is undesirable. For this reason, commitment protocols that are less likely to block are being developed. See Duchamp (1988) or Skeen (1982).

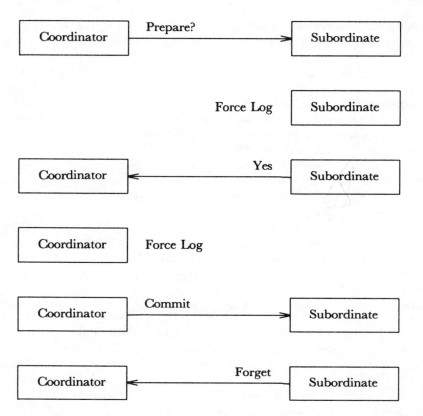

Figure 10.1 The two-phase commit protocol. The two-phase commit protocol contains two phases of message passing. One participant is the coordinator. All other participants are the subordinates. In the first phase, the coordinator asks each subordinate to prepare to commit the transaction. By responding positively, the subordinate relinquishes its rights to abort the transaction and agrees to commit or abort the transaction as instructed by the coordinator. If all the subordinates respond positively, the coordinator commits the transaction and notifies the subordinates of the decision.

Several optimizations are employed when there is a common log. With a common log, all servers on the same node spool log records to the same log. There is one transaction manager for each node. The transaction manager uses the same log as the servers. One of the participating nodes' transaction managers is selected to be coordinator. The other participating nodes' transaction managers are the subordinates. Whenever a transaction manager is asked to prepare a transaction, it asks all the local servers if they wish to prepare the transaction. If all the local servers respond positively, the transaction manager responds positively. After the transaction manager learns that the transaction has committed, it notifies the local participating servers.

If all servers participating in a transaction are on the same node, the local transaction manager can use an optimized form of the two-phase commit protocol with no subordinate nodes. If a server knows that it will be the only participant in a transaction, it can execute the transaction without contacting the transaction manager at all!

When a transaction aborts, each transaction manager notifies the participating servers that they must stop all processing on behalf of this transaction. Then each transaction manager tells its local recovery management component to undo the effects of this transaction. Finally, the transaction manager notifies the participating servers that the transaction has been aborted.

10.2.4 Concurrency

As described in Section 10.1, serializability is a strict concurrency control. It means that no matter how transactions are scheduled, the overall effect must be equivalent to that of some one-at-a-time (serial) schedule. Therefore, for any two transactions it must be possible to tell that one transaction preceded or succeeded the other, or that the transactions are unrelated and it does not matter which executed first. The serializability guarantee means that programmers can run transactions without worrying about whether they interfere with other concurrently running transactions.

Two-phase read/write locking

Two-phase *read/write* (or *shared/exclusive*) *locking* is a common technique used to guarantee serializability. With read/write locking, each transaction requests locks on the objects it accesses. To read an object, the transaction requests a (shared mode) read lock on that object. To write an object, the transaction requests an (exclusive mode) write lock on that object. This allows multiple transactions to read an object concurrently, but only one transaction to write the object.

	Read	Write
Read	Compatible	Conflict
Write	Conflict	Conflict

Figure 10.2 Conflicts for read/write lock. One writer will block all other readers and writers. There can be many simultaneous readers.

Figure 10.2 shows the compatibility of read/write locks. One writer will block all other readers and writers. There can be may simultaneous readers. If a transaction tries to get a write lock on an object, but there are already one or more transactions with read locks, the transaction must wait. Several transactions may wait for a write lock. Depending on this mix of reads and updates for the object, subsequent read requests may be granted or delayed. If the read requests are granted, the transactions waiting for write locks may *starve* and never continue. Similarly, if the write transactions are given priority, the transactions waiting for read locks may starve. Starvation can be avoided if readers and writers are queued on a first-in/first-out basis when there are waiting writers.

Read/write locking is *two-phase* if the transaction requests no additional locks after it begins releasing locks. Transaction systems implement two-phase locking by holding all locks until the transaction completes (commits or aborts).

In a nested transaction model, such as that developed by Moss (1981), a lock inheritance mechanism is introduced. A nested transaction may inherit locks from its parent. If a nested transaction aborts, the locks it obtained are dropped (or given back to its parent). If the nested transaction commits, the nested transaction's locks are transferred to its parent.

A *deadlock* is when two or more transactions are stuck because they are waiting for each other to drop locks; that is, there is a cycle in the who-waits-for-whom graph. Consider an example in which a transaction t_1 gets a write lock on object o_a and transaction t_2 gets a write lock on object o_b. Then transaction t_1 requests a write lock on object o_b and transaction t_2 requests a write lock on object o_a. The transactions are stuck waiting for each other.

There are three common techniques for handling deadlock: avoidance (Havender (1968)), detection (Obermarck (1982)), and time out. If locks are requested in a canonical order, deadlocks can be avoided because there can be no cycle in the who-waits-for-whom graph. Deadlocks can be detected by constructing and checking the who-waits-for-whom graph. If transactions (or RPCs) are short in duration, it is possible to impose a maximum amount of time for the transaction (or RPC) to execute; if the transaction (or RPC) does not complete within this time, a deadlock can be assumed. Whenever a deadlock is detected, one of the transactions is aborted and rerun.

In some instances, two-phase read/write locking may be too restrictive a technique. The serialization order is determined by the order in which locks are granted. Two-phase read/write locking does not allow all serial schedules, but it is simple and efficient to implement, and under current transaction loads it provides good throughput. As transaction systems are used for new and different purposes, transactions may run for a long time. Other techniques to increase concurrency are described in sections below.

Dropping locks early

Because of the potential for increased concurrency, it is tempting to drop locks early, that is, after the value has been accessed but before the transaction

	Read	Write	Increment
Read	Compatible	Conflict	Conflict
Write	Conflict	Conflict	Conflict
Increment	Conflict	Conflict	Compatible

Figure 10.3 Conflicts for increment locks. Increment locks are compatible with each other, but not with read or write locks.

completes. If a transaction reads an object only once per transaction there is no complication in releasing read locks early. However, if a transaction ever re-locks an object for reading, the read may not yield the same result as before. To guarantee *repeatable reads*, transactions cannot drop read locks early.

Because a transaction with a write lock on an object prevents all other trans-actions from reading or writing the object, it is especially tempting to drop write locks early. If a transaction dropped a write lock on an object before it com-pleted, some other transaction might read the updated value of the object. If the updating transaction subsequently aborted, the other transaction would also have to be aborted. This condition is known as a *cascading abort*. Because of the expense in detecting the cases that require a cascading abort, write locks are not dropped early. Holding write locks until the transaction completes prevents cas-cading aborts.

Type-specific locking

An abstract data type exports operations that have well known semantics. The implementation of these operations may be able to take advantage of *type-specific locking* (Korth (1983); Schwarz and Spector (1984)). Type-specific locking usu-ally involves additional lock modes and requires logical logging.

Consider a counter. In addition to allowing read and write locks on the counter, an increment lock might be allowed. Several transactions may incre-ment the counter in parallel. Figure 10.3 shows the compatibility of the incre-ment lock with other locks.

Non-serializable abstractions

As mentioned before, it is not always necessary to have strict serializability. For example, the weak queue described in Section 10.1 may be perfectly useful as an intermediate repository for mail that does not have to be delivered in an exact order.

Discussion

Two-phase read/write locking is a simple scheme for concurrency control. Other schemes are used to get higher throughput, although many schemes are *ad hoc*. As systems become more distributed and transactions more prevalent, other schemes than read/write locking may provide significant performance advantages. It is important not to preclude the use of these schemes when designing a transaction processing system. Systems that automatically do read/write locking in hardware do not allow these new concurrency control techniques to be used.

10.3 The Camelot transaction processing facility

To illustrate some of these implementation techniques, this section describes Camelot, a distributed transaction facility developed at Carnegie Mellon University. Camelot is intended to support wide-spread use of transaction processing techniques. Broadly speaking, the design of Camelot adheres to the philosophy outlined above. Camelot executes on a variety of uni- and multi-processors on top of the Unix-compatible, Mach operating system (Rashid (1986)).

The major functions of Camelot and their logical relationship are illustrated in Figure 10.4. All of these layers, except the library routines, are implemented by a collection of Mach processes, which run on every node in a distributed system. Each of these processes is responsible for supporting a particular collection of functions. Processes use Mach-provided threads of control to permit intra-process parallelism. Calls to Camelot are made to the Camelot library (e.g., to begin or commit a transaction), which in turn directs them to a particular Camelot process. Functions which are frequently called, such as log writes, are invoked by writing to memory queues that are shared between a data server and a Camelot process. Other functions are invoked using messages that are generated by MIG.

Figure 10.4 shows the seven processes in Camelot: Camelot process, master control, disk manager, communication manager, recovery manager, transaction manager, node server, and node configuration application.

- **Camelot.** This interactive process permits a user to set the Camelot configuration options, stores and retrieves these options from a Unix file, and restarts Camelot automatically after crashes. (Users are expected to store critical configuration data off-line as well as in the Unix file system for reliability reasons.)

- **Master control.** This process restarts Camelot after a node failure, parses all switches, and redirects diagnostic output.

- **Disk manager.** The disk manager allocates and deallocates recoverable storage, accepts and writes log records locally, and enforces the write-ahead log invariant. The disk manager works with dedicated network servers to support distributed logging. Additionally, the disk manager writes pages to/from the disk when Mach needs to service page faults on recoverable storage or to clean primary memory. Finally, it performs checkpoints to limit the amount of work during recovery and works closely with the recovery manager when failures are being processed. The disk manager is multithreaded to permit multiple I/O operations in parallel.

- **Communication manager.** The communication manager forwards inter-node Mach messages, and provides logical and real clock services. In addition, it knows the format of messages and keeps a list of all the nodes that are involved in a particular transaction. This information is supplied to the transaction manager for use during commit or abort processing. Finally, the communication manager provides a name service that creates communication channels to named servers. (The transaction manager and distributed logging service use IP datagrams, thereby bypassing the communication manager.)

- **Recovery manager.** The recovery manager is responsible for transaction abort, server recovery, node recovery, and media-failure recovery. Server and node recovery respectively require one and two backward passes over the log.

- **Transaction manager.** The transaction manager coordinates the initiation, commit, and abort of local and distributed transactions. It fully supports nested transactions.

- **Node server.** The node server is the repository of configuration data necessary for restarting the node. It stores its data in recoverable storage and is recovered before other servers.

- **Node configuration application.** The node configuration application permits Camelot's human users to update data in the node server and to crash and restart servers.

Camelot services are accessed via a powerful programmer library which can be viewed as a language extension (currently supporting C, C++, and Lisp). An easy-to-use library is part-way between full linguistic support, as in Argus or Avalon (Herlihy and Wing (1987); Liskov and Scheifler (1983)), and raw system calls. The *Camelot library* comprises routines and macros that allow a user to implement data servers and applications. For servers, it provides a common message handling framework and standard processing functions for system messages, for example, for performing recovery and participating in two-phase commit. Thus, the task of writing a server is reduced to writing procedures for the particular operations supported by the server.

The Camelot library for C provides `Begin_Transaction` and `End_Transaction` primitives that group operations into transactions. Code that executes between a `Begin_Transaction` and `End_Transaction` statement executes on behalf of that transaction. This includes local and remote procedure calls. Typically, an application will begin a transaction, execute one or more remote procedure calls to various servers using the `Server_Call` primitive, and end the transaction. See the code fragment in Section 10.1 for an example.

A data server writer specifies the RPC interface by using the MIG RPC specification language (Pausch and Eppinger (1989)). The interface specification is processed by the MIG stub generator which will create client-side

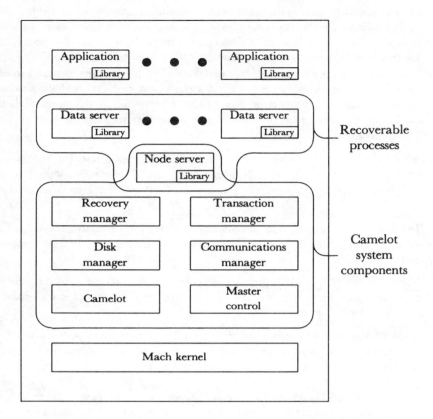

Figure 10.4 The structure of a Camelot node This figure depicts the structure of a Camelot node. Data servers and applications are written by Camelot users. Users view Camelot as a layer on top of Mach. Data servers maintain permanent data in recoverable virtual memory. Applications begin and end transactions that invoke operations on data servers by executing remote procedure calls. Data servers can act as applications, initiating transactions. The Camelot layer is composed of several processes: the transaction manager, the recovery manager, the disk manager, the communications manager, and the Camelot and master control tasks. The node server is a distinguished data server used to store configuration information. The transaction manager guarantees consensus among a transaction's participants as to whether the transaction commits or aborts. The recovery manager is responsible for restoring a transaction-consistent state after a failure. The disk manager is responsible for buffer management and maintaining the common log. The communications manager is responsible for transparently extending communications across the network and notifying transaction management when transactions become distributed. The Camelot and master control processes facilitate system initialization and serialize debugging output.

stubs that are loaded into the application and a server-side routine that is used by the Camelot library to decode incoming requests and encode the responses. The server writer must provide the interface routines that are called by the decoder when the server receives RPC requests. Upon receiving a request message from an application, the library code in the data server joins the transaction and sets up a call to the corresponding interface routine. The interface routine then executes as part of the transaction begun at the application.

Camelot provides a recoverable virtual memory abstraction that allows most of the data server's address space to be used for managing long-term data (Eppinger (1989)). In case of failure, recoverable virtual memory retains only changes made by committed transactions. The data server's interface routines can access recoverable virtual memory area quite transparently. The Camelot library allows statically allocated variables to be declared in between the `Begin_Recoverable_Declarations` and `End_Recoverable_Declarations` statements. Long-term storage can be dynamically allocated using transactional versions of `malloc` and `free`, called `Rec_Malloc` and `Rec_Free`. The library provides the `Rec` macro to access statically declared variables. The `Modify` macro is used to update recoverable virtual memory. (`Modify` is used in place of assignment for recoverable virtual memory). This macro takes care of spooling log records that describe the updates.

The Camelot architecture allows a good deal of flexibility in terms of concurrency control. The server writer must take explicit steps to control concurrent access to recoverable virtual memory. The library currently provides a shared/exclusive mode locking package. The interface routines issue `Lock` calls to obtain locks. Locks are automatically inherited by a parent transaction when a nested transaction commits. Locks are automatically dropped when the transaction completes.

On each node, Camelot maintains a local configuration database. This database can be accessed transactionally via RPCs. Camelot also provides a *node configuration application* that permits authorized users to create, delete, start, shutdown, and restart servers. It permits users to specify disk quotas for servers, the maximum recovery time that Camelot should take to recovery from a node failure, and the preferable times of the day for taking archival dumps. It also provides commands for authorizing and deauthorizing users, and for showing a node's current configuration.

In addition to these basic facilities, Camelot provides authentication and protection services. Together, these services are packaged in a facility called *Strongbox* and they make it easy for a client and server to prove their identities to each other, and to then encrypt their communication.

An example of an early Camelot application was the room reservation (RR) system. It graphically displayed (using the X.10 Window System) the reservations for departmental conference rooms and permits authorized users to make reservations. Almost all interaction is via mouse clicks. The RR application was designed to be run from any Mach workstation in the DARPA Internet and to automatically find a remotely located RR server which stores one year's worth of reservations. Internally, the server represented the room reservation database as a hash table of rooms, where each room points to a large one-dimensional array. Each array contained 365 days x 24 (half-hour) room reservation slots. The server also used a hash table for storing information about users. Not surprisingly, the overwhelming bulk of the code for RR was for the graphical interface, not the data server. The performance of the system on RT PC, Sun 3, and MicroVax II class workstations was fine. RR is no longer functioning, because it was difficult to port to X.11.

A more traditional application of Camelot is distributed ET-1 (Anonymous *et al.* (1985)). In the experimental implementation, workstations send debit-credit requests to Camelot nodes, each of which has two servers: Bank and BankData. The Bank server receives input requests from simulated terminals, executes transactions on BankData, and then returns responses to the workstation. Fifteen percent of all ET-1 transactions are distributed and require access to two Camelot nodes. BankData stores its data in large arrays, but hash tables could be substituted with little performance impact.

Camelot executes about 10 ET1 transactions/second/Camelot node, with 85 per cent of the transactions executing in less than 1 second on a Model IBM RT PC (APC). (This computer executes about three Vax MIPS.) We used two Camelot nodes running banking servers, and six workstations to drive the two nodes. While the zero second think time and number of workstations do not meet the specification of the ET1 benchmark, our test met the other substantive requirements.

With tens of thousands of lines of Camelot code for these test applications, the Coda replicated file system, Avalon, and Strongbox, we have been pleased with the programming interface to Camelot. It has seemed flexible enough, though programmers must buy into the Camelot programming model completely. We have noted that debugging servers has not been easy. Camelot's performance has been very satisfactory for a research prototype, and is probably sufficient for many types of applications. With Mach RPC times improving, Camelot performance should get even better.

10.4 Summary

This chapter has motivated the utility of transactions, discussed many of the key implementation techniques, and described the Camelot prototype facility. Surely, it is tricky to support failure atomicity, permanence, and serializability. All the multi-threading, synchronization, and recovery techniques, and the various distributed protocols are complex and difficult to implement. They also have real execution costs, particularly in terms of message passing, context swapping, and writes to stable storage.

However, it seems likely that once a transaction facility has been carefully implemented, its primitives can be used repeatedly for a variety of different applications. These range from a simple line printer daemon to a complex replicated, object-oriented database. Without question, enormous work is needed to program the many tens of thousands of lines of code required to support transactions. But, it seems valuable to implement this code once, rather than continuing to reimplement portions of it in system after system. The Camelot work, as well as the work on Argus (Liskov *et al.* (1987)) and Quicksilver (Haskin *et al.* (1988)), have attempted to demonstrate that a general purpose transaction facility is feasible and worthwhile.

Acknowledgements

I wish to acknowledge the help of my colleague, Jeffrey Eppinger, who graciously permitted me to use some of the survey prose from his Ph.D. thesis in Section 10.2. I am also indebted to the Camelot design team, as a whole, for providing me with great help in understanding the implementation of transaction processing systems.

10.5 References

P. A. Alsberg and J. D. Day (1976). 'A Principle for Resilient Sharing of Distributed Resources'. *Proceedings of the Second International Conference on Software Engineering*: 562—570, San Fancisco, CA, October 1976.

Anonymous *et al.* (1985). 'A Measure of Transaction Processing Power'. *Datamation* **31** (7), April 1985. (Also available as Technical Report Technical Report 85.2, Tandem Corporation, Cupertino, California, January 1985.)

M. M. Astrahan, M. W. Blasgen, D. D. Chamberlin, K. P. Eswaran, J. N. Gray, P. P. Griffiths, W. F. King, R. A. Lorie, P. R. McJones, J. W. Mehl, G. R. Putzolu, I. L. Traiger, B. W. Wade, and V. Watson (1976). 'System R: A Relational Approach to Database Management'. *ACM Transactions on Database Systems* **1** (2), June 1976.

A. D. Birrell and B. J. Nelson (1984). 'Implementing Remote Procedure Calls'. *ACM Transactions on Computer Systems* **2** (1): 39—59, February 1984.

J. J. Bloch (1989). 'The Camelot Library: A C Language Extension for Programming A General Purpose Distributed Transaction System'. *Proceedings Ninth International Conference on Distributed Computing Systems*, Newport Beach, CA, June 1989.

D. Duchamp (1988). *Transaction Management*. Ph.D. Thesis, CMU, 1988. (Forthcoming.)

J. L. Eppinger (1989). *Virtual Memory Management for Transaction Processing Systems*. Ph.D. Thesis, CMU, February 1989. (Also available as Technical Report CMU-CS-89-115 Carnegie Mellon University, February, 1989.)

J. L. Eppinger, L. B. Mummert, and A. Z. Spector (1989). *Guide to the Camelot Distributed Transaction Facility including the Avalon Language.* Prentice-Hall, Englewood Cliffs, NJ, 1989. (To appear.)

J. L. Eppinger and A. Z. Spector (1989). 'Transaction Processing in Unix: A Camelot Perspective'. *Unix Review* **7** (1): 58—67, January 1989.

R. S. Fabry (1974). 'Capability-based Addressing'. *Communications of the ACM* **17** (7): 403—411, July 1974.

J. N. Gray (1979). 'Notes on Database Operating Systems'. In R. Bayer, R. M. Graham, and G. Seegmuller (Eds.), *Operating Systems — An Advanced Course*, Volume 60, pages 393—481. Springer-Verlag, Lecture Notes in Computer Science, 1979. (Also available as Technical Report RJ2188 IBM Research Laboratory, San Jose, California, 1978.)

J. N. Gray (1980). *A Transaction Model.* Report RJ2895, IBM Research Laboratory, San Jose, California, August 1980.

J. N. Gray, P. McJones, M. Blasgen, B. Lindsay, L. Lorie, T. Price, F. Putzolu, and I. Traiger (1981). 'The Recovery Manager of the System R Database Manager'. *ACM Computing Surveys* **13** (2): 223—242, June 1981.

R. Haskin, Y. Malachi, W. Sawdon, and G. Chan (1988). 'Recovery Management in QuickSilver'. *ACM Transactions on Computer Systems* **6** (1): 82—108, February 1988.

J. W. Havender (1968). 'Avoiding Deadlock in Multitasking Systems'. *IBM Systems Journal* **7** (2): 74—84, 1968.

M. Herlihy and J. Wing (1987). 'Avalon: Language Support for Reliable Distributed Systems'. *Proceedings 17th International Symposium on Fault-Tolerant Computing*: 89—95, Pittsburgh, 1987. (Also published as CMU-Computer Science Department Technical Report CMU-Computer Science Department-86-167.)

H. F. Korth (1983). 'Locking Primitives in a Database System'. *Journal of the ACM* **30** (1): 55—79, January 1983.

B. Lampson (1981). 'Atomic transactions'. In Goos and Hartmanis (Ed.), *Distributed Systems — Architecture and Implementation*, Volume 105, pages 246—265. Springer-Verlag Lecture Notes in Computer Science, Berlin, 1981.

B. G. Lindsay, L. M. Haas, C. Mohan, P. F. Wilms, and R. A. Yost (1984). 'Computation and Communication in R*: A Distributed Database Manager'. *ACM Transactions on Computer Systems* **2** (1): 24—38, February 1984.

B. H. Liskov and R. W. Scheifler (1983). 'Guardians and Actions: Linguistic Support for Robust, Distributed Programs'. *ACM Transactions on Programming Languages and Systems* **5** (3): 381—404, July 1983.

B. Liskov, M. Day, M. Herlihy, P. Johnson, G. Leavens, R. Scheifler, and W. Weihl (1987). *Argus Reference Manual*. Technical Report-400, MIT Laboratory for Computer Science, Cambridge, MA, November 1987.

J. Eliot B. Moss (1981). *Nested Transactions: An Approach to Reliable Distributed Computing*. Ph.D. Thesis, MIT, April 1981.

R. Obermarck (1982). 'Distributed Deadlock Detection Algorithm'. *ACM Transactions on Database Systems* **7** (2): 187—208, June 1982.

R. Pausch and J. L. Eppinger (1989). 'Generating Interfaces for Camelot Data Servers'. In J. L. Eppinger, L. B. Mummert, and A. Z. Spector (Eds.), *Guide to the Camelot Distributed Transaction Facility including the Avalon Language*. Prentice-Hall, Englewood Cliffs, NJ, 1989.

R. J. Peterson and J. P. Strickland (1983). 'LOG Write-Ahead Protocols and IMS/VS Logging'. *Proceedings of the Second ACM SIGACT News-SIGMOD Symposium on Principles of Database Systems*: 216—243, March 1983.

R. F. Rashid (1986). 'Threads of a New System'. *Unix Review* **4** (8): 37—49, August 1986.

D. P. Reed (1978). *Naming and synchronization in a decentralized computer system*. Ph.D. Thesis, MIT, 1978. (Available as Technical Report MIT/LCS/Technical Report-205.)

J. H. Saltzer (1974). 'Protection and the Control of Information Sharing in Multics'. *Communications of the ACM* **17** (7), 1974.

P. M. Schwarz and A. Z. Spector (1984). 'Synchronizing Shared Abstract Types'. *ACM Transactions on Computer Systems* **2** (3): 223—250, August 1984. (Also available in Stanley Zdonik and David Maier (Eds.), *Readings in Object-Oriented Databases*. Morgan Kaufmann, 1988, and as Technical Report CMU-CS-83-163, Carnegie Mellon University, November 1983.)

P. M. Schwarz (1984). *Transactions on Typed Objects*. Ph.D. Thesis, CMU, December 1984. (Available as Technical Report CMU-CS-84-166 Carnegie Mellon University.)

M. D. Skeen (1982). *Crash Recovery in a Distributed Database System*. Ph.D. Thesis, University of California, Berkeley, May 1982.

A. Z. Spector and P. M. Schwarz (1983). 'Transactions: A Construct for Reliable Distributed Computing'. *Operating Systems Review* **17** (2): 18—35, April 1983. (Also available as Technical Report CMU-CS-82-143 Carnegie Mellon University, January 1983.)

A. Z. Spector, D. S. Daniels, D. J. Duchamp, J. L. Eppinger, and R. Pausch (1985). 'Distributed Transactions for Reliable Systems'. *Proceedings of the Tenth Symposium on Operating System Principles*: 127—146, December 1985. (Also available in *Concurrency Control and Reliability in Distributed Systems*, Bharat K. Bhargava, ed., pp. 214-249, Van Nostrand Reinhold Company, New York, and as Technical Report CMU-CS-85-117, Carnegie Mellon University, September 1985.)

Tandem (1987). *NonStop SQL Benchmark Workbook.* 84160, Tandem, March 1987.

Tuxedo (1988). *AT&T TUXEDO Processing System Release 3.0.* AT&T, Summit, NJ, 1988.

R.W. Watson (1981). 'Distributed System Architecture Model'. In B. W. Lampson (Ed.), *Distributed Systems — Architecture and Implementation: An Advanced Course*, Volume 105, pages 10—43. Springer-Verlag Lecture Notes in Computer Science, 1981.

W. Weihl and B. Liskov (1983). 'Specification and Implementation of Resilient, Atomic Data Types'. *Symposium on Programming Language Issues in Software Systems*, San Fancisco, CA, June 1983.

Chapter 11

Using Transactions in Distributed Applications

W. E. Weihl

As distributed systems become more widely used, there is an increasing need for effective ways of organizing *distributed programs*. Distributed programs can be hard to write because of the problems of concurrency inherent in distributed systems, and because of the possibility of part of the system failing while the rest continues to operate. In this section, an overview is presented of how *atomic transactions* can be used to solve some of the problems that arise in writing distributed programs. We illustrate the techniques with example programs written in Argus (Liskov and Scheifler (1983); Liskov *et al.* (1987)), an integrated programming language and system designed to support distributed applications.

Distributed applications typically have a number of requirements, including reliability, distribution, reconfigurability, concurrency, and consistency. Transactions are useful primarily for ensuring reliability and consistency in the presence of concurrency and failures. Transactions have two important properties. First, each transaction is *recoverable*: either it runs to completion and *commits*, or a failure occurs and it *aborts*. In the latter case, the net effect is as if the transaction never ran; in the former, the transaction's modifications are guaranteed to persist even if failures occur later. In other words, either all or none of the effects of a transaction occur; partial executions are not possible. Second, transactions are *serializable*: the effect of executing a collection of transactions concurrently is the same as if the transactions had been executed sequentially, one at a time.

Transactions were originally developed to provide a way of maintaining the consistency of a database. The serializability and recoverability properties of transactions allow one to guarantee that the database remains consistent by ensuring that each transaction, when run alone and to completion, preserves consistency. Given that each transaction preserves consistency, any serial execution of transactions without failures (where each transaction runs to completion)

215

also preserves consistency. In a transaction system, a concurrent execution with failures is equivalent to some serial execution without failures; thus, a concurrent execution with failures also preserves consistency.

More recently, transactions have been explored as a way of organizing programs for distributed systems. Here, the problem is not just to provide a way of keeping the state of the system consistent, but also to provide the programmer with mechanisms that simplify understanding and reasoning about programs. Failures and concurrency make it harder to reason about programs because of the complexity of the interactions among concurrent activities, and because of the multitude of failure modes. Transactions help here also, by allowing the programmer to view a complex piece of code as if it is run atomically: it appears to happen indivisibly, and it happens either completely or not at all.

An important extension, especially in distributed systems, is to allow transactions to be *nested*: a transaction can be composed of some number of *subtransactions*. Nested transactions are useful for two reasons:

1. They allow concurrency within a transaction. One transaction can run many subtransactions in parallel, with the guarantee that they will appear to have run sequentially, and each will appear to happen either completely or not at all.

2. They provide greater protection against failures, in that they allow checkpoints to be established within a transaction. When a subtransaction aborts, its parent can still continue, and may be able to complete its task using an alternative method. (The effects of a committed *sub*transaction can be lost in a crash; in this case, its parent will be forced to abort. When a *top-level* transaction commits, however, all of the effects of its committed descendants become permanent, and will survive crashes.)

In a distributed system, nested transactions can be used to implement remote procedure calls with a *zero or once* semantics: a call appears to happen exactly once or not at all; partial or multiple executions cannot happen. In the absence of a transaction mechanism of some sort, a weaker semantics must be accepted. In addition, nested transactions make building replicated systems convenient. Reading or writing replicas can be done as subtransactions — if some of the replicas fail to respond, causing their subtransactions to fail, the overall transaction can still succeed if enough of the replicas have responded.

Achieving adequate concurrency is an important concern in many applications. In recent years, much attention has been paid to concurrency control and recovery algorithms that exploit the semantics of applications to achieve higher levels of concurrency than is permitted by algorithms that view operations on data items as simple reads and writes. The motivation behind such algorithms is to alleviate the *concurrency bottlenecks* or *hot spots* that many systems contain. For example, if data is structured as a graph, the roots of the graph are likely to be accessed by most or all transactions. Aggregate data, such as the net assets of a bank or the stock held in an inventory control system, also tends to be accessed by many transactions. A simple approach to concurrency control can lead to an almost total loss of concurrency in accessing a hot spot, seriously limiting the throughput of the system. If transactions last a relatively long time, perhaps because they are interactive or involve several servers in a distributed system, the effect on overall performance of limited throughput can be severe.

Concurrency bottlenecks can often be avoided by using an application-specific concurrency control algorithm. Read-write locking is a simple example of an application-specific algorithm, whereby transactions executing read operations can be allowed to run concurrently without sacrificing atomicity. The correctness of this algorithm relies on the application-specific properties of the transactions — that certain operations do not modify the state of the system. A more interesting example involves aggregate data. Operations on an aggregate data item might include *increment*, *decrement*, and *read*. Using read-write locking, transactions executing *increment* and *decrement* operations must exclude each other. However, it is possible to design more permissive concurrency control algorithms, that allow transactions executing *increment* and *decrement* operations to run concurrently using the fact that these operations are commutable. The fundamental idea underlying such algorithms is to lock *logical* resources, thus avoiding unnecessary *physical* conflicts on the representation. For example, an aggregate data item can be viewed logically as a collection of individual items; operations to increment and decrement the aggregate can logically lock the items added to or deleted from the collection, rather than locking the physical representation of the aggregate. (Some low-level synchronization on the representation may be necessary, but the locks needed for this purpose can typically be held only for a short period of time, such as the duration of a single operation, rather than throughout an entire transaction.)

We have developed an approach to designing distributed applications that permits application-specific information to be used in concurrency control in a modular way. Atomicity is achieved through shared data objects, which must be implemented so that the transactions using them appear to be serializable and recoverable. Data objects that support atomicity are called *atomic objects*, and data types whose objects are atomic are called *atomic types*. Atomicity of activities is guaranteed only when all the objects shared by an activity are atomic objects.

This approach is based on identifying abstract data types during design that are natural for the application, and that can be implemented to provide adequate concurrency. Some types can be implemented quite simply by using a straightforward concurrency control algorithm such as read-write locking. Other types may need to be implemented using more complex type-specific concurrency control algorithms, such as that mentioned above for aggregate data. In some cases, likely concurrency bottlenecks will be obvious during design, but in other cases it may not be clear until a system is built that a given object is a concurrency bottleneck. Once concurrency bottlenecks have been identified, however, they can be re-implemented to provide more concurrency.

The concurrency requirements of the application must be considered when new data types are invented during design. The level of concurrency that can be achieved by a type-specific concurrency control algorithm depends strongly on the details of the type's specification. A typical way of increasing the allowable concurrency for a data type is to introduce non-determinism into the specifications of some of the type's operations. For example, consider a printer spooler that accepts requests from transactions to print files, and prints a file if the requesting transaction commits. If requests are spooled in a first in, first out queue, essentially no concurrency is possible among transactions issuing print requests. However, if we change the specification of the spool buffer so that 'dequeue' operations can remove *any* element in the buffer, not just the oldest one, transactions issuing print requests need not conflict at all.

In the remainder of this chapter we illustrate the use of transactions in a simple mail system implemented in Argus. We begin with a simple design for the mail system that provides relatively little concurrency, based on the example in Liskov and Scheifler (1983). We then show how some of the data types can be re-implemented to provide higher levels of concurrency. We also discuss how changes to the specifications of the data types would affect the achievable level of concurrency.

The mail system presented below is simple, and, in many ways, incomplete. It is designed somewhat along the lines of Grapevine (Birrell *et al.* (1982)), but, for pedagogical reasons, is greatly simplified. However, it does give some idea of how transactions could be used to solve many of the problems that arise in a real system.

The mail system provides operations to send mail to a user, to read a user's mail, to add users to the system, and to reconfigure the system. Most users would deal only with the first three operations, and would be unaware of the replicated and distributed nature of the implementation. The operations are quite simple; there is no protection, for example, so any user may read another user's mail. In addition, the reconfiguration operations are limited.

Users would normally interact with the mail system through some sort of user interface program, which would call the operations provided by the mail system. All operations are performed within the transaction system. This means, for example, that a message is not added to a mailbox unless the sending transaction commits.

11.1 Overall structure

The mail system is based on guardians — modules provided in Argus that acts as the unit of distribution. Each guardian encapsulates local data and processes, and resides at a single site. Local data in a guardian is stored in a garbage-collected heap. Each guardian provides a collection of operations, called *handlers*, that can be invoked by other guardians. The local data in one guardian cannot be accessed directly by processes in other guardians; instead, those

processes must call the guardian's handlers to access the guardian's local data.
Each handler invocation runs as a separate process. Some of the data in a guardian is *stable* and this data will be recovered after a crash, with a state reflecting
the effects of all committed top-level transactions. Three kinds of guardians are
distributed on various sites: mailers, maildrops, and registries. *Mailers* act as the
front end of the system — all use of the system occurs through calls of mailer
handlers. To ensure high availability, mailers should exist on many sites,
perhaps one on each site where a client might use the mail system. The other
guardians are internal to the system, and are used to store mail and
configuration information. A *maildrop* contains the mailboxes for some subset of
the users of the system. A mailbox for a given user is not replicated, so if a
maildrop is inaccessible the users whose mail is stored there will be unable to
read their mail. Multiple distributed maildrops are used to reduce contention
and to increase availability, so that the crash of one site will not make all mailboxes unavailable. *Registries* are used to keep track of the users whose mail is
stored at each maildrop. Registries are replicated — each registry knows about
all other registries — and contain the complete mapping from user IDs to

```
mailbox = data type is create, add_message, read_mail

    overview:  A mailbox is a sequence of messages.
               Mailboxes are atomic.

    create = proc() returns(mailbox)
        Effect:  Creates and returns a new empty mailbox.

    add_message = proc(mb: mailbox, msg: message)
        Effect:  Appends msg to mb.

    read_mail = proc(mb: mailbox) returns(array[message])
        Effect:  Returns a new array containing the messages in mb;
                 the messages are removed from mb.

end mailbox
```

Figure 11.1 Serial specification of the **mailbox** data type. The
specification for a data type consists of an **overview**, which defines
an 'abstract model' for objects of the type, together with
specifications for the operations provided by the type. The
specification of an operation consists of a *header*, describing the
types of the arguments, results, and exceptions, an optional
requires clause, describing any preconditions on the arguments,
and an **effect** clause, describing the results and any changes to
the states of objects. The specification constrains an implementation of the operation to satisfy the effect clause only when the
precondition described in the **requires** clause is satisfied; if the
requires clause is violated, the implementation can do anything.

maildrops. Thus, only one registry needs to be accessible at any time for it to be possible to send or read mail.

In designing the mail system, we invented several atomic data types to encapsulate implementation details, and to provide flexibility in concurrency control and recovery. Two types, mailbox and post_office, are used in the implementation of maildrop guardians; informal specifications for them are shown in Figure 11.1 and Figure 11.2. In writing the specifications, we focus on how the operations should behave in the absence of concurrency and failures (thus, we call them *serial specifications*); the additional assertion that the data type is atomic (or more precisely, dynamic atomic; see Chapter 12) requires the implementation to provide synchronization and recovery that ensure that transactions are serializable and recoverable.

As specified in Figure 11.1, a mailbox acts something like a FIFO queue: messages can be appended to the queue using the add_message operation, and the entire contents of the queue can be dequeued using the read_mail operation. Later, it will be discussed how this specification constrains the allowable concurrency, and how the specification might be changed to permit more concurrency. New mailbox objects can be created in a guardian's heap using the create operation; this will be done whenever a new user is added to the system.

A post_office stores a mailbox for each of some collection of users. It provides operations to create a new, empty post_office (one with no mailboxes), to add a user (creating a new empty mailbox for the user), and to find the mailbox for a given user. Some of the operations provided by the post_office data type can signal exceptions. Like CLU (Liskov and Snyder (1979); Liskov (1981)), Argus uses a termination model of exception handling — a procedure can

```
post_office = data type is create, add_user, lookup

    Overview:  A post_office is a mapping from users to mailboxes.
               Post_offices are atomic.

    create = proc() returns(post_office)
        Effect:  Creates and returns a new empty post_office.

    add_user = proc(p: post_office, u: user_id) signals(user_exists)
        Effect:  Signals user_exists if u is defined in p; otherwise
                 adds u to p, mapping it to a new empty mailbox.

    lookup = proc(p: post_office, u: user_id) returns(mailbox)
                        signals(no_such_user)
        Effect:  Returns the mailbox for u in p;
                 signals no_such_user if u is not defined in p.

    end post_office
```

Figure 11.2 Serial specification of the post_office data type.

```
user_map = data type is create, add_maildrop, add_user,
                         lookup, least_loaded

Overview:  A user_map is a relation between maildrops and user_ids.
           A maildrop is 'known' if it has been added; otherwise it
           is 'unknown'.
           User_maps are atomic.

create = proc() returns(user_map)
         Effect:  Creates and returns a new empty user_map.

add_maildrop = proc(um: user_map, drop: maildrop)
         Requires:  drop is not known in um.
         Effect:  Makes drop known in um.

add_user = proc(um: user_map, user: user_id, drop: maildrop)
             signals(user_exists, no_such_drop)
         Effect:  Signals user_exists if user already has an
                  associated maildrop in um; signals no_such_drop
                  if drop is not known in um; otherwise adds the
                  pair <user, drop> to um.

lookup = proc(um: user_map, user: user_id) returns(maildrop)
             signals(no_such_user)
         Effect:  Returns the maildrop for user in um; signals
                  no_such_user if user has no associated maildrop
                  in um.

least_loaded = proc(um: user_map) returns(maildrop)
         Effect:  Returns the maildrop with the fewest users in um;
                  if there are several such maildrops, any may be
                  returned.

end user_map
```

Figure 11.3 Serial specification of the user_map data type.

terminate either normally or by signalling any of the named exceptions listed in its interface. Result objects can be returned in either case.

An additional data type, user_map, is used in the implementation of registry guardians to keep track of where each user's mail is stored. The serial specification of user_map appears in Figure 11.3. A user_map stores associations between users and maildrops, with at most one maildrop per user. New associations can be added using the add_user operation. Only 'known' maildrops can be associated with users; the add_maildrop operation can be used to make a maildrop known. The maildrop for a user can be determined using the lookup operation. A maildrop with the fewest number of associated users can be found using the least_loaded operation.

```
maildrop = guardian is create
                    handles send_mail, read_mail, add_user

    stable boxes: post_office := post_office$create()

    create = creator() returns(maildrop)
        return(self)
        end create

    send_mail = handler(user: user_id, msg: message)
        box: mailbox := post_office$lookup(boxes, user)
        mailbox$add_message(box, msg)
        end send_mail

    read_mail = handler(user: user_id) returns(array[message])
        box: mailbox := post_office$lookup(boxes, user)
        return(mailbox$read_mail(box))
        end read_mail

    add_user = handler(user: user_id) signals(user_exists)
        post_office$add_user(boxes, user) resignal user_exists
        end add_user

end maildrop
```

Figure 11.4 Implementation of the **maildrop** guardian.

11.2 Implementations of guardians

Implementations of these data types are discussed below. First, however, we will present the implementations of the three guardians in the system. The implementation of the maildrop guardian is quite simple, and is shown in Figure 11.4. Its stable state is a **post_office**. When a maildrop is created (using the creator **create**), the stable state is initialized to a new empty **post_office**, and the name of the new maildrop guardian is returned. To send a message to a user, the user's mailbox is found in the **post_office**, and the message is added to the mailbox. We assume here that the user exists; the other guardians will never call the **send_mail** handler of a maildrop unless the user has a mailbox at that maildrop. Similarly, to read a user's mail, the **read_mail** handler finds the user's mailbox, and removes and returns the messages stored there. Adding a user involves calling the corresponding operation provided by the **post_office**; if the user already has a mailbox at this maildrop, the exception signalled by the call of **post_office$add_user** is resignalled to the caller of the handler. (The notation T$op means the operation op provided by the data type T.)

The implementation of the mailer guardian is presented in Figure 11.5. The stable state of the mailer contains a single registry in the stable variable **some**. This registry is provided as an argument to the creator **create**, and is used by the mailer to find the other parts of the mail system after a crash. The mailer also has a volatile variable, best; registries are polled periodically in the background process of the mailer, and the one that responds first is remembered in best. After a crash, best is re-initialized to equal some.†

The background process periodically runs a top-level transaction that finds all the registries (via the handler call best.all_registries, which calls the handler all_registries provided by the guardian best), and then polls the registries concurrently using the ping handler. The first registry to respond is remembered in best, and the other calls of ping are aborted by forcing control to exit the coenter statement (the exit done statement transfers control to the exception handler for done). In Argus, any handler call can potentially signal unavailable if the system is unable to complete the call for some reason. If one of the calls in the background process of the mailer signals unavailable, its arm of the coenter is terminated (using the leave statement), but the other concurrent calls continue. When one call responds (making it best) or all calls signal, the top-level transaction ends, and the process blocks and tries again later.

The send_mail handler uses the best registry to find the maildrop for the user, and then uses the send_mail handler of the maildrop to send the mail. Similarly, the read_mail handler finds the maildrop for the user, and then calls the read_mail handler of that maildrop to get the user's mail. If the registry or the maildrop is unavailable, the mailer reflects this back to the caller by resignalling. (Notice that the mail system will appear to be unavailable to a user of the system if the best registry used by the user's mailer is unavailable. A more robust implementation would provide a way for the mailer to contact other registries in such situations.)

The add_user handler is more interesting. It first uses the select handler of the best registry to select a maildrop for the user. Select will signal user_exists if the user already has a mailbox at some maildrop; this is resignalled to the caller of add_user. If select returns a maildrop, a mailbox is created for the user at the maildrop (using the handler call *drop.add_user*), and the association between the user and the selected maildrop is added concurrently to each registry. If any of these handler calls signals unavailable, the entire add_user handler is aborted, and unavailable is resignalled to the caller. This is facilitated by running each handler or creator call as a subtransaction. Thus, aborting the handler call in this case ensures that either the handler call (including the calls it makes) has no effect, or the selected maildrop and all registries are updated appropriately. It is not possible for some, but not all, of the registries to record the association between the user and the maildrop, or for the registries to record it but for the maildrop not to create a mailbox for the user.

A new maildrop can be created using the add_maildrop handler. This handler creates a new maildrop at the specified node, and then makes the maildrop known at all registries. As with add_user, if any of the subsidiary calls signals

† The recover code section is run after a crash before the background process is restarted or new handler calls are accepted.

```
mailer = guardian is create
          handles send_mail, read_mail, add_user, add_maildrop,
              add_registry, add_mailer

    reg_list = atomic_array[registry]     % A type abbreviation.

    stable some: registry      % stable reference to some registry
    best: registry             % volatile reference to the 'best'
                               % registry
    recover
        best := some           % re-initialize after a crash
        end

    background
        while true do          % periodically find a new best registry
            enter topaction
                regs: reg_list := best.all_registries()
                               % get a list of all registries
                coenter        % runs concurrent subactions, one for
                               % each registry in regs
                action foreach reg: registry in
                           reg_list$elements(regs)
                        reg.ping()     % see if it responds
                            except when unavailable(*): leave end
                        best := reg
                        exit done      % abort all others
                    end except when done: end
                end
            sleep(...)         % some amount of time
            end
        end

    create = creator(reg: registry) returns(mailer)
        some := reg
        best := reg
        return(self)
    end create

    send_mail = handler(user: user_id, msg: message)
            signals(no_such_user, unavailable(string))
        drop: maildrop := best.lookup(user)
            resignal no_such_user, unavailable
        drop.send_mail(user, msg) resignal unavailable
    end send_mail

    read_mail = handler(user: user_id) returns(array[message])
            signals(no_such_user, unavailable(string))
        drop: maildrop := best.lookup(user)
            resignal no_such_user, unavailable
        return(drop.read_mail(user)) resignal unavailable
    end read_mail
```

Figure 11.5 Implementation of the mailer guardian (Part I).

```
     add_user = handler(user: user_id)
          signals(user_exists, unavailable(string))
       begin
          drop: maildrop := best.select(user_id)
          regs: reg_list := best.all_registries()
          coenter      % run the call to drop.add_user concurrently
                       % with the calls
                       % to reg.add_user, for each reg in regs
             action drop.add_user(user)
             action
                  foreach reg: registry in reg_list$elements(regs)
                       reg.add_user(user, drop)
                  end
             end
          resignal user_exists
          abort resignal unavailable
       end add_user

   add_maildrop = handler(home: node) signals(unavailable(string))
       begin
          drop: maildrop := maildrop$create()@home
          regs: reg_list := best.all_registries()
          coenter
             action
                  foreach reg: registry in reg_list$elements(regs)
                       reg.add_maildrop(drop)
                  end
             end
          abort resignal unavailable
       end add_maildrop

   add_registry = handler(home: node) signals(unavailable(string))
       best.new_registry(home) resignal unavailable
   end add_registry

   add_mailer = handler(home: node) returns(mailer)
          signals(unavailable(string))
       m: mailer := mailer$create(best)@home resignal unavailable
       return(m)
   end add_mailer

end mailer
```

Figure 11.5 contd.

unavailable, the entire handler call is aborted. The newly created maildrop will become permanent only if the calling transaction commits; if the handler call or an ancestor transaction is aborted, the maildrop will be destroyed.

A new registry can be created by calling the add_registry handler, which asks the best registry to create the new registry. Similarly, a new mailer can be created via the add_mailer handler, which creates a new mailer at the specified node, giving it the current mailer's best registry as its connection to the rest of

```
registry = guardian is create
    handles lookup, select, all_registries, ping, add_user,
            add_maildrop, new_registry, add_registry

    reg_list = atomic_array[registry]        % A type abbreviation.

    stable regs: reg_list          % all registries
    stable users: user_map         % locations of mailboxes for all
                                   % users

    create = creator(rs: reg_list, um: user_map) returns(registry)
        reg_list$addh(rs, self)  % appends the new guardian to the
                                 % end of the array
        regs := rs
        users := um
        return(self)
    end create

    lookup = handler(user: user_id) returns(maildrop)
            signals(no_such_user)
        return(user_map$lookup(users, user)) resignal no_such_user
    end lookup

    select = handler(user: user_id) returns(maildrop)
            signals(user_exists)
        user_map$lookup(users, user)
            % if this returns normally, the user exists;
            % the maildrop returned is ignored.
                except when no_such_user:
                    return(user_map$least_loaded(users)) end
        signal user_exists
    end select

    all_registries = handler() returns(reg_list)
        return(regs)
    end all_registries

    ping = handler()
    end ping

    add_user = handler(user: user_id, drop: maildrop)
            signals(user_exists)
        user_map$add_user(users, user, drop) resignal user_exists
    end add_user

    add_maildrop = handler(drop: maildrop)
        user_map$add_maildrop(users, drop)
    end add_maildrop
```

Figure 11.6 Implementation of the Registry Guardian. Each handler or creator call runs as a subtransaction.

```
new_registry = handler(home: node) signals(unavailable(string))
   begin
      new: registry := registry$create(regs, users) a home
      coenter
         action foreach reg: registry in
                  reg_list$elements(regs)
            reg.add_registry(new)
         end
      end abort resignal unavailable
   end new_registry

add_registry = handler(reg: registry)
   reg_list$addh(regs, reg)
end add_registry

end registry
```

Figure 11.6 contd.

the mail system.

Finally, the implementation of the registry guardian is shown in Figure 11.6. Each registry has a list of all the registries in stable storage, along with a user_map recording the maildrop where each user's mail is stored. New registries are created by calls to the new_registry handler, which uses the creator create to create the new registry at the specified node, and then adds the new registry to the list of registries at all existing registries by calling the add_registry handler. (The first registry must be created by calling create explicitly; the system could be started by creating one registry and one mailer with direct calls to their creators — passing an empty reg_list and user_map to the registry, and the single registry to the mailer — and then using the handlers provided by existing mailers to extend or reconfigure the system.) Create takes an initial registry list and user_map, and initializes its stable state by adding the new registry to the registry list and recording the registry list and the user_map in stable storage. Add_registry simply adds the new registry to the list of registries in stable storage. Recall that each of these handlers runs as a subtransaction; if the calling transaction aborts, the effects will be undone.

The other handlers should be mostly self-explanatory. The select handler simply finds a lightly loaded maildrop, first checking that the user is not already assigned to some maildrop. A better implementation might give higher priority to a maildrop 'close' to the user's home node.

11.3 How transactions were used

The example programs above illustrate a number of places where transactions are useful. In several cases, it is important that either all or none of a set of updates happen. For example, either a user should be added to a maildrop and recorded at all registries, or nothing should be changed. The recoverability property of transactions makes it easy to ensure the appropriate behaviour in these cases, by aborting the transaction when one of the updates cannot be performed. Similarly, either a new maildrop is created, made permanent, and recorded at all registries, or the registries are not changed and the newly created maildrop is destroyed.

The serializability property of transactions is also useful in several places. For example, if two clients try to add the same user_id concurrently, the effect will be as if they ran sequentially. As a result, one of the clients will succeed, and the other will be told that the user already exists. Similarly, if two clients try to create new registries concurrently, one will appear to be created first, and then the second one will be created with an initial registry list that contains the first one. Without some synchronization here, we could create two new registries that know about the old registries, but not about each other. (Compare the effects of such concurrency in this system with the complex behaviour that can arise in a system such as Grapevine (Birrell *et al.* (1982)), which does not use transactions.)

11.4 Application-specific concurrency control

Let us now consider the level of concurrency provided by this system. The built-in atomic types in Argus, such as atomic_array, use two-phase locking with read and write locks to ensure serializability. Since at most one transaction can hold a write lock at a time, concurrent modification of the reg_list stored in each registry is prevented. As long as adding a new registry is not expected to occur very often, this lack of concurrency is probably okay.

There are other places, however, where highly concurrent access is probably important. For example, every transaction that sends or reads mail for a user accesses the post_office in some maildrop. A simple implementation of post_office is shown in Figure 11.7.† This implementation uses a representation based on the built-in atomic types, which use read-write locking. Thus, if a new user is being added by one transaction, attempts by other transactions to read the post_office to send mail or read mail for another user may be forced

---

† In Argus, as in CLU (Liskov (1981)), a data type is implemented using a cluster, which contains a definition of the representation for the type together with implementations for the operations on the type. The representation is defined by the type abbreviation 'rep = ...'. The reserved word cvt used as the type of an argument or result in the interface of an operation indicates that the type of the given argument or result is changed on entry to or exit from the operation: outside the cluster, its type is the type defined by the cluster, while inside the cluster, its type is the representation type. Thus, in Figure 11.7, the type of the argument po to the lookup operation is post_office outside the cluster, and is rep (= atomic_array[pair]) inside the cluster. These type conversions allow the implementation of the operations on a type to access the representation of an object of the type while ensuring that code in other modules cannot access the representation; they are used solely for type-checking purposes, and involve no run-time computation.

```
post_office = cluster is create, lookup, add_user

    pair = struct[u: user_id, mb: mailbox]
    rep = atomic_array[pair]

    create = proc() returns(cvt)
        return(rep$new())
    end create

    lookup = proc(po: cvt, user: user_id) returns(mailbox)
            signals(no_such_user)
        for p: pair in rep$elements(po) do
            if p.u = user then return(p.mb) end
            end
        signal no_such_user
    end lookup

    add_user = proc(po: cvt, user: user_id) signals(user_exists)
        for p: pair in rep$elements(po) do
            if p.u = user then signal user_exists end
            end
        rep$addh(po, pair${u: user, mb: mailbox$create()})
    end add_user

end post_office
```

Figure 11.7 A simple implementation of post_office.

to wait until the first transaction completes. As long as the transaction adding the user does not last very long, the delay experienced by other transactions should not be too great. However, if transactions are interactive, or a single transaction adds many users, there may be a long delay. Since transactions are distributed, it is also possible for a failure during two-phase commit to cause locks to be held for a long time.

Fortunately, operations on a post_office involving different users are logically independent. As a result, it is possible to implement the post_office to allow transactions executing lookup operations to proceed concurrently with transactions adding users and maildrops. An implementation of post_office that allows this kind of concurrency is shown in Figure 11.8. The implementation follows a typical strategy used in Argus for highly concurrent implementations of atomic types. The representation of a post_office is an ordinary nonatomic array, protected by a *mutex*, which can be used to ensure mutually exclusive access to the objects contained in it. (Since the array is not atomic, some synchronization is needed between concurrent operations to ensure that they do not interfere in their use of the array.) The elements of the array are pairs consisting of a user_id and a possible_mailbox. A possible_mailbox is an atomic variant with two possible tags. The possible_mailbox associated with a given user_id in the array acts as a kind of logical lock on that user_id.

```
post_office = cluster is create, lookup, add_user

    possible_mailbox = atomic_variant[none: null, some: mailbox]
    pair = struct[u: user_id, mb: possible_mailbox]
    rep = mutex[array[pair]]

    create = proc() returns(cvt)
        return(rep$create(array[pair]$new()))
    end create

    lookup = proc(po: cvt, user: user_id) returns(mailbox)
            signals(no_such_user)
        cleanup(po)      % Call the internal routine cleanup
        seize po do
            while true do % loop while possible_mailbox locked
                pm: possible_mailbox := find_user(po.value, user)
                tagtest pm do
                    tag none:  signal no_such_user
                    tag some(mb: mailbox):  return(mb)
                end
                pause % if it's locked, pause and try again
            end
        end
    end lookup

    add_user = proc(po: cvt, user: user_id) signals(user_exists)
        cleanup(po)
        seize po do
            while true do
                pm: possible_mailbox := find_user(po.value, user)
                tagtest pm do
                    wtag none:  possible_mailbox$change_some(pm,
                                        mailbox$create())
                                rep$changed(po)
                    tag some:   signal user_exists
                end
                pause % wait and try again later
            end
        end
    end add_user

    find_user = proc(pairs: array[pair], user: user_id)
            returns(possible_mailbox)
        for p: pair in array[pair]$elements(pairs) do
            if p.u = user then return(p.mb) end
        end
        null_mb: possible_mailbox := possible_mailbox$make_none(nil)
        phantom: pair := pair${u: user, mb: null_mb}
        array[pair]$addh(pairs, phantom)
        return(null_mb)
    end find_user
```

Figure 11.8 A highly concurrent implementation of post_office.

```
cleanup = proc(po: rep)
    enter topaction
        seize po do
            pairs: array[pair] := po.value
            current: int := array[pair]$low(pairs)
            while true do
                tagtest pairs[current].mb
                    wtag none:
                        top_elem: pair := array[pair]$remh(pairs)
                        % removes and returns the top
                        % element of the array
                        pairs[current] := top_elem
                    others:  current := current + 1
                end
            end except when bounds: end
        end
    end
end cleanup

end post_office
```

Figure 11.8 contd.

If a transaction looks up a user_id, and finds that the associated possible_mailbox has tag none (meaning that the user has no mailbox in the post_office), the transaction will retain a read lock on the possible_mailbox, preventing some other transaction from adding a mailbox for the user before the first transaction completes. This is necessary to avoid a 'phantom record' problem (cf. Eswaran *et al.* (1976)).

The lookup and add_user operations are implemented similarly. Each begins by calling the internal routine cleanup, which is explained below. Each then seizes the mutex and loops, trying to get the appropriate lock on the possible_mailbox for the user. If an appropriate lock cannot be obtained, the mutex is released, the operation pauses for a system-determined amount of time, and then the mutex is re-acquired and the lock on the possible_mailbox is checked again. The internal routine find_user is used to find the possible_mailbox for a user; it maintains the abstraction that every user_id has a possible_mailbox, by creating one (with tag none) if none exists. Given the possible_mailbox for a user, lookup uses the **tagtest** statement to examine the tag. If the tag is none, lookup signals; if the tag is some, lookup returns the associated mailbox. However, if a read lock cannot be obtained to read the tag, the tagtest statement terminates, causing the lookup routine to execute the pause statement.

Add_user requires a write lock if the tag is none (indicated by the reserved word wtag), and, in that case, changes the state of the possible_mailbox to have tag some with an associated new mailbox. (The changed operation is called on the rep to inform the system that the array inside the mutex has been modified, so that the change can be saved on stable storage before the transaction commits to the top level.) If the tag is some and a read lock can be obtained, add_user signals. If the appropriate lock for each tag cannot be obtained, add_user pauses, releasing the mutex, and then tries again.

If a transaction executing add_user changes a possible_mailbox to have tag some and then aborts, the change will be undone (since atomic_variants ensure recoverability), and the abstract effect will be as if the transaction never ran. The representation of the post_office, however, will still contain an entry for the user_id, with a possible_mailbox with tag none. Similarly, if a lookup operation is invoked for a user that does not have an associated mailbox, a possible_mailbox with tag none will be created for the user (unless one already exists), and will remain in the array after the lookup's transaction completes. To keep large numbers of these 'phantom' users from accumulating in the array, the internal routine cleanup is used to find array elements for users without mailboxes and to remove them from the array. In this implementation, cleanup is called once for each invocation of an operation on the post_office. A more realistic implementation would call cleanup only occasionally.

Cleanup can remove an array element only if no active transaction has a lock on the element's possible_mailbox. It finds these elements by starting an independent top-level transaction and trying to obtain a write lock on the possible_mailbox; if the write lock can be obtained by the top-level transaction, no other transaction can have a lock (of any kind). If the write lock can be obtained and the possible_mailbox has tag none, the storage for the element can be reclaimed. Cleanup works by searching the array starting at the smallest index. If the current element cannot be reclaimed, the search continues with the next index in the array. If the current element can be reclaimed, it is replaced in the array with the element from the high end of the array, and the high end of the array is shortened (using the remh operation on array[pair]). The loop terminates when bounds is signalled by one of the operations that indexes into the array; this will happen when the current index exceeds the high bound of the array (either because the current index was incremented, or because the high end was trimmed), meaning there are no more elements to be checked.

Other types used in the mail system may also require highly concurrent implementations. For example, in the user_map it may be important to avoid conflicts between operations involving different users, so that adding one user (or a maildrop) does not delay sending or reading mail for another user. There is no logical conflict between adding one user and looking up another, and techniques similar to those used in Figure 11.8 could be used to implement user_map to avoid such conflicts. However, concurrent attempts to add two users may conflict regardless of the implementation, since each selects the least loaded maildrop and then adds the user to that maildrop, changing its load (and possibly whether it is the least loaded). We might prefer an implementation in which the least_loaded operation does not exclude attempts to add users to maildrops, by having it find the known maildrop that appears to be least loaded, but not set any locks that exclude adding users to maildrops. One way of viewing such an implementation is that we have sacrificed atomicity to increase concurrency. Another view is that the type is still atomic, but the specification is weaker: least_loaded is specified non-deterministically to be able to return any known maildrop. This second view allows us to continue to use atomicity to reason about our programs, but tells us very little about the behaviour of the least_loaded operation. An additional probabilistic specification that the maildrop returned by least_loaded is likely to be the least loaded maildrop, or to have a load close to the lightest load, would be useful (since the implementation sketched above returns the least loaded maildrop as long as there is no concurrency). Such specifications are discussed further in Chapter 16.

The mailbox is another example where concurrency could be important. For example, if transactions that send mail last a long time, perhaps because they are interactive or because they involve sending mail to many users (for example, a mailing list), it might be desirable that concurrent attempts to send mail to the same user do not conflict. However, since the mailbox was specified to act like a FIFO queue, only one transaction at a time can execute an add_message operation on a given mailbox. More concurrency could be obtained by relaxing the specification of the read_mail operation on mailboxes, allowing it to remove and return any subset of the messages in the mailbox. In the absence of concurrency, mailboxes would behave like FIFO queues; if one transaction adds a message to a mailbox while a concurrent transaction reads the messages in the mailbox, the read_mail operation may return some subset of the messages in the mailbox, while if concurrent transactions add messages to the same mailboxes, the order in which the messages are returned by a read_mail operation may be arbitrary. Thus, mailboxes would behave more like *semiqueues* (Weihl and Liskov (1985)) than first in, first out queues. As with the alternative specification of user_map$least_loaded discussed above, it would be useful to have an additional probabilistic guarantee that a message added to a mailbox by one transaction would be unlikely to remain in the mailbox for very long without being returned as the result of some read_mail operation.

11.5 Discussion

The example above provides several illustrations of the utility of transactions in distributed applications. The serializability and recoverability properties of transactions simplify reasoning about programs by allowing the programmer to think of each transaction as occurring indivisibly: interleavings of the steps of concurrent transactions can be ignored, as can partial executions of transactions.

It is important to realize that transactions are quite flexible. As illustrated above, atomicity is necessary only at the level of the specification of an abstract data type, not its implementation. In other words, delays are necessary to handle logical conflicts, but delays due to physical conflicts can frequently be avoided through careful programming. Type-specific concurrency control algorithms can be used in the implementation of an atomic data type to provide high levels of concurrency by avoiding unnecessary physical conflicts. Such highly concurrent implementations are typically more complex, but the complexity is localized to the implementation of each individual type.

The designer of a system also has flexibility in choosing the granularity of transactions. A given activity, such as sending a message in a mail system, could be implemented as a single transaction, or as a sequence of transactions, depending on the needs of the application. A finer granularity of transactions may lead to greater concurrency, but typically at the expense of a more complicated program. Too fine a granularity of transactions could, in fact, hurt performance, since each transaction introduces some overhead, such as the cost of two-phase commit. If activities are structured as sequences of transactions, their concurrent interactions will be more complex. In addition, an activity is no longer recoverable in its entirety: it is possible for some of its transactions, but not all, to complete. Some way of compensating for partially executed activities must be designed into the application.

Addressing these trade offs between concurrency and complexity is an important part of designing a distributed program. An appropriate granularity of transactions must be chosen. In addition, appropriate operations should be designed for the shared data objects so that they can be implemented to support the desired level of concurrency. In several examples above, we discussed how alternative specifications affect the level of concurrency that is achievable. Similar issues arise in replicated systems. Type-specific replication algorithms can be used to provide higher availability (for example, see Herlihy (1986)). In addition, relaxing the specifications of operations can permit greater availability.

11.6 References

A. D. Birrell, R. Levin, R. M. Needham, and M. Schroeder (1982). 'Grapevine: An Exercise in Distributed Computing'. *Communications of the ACM* **25**: 260—274, April 1982.

K. P. Eswaran, J. N. Gray, R. A. Lorie, and I. L. Traiger (1976). 'The Notions of Consistency and Predicate Locks in a Database System'. *Communications of the ACM* **19** (11): 624—633, November 1976.

M. Herlihy (1986). 'A quorum-consensus replication method for abstract types'. *ACM Transactions on Computer Systems* **4** (1): 32—53, Feb. 1986.

B. Liskov and A. Snyder (1979). 'Exception handling in CLU'. *IEEE Transactions on Software Engineering*: 546—558, 1979.

B. Liskov (1981). 'CLU reference manual'. In Goos and Hartmanis (Ed.), *Lecture Notes in Computer Science*, Volume 114. Springer-Verlag, Berlin, 1981.

B. Liskov and R. Scheifler (1983). 'Guardians and Actions: Linguistic Support for Robust, Distributed Programs'. *ACM Transactions on Programming Languages and Systems* 5 (3): 381—404, July 1983.

B. Liskov, D. Curtis, P. Johnson, and R. Scheifler (1987). 'Implementation of Argus'. *Proceedings of the Eleventh Symposium on Operating System Principles*: 111—122, Austin, TX, 8-11 November 1987.

W. E. Weihl and B. Liskov (1985). 'Implementation of Resilient, Atomic Data Types'. *ACM Transactions on Programming Languages and Systems* 7 (2): 244—269, April 1985.

Chapter 12

Theory of Nested Transactions

W. E. Weihl

As discussed in Chapter 11, nested transactions are useful for two reasons: they allow concurrency within a transaction, and they provide greater protection against failures by allowing checkpoints to be established within a transaction. The notion of correctness for a nested transaction system is similar to that for a single-level transaction system — transactions should be serializable and recoverable — but there are some subtle differences. In this section we present a theory of correctness for nested transaction systems. The theory described here deals with concurrency and aborts, but does not cope with crashes; this is the subject of current research.

Because of space limitations, our presentation here is informal and is designed to emphasize the issues and the intuition underlying the approach. Details can be found in Fekete *et al.* (1987b), Fekete *et al.* (1987a), and Aspnes *et al.* (1988).

12.1 Issues raised by nesting

Nested transactions as used in Argus (Liskov and Scheifler (1983)) and Camelot (Spector and Swedlow (1987)) differ from classical single-level transactions in two important ways. First, a child transaction can abort without forcing its parent to abort. In fact, the parent can be informed that the child has aborted, and can take different steps than when the child commits. This means that aborts must be included explicitly in the model — unlike most theoretical work on concurrency control for single-level transaction systems (Bernstein and Goodman (1981); Bernstein, Hadzilacos, and Goodman (1987); Papadimitriou (1979)). Second, a transaction can run several subtransactions concurrently. This requires us to extend the notion of 'serializability', since a transaction can request several children to be run concurrently, yet in a serial execution no concurrency should occur.

12.2 Goals

Our goal in this chapter is to present a rigorous framework for describing and analysing transaction management algorithms, including concurrency control and recovery algorithms, replication algorithms, commit protocols, and orphan detection algorithms. A rigorous framework is important because the algorithms and their interactions can be quite subtle. We need to give precise definitions of correctness, which then serve as specifications for algorithms. In addition, rigorous proofs of correctness are needed.

In developing this framework, we have two primary goals:

- *Generality*. It should be possible to describe a wide variety of algorithms in a common framework, and to state general results that apply to many algorithms.

- *Modularity*. It should be possible to analyse different algorithms as independently as possible. For example, concurrency control algorithms, recovery algorithms, commit protocols, and orphan detection algorithms may all be used simultaneously in the same system. The requirements for each algorithm should be stated as independently of the others as possible, so that one algorithm can be verified without having to consider how it interacts with others.

One important issue in achieving generality is to state the correctness requirements for systems in a way sufficiently abstract that interesting algorithms are not excluded. Most existing theoretical work on concurrency control makes assumptions about the underlying model that preclude certain algorithms. For example, operations are frequently assumed to be either reads or writes, objects are assumed to have a single version, and an 'update-in-place' model is used for executing operations. We would like to be able to describe and analyse algorithms that use application semantics to achieve higher concurrency (for example, see Chapter 11), that use multiple versions, and that use recovery methods other than update-in-place, and to do this within a single common framework. We would also like our definitions to be as independent as possible of any particular programming language or system.

Modularity can be achieved in part by using a formal framework that naturally allows the description and analysis of a system to be decomposed into pieces, and that allows a system to be analysed at different levels of abstraction. To this end, we use an operational model based on *input/output automata*, a model developed by Lynch and Tuttle (1987). Such a model is perhaps necessary for achieving the kind of modularity aimed at, but is not by itself sufficient. Careful analysis of the algorithms is required to understand exactly how they interact; for example, how concurrency control algorithms depend on recovery algorithms, and vice-versa, and how commit protocols and orphan detection algorithms depend on each other and on recovery algorithms. In some cases algorithms can be analysed independently, but in others there are interesting dependencies that cannot be avoided.

Another aspect of modularity is our desire to model distributed transaction systems. The state of a distributed system can be viewed as composed of a number of independent objects, with concurrency control and recovery performed separately at each object. How correctness can be defined *locally* for individual objects, rather than just for the system as a whole is discussed below. A local notion of correctness affords useful modularity, since different concurrency control algorithms can be chosen for different objects, as long as each satisfies the local notion of correctness.

12.3 Relation to other work

Most work on concurrency control and recovery treats concurrency control and recovery as two separate problems. As discussed in Weihl (1989), concurrency control and recovery interact in subtle ways. For generality, it is important to consider the two together when defining correctness. Most work on concurrency control makes assumptions about recovery that rule out interesting recovery algorithms. To analyse particular algorithms, it may be convenient to treat them separately, but in defining correctness it is important not to introduce restrictive assumptions or structure. In the approach discussed here, correctness is defined for whole system, and structure appropriate for analysing particular algorithms is introduced after that.

A number of papers have been published in recent years on 'nested transactions'. There are actually two kinds of nesting in transactions that are discussed in the literature. Since they are frequently confused, it is worth distinguishing them here. The two kinds of nesting correspond loosely to the nesting of procedures and the nesting of layers of data abstractions. In the first kind, represented by systems such as Argus and Camelot, a subtransaction is not visible outside its parent. If the parent aborts, the subtransaction is also aborted. In the second kind, represented by type-specific concurrency control algorithms as discussed in Weihl (1984), Weihl and Liskov (1985), Beeri, Bernstein, and Goodman (1986), and Moss, Griffeth, and Graham (1986), a subtransaction's modifications are visible to other transactions at the same level of abstraction as soon as it commits, even if its parent is still active. If the parent then aborts, a compensating 'undo' operation must be run to remove the effects of the already committed subtransaction. In the work described here, only 'procedural' nesting is addressed; models for 'layered' systems are still being studied.

Examples of type-specific concurrency control algorithms can be found in Weihl (1984), Weihl (1989), Herlihy (1987), Herlihy and Weihl (1988), and Herlihy (1986). The need for a definition of correctness that encompasses both concurrency control and recovery is illustrated by the locking algorithms in Weihl (1989), which shows how different recovery algorithms place different constraints on concurrency. More details of the work described here can be found in Fekete *et al.* (1987b), and Fekete *et al.* (1987a).

12.4 Basic model

Input/output automata are used as the underlying formal model for our theory. A system is modelled as a collection of communicating automata; for example, each transaction and each object will be modelled as a separate automaton. An I/O automaton has a potentially infinite set of *states*, some of which are designated as *initial states*. It has *actions*, which are divided into *input actions* and *output actions*. (I/O automata can also have *internal actions*, but that is a level of detail that need not concern us here.) The input and output actions are used for communicating with other automata. In addition, an automaton has a *transition relation*, which is a set of triples of the form (s', π, s), where s' and s are states and π is an action. Such a triple means that in state s' the automaton can atomically do action π and change to state s. In this case we say that π is *enabled* in state s'. An element of the transition relation is called a *step* of the automaton.

An automaton executes by taking one step at a time according to its transition relation. We model a finite *execution* of an automaton as an alternating sequence $s_0, \pi_1, s_1, \pi_2, \ldots, \pi_n, s_n$ of states and actions, starting and ending with a state, such that each triple (s', π, s) that occurs as a consecutive subsequence is a step of the automaton. Frequently, we will be concerned only with how an automaton interacts with its environment, and not with the details of its internal state. Thus, we will look at *schedules* of an automaton, which are sequences of actions that are obtained from executions by deleting the states.

Input actions of an automaton are generated by the environment of the automaton, while the outputs are generated by the automaton itself. In this model, the automaton cannot control its environment. Thus, we require the automaton to be prepared for any input to happen at any time. More formally, the transition relation of an automaton is restricted to be *input-enabled*: each input action must be enabled in every state. This differs from CSP-like models (Hoare (1978)) in which an input is delayed until the automaton is prepared to accept it.

We describe systems as consisting of interacting components, each of which is an I/O automaton. It is convenient and natural to view systems as I/O automata, also. A state of the composition is just a tuple of states of the individual components. The set of actions of the composition is the union of the sets of actions of the components. We restrict compositions so that each action is controlled by one automaton: no action can be an output of more than one automaton. In this way, each action is controlled either by the environment of the system, or by a single component. When a component or the environment generates an action, that action occurs simultaneously at all other components for which it is an input. Given a schedule α of a system with a component A, we denote the subsequence of α containing all the actions of A by $\alpha|A$.

The following fundamental property of I/O automata expresses our ability to reason about a system by reasoning locally at each component:

Proposition:

Let S be the composition of a collection of automata. Then α is a schedule of S if and only if, for every component A of S, $\alpha|A$ is a schedule of A.

We will now use I/O automata to define *serial systems*, whose schedules serve as the basis of our correctness definitions. A serial system consists of a collection of *transaction automata* and *serial object automata* communicating with a *serial scheduler automaton*. Transactions and serial objects describe user programs and data, respectively. The serial scheduler controls communication between the other components, and thereby controls the orders in which the transactions can take steps. It ensures that no subtransactions of a given transaction are active concurrently, and that no transaction fails after taking its first step. In other words, in an execution of a serial system, siblings execute serially, and aborted transactions have no effect. A real system will permit concurrency, as well as aborts of partially executed transactions. As discussed below in Section 12.5, a real system with concurrency and failures is required to 'simulate' a serial system in the sense that transactions cannot distinguish one from the other.

12.4.1 Transactions

We model the pattern of transaction nesting by a tree of transaction names, with T_0 as the root. The leaves of this tree are called *accesses* (because they are the transactions that directly access data). This tree can be thought of as a predefined naming scheme for all possible transactions that might ever be invoked. In any particular execution, only some of these transactions will actually take steps. For example, suppose that an Argus guardian contains the following background code:

```
background
    while true do
        enter topaction
            coenter
                action ...
                action ...
                end
            end
        end
    end
```

Each time around the loop, this code runs a top-level transaction, which runs two children in parallel. The tree corresponding to this code would look like the one in FIGURE 12.1. T_0 represents the environment in which the top-level transactions run. The children of T_0 represent the top-level transactions, one for each iteration of the loop. Each of these has two children, for the two subtransactions created by the coenter statement.

We introduce the root T_0 for uniformity. It models the external world, which creates top-level transactions. It is different from other transactions in that it

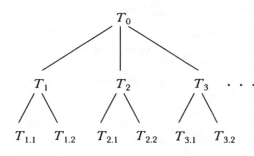

Figure 12.1

will never commit or abort. However, like other transactions, it has actions that describe the invocation and return of its children. Thus, it is convenient to model it in a uniform way.

Each transaction T (except for the accesses, which are described in the next section is modelled as a transaction automaton with the following input and output actions:

> Input:
>> `Create(`T`)`
>> `Report_Commit(`T'`,` v`)`, for T' a child of T and v a value
>> `Report_Abort(`T'`)`, for T' a child of T
>
> Output:
>> `Request_Create(`T'`)`, for T' a child of T
>> `Request_Commit(`T`,` v`)`, for v a value

The `Create(`T`)` input action 'wakes up' the transaction T. T generates the `Request_Create(`T'`)` output action whenever it wants to run a particular child transaction T'. The `Report_Commit(`T'`,` v`)` input action informs T that a child T' has completed successfully, and returns a value v recording the results of the child's execution. (An argument value in the `Request_Create(`T'`)` action is not included since children with different input parameters can be considered to be different transactions in the tree; T can choose which child to request based on the argument value it wishes to pass to the child.) The `Report_Abort(`T'`)` input action informs T that a child T' has failed, without returning any other information. Finally, the `Request_Commit(`T`,`v`)` output action is an announcement by T that it has finished its work, and includes a value recording the results of this work. (Notice that there is no `Request_Abort(`T`)` output action. Instead, decisions to abort transactions are assigned to another component of the system. A request to abort can be viewed as a 'hint' to this other component that the transaction should be aborted. Modeling these hints explicitly would be easy and would merely add an extra case to the analysis in many of the proofs.)

We do not assume much about particular transaction automata; they could be derived from Argus programs, or from programs in some other language such as Avalon (Herlihy and Wing (1987)). However, we do assume that schedules of transactions obey certain syntactic constraints. In particular, if α is a schedule of the transaction automaton T, then α is *well formed* if:

- the first action in α, if any, is a Create(T) action;

- no action appears twice in α;

- if a report for a child T' of T appears in α, it is preceded by a Request_Create(T');

- at most one report occurs for each child; and

- if a Request_Commit(T,v) appears in α, it is the last action in α, and it is preceded by a report action for each child T' for which there is a Request_Create(T') in α.

Technically, it is assumed that transaction automata *preserve* well-formedness, which means that they will not generate an output that violates well-formedness unless their environment has already provided an input that violates it. As it turns out, transactions will always be placed in environments that also preserve well-formedness, so only well formed schedules will be examined. Thus, according to the well-formedness constraints above a transaction must not do anything until it has been created or after it has requested to commit, and must not request to commit until it has heard responses from all requested children. In addition, it must not request the same child twice. The environment in which the transaction is placed must not generate a report for a child unless the child has been requested, and must not generate more than one report for a given child.

Notice that a transaction T and its children cannot be connected directly: the output Request_Create(T') of T and the input Create(T') of T' are different actions. This is intentional, and allows us to take the same transaction automata and place them in different contexts. For example, in a serial system, the context will ensure that siblings run one at a time, while in a concurrent system, siblings may run concurrently. In Section 12.4.3, we describe how communication between transactions and their children in a serial system is mediated by the serial scheduler.

12.4.2 Serial objects

As mentioned earlier, direct access to data is performed only by the leaves of the transaction tree, which are called *access transactions*, or simply *accesses*. Each access models a single operation on the shared state. Thus, the internal nodes model transactions whose function is to create and manage subtransactions, but not to access data directly. (Distinguishing in this way between internal nodes and accesses simplifies the formal model. Real systems such as Argus and Camelot allow a transaction both to create subtransactions and to access data. Such systems are easily modelled in our framework by introducing a new subtransaction for each operation on the shared state.) In a distributed system, it is natural to view the state of the system as being stored in a number of independent *objects*. Thus, we partition the accesses according to the objects they access.

Since accesses to the same object need to communicate, we associate a single automaton, called a *serial object automaton*, with each object, rather than one with each access. The serial object automata serve as *specifications* of the behavior of the operations on the objects in the absence of concurrency and failures. (They correspond to the serial specifications of Weihl (1984), and Weihl (1987a).) Each serial object X is modelled as a serial object automaton $S(X)$ with the following input and output actions:

Input:
  Create(T), for T an access to X

Output:
  Request_Commit(T,v), for T an access to X and v a value

Although these actions are given the same names as the actions of non-access transactions, it is helpful to think of them in other terms also: a Create(T) corresponds to an invocation of an operation on the object, while a Request_Commit(T,v) corresponds to a response by the object to an invocation, returning the value v.

As with transactions, little needs to be assumed about the details of particular serial objects. However, it is convenient to assume that schedules of serial objects obey certain syntactic constraints. In particular, a schedule α of a serial object is well formed if:

- no action appears twice in α;

- α is an alternating sequence of Creates and Request_Commits, starting with a Create; and

- a Request_Commit(T,v) action is immediately preceded by a Create(T) action.

In other words, operations on the object execute one at a time, no access is executed more than once, and a response returned by the object is for the most recent invocation. It is assumed that serial objects preserve well-formedness; as with transactions, serial objects are only placed in contexts that also preserve well-formedness, so only well-formed schedules are of concern.

For example, an object with read and write operations might be specified by a serial object automaton file described as follows. A state s of file has two components, s.pending, which is either null or an access to file, and s.value, which is a value representing the current state of the file. The transition relation consists of all triples (s', π, s) satisfying the pre- and post-conditions described below, where π is the indicated action. (If a component of the state is not mentioned in the postcondition, we assume that it is the same in s as in s'.)

Create(T), for T an access to file
    Postcondition: s.pending $= T$

Request_Commit(T,ok), for T a write(v) access to file
    Precondition: s'.pending $= T$
    Postcondition: s.pending $=$ null
                s.value $= v$

Request_Commit(T,v), for T a read access to file
    Precondition: s'.pending $= T$
                s'.value $= v$
    Postcondition: s.pending $=$ null

An invocation can occur at any time (though remember that only well-formed schedules are of interest), and simply records the pending access in s.pending. A response to an invocation can be generated when the access is pending. If the access is a write operation with argument v, it records the new value in s.value and changes s.pending to indicate that the invocation is no longer pending. The single result 'ok' is always returned by a write operation. Similarly, a response to a read operation with result v can occur only when s'.value $= v$, since a read operation should return the current state of the file.

If all serial objects are given specifications similar to that for file, so that each operation is either a read or a write, a model similar to that used in most of the literature on concurrency control is obtained, in which operations are treated as reads and writes. However, more complex operations can also be specified. For example, a bank account object with *deposit*, *withdraw*, and read_balance operations might be specified by a serial object automaton *bank* described as follows. A state s of *bank* has two components, s.pending, which is either null or an access to *bank*, and s.balance, which is an integer representing the current balance of the account. The transition relation consists of all triples (s', π, s) satisfying the pre- and post-conditions described below, where π is the indicated action.

Create(T), for T an access to *bank*
    Postcondition: s.pending $= T$

Request_Commit(T,ok), for T a *deposit(amt)* access to *bank*
    Precondition: s'.pending $= T$
    Postcondition: s.pending $=$ null
                s.balance $= s'$.balance $+$ *amt*

Request_Commit(T,*ok*), for T a *withdraw(amt)* access to *bank*
   Precondition: s'.pending $= T$
                    s'.balance $\geqslant amt$
   Postcondition: s.pending $=$ null
                    s.balance $= s'$.balance $- amt$

Request_Commit(T,*refused*), for T a *withdraw(amt)* access to *bank*
   Precondition: s'.pending $= T$
                    s'.balance $< amt$
   Postcondition: s.pending $=$ null

Request_Commit(T,*amt*), for T a **read_balance** access to *bank*
   Precondition: s'.pending $= T$
                    s'.balance $= amt$
   Postcondition: s.pending $=$ null

As with **file**, an invocation can occur at any time, and is recorded as pending. A response to a pending deposit operation increments the current balance by the amount to be deposited. A response with value 'ok' to a pending withdraw operation can be generated whenever the current balance is large enough to cover the requested withdrawal, and decrements the current balance by the specified amount. If the current balance is too small to cover a requested withdrawal, then the response to the withdrawal must return the value 'refused', and the balance is not changed. Finally, **read_balance** operations are similar to read operations on **file**.

The ability to specify the behavior of an object using a serial object automaton is essential for modelling type-specific concurrency control algorithms. As discussed earlier, concurrency can be enhanced by using information about the semantics of operations — for example, that two operations commute — in synchronizing concurrent transactions. When a system has a *hot spot*, such as an aggregate quantity (e.g., net assets for a bank, or quantity on hand for an inventory system) or a data structure representing a collection, type-specific algorithms can be essential for achieving good performance. Many examples of type-specific algorithms can be found in the literature; e.g., see IBM (), Reuter (1982), O'Neil (1986), Weihl (1989), Herlihy (1987), and Herlihy and Weihl (1988). In Section 12.6.2, a locking algorithm is described that uses the specifications of operations to allow operations that commute to run concurrently.

12.4.3 The serial scheduler

Notice that all the automata in a system are 'running' at the same time. Any transaction that has been created can generate outputs, for example to request the creation of children. Furthermore, once a transaction has requested the creation of one child, it can request further children without waiting for a response from the first. This allows us to model constructs such as the `coenter` statement in Argus, with which a transaction can create several children concurrently.

While a parent can request the creation of several children without waiting for responses from any of them, the children should not actually execute concurrently in a serial system. Recall that transactions and their children do not communicate directly. Instead, all communication between a transaction and its children in a serial system occurs through a *serial scheduler automaton*, which accepts requests (such as `Request_Create`(T') from a parent T to create a child T') and at some later point actually carries out the requests. The serial scheduler has two important properties:

- It runs sibling transactions one at a time. Even if a parent requests the creation of several children one right after the other, the serial scheduler will delay the `Create` actions for the children so that only one child is running at a time.

- It aborts a transaction only if it has been requested but has not started running. Thus, an aborted transaction never takes any steps, so it has no effect on the shared state.

Thus, transactions can abort in a serial execution, and a parent can create several children that appear to overlap (the parent requests one without waiting for the report from the previous one), but aborted transactions have no effect and overlapping children run in some serial order.

In more detail, the serial scheduler has the following input and output actions:

Input:
    `Request_Create`(T), for $T \neq T_0$
    `Request_Commit`(T,v)
Output:
    `Create`(T)
    `Commit`(T), for $T \neq T_0$
    `Abort`(T), for $T \neq T_0$
    `Report_Commit`(T,v), for $T \neq T_0$ and v a value
    `Report_Abort`(T), for $T \neq T_0$

The `Request_Create` and `Request_Commit` inputs are intended to be identified with the corresponding outputs of transaction and serial object automata, and correspondingly for the `Create`, `Report_Commit` and `Report_Abort` output actions. The `Commit` and `Abort` actions mark the point in time at which the decision about the fate of the transaction is irrevocable.

Each state s of the serial scheduler consists of six sets: $s.\texttt{create\_requested}$, $s.\texttt{created}$, $s.\texttt{commit\_requested}$, $s.\texttt{committed}$, $s.\texttt{aborted}$, and $s.\texttt{reported}$. The set $s.\texttt{commit\_requested}$ is a set of (transaction,value) pairs, and the others are sets of transactions. There is exactly one start state, in which the set `create_requested` is $\{T_0\}$, and the other sets are empty. *s.*completed is equivalent to *s.*committed $\cup$ *s.*aborted.

The transition relation of the serial scheduler consists of exactly those triples (s',π,s) satisfying the pre- and postconditions described below, where π is the indicated action:

    Request_Create(T), for $T \neq T_0$
      Postcondition: *s.*create_requested $= s'.$create_requested $\cup \{T\}$

    Request_Commit(T,v)
      Postcondition: *s.*commit_requested $= s'.$commit_requested $\cup \{(T,v)\}$

    Create(T)
      Precondition: $T \in s'.$create_requested $-$ *s.*created
                   $T \notin s'.$aborted
                   siblings(T) $\cap s'.$created $\subset s'.$completed
      Postcondition: *s.*created $= s'.$created $\cup \{T\}$

    Commit(T), for $T \neq T_0$
      Precondition: $(T,v) \in s'.$commit_requested for some v
                   $T \notin s'.$completed
      Postcondition: *s.*committed $= s'.$committed $\cup \{T\}$

    Abort(T), for $T \neq T_0$
      Precondition: $T \in s'.$create_requested $- s'.$completed
                   $T \notin s'.$created
                   siblings(T) $\cap s'.$created $\subset s'.$completed
      Postcondition: *s.*aborted $= s'.$aborted $\cup \{T\}$

    Report_Commit(T,v), for $T \neq T_0$ and v a value
      Precondition: $T \in s'.$committed
                   $(T,v) \in s'.$commit_requested
                   $T \notin s'.$reported
      Postcondition: *s.*reported $= s'.$reported $\cup \{T\}$

    Report_Abort(T), for $T \neq T_0$
      Precondition: $T \in s'.$aborted
                   $T \notin s'.$reported
      Postcondition: *s.*reported $= s'.$reported $\cap \{T\}$

The input actions, Request_Create and Request_Commit, simply result in the request being recorded in the appropriate component of the state. A Create action can occur only if a corresponding Request_Create has occurred and the Create has not already occurred, if the transaction has not already aborted, and if each of the previously created siblings has committed or aborted. That is, siblings are run sequentially. The second precondition on the Abort action, together with the second precondition on the `Create` action, ensures that a transaction is either created or aborted but not both. The result of a transaction can be reported to its parent at any time after the commit or abort has occurred.

12.5 Alternative notions of correctness

Schedules of a serial system capture the notion that an aborted transaction has no effect, and that siblings execute sequentially. Thus, they serve as the basis against which correctness is defined for more complicated real systems, which may allow concurrency among siblings and failures of partially completed transactions. In modelling more complex systems, the same transactions are used as in serial systems, but the other components may be different. For example, there might be a communication controller component and separate components for each object, or there might be a single component that performs concurrency control and recovery for all objects.

Many possible notions of correctness for a real system can be defined, all based on the idea that the schedules of the real system should 'look like' serial schedules to the transactions. More precisely, if α is a schedule of a real system, α is called *serially correct* for T if there exists a serial schedule β such that $\beta|T = \alpha|T$. (The expression 'T sees a serial view β' is sometimes used.) In other words, T sees the same thing in α that it could see in some serial schedule. There are a variety of correctness criteria we could require, ranging from relatively weak to quite strong:

- Schedules must be serially correct for T_0.

- Schedules must be serially correct for non-orphan transactions (an *orphan* is a transaction with an aborted ancestor).

- Schedules must be serially correct for all transactions.

The first requirement, serial correctness for T_0, is relatively weak compared to the others. However, it guarantees that the results returned by the top-level transactions will be consistent with a serial execution of those transactions, so the 'external world' will see what appears to be a serial execution. In addition, top-level transactions that do not overlap will appear to execute in the order in which they actually run. In this respect, serial correctness for T_0 is similar to the 'external consistency' requirement sometimes discussed in the database concurrency control literature.

Serial correctness for T_0 is probably a sufficient condition for the end-users of the system to understand its behavior. (Henceforth, when we simply say 'serially correct', we mean 'serially correct for T_0'.) Most systems, however, ensure stronger properties. For example, pessimistic concurrency control algorithms ensure serial correctness for all non-orphans. In contrast, however, optimistic algorithms (Herlihy (1986); Kung and Robinson (1981)), in which a transaction must 'validate' before it can commit, can violate serial correctness for non-orphans, as long as such transactions eventually fail validation.

Serial correctness for all transactions, including orphans, is desirable because it allows the code for any transaction to be written as if the transaction will run in a serial system; the effects of concurrency and failures can be completely ignored. If serial correctness is not guaranteed for orphans, an orphaned transaction may execute in an unexpected way; it might loop forever, or otherwise behave undesirably. This can make systems harder to test and debug, since the cause of unexpected behavior could be either that the code is wrong, or that the transaction that was running it was an orphan. In general, however, ensuring serial correctness for all transactions including orphans requires the use of an orphan detection algorithm (see Liskov *et al.* (1987)) in addition to the usual concurrency control and recovery algorithm.

The notion of serial correctness for a transaction is similar to the notion of 'view serializability' used in the database concurrency control literature (Bernstein and Goodman (1981)), which requires the values read by each transaction to be the same as in some 'equivalent' serial execution, and requires the final state of the database to be the same as after the 'equivalent' serial execution. However, it differs in several important ways:

- The notion of serial correctness followed here allows arbitrary operations on objects, not just reads and writes.

- Serial correctness does not require the state of the system to be the same as after the corresponding serial execution.

- Serial correctness allows different transactions to see different views.

The ability to specify arbitrary operations on objects, rather than just reads and writes, is essential for modelling and analysing type-specific concurrency control algorithms. The lack of any constraints on the state of the real system allows us to focus on the observable behavior of the system as seen by the transactions, rather than on the details of how it is implemented. As a result, fewer constraints are placed on the structure of the real system, and obtain more general correctness criteria that can be applied to a broader range of algorithms.

Different transactions can see different views in the following manner. If two siblings T_1 and T_2 are running concurrently in a schedule α of a real system and neither has completed, there cannot be a single serial schedule β such that $\beta|T_1 = \alpha|T_1$ and $\beta|T_2 = \alpha|T_2$. If there were, then T_1 and T_2 would both be active in β, yet in a serial schedule siblings must run sequentially. However, α could still be serially correct for T_1 and serially correct for T_2, since there might be distinct serial schedules β_1 and β_2 such that $\beta_1|T_1 = \alpha|T_1$ and $\beta_2|T_2 = \alpha|T_2$. In a system that ensures serial correctness for non-orphan transactions, concurrently active siblings that are not orphans will necessarily see different serial views. A similar scenario illustrates that orphans will in general see different views from non-orphans in a system that ensures serial correctness for all transactions.

While different transactions are allowed to see different views, and as illustrated in the previous paragraph, must see different views in some cases, most real systems guarantee that there is a single serial schedule that looks the same to all transactions that are visible to T_0. (T_1 is visible to T_2 if every ancestor of T_1 up to but not including the least common ancestor with T_2 has committed. If a transaction is visible to T_0, it and each of its ancestors up through its top-level ancestor have committed.) It can be useful to prove this stronger condition when verifying the correctness of an algorithm.

12.6 Modeling algorithms

As mentioned earlier, there are many components to a transaction management system — concurrency control, recovery, commit protocols, and orphan detection — that work together to ensure correctness. In this section we discuss how concurrency control and recovery algorithms can be modelled. (As mentioned earlier, our analysis of recovery covers only recovery from aborts, not crashes.)

One approach to modelling concurrency control and recovery is to use a single automaton — the 'database' — that handles concurrency control and recovery for all objects. A more useful approach for distributed systems that more directly captures the modular decomposition of programs written in a language like Argus is to model each object as a separate automaton. We can then think of concurrency control and recovery as being done separately at each object. Many concurrency control algorithms can be viewed in this way.

Regarding concurrency control and recovery as being done separately at each object provides useful modularity in building systems, since different algorithms can be used at different objects in the system. For example, an object that is accessed frequently by many transactions may need a complex concurrency algorithm that uses the semantics of the operations on the object to provide a high level of concurrency. However, the concurrency control algorithms at different objects cannot be chosen completely independently. For example, suppose that one object uses two-phase locking (Eswaran *et al.* (1976)) and another object uses multi-version timestamping (Reed (1983)). Suppose we have two top-level transactions A and B, with timestamps 1 and 2 respectively. The multi-version timestamping object will ensure that A and B are serializable in the order of their timestamps, namely A followed by B. However, if B writes the two-phase locking object and A reads it, then the two-phase locking object will ensure that A is serialized *after* B. In this case there is no single serialization order that works for all objects, and the system will not ensure serial correctness.

The fundamental problem that must be solved is to ensure that the objects in the system agree on a serialization order for the transactions. The problem in the example above is that the different algorithms choose different orders: multi-version timestamping chooses an order based on the timestamps, which might be assigned when each transaction starts running, while two-phase locking chooses an order based on the order in which the transactions access the object.

We can classify concurrency control algorithms based on the serialization order they produce. Informally, *dynamic atomic* algorithms, such as two-phase locking (Eswaran *et al.* (1976)), ensure that transactions are serializable in the order in which they commit. *Static atomic* algorithms, such as multi-version timestamping (Reed (1983)), ensure that transactions are serializable in the order of time-stamps assigned to each transaction when it starts running. *Hybrid atomic* algorithms, such as the methods described in Weihl (1987b), distinguish between read-only and update transactions; update transactions are serialized in commit order based on timestamps assigned when they commit, while read-only trans-actions are serialized based on timestamps assigned when they start running.

In designing a system, a *global* decision must be made about the serialization order to be used. One way of documenting this decision is to define a *local atomicity property* to be satisfied by all objects in a system. A local atomicity property is a property P of individual objects such that if all objects satisfy P, the system is serially correct. This definition of local atomicity properties corresponds to the three classes of algorithms described above. The choice of a local atomicity pro-perty can be hard to make, and is also difficult to change. Once the choice is made, the question of correctness can be addressed independently at each object. Thus, a system can be modified by adding, deleting, or changing transactions and objects; as long as each object satisfies the local atomicity property for the system, serial correctness is guaranteed.

In the remainder of this section, ways in which a particular locking algorithm can be described and analysed are shown. We describe the algorithm for a sin-gle object, and show that it ensures *dynamic atomicity*. Thus, this algorithm could be used at some objects and other algorithms at other objects; as long as the oth-ers also ensure dynamic atomicity, the system will be serially correct.

The algorithm uses the specification of the object (given by the serial object automaton) to eliminate some conflicts: operations are required to conflict only if they do not commute. Before describing how the algorithm works at an object, we show how to model a concurrent system.

12.6.1 Concurrent systems

In a serial system, as described earlier, siblings execute sequentially and aborted transactions have no effect. In a concurrent system, siblings can execute con-currently and partially executed transactions can abort. Concurrency control and recovery algorithms must ensure that concurrently executing siblings *appear* to execute sequentially, and that aborted transactions *appear* to have no effect. The transactions in a concurrent system are the same as in a serial system. However, the rest of the system is different. Instead of a serial object automaton, a *concurrent object automaton* $C(X)$ is used for each object X and, instead of the serial scheduler, a *concurrent controller automaton* is used. The concurrent controller serves the same role as the serial scheduler, handling communication among transactions and objects. However, it allows siblings to run concurrently and it allows partially executed transactions to abort.

The concurrent object automaton $C(X)$ has the following input and output actions:

Input:
  Create(T), for T an access to X
  Inform_Commit_At(X)OF(T), for $T \neq T_0$
  Inform_Abort_At(X)OF(T), for $T \neq T_0$
Output:
  Request_Commit(T,v), for T an access to X and v a value

To do concurrency control and recovery, it must be known when transactions have committed and aborted. Thus, in addition to the Create and Request_Commit actions of a serial object, a concurrent object has Inform_Commit and Inform_Abort actions.

As with serial objects, some simple syntactic constraints on concurrent objects must be assumed. In particular, we assume that the concurrent object $C(X)$ preserves the following well-formedness properties:

● No Create or Request_Commit action appears twice;

● a Request_Commit(T,v) output action is preceded (not necessarily immediately) by a Create(T) action;

● there is at most one Request_Commit for a given access to X; and

● if T is an access to X, then Inform_Commit_At(X)OF(T) is preceded by a Request_Commit(T,v) for some v.

In other words, the object does not respond to an operation that has not been invoked, and does not respond more than once to the same access; the environment is required not to invoke the same access twice, and not to inform the object that an access has committed unless the access actually ran. Notice that, in contrast to the constraints on serial objects, we do not require the accesses to be non-overlapping.

A concurrent system also includes a *concurrent controller automaton*, which has the same actions as the serial scheduler, along with Inform_Commit and Inform_Abort output actions:

Input:
  Request_Create(T), for $T \neq T_0$
  Request_Commit(T,v)
Output:
  Create(T)
  Commit(T), for $T \neq T_0$
  Abort(T), for $T \neq T_0$
  Report_Commit(T,v), for $T \neq T_0$ and v a value
  Report_Abort(T), for $T \neq T_0$
  Inform_Commit_At(X)OF(T), for X an object and $T \neq T_0$
  Inform_Abort_At(X)OF(T), for X an object and $T \neq T_0$

As in a serial system, the input actions are intended to be identified with the corresponding outputs of transaction and concurrent object automata, and similarly for the output actions.

Each state s of the concurrent controller consists of six sets: s.create_requested, s.created, s.commit_requested, s.committed, s.aborted, and s.reported. The set s.commit_requested is a set of (transaction,value) pairs, and the others are sets of transactions. There is exactly one start state, in which the set create_requested is $\{T_0\}$, and the other sets are empty. define s.completed to be s.committed $\cup$ s.aborted.

The transition relation of the concurrent controller is as follows:

Request_Create(T), for $T \neq T_0$
  Postcondition: s.create_requested = s'.create_requested $\cup$ $\{T\}$

Request_Commit(T,v)
  Postcondition: s.commit_requested = s'.commit_requested $\cup$ $\{(T,v)\}$

Create(T)
  Precondition: $T \in s'$.create_requested — s'.created
  Postcondition: s.created = s'.created $\cup$ $\{T\}$

Commit(T), for $T \neq T_0$
  Precondition: $(T,v) \in s'$.commit_requested for some v
               $T \notin s'$.completed
  Postcondition: s.committed = s'.committed $\cup$ $\{T\}$

Abort(T), for $T \neq T_0$
  Precondition: $T \in s'$.create_requested — s'.completed
  Postcondition: s.aborted = s'.aborted $\cup$ $\{T\}$

Report_Commit(T,v), for $T \neq T_0$ and v a value
  Precondition: $T \in s'$.committed
               $(T,v) \in s'$.commit_requested
               $T \notin s'$.reported
  Postcondition: s.reported = s'.reported $\cup$ $\{T\}$

Report_Abort(T), for $T \neq T_0$
  Precondition: $T \in s'$.aborted
               $T \notin s'$.reported
  Postcondition: s.reported = s'.reported $\cup$ $\{T\}$

Inform_Commit_At(X)OF(T), for $T \neq T_0$
  Precondition: $T \in s'$.committed

Inform_Abort_At(X)OF(T), for $T \neq T_0$
  Precondition: $T \in s'$.aborted

There are two main differences between the concurrent controller and the serial scheduler. First, the Create(T) and Abort(T) actions no longer have the preconditions requiring siblings to run sequentially and preventing a transaction from being aborted if it has been created. Second, the Inform actions have been added, and can occur whenever the corresponding decision (Commit or Abort) has occurred.

12.6.2 Type-specific locking

A locking algorithm will now be described for a single object X. First, we need to define when two operations commute. The formal notion of an operation used here includes the value returned by an invocation, allowing us to use the value returned by an operation in testing for conflicts. In effect, this gives us a finer granularity of locking. Formally, if T is an access to X, we call the sequence Create(T); Request_Commit(T,v) an *operation* of X; informally, this corresponds to a single execution of the access T. Commutativity for operations is defined in this formal sense, rather than just for accesses. The letters P and Q will denote operations.

A technical definition is needed first. Let α and β be finite sequences of actions of $S(X)$; then α is *equieffective* to β if, for every sequence γ of actions of $S(X)$ such that both $\alpha\gamma$ and $\beta\gamma$ are well formed, $\alpha\gamma$ is a schedule of $S(X)$ if and only if $\beta\gamma$ is a schedule of $S(X)$. Informally, two sequences are equieffective if they cannot be distinguished by later computations; their 'future histories' as determined by the automaton $S(X)$ are the same. (The restriction to well-formed extensions is a technicality that does not affect the intuition underlying the definition.) Two schedules that leave $S(X)$ in the same state are clearly equieffective. In addition, schedules with different final states can be equieffective if the differences in the states cannot be observed (for example, if the state includes internal bookkeeping information that does not affect the values returned by operations).

Now, two operations P and Q are defined to *commute* if, for any sequence of operations ψ such that ψP and ψQ are well-formed schedules of $S(X)$, ψPQ and ψQP are equieffective well-formed schedules of $S(X)$. In other words, if P can be executed after ψ, and so can Q, then P and Q can both be executed in either order after ψ, and the order in which they are executed cannot be determined by later computations.

The locking algorithm allows transactions to execute concurrently as long as their operations commute in the sense defined above. The algorithm works by maintaining an 'intentions list' for each transaction. When a transaction commits, its intentions list is appended to its parent's; when it aborts, its intentions list is discarded. Also, before executing an operation P for a transaction, the intentions lists for all concurrent transactions are first checked to make sure that none of the operations already executed by those transactions conflict (do not commute) with P. If there are no conflicts with concurrent transactions, the operation can be executed; otherwise, it must block.

The algorithm is described by a particular concurrent object automaton CBL(X) (for 'conflict-based locking') defined as follows. A state s of CBL(X) has components s.created, s.run, and s.intentions. Of these, created and run are

sets of accesses to X, initially empty, and `intentions` is a function from transactions to sequences of operations of X, initially mapping every transaction to
the empty sequence Λ. When the operation P is in the sequence
s.`intentions`(T), T *holds a P-lock* in s. Given a state s and a transaction T,
$view(T,s)$ (the view of T in state s) is defined recursively as follows: $view(T_0,s) =$
s.`intentions`(T_0); $view(T,s)$ = $view(parent(T),s)s$.`intentions`(T). In other
words, a transaction's 'view' is the concatenation of the intentions lists for its
ancestors, starting with T_0. The transition relation is as follows:

> `Create`(T), for T an access to X
>   Postcondition: s.`created` $= s'$.`created` $\cup \{T\}$

> `Inform_Commit_At`(X)OF(T), $T \neq T_0$
>   Postcondition: s.`intentions`$(T) = \Lambda$
> s.`intentions`$(parent(T)) = s'$.`intentions`$(parent(T))s'$.`intentions`(
> s.`intentions`$(U) = s'$.`intentions`(U), for $U \neq T$, $parent(T)$

> `Inform_Abort_At`(X)OF(T), $T \neq T_0$
>   Postcondition: s.`intentions`$(U) = \Lambda$, for U a descendant of T
> s.`intentions`$(U) = s'$.`intentions`(U) for U not a descendant of T

> `Request_Commit`(T,v), for T an access to X
>   Precondition: $T \in s'$.`created` $- s'$.`run`
>   let P be the operation `Create`(T)`Request_Commit`(T,v)
>   for every U that is not an ancestor of T, and every operation Q
>   in s'.`intentions`(U), P commutes with Q
> $view(T,s')P$ is a schedule of $S(X)$
>   Postcondition: s.`run` $= s'$.`run` $\cup \{T\}$
> s.`intentions`$(T) = s'$.`intentions`$(T)P$
> s.`intentions`$(U) = s'$.`intentions`(U), for $U \neq T$

When an access transaction is created, it is recorded in the set s.`created`. When
an `Inform_Commit_At`(X)OF(T) is received, T's intentions list is appended to its
parent's; when an `Inform_Abort_At`(X)OF(T) is received, T's intentions list is
discarded, as are the intentions lists of T's descendants (since aborting a transaction effectively aborts all its descendants as well). This generalizes the
approach taken by Moss, Griffeth, and Graham (1986) in implementing read-
write locking for nested transactions, in which locks and versions are passed to
the parent when a transaction commits, and are discarded when a transaction
aborts. Finally, a response containing the return value v to an access T can be
returned only if T has been created but not yet responded to, every holder of a
conflicting lock is an ancestor of T, and v is a value that can be returned by T
in T's view according to the serial object $S(X)$.

The algorithm described above ensures *dynamic atomicity*, a local atomicity property that characterizes the behavior of concurrency control algorithms that serialize transactions in the order that they complete. In a nested transaction system, the appropriate notion for a serialization order is what we call a *sibling*

order. A sibling order is a partial order on transactions that only relates siblings. Alternatively, a sibling order can be thought of as a family of partial orders, one for the children of each transaction. Recall that in an execution of the serial system siblings execute sequentially; this sequential order can be described by a sibling order.

For dynamic atomic algorithms, the appropriate sibling order is the *completion order*, defined as follows. Given a schedule α of a concurrent system, *completion*(α) is defined to be the binary relation on siblings such that $(U, U') \in$ completion(α) if either both U and U' complete (commit or abort) in α and U completes before U', or U completes in α and U' does not. Dynamic atomic algorithms ensure serial correctness for all non-orphans by giving each non-orphan T a serial view that consists of the accesses visible to T, ordered according to the completion order. Notice that the completion order relates siblings; if U and U' are siblings such that $(U, U') \in$ completion(α), we can extend the order to the descendants of U and U' by ordering all descendants of U before all descendants of U'. This corresponds to the order of execution in a serial system in which U completes before U', since the descendants of U must complete before U itself can complete, and U' and its descendants don't start running until U has finished in a serial execution.

If β is a schedule of $C(X)$, dynamic atomicity requires, for each non-orphan transaction T, that the accesses visible to T must be serializable in the completion order. In other words, there must be a schedule of $S(X)$ containing the accesses in β that are visible to T in the order given by the completion order, and the accesses must return the same results in the schedule of $S(X)$ as in β. Note, however, that the notions of 'non-orphans', 'visible accesses', and 'completion order' depend on Commit and Abort actions, which occur in a schedule of a concurrent system, but not in the local schedule at $C(X)$. The problem here is to use the information available locally to $C(X)$ to ensure dynamic atomicity. It is easy to define local versions of 'orphan' and 'visible accesses', based on the Inform actions that have occurred. For the completion order, however, we can only approximate it given local information. The following example illustrates the problem. Suppose T and T' are sibling accesses to X that are running concurrently, and that the following schedule occurs (for the entire system):

```
...
Create(T)
Request_Commit(T,v)
Create(T')
Request_Commit(T', v')
Commit(T)
Commit(T')
Inform_Commit_At(X)OF(T)
Inform_Commit_At(X)OF(T')
```

In this schedule, T completed before T', but, based on what happened at X, it is not certain which completed first. This is because the following schedule contains the same sub-schedule at X:

```
...
Create(T)
Request_Commit(T,v)
Create(T')
Request_Commit(T', v')
Commit(T')
Commit(T)
Inform_Commit_At(X)OF(T)
Inform_Commit_At(X)OF(T')
```

The only difference between this schedule and the previous one is that the order of the Commit actions is reversed; the Inform_Commit actions appear in the same order. Thus, X cannot know which actually completed first. However, there are situations in which an object *can* know that one transaction completed before another; for example, consider the following schedule:

```
...
Create(T)
Request_Commit(T,v)
Create(T')
Commit(T)
Inform_Commit_At(X)OF(T)
Request_Commit(T', v')
Commit(T')
Inform_Commit_At(X)OF(T')
```

Since Inform_Commit_At(X)OF(T) occurred before Request_Commit(T',v'), X can tell that T must have completed before T', since Commit(T) must occur before Inform_Commit_At(X)OF(T), and Commit(T') must occur after Request_Commit(T',v').

The local information available to X about the completion order gives us a partial order on accesses; the actual completion order could be any total order consistent with that partial order. To ensure dynamic atomicity, an object must ensure that the accesses (locally) visible to a (local) non-orphan transaction T are serializable in all orders consistent with its local knowledge of the completion order. (To be able to prove inductively that an algorithm ensures dynamic atomicity, it is also useful to require that all serialization orders consistent with the local knowledge at X are 'equivalent', in the sense that the resulting schedules of $S(X)$ are all equieffective.)

This can be illustrated by considering how the algorithm described by CBL(X) behaves in the three scenarios above. For simplicity, assume that nothing happens at X before the actions shown in the schedules above. Let P be the operation Create(T)Request_Commit(T,v), and let Q be the operation Create(T')Request_Commit(T',v'). The first two schedules do not differ at X, so they are considered together. In these schedules, T and T' run one after the other before any Inform actions occur, so each gets a 'view' that is an empty sequence of operations (corresponding to an initial state of $S(X)$). Then, by the precondition on Request_Commit actions in CBL(X), the operation sequence consisting of P alone is a schedule of S(X), as is the operation sequence consisting of Q alone. Now consider the parent of T and T'. At the end of each of the first two schedules, T and T' are both visible to their parent. Since the local information at X does not tell us whether T or T' completed first, dynamic atomicity requires them to be serializable in both orders; in other words, the operation sequences PQ and QP must be schedules of $S(X)$. Notice that the precondition on Request_Commit actions in CBL(X) also requires P to commute with Q; since P is a schedule of $S(X)$, and so is Q, it follows from the definition of commutativity that PQ and QP are both schedules of $S(X)$, and that they are equieffective. This is exactly what is required for dynamic atomicity.

In the third schedule above, the Request_Commit(T',v') action uses a view consisting of the operation P, so by the precondition on Request_Commit(T',v'), the operation sequence PQ is a schedule of $S(X)$. If the parent of T and T' at the end of the schedule are considered again, it can be seen that it is necessary to ensure that T and T' are serializable in all orders consistent with the local information at X. As discussed above, however, it can be deduced from what happened at X that T completed before T', so we only need to ensure that T is serializable before T', that is, that PQ is a schedule of $S(X)$. As argued above, the precondition on Request_Commit actions ensures this.

The examples given above illustrate the basic idea underlying the algorithm. They can easily be extended to construct an inductive proof of correctness.

12.7 Discussion

Nested transactions introduce two modelling problems not raised by single-level transactions: the meaning of aborted subtransactions, and modelling concurrent children. Serial systems, as discussed above, give a precise semantics to aborts and to concurrent children. In a serial system, aborted transactions take no steps, and hence have no effect; in addition, siblings that appear to overlap actually execute sequentially. Serial systems are used to define correctness of more complex systems: a system that allows siblings to run concurrently or to abort after a partial execution must 'look like' a serial system to the transactions. Several alternative definitions of correctness, which vary in their requirements for subtransactions and for orphans were discussed.

An important aspect of the approach to defining correctness taken here is that the focus is on the interface between the transactions and the rest of the system, and properties of the observable behavior at that interface are defined. This leads to a definition of correctness that is quite general, and can be applied to a wide variety of algorithms. For example, it allows us to deal easily with type-specific algorithms, as well as with algorithms in which concurrency control and recovery are tightly coupled.

Other transaction management algorithms, such as commit protocols and orphan detection algorithms, can also be modelled within the framework described above. For example, orphan detection algorithms can be modelled as modified controllers in the concurrent system (see Herlihy et al. (1987)).

A type-specific locking algorithm has also been defined, and the steps involved in verifying the algorithm have been sketched. A similar approach can be used to verify many other concurrency control algorithms. One of the most important steps in verifying (or designing) a concurrency control algorithm is to identify the serialization order produced by the algorithm; this corresponds to defining a local atomicity property. In the case of dynamic atomic algorithms, the serialization order is the completion order, while in the case of timestamp-based algorithms, it is the timestamp order (which might correspond to the order in which the transactions are started). Given the serialization order, the constraints on the behavior of each object can be determined by considering the local information available to the object about the global execution. This was illustrated by showing how each object has only partial information about the global completion order; an object must ensure that transactions are serializable in all orders consistent with its local information.

12.8 References

J. Aspnes, A. Fekete, N. Lynch, M. Merritt, and W. Weihl (1988). 'A Theory of Timestamp-Based Concurrency Control for Nested Transactions'. *Proceedings 14th International Conference on Very Large Data Bases*, Los Angeles, CA, 1988.

C. Beeri, P. Bernstein, and N. Goodman (1986). *A Model for Concurrency in Nested Transaction Systems*. Technical Report-86-03, Wang Institute of Graduate Studies, 1986.

P. A. Bernstein and N. Goodman (1981). 'Concurrency Control in Distributed Database Systems'. *ACM Computing Surveys* 13 (2): 185—221, June 1981.

P. A. Bernstein, V. Hadzilacos, and N. Goodman (1987). *Concurrency Control and Recovery in Database Systems*, Volume . Addison Wesley, Reading, MA, 1987.

K. P. Eswaran, J. N. Gray, R. A. Lorie, and I. L. Traiger (1976). 'The Notions of Consistency and Predicate Locks in a Database System'. *Communications of the ACM* 19 (11): 624—633, November 1976.

A. Fekete, N. Lynch, M. Merritt, and W. Weihl (1987a). 'Nested Transactions and Read/Rrite Locking'. *Proceedings 6th Symp. on Principles of Database Systems*: 97—111, San Diego, CA, 1987. (A longer version with complete proofs can be found in MIT/LCS/TM-324.)

A. Fekete, N. Lynch, M. Merritt, and W. Weihl (1987b). *Nested Transactions, Conflict-Based Locking, and Dynamic Atomicity.* MIT/LCS/TM-340, MIT Laboratory for Computer Science, 1987.

M. Herlihy (1986). 'Optimistic Concurrency Control for Abstract Data Types'. *Proceedings 5th Symposium on Principles of Distributed Computing*: 206—217, Calgary, Alberta, Canada, 1986.

M. Herlihy (1987). 'Extending Multiversion Time-Stamping Protocols to Exploit Type Information'. *IEEE Transactions on Computers* **C-36** (4), 1987.

M. Herlihy, N. Lynch, M. Merritt, and W. Weihl (1987). 'On the correctness of orphan elimination algorithms'. *Proceedings 17th International Symposium on Fault-tolerant Computing*: 8—13, Pittsburgh, PA, 1987. (Longer version with complete proofs in MIT/LCS/TM-329.)

M. Herlihy and J. Wing (1987). 'Avalon: Language Support for Reliable Distributed Systems'. *Proceedings 17th International Symposium on Fault-Tolerant Computing*: 89—95, Pittsburgh, 1987. (Also published as CMU-Computer Science Department Technical Report CMU-Computer Science Department-86-167.)

M. Herlihy and W. Weihl (1988). 'Hybrid Concurrency Control for Abstract Data Types'. *Proceedings of the ACM Symposium on Principles of Database Systems*, Austin, 1988.

C. A. R. Hoare (1978). 'Communicating Sequential Processes'. *Communications of the ACM* **21** (8): 666—677, August 1978.

IBM. *IBM Program Product General Information Manual.* GH20-9069-2, IMS/VS Version 1 Fast Path Feature.

H. T. Kung and J. T. Robinson (1981). 'On Optimistic Methods for Concurrency Control'. *ACM Transactions on Database Systems* **6** (2): 213—226, June 1981.

B. Liskov and R. Scheifler (1983). 'Guardians and Actions: Linguistic Support for Robust, Distributed Programs'. *ACM Transactions on Programming Languages and Systems* **5** (3): 381—404, July 1983.

B. Liskov, R. Scheifler, E. F. Walker, and W. Weihl (1987). *Orphan Detection.* Programming Methodology Group Memo 53, MIT Laboratory for Computer Science, 1987. (Appeared in the Seventeenth Internation Symposium on Fault-Tolerant Computing, July 1987.)

N. Lynch and M. Tuttle (1987). 'Hierarchical correctness proofs for distributed algorithms'. *Proceedings 6th ACM Symposium on Principles of Distributed Computing*: 137—151, Vancouver, 1987. (For more details see MIT/LCS/Technical Report-387.)

J. Moss, N. Griffeth, and M. Graham (1986). *Abstraction in concurrency control and recovery management (revised)*. COINS Technical Report 86-20, University of Massachusetts at Amherst, 1986.

P. O'Neil (1986). 'The Escrow Transactional Method'. *ACM Transactions on Database Systems* 11 (4): 405—430, 1986.

C. H. Papadimitriou (1979). 'The Serializability of Concurrent Database Updates'. *Journal of the ACM* 26 (4): 631—653, October 1979.

D. P. Reed (1983). 'Implementing Atomic Actions on Decentralized Data'. *ACM Transactions on Computer Systems* 1: 3—23, Feb 1983.

A. Reuter (1982). 'Concurrency on high-traffic data elements'. *Proceedings Symposium on Principles of Database Systems*: 83—92, Los Angeles, CA, 1982.

(1987). A. Spector and K. Swedlow (Eds.). *Guide to the Camelot Distributed Transaction Facility*. CMU Computer Science Department, 1987.

W. E. Weihl (1984). 'Specification and implementation of atomic data types'. *Ph.D. Thesis*, 1984. (Available as Technical Report MIT/LCS/Technical Report-314.)

W. E. Weihl and B. Liskov (1985). 'Implementation of Resilient, Atomic Data Types'. *ACM Transactions on Programming Languages and Systems* 7 (2): 244—269, April 1985.

W. E. Weihl (1987a). 'Local atomicity properties: modular concurrency control for abstract data types'. *ACM Transactions on Programming Languages and Systems*, 1987. (To appear.)

W. E. Weihl (1987b). 'Distributed version management for read-only actions'. *IEEE Transactions on Software Engineering* SE-13 (1): 55—64, 1987.

W. E. Weihl (1989). 'The Impact of Recovery on Concurrency Control'. *Proceedings 8th Symposium on Principles of Database Systems*, Philadelphia, PA, 1989.

PART VI

Replication

Replication is the fundamental method for achieving fault tolerance in a distributed system. If information were not replicated, a failure of the device holding that information would cause it to be lost. Replicating data is far from simple, however. If there are no sufficient guarantees as to the consistency of the replicated data, different data may be observed depending on the replica consulted.

Part VI presents two viewpoints on replication. In Chapter 13, Davidson discusses the problems of partition failures for maintaining replicated data consistency. Forbidding updates is often not viable, because of the nature of the information stored and the time it takes to repair the connection.

Chapter 14 describes a method of replicating data using reliable broadcast protocols. Joseph and Birman use event-ordering techniques with their reliable broadcast protocols in order to make node failures as transparent as possible. In Chapter 15, they describe how reliable broadcast and event ordering are used in the ISIS system to build a programming platform in which failures are made as transparent as possible.

Chapter 13

Replicated Data and Partition Failures

S. B. Davidson

In a distributed database system, data is often replicated to improve performance and availability. By storing copies of shared data on processors where it is frequently accessed, the need for expensive, remote read accesses is decreased. By storing copies of critical data on processors with independent failure modes, the probability that at least one copy of the data will be accessible increases. In theory, data replication makes it possible to provide arbitrarily high data availability.

In practice, realizing the benefits of data replication is difficult since the *correctness* of data must be maintained. One important aspect of correctness with replicated data is *mutual consistency*: all copies of the same logical data item must agree on exactly one 'current value' for the data item. Furthermore, this value should 'make sense' in terms of the transactions executed on copies of the data item. When communication fails between sites containing copies of the same logical data item, mutual consistency between copies becomes complicated to ensure. The most disruptive of these communication failures are *partition failures*, which fragment the network into isolated subnetworks called *partitions*. Unless partition failures are detected and recognized by all affected processors, independent and uncoordinated updates may be applied to different copies of the data, thereby compromising the correctness of data. Consider, for example, an airline reservation system implemented by a distributed database which splits into two partitions when the communication network fails. If, at the time of the failure, all the nodes have one seat remaining for a certain flight, reservations could be made in both partitions. This would violate correctness: who should get the last seat? There should not be more seats reserved for a flight than physically exist on the plane, although some airlines

Parts of this chapter were reprinted with permission from 'Consistency in Partitioned Networks' by Susan B. Davidson, Hector Garcia-Molina and Dale Skeen, ACM Computing Surveys 17(3) (Sept. 1985) pp 341-370.

do not implement this constraint and allow overbookings.

The design of a replicated data management algorithm tolerating partition failures (or *partition-processing strategy*) is notoriously hard. Typically, the cause or extent of a partition failure cannot be discerned by the processors themselves. At best, a processor may be able to identify the other processors in its partition; but, for the processors outside of its partition, it will not be able to distinguish between the case where those processors are simply isolated from it and the case where those processors are down. In addition, slow responses can cause the network to appear partitioned even when it is not, further complicating the design of a fault-tolerant algorithm.

However, the problems associated with maintaining correct operation in a partitioned distributed database system are not limited to the problems associated with the correctness of data. Due to the expense and complexity of maintaining replicated data, most distributed database systems limit the amount of replication to a few copies. Since data is not replicated at every site in the network, it is possible to pose *queries* (transactions that do *not* perform updates, also known as *read-only* transactions) during network partitioning for which not all data are available. Ideally in such a situation, the system should attempt to provide some level of service by providing *as good an answer as possible*. For example, if a doctor at a hospital wanted to query a distributed blood bank database to find how many pints of blood were available throughout the system, but only blood bank A were accessible due to a partition failure, a useful answer would be 'Blood bank A has 20 pints, but there may be more at other (currently inaccessible) sites.'

In this chapter, the tradeoffs involved in designing a partition-processing strategy will be discussed first. A formal notion of correctness in a replicated database system ('one-copy serializability') will then be given, along with an overview of several 'quorum-based' partition-processing strategies. We will then shift our attention away from the problem of *updating* during partition failures to the problem of answering *queries*, and present methods of providing partial answers in the face of unavailable data.

Although the discussion on updating transactions is couched within a database context, most results have more general applications. In fact, the only essential notion in many cases is that of a transaction. This means that these strategies are immediately applicable to mail systems, calendar systems, object-oriented systems, and other applications using transactions as their underlying model of processing.

13.1 Correctness versus availability

When designing a system that will operate when it is partitioned, the competing goals of availability (the system's normal function should be disrupted as little as possible) and correctness (data must be correct when recovery is complete) must somehow be met. These goals are not independent; hence, trade-offs are involved.

Correctness can be achieved simply by suspending operation in all but one of the partition groups and forwarding updates at recovery; but this severely compromises availability. In applications where partitions either occur frequently or occur when access to the data is imperative, this solution is not acceptable. For example, in the Airline Reservation System it may be too expensive to have a high connectivity network and partitions may occasionally occur. Many transactions are executed each second — TWA's centralized reservations system estimates 170 transactions per second at peak time (Gifford and Spector (1984)) — and each transaction that is not executed may represent the loss of a customer. In a military command and control application, a partition can occur because of an enemy attack, and it is precisely at this time that transaction processing must not be halted.

On the other hand, availability can be achieved simply by allowing all nodes to process transactions 'as usual' despite the partitioning (note that transactions can only execute if the data they reference is accessible). However, correctness may be compromised. Transactions may produce 'incorrect' results (such as more seats on a plane than are physically available) and the databases in each group may diverge. In some applications, such 'incorrect' results may be acceptable in light of the higher availability achieved: when partitions are reconnected, the problems may be corrected by executing transactions missed by a partition, and by choosing certain transactions to 'undo'. If the chosen transactions have had no real-world effects, they can be undone using standard database recovery methods. If, on the other hand, they have had real-world effects, then appropriate *compensating transactions* must be run, transactions which not only restore the values of the changed database items but also issue real-world actions to nullify the effects of the chosen transactions (for example, by cancelling certain reservations and sending messages to affected users). Alternatively, *correcting transactions* can be run, transforming the database from an incorrect state to a correct state without undoing the effects of any previous transactions. For instance, in a banking application, the correcting transaction for overdrawing a checking account during a partitioning would apply an overdraft charge. Of course, in some applications incorrect results are either unacceptable or incorrectable. For example, it may not be possible to undo or correct a transaction that effectively hands $1,000,000 to a customer.

Since it is clearly impossible to satisfy both goals simultaneously, one or both must be relaxed to some extent. Several partition processing strategies have been suggested that either *relax* correctness, or rely on compensating or correcting transactions to regain consistency once the partition is repaired (Davidson (1984); Garcia *et al.* (1983); Garcia and Kogan (1988); Kogan and Garcia (1987); Lynch, Blaustein, and Siegel (1986); Parker *et al.* (1983)). Other partition processing strategies have been suggested that *pre-analyze* transactions or use *type-specific* information to increase availability while guaranteeing correctness (Blaustein *et al.* (1983); Garcia and Kogan (1988); Herlihy (1986); Wright (1983)). Since most of these techniques require extensive knowledge about what the information in the database represents, how applications manipulate the information, and how much undoing, correcting, or compensating inconsistencies will cost, discussion of partition-processing strategies will be limited to a class that *guarantees* correctness, and does so in a *syntactic* manner (that is, no semantic understanding of the database is required). A more complete survey of these techniques can be found in Davidson, Garcia, and Skeen (1985), and an analysis of the limitations on availability for strategies that guarantee correctness can be found in Coan, Oki, and Kolodner (1986).

13.2 The notion of correctness

What does 'correct processing' mean in a database system? Informally, a database is correct if it correctly describes the external objects and processes that it is intended to model. In theory, such a vague notion of correctness could be formalized by a set of static constraints on objects and their attributes, and a set of dynamic constraints on how objects can interact and evolve. In practice, a complete specification of the constraints governing even a small database is impractical (besides, even if it were practical, enforcing the constraints would not be). Consequently, database systems use a less ambitious, very general notion of correctness based on the order of transaction execution, *one-copy serializability*, and on a small set of static data constraints known as *integrity constraints*.

In this section, the notion of correctness is examined, beginning informally with examples illustrating incorrect behaviour, followed by a more formal definition of correctness in the traditional database system. When referring to the state of the database, the terms 'correct' and 'consistent' are used interchangeably.

13.2.1 Anomalies

Consider a banking database that contains a checking account and a savings account for a certain customer, with a copy of each account stored at sites A and B. Suppose a communication failure isolates the two sites. Figure 13.1 shows the result of executing a checking account withdrawal at A (for \$100) and two checking account withdrawals at B (totalling \$100). Although the resulting copies of the checking account contain the same value, we know intuitively that the actions of the system are incorrect: The account owner withdrew \$200 from a checking account actually containing only \$100. The anomaly is caused by conflicting write operations issued in parallel by transactions executing in different partitions.

An interesting aspect of this example is that in the resulting database all copies are mutually consistent, that is, all copies of a data item contain the same value.† Thus, although it is commonly used as the correctness criterion for replicated file systems and information databases, such as telephone directories, mutual consistency is not a sufficient condition for correctness in a transaction-

---

† This is the narrowest interpretation of several uses of the term 'mutual consistency' that appear in the literature. Some authors use mutual consistency synonymously with one-copy serializability (defined in the next section).

Site A   **Site B**

Checking:	$ 100
Savings:	$ 200

Checking:	$ 100
Savings:	$ 200

$$\text{Checking} := \text{Checking} - \$25$$

$$\text{Checking} := \text{Checking} - \$100$$

$$\text{Checking} := \text{Checking} - \$75$$

Checking:	$ 0
Savings:	$ 200

Checking:	$ 0
Savings:	$ 200

Figure 13.1 An anomaly resulting from concurrent write operations on the same data item in separate partitions.

oriented database system. It is also not a necessary condition: consider the example where A executes the $100 withdrawal while B does nothing. Although the resulting copies of the checking account contain different values, the resulting database is correct if the system recognizes that the value in A's copy is the most recent one.

A different type of anomaly on the same database is illustrated in Figure 13.2. It shows the result of executing a checking withdrawal of $200 at site A, and a savings withdrawal of $200 at site B. Here, we assume that the semantics of the checking withdrawal allow the account to be overdrawn as long as the overdraft is covered by funds in the savings account (Checking + Savings $\geq$ 0). The semantics of the savings withdrawal are similar.

In the execution illustrated, however, these semantics are violated: $400 is

Site A   **Site B**

Checking:	$ 100
Savings:	$ 200

Checking:	$ 100
Savings:	$ 200

if Savings + Checking > $200 then
  Checking := Checking — $200

if Savings + Checking > $200 then
  Savings := Savings — $200

Checking:	— $ 100
Savings:	$ 200

Checking:	$ 100
Savings:	$ 0

Figure 13.2 An anomaly resulting from concurrent read and write operations in different partitions.

withdrawn, whereas the accounts together contain only $ 300. The anomaly was not caused by conflicting writes (none existed since the transactions updated different accounts), but rather because accounts are allowed to be read in one partition and updated in another.

Concurrent reads and writes in different partitions are not the only sources of inconsistency in a partitioned system, nor do they always cause inconsistencies. For example, if the savings withdrawal in Figure 13.2 is changed to a deposit, the intended semantics of the database would not be violated. However, the above are typical anomalies that can occur if conflicting transactions are executed in different partitions.

13.2.2 One-copy serializability

A database is a set of *logical data items* that support the basic operations *read* and *write*. The granularity of these items is not important: they could be records, files, relations, etc. The *state* of the database is an assignment of values to the logical data items. For brevity, logical data items are subsequently called data items or, more simply, items.

A *transaction* is a program that issues read and write operations on the data items, and either terminates successfully (*commits*) or fails (*aborts*). In addition, a transaction may have effects that are external to the database, such as dispensing money or displaying results on a user's terminal. The items read by a transaction constitute its *readset*; the items written, its *writeset*. A *read-only transaction* (or *query*) neither issues write requests nor has external effects. Transactions are assumed to be correct, that is a transaction, when executed alone, transforms an initially correct database state into another correct state (Traiger *et al.* (1982)).

Transactions interact with one another indirectly by reading and writing the same data items. Two operations on the same item are said to *conflict* if at least one of them is a write. Conflicts are often labelled either *read-write*, *write-read*, or *write-write* depending on the types of data operations involved and their order of execution (Bernstein and Goodman (1981)). Conflicting operations are significant because their order of execution affects the final database state.

A generally accepted notion of correctness for a database system is that it executes transactions so that they appear to users as indivisible, isolated actions on the database. This property, referred to as *atomic* execution, is achieved by guaranteeing the following properties:

1. The execution of each transaction is 'all or nothing': either all of the transaction's writes and external operations are performed or none are performed. (In the former case the transaction is said to be *committed*; in the latter case, *aborted*.) This property is often referred to as *atomic commitment*.

2. The execution of several transactions concurrently produces the same database state as some serial execution of the same transactions. The execution is then said to be *serializable*.

The first property is established by the commit and recovery algorithms of the database system (such as logging techniques (Gray *et al.* (1981); Verhofstad (1978))); the second, by the concurrency control algorithm. For now, we will concentrate on the concurrency control aspects of transaction processing and assume that site and transaction failures are tolerated correctly.

> **EXAMPLE:** As an example of how concurrent execution can produce incorrect results in a *centralized* database, consider the concurrent activity at site B in Figure 13.1. Here, two transactions, T_1 and T_2, concurrently withdraw money from a checking account, represented as x. A withdrawal transaction T_i could be represented by the following operations:
>
> $$T_i : r_i(x), w_i(x),$$
>
> where r_i represents a read operation and w_i a write operation of the new value of x by transaction T_i. For transaction T_1, $w_1(x)$ writes a value of x that is \$25 less than the value read by $r_1(x)$; for transaction T_2, $w_2(x)$ writes a value of x that is \$75 less than the value read by $r_2(x)$. The following sequence of operations (or *history*) represents an execution that is intuitively incorrect:
>
> $$H = r_1(x), r_2(x), w_1(x), w_2(x).$$
>
> Although the customer withdrew a total of \$100 from the account, H only reflects the execution of *one* withdrawal transaction. Since both transactions read the same initial value of x (\$100), the final value of x, written by T_2, is \$25. H is not serializable; there is also no serial execution of T_1 and T_2 that results in a final value of \$25 for x. For example, the serial execution of T_1 before T_2 would be:
>
> $$H_s = r_1(x), w_1(x), r_2(x), w_2(x).$$
>
> Since T_2 reads the value of x produced by T_1 (\$75), the final value written by T_2 is \$0. This would also be the final value for x if T_2 were executed before T_1.
>
> One concurrency control technique that would have avoided this anomaly is *strict two-phase locking* (Eswaran *et al.* (1976)). Before executing a write operation, the transaction must acquire an exclusive lock on the data item; before executing a read operation, the transaction must acquire at least a shared lock (if the transaction will later write the data item, an exclusive lock may be obtained). Exclusive locks are said to *conflict* with other shared or exclusive locks on the same data item; however, shared locks only conflict with exclusive locks on the same data item. Under strict two-phase locking, conflicting locks may not be granted, and any lock that is granted is held until the transaction terminates. If this technique had been used in H, T_1 would have acquired an exclusive lock on x before reading it, thus preventing T_2 from reading x until T_1 had written its new value for x. The result would have been the serial execution H_s.

Atomic transaction execution (the concurrent execution of transactions is serializable) together with the assumption that transactions are correct (a transaction executed alone transforms an initially correct database state into another correct state) imply by induction that the execution of any set of transactions transforms an initially correct database state into a new, correct state. While atomic execution is not always necessary to preserve correctness, most real database systems implement it as their sole criterion of correctness. This is because atomic execution corresponds to users' intuitive model that transactions are processed sequentially, and can be enforced by very general mechanisms that determine the order of conflicting data operations (such as strict two-phase locking, shown in the previous example). These mechanisms are independent of both the semantics of the data being stored and of the transactions manipulating it.

Some systems allow additional correctness criteria to be expressed in the form of *integrity constraints*. Unlike atomicity, these are semantic constraints. They may range from simple constraints (the balance of checking accounts must be non-negative) to elaborate constraints that relate the values of many data items. In systems enforcing integrity constraints, a transaction is allowed only if its execution is atomic and its results satisfy the integrity constraints. To simplify the discussion, it will be assumed that integrity constraints are checked as part of the normal processing of a transaction (the withdrawal transaction fails if the checking account balance becomes negative).

Notice that it has not been specified whether a centralized or a distributed database system is being discussed; it has not been necessary to do so since the definitions, the properties of transaction processing, and the correctness criteria are the same in both. Of course, the algorithms for achieving correct transaction processing differ markedly between the two types of implementations.

In a *replicated database*, the value of each logical item x is stored in one or more *physical data items*, which are referred to as the *copies* of x. Each read and write operation issued by a transaction on some logical data item must be mapped by the database system to corresponding operations on physical copies. To be correct, the mapping must ensure that the concurrent execution of transactions on replicated data is equivalent to a serial execution on nonreplicated data, a property known as *one-copy serializability*. The logic that is responsible for performing this mapping is called the *replica control algorithm*.

> EXAMPLE: Continuing with the previous banking example, consider the situation in Figure 13.1. Here, transactions T_1 and T_2 execute at site B, while transaction T_3 executes at site A. If the concurrency control used at each site is strict two-phase locking, we know that the *local* execution will be serializable. However, the global execution may be incorrect due to an incorrect replica control algorithm. If we adopt a 'read-one, write-one' replica control (the *local copy* of a data item is read and updated), we get the execution in Figure 13.1. Letting the copies of x at A and B be x_A and x_B respectively, the withdrawal transactions become the following sequences of operations on physical copies:
>
> $T_3 : r_3(x_A), w_3(x_A),$
>
> $T_1 : r_1(x_B), w_1(x_B).$
>
> $T_2 : r_2(x_B), w_2(x_B).$

As shown in Figure 13.1, site A executes T_3 while site B executes T_1 followed by T_2. While mutual consistency is preserved ($x_A = x_B = \$200$), the result is incorrect since only $\$100$ was withdrawn from the logical data item x. The execution is *not* one-copy serializable since the execution of T_1, T_2 and T_3 in the distributed system does not reflect a serial execution of the transactions on the logical data item x.

However, if the replica control algorithm used in were 'read-one, write-all', this anomaly would have been avoided: A transaction must read one copy of a data item (usually, the nearest copy), but must update *all* copies. In this case, the withdrawal transactions become the following sequences of operations on physical copies:

$$T_3 : r_3(x_A),\ w_3(x_A),\ w_3(x_B)$$

$$T_1 : r_1(x_B),\ w_1(x_A),\ w_1(x_B)$$

$$T_2 : r_2(x_B),\ w_2(x_A),\ w_2(x_B).$$

Since each site uses strict two-phase locking as its concurrency control, if T_3 and T_1 both read the original value of x, deadlock will occur when they try to update the remote copies of x: T_3 holds an exclusive lock on x_A and cannot release the lock until it acquires an exclusive lock on x_B and completes, while T_1 holds an exclusive lock on x_B and cannot release the lock until it acquires an exclusive lock on x_A and completes. However, the following execution sequences at sites A and B respectively would avoid deadlock and are one-copy serializable:

$$H_A = r_3(x_A),\ w_3(x_A), \qquad\qquad\qquad w_1(x_A), \qquad w_2(x_A)$$
$$H_B = \qquad\qquad\qquad w_3(x_B),\ r_1(x_B),\ w_1(x_B),\ r_2(x_B),\ w_2(x_B)$$

Note that the joint execution of H_A and H_B corresponds to executing T_3, T_1 and then T_2 using the logical data item x.

Similar reasoning will lead the reader to conclude that the anomaly shown in Figure 13.2 would also be avoided using 'read-one, write-all' replica control together with strict two-phase locking.

As a correctness criterion, one-copy serializability is attractive for the same reasons that (normal) serializability is: it is intuitive, and it can be enforced using general-purpose mechanisms that are independent of the semantics of the database and of the transactions executed.

13.2.3 Partitioned operation

Let us now consider transaction processing in a partitioned network, where the communication connectivity of the system is broken by failures or by anticipated communication shutdowns. To keep the exposition simple, let us assume that the network is 'cleanly' partitioned (that is, any two sites in the same partition can communicate and any two sites in different partitions cannot communicate), the database is *completely replicated* (a copy of every item is at every site throughout the system), and one-copy serializability is the correctness criterion in use.

While the system is partitioned, each partition must determine which transactions it can execute without violating the correctness criteria. Actually, this can be thought of as two problems:

1.   Each partition must maintain correctness within the part of the database stored at the sites comprising the partition, and

2.   Each partition must make sure that its actions do not conflict with the actions of other partitions, so that the database is correct across all partitions.

If we assume that each site in the network is capable of detecting partition failures, then correctness *within* a partition can be maintained by adapting one of the standard replica control algorithms for nonpartitioned systems. For example, the sites in a partition can implement a write operation on a logical object by writing all available copies in the partition ('read-one, write-all-available'). This, along with a standard concurrency control protocol, ensures one-copy serializability in the partition.

The really difficult problem is ensuring one-copy serializability *across* partitions: it is not sufficient to run a replica control algorithm that is correct in each partition to ensure that overall transaction execution is one-copy serializable.

> **EXAMPLE**: Continuing with the banking example, suppose that a partition failure occurs before T_3 is executed at site A and T_1 and T_2 are executed at site B. If a 'read-one, write-all-available' replica control strategy were used, the resulting execution would be the same as the 'read-one, write-one' strategy in the previous section. Although the execution of T_1, T_2 and T_3 in their respective partitions is trivially one-copy serializable, conflicting operations occurred in different partitions, and the joint execution of both partitions is *not* one-copy serializable.

In addition to solving the problem of global correctness, a partition processing strategy must solve two problems of a different sort. First, when the partitioning occurs, the database is faced with the problem of atomically committing ongoing transactions. The complication is that the sites executing the transaction may find themselves in different partitions, and thus unable to communicate a decision regarding whether to complete the transaction (commit) or to undo it (abort). In many cases, it is impossible to make a decision within each partition that is consistent across partitions, and the transaction is forced to *wait* until the failure is repaired. In this case, the transaction is said to be *blocked*. Blocking is clearly undesirable since the availability of data is reduced; for example, locks on data items cannot be released until the transaction terminates. Unfortunately, while there are methods of reducing the likelihood of blocking, there are no nonblocking commit protocols for network partitions (Skeen (1982)). Note that the problem of atomic commitment in multiple partitions does not arise for a transaction submitted after the partitioning occurs (such a transaction will be executed in only one partition), and that this problem arises in any partitioned database system whether it is replicated or not.

Second, when partitions are reconnected, mutual consistency between copies in different partitions must be re-established. That is, the updates made to a logical data object in one partition must be propagated to its copies in the other partitions. Conceptually, this problem can be solved in a straightforward manner by extra bookkeeping whenever the system partitions. For example, each update applied in a partition can be logged, and this log can be sent to other partitions upon reconnection. (Such a log may be integrated with the 'recovery log' that is already kept by many systems.) In practice, an *efficient* solution to this problem is likely to be intricate and to depend on the normal recovery mechanisms employed in the database system. For this reason, it is not discussed further.

13.2.4 Modelling partitioned behaviour

To model the conflict between transactions in partitioned systems, we will use a *precedence graph†* (Davidson (1984)). A precedence graph models the necessary ordering between transactions, and is used to check serializability across partitions. They are adapted from serialization graphs, which are used to check serializability within a site (Papadimitriou (1979)). In the following, it is assumed that the readset of a transaction contains its writeset. The reason for this assumption is to avoid certain NP-complete problems in checking serializability, see Ullman (1988).

The transactions executed in each partition group during the failure are represented by a serial history of transactions, their readsets and writesets. Such a history must exist since, by assumption, transaction execution within a partition is serializable. For partition i, let T_{i1}, T_{i2}, . . . , T_{in} be the set of transactions, in serialization order, executed in i.

The nodes of the precedence graph represent transactions; the edges, interactions between transactions. The first step in the construction of the graph is to model conflicts between transactions *in the same partition* with precedence edges. A *precedence edge* $(T_{ij} \rightarrow T_{ik})$ represents the fact that T_{ij} wrote a copy that was later read by T_{ik} (write-read conflict), or that T_{ij} read a copy that was later changed by T_{ik} (read-write conflict). Since it is assumed that the readset of a transaction contains its writeset, write-write conflicts are subsumed by write-read conflicts. Note that both T_{ij} and T_{ik} are in the same partition group. In both cases, an edge from T_{ij} to T_{ik} indicates that in any equivalent serial execution, T_{ij} must precede T_{ik}. Note that the graph constructed so far must be acyclic since the orientation of an edge is always consistent with the serialization order.

To complete the precedence graph, conflicts between transactions in *different partitions* must be represented. This is modelled by interference edges. An

---

† A more complete modelling of partitioned behaviour is replicated data serialization graphs (Bernstein, Hadzilacos, and Goodman (1987)), however, precedence graphs are sufficient for this discussion.

interference edge ($T_{ij} \rightarrow T_{lk}$, $i \neq l$) indicates that T_{ij} read an item that is written by T_{lk} in another partition. The meaning of an interference edge is the same as a precedence edge: an interference edge from T_{ij} to T_{lk} indicates that T_{ij} logically 'executed before' T_{lk} since it did not read the value written by T_{lk}. An interference edge signals a read-write conflict between the two transactions, and indicates that any equivalent serial execution must maintain this order. (A write-write conflict manifests as a pair of read-write conflicts since each transaction's readset contains its writeset.)

> **EXAMPLE**: Suppose the serial history of transactions executed in P_1 is T_{11}, T_{12}, T_{13}, and that of P_2 is T_{21}, T_{22}. The precedence graph for this execution is given in Figure 13.3, where the readset of a transaction is given above the line and the writeset below the line. (Thus, transaction T_{12} reads b, c and writes c.) Note that the precedence graph contains the cycle
>
> $$T_{11} \rightarrow T_{12} \rightarrow T_{13} \rightarrow T_{21} \rightarrow T_{22} \rightarrow T_{11}$$

Intuitively, cycles in the precedence graph are bad because there is no equivalent serial execution: if T_{ij} and T_{kl} are in a cycle then the database reflects the results of T_{ij} executing before T_{kl} and of T_{kl} executing before T_{ij}, a contradiction. Conversely, the absence of cycles is good: the precedence graph for a set of partitions is acyclic if and only if the resulting database state is consistent (Davidson (1984)). An acyclic precedence graph indicates that the transactions from both groups are equivalent to a single serial history, and the last updated copy of each data item is the correct value. A serialization order for the transactions can be obtained by topologically sorting the precedence graph. Thus, the combined execution within the two groups is *one-copy serializable*.

In the previous example, since a cycle resulted in the precedence graph, the combined execution within the two partition groups is *not* one-copy serializable.

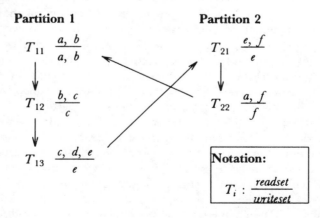

Figure 13.3 Conflict between transactions executed in different partitions indicated by a cycle in precedence graph.

In the next section, *quorum-based* partition processing strategies that guarantee acyclic precedence graphs will be discussed.

13.3 Quorum-based approaches

Quorum-based partition processing strategies attempt to increase the availability of data while guaranteeing one-copy serializability by adjusting the number of copies that must be accessed to successfully read and write within a partition. For example, in 'read-one, write-all' replica control, data items cannot be written by transactions in either partition after a single failure since at least one copy becomes inaccessible in both groups (bearing in mind that all data items are completely replicated). However, if a replica control strategy required that only *some* copies be accessed, write operations could be performed in a group that contained *enough* copies after a partition failure.

Quorum-based approaches also model the varying 'importance' of different copies of data items by assigning each copy some number of *votes*. A replica control strategy then uses the total number of votes assigned to a data item to dictate a read quorum r and write quorum w; that is, it dictates how many votes must be 'collected' to read and write a data item. If access is granted to a copy that has a vote of n, the transaction collects n votes from that copy. For example, to model the fact that a customer withdraws money from site A more frequently than site B, more votes could be assigned to x_A than to x_B.

In order to guarantee one-copy serializability, quorums must satisfy two constraints (Gifford (1979)):

1. $r + w$ exceeds the total number of votes v assigned to the item, and

2. $w > v/2$.

The first constraint ensures that there is a non-null intersection between every read quorum and every write quorum. Any read quorum is therefore guaranteed to have a current copy of the item. The most recent copy can be identified by *version numbers*; the copy with the highest version number is the copy read.

In a partitioned system, the first constraint guarantees that an item cannot be read in one partition and written in another; the second constraint ensures that two writes cannot occur in two different partitions on the same data item. Hence, no interference edges can appear in the precedence graph of any execution, and one-copy serializability is guaranteed by the fact that correctness is maintained within each partition.

> **EXAMPLE:** Suppose that sites A, B and C all contain copies of items x and y, and that a partition P_1 occurs, isolating A and B from C. Initially, $x = y = 0$, each site has 1 vote for each of x and y, and $r = w = 2$ for both x and y (see Figure 13.4(a)).

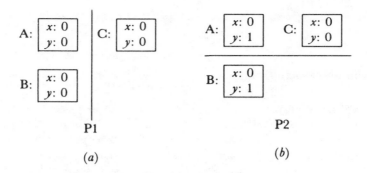

Figure 13.4 Correct transaction processing during partitioning using voting.

During the partitioning, transaction T_1 wishes to update y based on values read for x and y. Although it cannot be executed at C since it cannot obtain a read quorum for x, or read and write quorums for y, it can be executed at A, and the new value $y = 1$ is propagated to B (see Figure 13.4(b)).

Now suppose P_1 is repaired, and a new failure P_2 isolates A and C from B. During this new failure, transaction T_2 wishes to update x based on values read for x and y. It cannot be executed at B since it cannot obtain a read quorum for y, or read and write quorums for x. However, it can be executed at C. Using the most recent copy of $y = 1$ (obtained by reading copies at both A and C and taking the latest version) T_2 computes the new value $x = 1$ and propagates the new value to A.

Note that read accessibility can be given a high priority by choosing r small; if $r < v/2$, it is possible for an item to be read accessible in more than one partition, in which case it will be write accessible in none. Note also that the algorithm does not distinguish between communication failures, site failures, or just slow response.

13.3.1 Assigning votes

Different choices of vote assignments and quorums yield different 'flavours' of partition processing strategies with different performance characteristics. For example, if all v votes are assigned to one copy, x_p, and $r = q = v$, then a 'primary copy' strategy is emulated (Alsberg and Day (1976); Stonebraker (1979)): x_p is responsible for all the read and write activity on x in the system. During a partition failure, only the partition group containing x_p can process transactions accessing x. Unfortunately, if the site containing the primary copy of a data item fails and site failure cannot be distinguished from network partitioning, the data item becomes inaccessible everywhere. As another example, if every copy is given a single vote, and $r = w = \lfloor v/2 \rfloor + 1$, we have a simple 'majority consensus' algorithm (Thomas (1979)); in the event of a partition failure, a partition containing a majority of sites can process transactions. In this scheme, the data item may become inaccessible everywhere if the network breaks up into fragments so that no group contains a majority of the sites; however, since partition failures are assumed to be 'infrequent catastrophes', this is an unlikely occurrence.

Although the 'majority consensus' approach might seem natural, there are cases in which it does not perform well (Garcia and Barbara (1985)). For example, consider a system with data item x replicated at four sites A, B, C and D. Each copy is given a single vote, and $r = w = 3$. The set of groups of nodes that could execute transactions against x would be:

$$S = \{\{A, B, C\},\{A, B, D\},\{A, C, D\},\{B, C, D\}\}.$$

However, if x_A was assigned a vote of 2, and other copies a single vote, the majority is still 3 ($r = w = 3$), but a *better* vote assignment is achieved. There are *more* groups of nodes that can execute transactions against x in the event of a network partition:

$$R = \{\{A, B\},\{A, C\},\{A, D\},\{B, C, D\}\}.$$

Note that every group of nodes that can operate under S can also operate under R, but not the other way round. It is therefore important to consider the vote assignments and failure characteristics of the network carefully when choosing the *best* assignment for a given application.

Another 'quorum-like' partition processing strategy that appears to be similar to this simple form of voting is called *coteries* (Lamport (1978)). In this approach, groups of nodes that may perform the read and write operations for each data item are selected. Each pair of groups must have a node in common to guarantee mutual exclusion. For example, R (given above) is a coterie; if read and write operations are only allowed to be performed in partitions that are a superset of one of the groups in R, one-copy serializability is guaranteed. Surprisingly, it turns out that coteries are more powerful than vote assignments (Garcia and Barbara (1985)) in that there are sets of groups for which there exists no vote assignments. However, since voting is easier to implement, most systems do not use coteries.

A weakness of *static* vote and quorum assignments is that reading an item can be expensive. Furthermore, it is *unnecessarily* expensive when there are no failures (Bernstein and Goodman (1983); Eager and Sevcik (1983)). In the next subsections, we will discuss ways of reducing this overhead by *dynamically* adjusting the read- and write quorums.

13.3.2 Failure-mode quorums

Requiring a readset quorum significantly degrades performance when there are no failures, but is necessary to guarantee correctness when there are failures. Thus, an enhancement of the 'static' voting strategy is to allow transactions to run in two modes, normal and failure. When in *normal mode*, transaction T reads one copy of each data item in its readset, and updates all copies in its writeset.

If some copy cannot be updated, T becomes 'aware' of a *missing update*, and must run in *failure mode*, in which quorums must be obtained for each data item in the readset and writeset. This 'missing update information' is then passed along to all following transactions that need the information — all transactions in the precedence graph of future execution connected to T by a path of precedence edges originating at T. These transactions also become aware of missing updates, and must run in failure mode. Since T cannot see the future and does not know what later transactions will be affected, a level of indirection is used: missing update information is posted at sites along with a description of what transactions need the information. When the failure is repaired, the missing update information will eventually be posted at the sites that 'caused' the missing updates, that is, the sites that did not receive the updates. The updates can then be applied, and postings removed from other sites throughout the system.

The algorithm hinges on the ability to recognize 'missing writes' and to propagate the information to later transactions so that cycles in the precedence graph of committed transactions are avoided. Note that certain transactions may be able to execute without restriction even if there are partition failures present in the system; there is no harm in allowing read-only transactions to 'run in the past', read an old value of a data item during a failure, as long as no cycles are created in the precedence graph of committed transactions. This ability to run in the past allows a site that has become isolated from the rest of the network to execute read-only transactions even if updates are being performed on remote copies of the data items stored at that site.

Example: Suppose that there are four sites in the system A, B, C and D. Sites A, B and C contain copies of data item x; site B, C and D contain copies of data item y. Now suppose a failure occurs, isolating sites A and B from sites C and D. Transactions T_1, T_2, T_3 are initiated at site A (in that order), while transaction T_4 is initiated at D. The readsets, writesets and precedence graph are depicted in Figure 13.5. (The graph shown is of *uncommitted* transactions since cycles in the graph of *committed* transactions will obviously be avoided.)

T_1 is unaware of the failure, since it can obtain a copy of x and y at A; it can happily run in the past. T_2 becomes aware of the failure when it is unsuccessful at updating the copy of x at C. It is allowed to commit, however, since it can receive a quorum for each data item in its read and write sets (assuming that each copy has a weight of 1). T_2 is then required to pass all of its missing update information to transactions that are incoming nodes for outgoing edges from T_2, such as T_3 in this example. If T_3 were to successfully commit, it would also be required to pass on the missing update information. However, in this example, T_3 is not allowed to commit; since it is aware of missing updates, it is required to obtain a quorum for data items in its readset, which it cannot for y (its group only contains the copy y_A). Transaction T_4 would also not be allowed to commit since although it can obtain a quorum for y, it finds that it cannot update the copy of y at B, and must then run in failure mode. Since it cannot obtain a quorum for x, it cannot complete successfully. Thus, in this example (as well in all others),

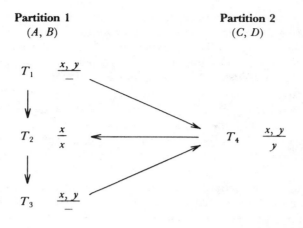

Figure 13.5 Potential conflict between transactions in different partitions is avoided by requiring transactions aware of missing updates to collect read and write quorums.

there are no cycles in the graph of *committed* transactions. Note that the restriction that T_2 and T_4 be rerun in failure mode is necessary — suppose that T_2 and T_4 both read x and y, but T_2 updated x while T_4 updated y. If they both executed in normal mode and did not switch to failure mode when they became aware of missing updates, a cycle would result in the graph of committed transactions.

Using different techniques, this scheme can be generalized to *multiple* levels of quorums. That is, 'normal' transaction processing is level 1, and levels 2, 3,..., correspond to various vote assignments that optimize availability for different failure modes (Herlihy (1986)). It can also be adapted to use *abstract data type* information for increased availability (Herlihy (1986)).

13.3.3 One-copy reads

A disadvantage of the 'failure mode' quorums described in earlier sections is that a read quorum must still be accessed in the event of a partition failure. Virtual partitions (El Abbadi, Skeen, and Cristian (1985); El Abbadi and Toueg (1986)) ensure that a transaction never has to access more than *one copy* for a read operation.

In this partition processing strategy, each site S maintains a 'view' (or *virtual partition*) of what sites it believes it can communicate with, called $view(S)$. To be able to process a read (or write) operation on item x, $view(S)$ must contain a read (or write) quorum for x. To read x, a transaction executing at S accesses the nearest copy in its view; $w_i(x)$ is translated to writing every copy in $view(S)$.

Note that determining whether a read and write quorum are available can be determined using local information (*i.e.*, by consulting its view).

Since views only *approximate* the actual state of the network, site S may discover that *view*(S) is out of date. This may happen, for example, when a transaction executing at S is unable to update a copy in *view*(S), or when a transaction originating at a site that is not in *view*(S) attempts to write some copy at S (in which case the write will be rejected). S must then abort all active transactions originating at S and initiate a *creation protocol* to update its view. This protocol ensures that all sites in the new view agree on the view, and that all copies of data items for which there is a read quorum in the new view are up-to-date.†

To motivate the correctness of this approach, recall that the basic property of read and write quorums is that they are mutually exclusive: if one partition has a read quorum, then no other partition can have a write quorum. If site S *believes* it has a write quorum but in fact does not, the fact that *view*(S) is incorrect will be discovered at the time a 'write-all' is attempted. If site S incorrectly believes it has a read quorum, however, it may read an *old* value and not discover the mistake until an inaccessible update is performed in its view. Fortunately, these 'incorrect' read operations can safely be 'run in the past', as in the previous scheme.

13.4 Querying in the face of partitions

In the previous section, the problems of updates and of maintaining the correctness of data in the face of partition failures were the main focus of attention. The observant reader will have noticed that even read-only transactions or *queries* for which *all data is available* may be forced to wait if one-copy serializability is the correctness criteria. For example, consider a database containing two data items, x and y, that is completely replicated over two sites, A and B. A partition failure occurs so that A and B can no longer communicate. During the failure, transactions T_1 and T_2 execute at site A: T_1 updates x; T_2 then reads the values of x and y. Meanwhile, transactions T_3 and T_4 execute at site B: T_3 updates y; T_4 then reads the values of x and y. Note that the query T_2 requires T_1 to be serialized before T_3 in an equivalent global schedule, while the query T_4 requires T_3 to be serialized before T_1, a contradiction (see Figure 13.6).

Although such anomalies are theoretically disturbing, in practice queries are frequently allowed to execute without restriction despite the fact that they may see an inconsistent database state. In this section, the problem of updates and serializability will therefore be ignored. That is, it will be assumed that the database is *static* during the failure, and concentrate on providing approximate answers to queries in the face of network partitions. Furthermore, the discussion

---

† The creation protocol given in El Abbadi, Skeen, and Cristian (1985) and El Abbadi and Toueg (1986) tolerates additional partition failures occurring during its execution.

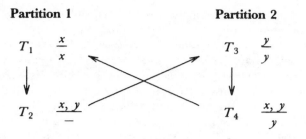

Figure 13.6 Conflict involving queries.

will be limited to systems in which data is stored as simple tables or *relations*, although the results are applicable to a variety of other types of systems.

13.4.1 Approximating queries

Due to the expense and complexity of maintaining replicated data, most distributed database systems limit the amount of replication. Data is fragmented to mirror the usage patterns in the database, and partially replicated to minimize cost and provide fault tolerance (Ceri and Pelegatti (1984)). Since data is not completely replicated, it is possible to pose queries during network partitioning for which not all data is available.

Queries which require access to unavailable data are typically either delayed until the data becomes available (the partition is repaired), or are aborted with some explanation to the user. If the query is aborted, the user may decide to rephrase the query using only data that is available within the partition. However, this requires a knowledge of system-level issues, such as what nodes are within the same partition group and where data is stored. This not only violates the notion of *transparency of data*, but may be impossible to determine if the network is in a state of flux. What is needed is an automatic method of providing an *approximate answer* to the original query, using the available data. The approximate answer should be *monotonic* in the sense that any fact which is said to be true remains true as data structures become available, and any fact which is said to be false remains false. In other words, if the answer that would be given if the network were not partitioned is called the *complete answer*, the requirement is that anything the approximation says to be true is true in the complete answer, and anything the approximation says to be false is false in the complete answer.†

To illustrate what is meant by monotonic computation, we will digress from databases for the moment and consider the bisection method for obtaining the

---

† Recall that we are assuming a *static* database for now, and are ignoring any updates that may be performed in other partitions.

root of a function, f. For simplicity, f is assumed to have exactly one root, r. At any point in computation, r is represented by an interval, (a, b), where $a \leqslant r \leqslant b$. The computation successively halves the interval: if $f(a) \cdot f((a + b)/2) \leqslant 0$, the new interval becomes $(a, (a + b)/2)$; otherwise the interval becomes $((a + b)/2, b)$. Assuming that the initial estimate of r is correct, the interval is correct at any later point in the computation: the root is possibly any of the points between a and b, and definitely not any of the points outside of that interval. Furthermore, the answer improves as computation progresses.

Since the answer to a query in a database is a set of tuples, an obvious analogy of an 'interval' in the database realm is a *bounding pair* (A, B), where A is a 'superset' of the answer T and B is a 'subset' of T. A is called a *complete approximation* of T: Every tuple in A is *possibly* an approximation of one or more tuples in T, and anything not approximated by something in A is *definitely not* in T. B is called a *consistent approximation*: Every tuple in B is *definitely* an approximation of one or more tuples in T.

More precisely, we say that a tuple x *approximates* another tuple y (written $x \leqslant y$) if every field (or *attribute*) in x is contained in y and agrees on the value. However, y may contain additional fields as well. For example, if x and y are given as

$$x = [Name \Rightarrow \text{'John Doe'}], \ y = [Name \Rightarrow \text{'John Doe'}; \ Age \Rightarrow 21],$$

then $x \leqslant y$ since x is not defined on *Age* but agrees on the *Name* value. However, if

$$u = [Name \Rightarrow \text{'John Adams'}]$$

then neither x nor y are related to u since they disagree on *Name*. Finally, if

$$v = [Name \Rightarrow \text{'John Doe'}; \ City \Rightarrow \text{'Philadelphia'}],$$

then $x \leqslant v$, but y and v are unrelated. Extending this ordering to sets, if A, B and T are *sets of tuples*, then A is called a *complete approximation* of T if for every t in T there exists an a in A such that $a \leqslant t$ (extending $A \supseteq T$). B is a *consistent approximation* of T if for every b in B there exists a t in T such that $b \leqslant t$ (extending $B \subseteq T$). If A is a complete approximation for T and B is a consistent approximation for the same set T, then (A, B) is a *bounding pair* for T.

Using this ordering of approximation, the *smallest tuple* is [ ]: [ ] approximates every other tuple since no attributes are known. The set containing no tuples (empty set) is the *smallest consistent approximation* for any set T (trivially) and the set containing the smallest tuple, $\{[\ ]\}$, is the *smallest complete approximation* for any set T since every tuple in T is approximated by [ ].

Note that if a bounding pair (A, B) approximates T, and A, B and T are all *stored* within the distributed database, the statement '(A, B) approximates T' is an integrity constraint, and expresses *implicit redundancy*. Since A is a complete approximation of T, every tuple in T must agree with some tuple in A on common attributes. Since B is a consistent approximation of T, every tuple in B must agree with some tuple in T on common attributes. It is due to this implicit redundancy that useful, approximate answers in the presence of unavailable data can be provided.

In the past five years, attempts to 'marry' knowledge-base systems and database systems have provided powerful logic-based languages for expressing a semantic understanding of data in addition to expressing queries (Gallaire, Minker, and Nicolas (1984)). In the next section, an example of how a 'rule based' system (Ullman (1988)) could be used to give an approximate answer in the face of partition failures is given.† It should be emphasized that providing approximate answers is a current area of research, and that such techniques are not currently being used in the commercial world.

13.4.2 Example of an approximating query

Suppose there are five tables of information distributed throughout the system: one for teaching fellows, one for graduate students, one for university employees and one each for all the teachers of all sections of the classes CS4 and CS5.

Name	Salary	TPhone
Liza	11K	4093
Joe	11K	8599
Ella	10K	8789
Burt	7K	1423

Figure 13.7 The teaching fellows (*TF*) relation.

(See FIGURES 13.7, 13.8 and 13.9 for the particular example tables used.) These tables have the following column entries:

- *TF* (Teaching Fellows) *Name*, *Salary* and *TPhone*.

- *GS* (Graduate Students) *Name*, *Degree* and *Phone*

- *UE* (University Employee) *Name* and *Salary*

- *CS*4 (Teachers of CS4) *Name*, *Section* and *Office*

- *CS*5 (Teachers of CS5) *Name*, *Section* and *TPhone*.

For now, assume that the tables are all correct and complete (that all university employees are listed in the *UE* table and everyone listed in *UE* is a university employee), and that the names listed are unique (e.g., our database does not have more than one person named Burt).

† For complete definitions of these concepts, along with proofs of correctness, see Buneman, Davidson, and Watters (1989b) and Buneman, Davidson, and Watters (1989a).

Name	Degree	Phone
Joe	PhD	1324
Mary	PhD	3241
Burt	MS	1423
Ella	PhD	4123
Nancy	MS	3214
Chuck	MS	1342
Liza	PhD	1432

Name	Salary
Karen	35K
Liza	11K
Steve	60K
Rose	71K
Joe	11K
Ella	10K
Paul	13K
Burt	7K
Edward	40K
Mary	10K

Figure 13.8 The graduate students (*GS*), and university employees (*UE*) relations.

Name	CS4Section	Office
Joe	2	023
Burt	1	126

Name	CS5Section	TPhone
Ella	2	8789
Burt	1	1423

Figure 13.9 The *CS*4 and *CS*5 Relations.

In addition to the tabular data, semantic relationships between the tables have been specified as *rules* of the form

$$p \rightarrow q.$$

Such a rule can be interpreted as: 'Whenever a pattern is found that matches p, there must be a pattern that matches q'. In this example, 'patterns' can be thought of as tuples in named relations. The notation '—' for an attribute indicates that the value is unimportant; attributes that must match in value are given the same name variable (*e.g.*, '*Name*' in the first rule). The semantic relationships for this example are:

(a) *TF*(*Name, Salary,* −) → *UE*(*Name, Salary*): Every teaching fellow is a university employee.

(b) *TF*(*Name,* −, −) → *GS*(*Name,* −, −): Every teaching fellow is a graduate student.

(c) *CS*4(*Name,* −, −) → *TF*(*Name,* −, −): Only teaching fellows teach CS4.

(d) *CS*5(*Name,* −, *TPhone*) → *TF*(*Name,* −, *TPhone*): Only teaching fellows teach CS5. Note that the phone number that appears in CS5 is the phone number that appears in TF.

In the absence of any partition failures, these rules act as *integrity constraints*. If the system had an integrity subsystem, the appropriate rule(s) would be evaluated at the end of any transaction that might violate the rule (see Blaustein (1981) and Buneman and Clemons (1979) for a discussion of efficiently monitoring integrity constraints). If a violation was detected, the transaction would be aborted. Unfortunately, due to the overhead introduced, few systems implement integrity subsystems of this complexity.

Now suppose that a query to retrieve *TF* is submitted; unfortunately, a partition failure has occurred and *TF* is no longer available. We therefore want the system to automatically determine an approximation of *TF* using the remaining information (*GS*, *UE*, *CS*4 and *CS*5). We will now mimic how the system might approximate *TF* using these rules:

1.   Create an initial bounding pair of tables, (TF_A, TF_B). TF_A is the smallest complete approximation of *TF*, {[ ]} (*i.e.*, the table with one entry consisting of null values everywhere), and TF_B the smallest consistent approximation of *TF*, the empty set (see Figure 13.10).

Name	Salary	TPhone
—	—	—

Name	Salary	TPhone

Figure 13.10 The initial bounding pair, (TF_A, TF_B).}

2.   Rule (a) says that every teaching fellow must be a university employee. A restatement of this is that it is only possible for *TF* to contain tuples that approximate something in *UE*. We can therefore replace TF_A with the *Name* and *Salary* values of all tuples in the *UE* table, placing null values for the *TPhone* column.

3.   Rule (b) says that every teaching fellow must also be a graduate student. Using similar reasoning, we can therefore cross off any entry in TF_A whose name does not appear in the *GS* table — Karen, Steve, Rose, Paul and Edward. Figure 13.11 represents TF_A at this point.

Name	Salary	TPhone
Liza	11K	—
Joe	11K	—
Ella	10K	—
Burt	7K	—
Mary	10K	—

Figure 13.11 The complete approximation, TF_A, after comparison with *UE* and *GS*.

Name	Salary	TPhone
Joe	—	—
Ella	—	8789
Burt	—	1423

Figure 13.12 The consistent approximation, TF_B, after comparison with $CS4$ and $CS5$.

4. Insert into TF_B the *Name* fields of tuples in $CS4$ with nulls everywhere else, since teachers of CS4 are definitely teaching fellows by Rule (c).

5. Using Rule (d), repeat the previous step for the $CS5$ table, filling in the appropriate *TPhone* value as well as *Name*. If a tuple with the same name already appears in TF_B, just fill in the *TPhone* value (as with Burt, for example). Figure 13.12 represents TF_B at this point.

6. We now notice that since *Names* are unique, the only possible *Salary* value for tuples in TF_B are those found in the corresponding tuples of TF_A. We can therefore improve the approximations in TF_B by filling in the *Salary* fields. Likewise, we can improve the approximations in TF_A by filling in the appropriate *TPhone* values from TF_B.

At this point, we have done all we can to approximate teaching fellows using the available data, and the final bounding pair is as shown in Figure 13.11. Referring to Figure 13.7, note that TF_A is indeed a complete approximation of TF since every name in TF appears in TF_A. Note that in TF_A, the *TPhone* is sometimes undefined; a tuple in TF_A is only an *approximation* of a tuple in TF. TF_B is also a consistent approximation of TF since every tuple in TF_B is in TF. Again, in TF_B the *TPhone* is sometimes undefined since tuples in TF_B only *approximate* those in TF.

During this process, the system might also identify *anomalies* in the database. For example, if an entry for a student with name 'Rose' were added to the CS4

Name	Salary	TPhone		Name	Salary	TPhone
Liza	11K	—		Joe	11K	—
Joe	11K	—		Ella	10K	8789
Ella	10K	8789		Burt	7K	1423
Burt	7K	1423				
Mary	10K	—				

Figure 13.13 The final bounding pair, (TF_A, TF_B).

† This is also due to the fact that any other value for *Salary* would violate Rule (a).

table, the system would detect an anomaly in step (5) outlined above: There is no entry in the complete approximation TF_A for Rose; Rose was crossed off TF_A in step (2) since she is not in the table of graduate students (see Figure 13.11). This is a violation of the semantic relationships: an entry for a student with name 'Rose' should either appear in GS, or CS4 should not contain an entry for a student with name 'Rose'. This would be caught at the time the incorrect deletion or insertion were made if an integrity subsystem were being used.

It should also be noted that TF is correctly approximated at any point in this computation. For example, if only GS and UE are available, TF is approximated by the bounding pair (A,B) where A is the table in Figure 13.11, and B is the empty relation. If only $CS4$ and $CS5$ were available, TF is approximated by the the bounding pair with A the relation consisting of one tuple with nulls everywhere (see Figure 13.10), and B as in Figure 13.12.

13.5 Conclusions

Although partition failures may occur infrequently, their effects on distributed systems can be devastating: the availability of data may be severely restricted, and its correctness threatened. In this chapter, 'correct' transaction processing has been defined, and the problems and trade offs involved in maintaining correctness have been discussed. A class of partition-processing strategies that maintain correctness during partitioning was also discussed. They have the additional advantage of working when network partitions are not 'clean', and do not distinguish between communication failures, site failures, or slow responses. Thus, correctness is maintained even when the cause and extent of partitioning cannot be accurately determined.

Due to the overhead of maintaining the correctness of replicated data, most systems limit the number of copies to at most two or three. During network partitioning, queries may therefore be rejected if the data they access is unavailable. However, data is often 'implicitly' replicated; integrity constraints define relationships that must exist between different data items. Using these relationships, it is possible to construct 'approximate' answers to queries even when the data needed is unavailable. While the research in this area is still young, initial results are promising.

13.6 References

P. A. Alsberg and J. D. Day (1976). 'A Principle for Resilient Sharing of Distributed Resources'. *Proceedings of the Second International Conference on Software Engineering*: 562—570, San Fancisco, CA, October 1976.

P. A. Bernstein and N. Goodman (1981). 'Concurrency Control in Distributed Database Systems'. *ACM Computing Surveys* **13** (2): 185—221, June 1981.

P. A. Bernstein and N. Goodman (1983). 'The Failure and Recovery Problem for Replicated Databases'. *Proceedings 2nd ACM Symposium on Principles of Distributed Computing*: 114—122, August 1983.

P. A. Bernstein, V. Hadzilacos, and N. Goodman (1987). *Concurrency Control and Recovery in Database Systems*. Addison Wesley, Reading, MA, 1987.

B. Blaustein (1981). *Enforcing Database Assertions: Techniques and Applications*. Ph.D. thesis, Harvard University, Cambridge, Ma, 1981.

B. Blaustein, H. Garcia, D. R. Ries, R. M. Chilenskas, and C. W. Kaufman (1983). 'Maintaining Replicated Databases Even in the Presence of Network Partitions'. *Proceedings IEEE 16th Electrical and Aereospace Systems Conference*: 353—360, Sept. 1983.

P. Buneman and E. K. Clemons (1979). 'Efficiently Monitoring Relational Databases'. *ACM Transactions on Database Systems* **4** (3): 368—382, September 1979.

P. Buneman, S. Davidson, and A. Watters (1989a). 'Querying Independent Databases'. *Information Sciences: An International Journal*, 1989. (To appear.)

P. Buneman, S. Davidson, and A. Watters (1989b). 'A Semantics for Complex Objects and Approximate Queries'. *Journal of Computer and System Sciences*, 1989. (To appear.)

S. Ceri and G. Pelegatti (1984). *Distributed Databases: Principles and Systems*. McGraw-Hill, New York, NY, 1984.

B. Coan, B. Oki, and E. Kolodner (1986). 'Limitations on Database Availability when Networks Partition'. *Proceedings 5th ACM Symposium on Principles of Distributed Computing*: 187—194, 1986.

S. B. Davidson (1984). 'Optimism and Consistency in Partitioned Distributed Database Systems'. *ACM Transactions on Database Systems* **9** (3): 456—481, Sept. 1984.

S. B. Davidson, H. Garcia, and D. Skeen (1985). 'Consistency in Partitioned Networks'. *ACM Computing Surveys* **17** (3): 341—370, Sept. 1985.

D. L. Eager and K. C. Sevcik (1983). 'Achieving Robustness in Distributed Database Systems'. *ACM Transactions on Database Systems* **8** (3): 354—381, Sept. 1983.

A. El Abbadi, D. Skeen, and F. Cristian (1985). 'An Efficient, Fault-tolerant Algorithm for Replicated Data Management'. *Proceedings 4th ACM Symp. on the Principles of Database Systems*: 215—229, March 1985.

A. El Abbadi and S. Toueg (1986). 'Availability in Partitioned Replicated Databases'. *Proceedings 5th ACM Symposium on the Principles of Database Systems*: 240—251, March 1986.

K. P. Eswaran, J. N. Gray, R. A. Lorie, and I. L. Traiger (1976). 'The Notions of Consistency and Predicate Locks in a Database System'. *Communications of the ACM* 19 (11): 624—633, November 1976.

H. Gallaire, J. Minker, and J. Nicolas (1984). 'Logic and Databases: A Deductive Approach'. *ACM Computing Surveys* 16 (2): 153—185, June 1984.

H. Garcia, T. Allen, B. Blaustein, R. M. Chilenskas, and D. R. Ries (1983). 'Data-Patch: Integrating Inconsistent Copies of a Database After a Partition'. *Proceedings Third IEEE Symposium on Reliability in Dist. Software and Database Systems*: 38—48, Oct. 1983.

H. Garcia and D. Barbara (1985). 'How to Assign Votes is a Distributed System'. *Journal of the ACM* 32 (4): 841—860, October 1985.

H. Garcia and B. Kogan (1988). 'Achieving High Availability in Distributed Databases'. *IEEE Transactions on Software Engineering* 14 (7): 886—896, July 1988.

D. K. Gifford (1979). 'Weighted Voting for Replicated Data'. *Proceedings of the Seventh Symposium on Operating System Principles*: 150—162, December 1979.

D. K. Gifford and A. Spector (1984). 'The TWA Reservation System'. *Communications of the ACM* 27 (7): 650—665, July 1984.

J. N. Gray, P. McJones, M. Blasgen, B. Lindsay, L. Lorie, T. Price, F. Putzolu, and I. Traiger (1981). 'The Recovery Manager of the System R Database Manager'. *ACM Computing Surveys* 13 (2): 223—242, June 1981.

M. Herlihy (1986). 'A quorum-consensus replication method for abstract types'. *ACM Transactions on Computer Systems* 4 (1): 32—53, Feb. 1986.

B. Kogan and H. Garcia (1987). 'Update Propagation in Bakunin Data Networks'. *Proceedings 6th ACM Symposium on Principles of Distributed Computing*: 13—26, 1987.

L. Lamport (1978). 'Time, Clocks, and the Ordering of Events in a Distributed System'. *Communications of the ACM* 21 (7): 558—565, July 1978.

N. Lynch, B. Blaustein, and M. Siegel (1986). 'Correctness conditions for highly available replicated databases'. *Proceedings 5th ACM Symposium on Principles of Distributed Computing*: 11—28, Calgary, Canada, Aug. 1986.

C. H. Papadimitriou (1979). 'The Serializability of Concurrent Database Updates'. *Journal of the ACM* 26 (4): 631—653, October 1979.

D. S. Parker, G. J. Popek, G. Rudisin, A. Stoughton, B. Walker, E. Walton, J. Chow, D. Edwards, S. Kiser, and C. Kline (1983). 'Detection of Mutual Inconsistency in Distributed Systems'. *IEEE Transactions on Software Engineering* 9 (3),

May 1983.

D. Skeen (1982). 'On Network Partitioning'. *IEEE COMPSAC*: 454—455, Nov. 1982.

M. Stonebraker (1979). 'Concurrency Control and Consistency of Multiple Copies in Distributed INGRES'. *IEEE Transactions on Software Engineering* **SE-5** (3): 188—194, May 1979.

R. H. Thomas (1979). 'A Majority Consensus Approach to Concurrency Control'. *ACM Transactions on Database Systems* **4** (2): 180—209, June 1979.

I. L. Traiger, J. N. Gray, C. A. Galtieri, and B. G. Lindsay (1982). 'Transactions and Consi stency in Distributed Database Systems'. *ACM Transactions on Database Systems* **7** (3): 323—342, September 1982.

J. D. Ullman (1988). *Database and Knowledge-Base Systems, Vol. I.* Computer Science Press, 1988.

J. S. M. Verhofstad (1978). 'Recovery Techniques for Database Systems'. *ACM Computing Surveys* **10** (2): 167—196, 1978.

D. D. Wright (1983). *Managing Distributed Databases in Partitioned Networks.* Ph.D. thesis, Cornell University, Dept. of Computer Science, Ithaca, NY, Sept. 1983.

Chapter 14

Reliable Broadcast Protocols

T. A. Joseph and K. P. Birman

The distinguishing feature of a distributed program is not just that its various parts are distributed over a number of processors, but that these parts communicate with one another. The hardware in a distributed system allows a processor to send messages to other processors; the operating system usually extends this facility to allow a process on one machine to send messages to a process on another. The operating system may also provide facilities to set up virtual circuits between processes and may include protocols that ensure a certain degree of reliability in the communication. From the point of view of a programming language, however, these facilities are still rather low-level, and this has led to a search for appropriate high-level abstractions for inter-process communication. Some researchers suggest that distribution should be completely hidden from the programmer. They argue for an abstraction that looks like a global shared memory. This abstraction has the advantage that it is simple to program with — writing a distributed program is no different from writing a non-distributed one. However, hiding distribution is not appropriate for all applications — some applications need to have explicit knowledge of location, either to obtain fault-tolerance or for better performance. Moreover, implementing the abstraction of a global shared memory on a network of computers could be extremely inefficient, especially if the network is large. It becomes increasingly difficult to justify the overhead of a shared memory abstraction as the network size becomes larger and a typical application runs only on a small fraction of the sites in the network.

A commonly used high-level abstraction for inter-process communication is the *remote procedure call* (RPC), introduced by Birrell and Nelson (1984). A process communicates with another using an interface that looks just like a call to a procedure. The advantage of this abstraction is that it simplifies distributed programming by making communication with a remote process look like communication within a process. Its limitation, however, is that it can only be employed for two-

293

way communication, between a calling process and a called process. Remote procedure calls are therefore most useful in distributed programs that fit the 'client-server' model — client processes request services from server processes; server processes accept such requests and respond to each of them individually. In contrast, RPC is not a particularly convenient abstraction when a distributed program is composed of a number of processes that have a high degree of inter-dependence on one another and where the communication among them reflects this inter-dependence. In such programs the communication often takes place from one process to *a number of* processes rather than from a calling process to a called process, as in RPCs. An example of such a program would be a server that, for reasons of fault-tolerance or load sharing, is implemented as a group of processes on a number of sites. It would be convenient if a client requesting a service from such a server could send requests to the group as a whole, rather than being required to know the group's membership and to communicate with members on a one-to-one basis. This is especially important if the server group could change its membership or location from time to time. Also, if the members of the group wish to divide up the work of responding to a request, each of them must ensure that its actions are consistent with what the other members are doing, and so they will need to communicate with one another. What is needed here is a facility that enables a process to send a message to *a set of processes*. We will call the act of sending a message to a set of processes a *broadcast*.†

In its simplest form, a broadcast causes a copy of a message to be sent to each destination process. What makes broadcasts interesting is that they must handle the possibility that some of the processes taking part in the broadcast may fail in the middle of a broadcast. For example, a failure of the sender could cause a broadcast message to be delivered to some but not all of its intended destinations — a possibility that never occurs when only two processes communicate with each other. To be useful to a programmer, a broadcast must have well-defined behaviour even when failures may occur. Broadcasts that provide such guarantees are called 'reliable broadcasts.' Reliable broadcasts are implemented using special protocols that detect failures and/or take compensating actions. The definition of broadcast used here is general enough to cover protocols like 2- and 3-phase transaction commit protocols, and indeed some of the broadcast protocols described in this chapter are similar to these protocols. The discussion begins with a description of the system model and the model of failures.

14.1 System model

Figure 14.1 shows a model of a distributed system. It consists of a number of processors (sites) connected to one another by a communications network. Each

---

† This use of the term *broadcast* does not refer to any hardware broadcast facility. On the contrary, we assume only that the network provides point-to-point communication. If the network does have a broadcast capability, some of the protocols described in this chapter can take advantage of it.

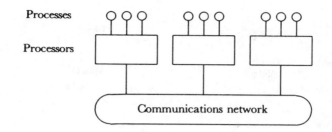

Figure 14.1 System model

processor may have a number of user processes executing on it. There is no shared memory between sites and so the only form of communication between sites is through the network, which enables messages to be transmitted from any processor to any other processor in the system. Message transmission is asynchronous: sending and receiving processes do not have to wait for one another for communication to occur, and message transmission times are variable. Figure 14.2 shows the structure of the communication sub-system at each site (the meaning of the arrows will be described later). The communication sub-system may be part of the operating system kernel, a separate system process, part of the user process, or any combination of these. The issue here is its *function* rather than its *location*. The transport layer contains the hardware and the software that enables a message to be sent from one processor to another. It is assumed that the transport layer provides reliable, sequenced point-to-point communication. That is, a message sent from one site to another is eventually delivered (unless the sending or the receiving site fails), and that messages between any pair of sites are delivered in the order they were sent. This form of reliability is achieved using protocols that sequence messages, detect lost or garbled messages (with high probability), and retransmit such messages. Many such protocols are described in Tanenbaum (1988).

The broadcast layer implements the facility to send a message from one process to a set of processes, possibly on different machines. A process wishing to perform a broadcast presents the broadcast layer with a message and a list of destination processes for that message. The broadcast layer uses the destination list to compute a set of sites that must receive this message, and uses the transport layer to send a copy of the broadcast message to each of these sites. It typically includes other information with the message, which is used by the broadcast layer at the receiving site. Depending on the broadcast protocol being executed, there may be further rounds of communication among the sites before the message is finally delivered to the destination processes at each of the sites. In what follows the site from which a broadcast is made is called its *initiator*, and the sites to which it is sent its *recipients*. The arrows in Figure 14.2 shows a pattern of message exchange that could arise when a process at site 1 does a

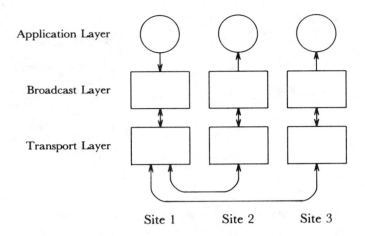

Application Layer

Broadcast Layer

Transport Layer

Site 1   Site 2   Site 3

Figure 14.2 Communication sub-system

broadcast to processes at sites 2 and 3. In this figure, the broadcast layer at site 1 sends a message to the broadcast layers at sites 2 and 3, which engage in further communication with the broadcast layer at site 1 before they deliver the message to the application.

The protocol executed by the broadcast layer depends on the level of fault-tolerance it provides and on the way in which it orders the delivery of broadcasts relative to one another. A number of such broadcast protocols will be considered and their cost-performance trade offs will be examined, beginning with a protocol that achieves a simple form of fault tolerance and then moving on to more complex protocols providing various delivery ordering properties. The detailed examples will be the broadcast protocols of the ISIS system (Birman and Joseph (1987a); Birman and Joseph (1987b)), but other, similar protocols will be discussed in passing.

14.2 Failure model

To talk about reliable broadcasts we must first talk about what kinds of failures we are trying to overcome. The simplest failure model is the 'crash model.' In this model, the only kind of failure that can occur in the system is that a processor may suddenly halt, killing all the processes that are executing there. Operational processes never perform incorrect actions, nor do they fail to perform actions that they are supposed to carry out. Furthermore, all operational processes can *detect* the failure of a processor, much as if there were a special device connected to each processor and giving the status — operational or failed — of all other processors in a mutually consistent manner. For most of this chapter it is assumed that only crash failures can occur. There are a couple of reasons for restricting our attention to crash failures. First, the abstraction of crash failures can be implemented on top of a system subject to more complex failures by running an appropriate software protocol. The ISIS failure detector (Birman and Joseph (1987a)) and the protocol described in Schlichting and Schneider (1983) are examples of such protocols. Second, techniques are available to automatically translate a protocol that tolerates crash failures into protocols that tolerate larger classes of failures (Neiger and Toueg (1988)). Since protocols that tolerate only crash failures are simpler to develop and to understand, it is easiest to describe such protocols here, and then to either implement them on top of an appropriate base layer or to use translation techniques to obtain versions that are more fault-tolerant.

14.3 Atomic broadcast protocols

One of the simplest properties provided by a broadcast protocol is *atomicity*, that is, a broadcast message is either received by *all* destinations that do not fail or by *none* of them.† Moreover, non-delivery may occur only if the sender fails before the end of the protocol. An atomic broadcast protocol will never cause a message to remain undelivered at some non-faulty destinations if it has been delivered at some others (even if some destinations fail before the protocol completes). This is a very useful property because a process that receives such a broadcast can act with the knowledge that all the other operational destinations will also receive a copy of the same message. This reduces the danger of a recipient taking actions that are inconsistent with the actions taken by other processors. Consider the case where a number of processes each maintain a copy of a replicated set of items and a broadcast is made to these processes requesting them to add a particular item to this set. If an atomic broadcast protocol is used, each recipient can add the item to its copy of the set in the knowledge that all other destinations will do the same, and so their sets will all contain identical information. Without atomicity, the implementor of the replicated set will have to take steps to ensure that a failure will not cause some processes to miss updates, which would result in the copies of the set becoming inconsistent.

At first glance, an atomic broadcast protocol might seem trivial to implement, especially if the transport layer gives reliable point-to-point transmission. The initiator could simply send the message to each destination site, and a recipient could simply deliver it to any destination process at that site. But what happens if the initiator crashes after it has sent the message to some (but not all) of the destination sites? This leaves us in precisely the situation that we are trying to avoid: some destinations have received the message, while others have not. To make matters worse, the destinations that have not received the message have no

---

† Some researchers have used the term *atomicity* to refer to stronger properties. Here, it is used to mean all-or-nothing delivery only.

idea that they should receive one. This means that it is necessary for one or more of the recipients to detect that the initiator has failed and to forward the message to the sites that did not receive it. This, of course, also means keeping a copy of the message around for a while — at least until it is known that all destinations have received it. And, since copies of messages cannot be kept around forever, some means must also be provided for a recipient to obtain the knowledge that a message has been received everywhere, so that it can then discard the message. This introduces further complexity. If a duplicate copy of a message were to turn up at a site after knowledge about the message was discarded there, it might be (erroneously) delivered a second time. Thus, one needs to be certain that before the system discards a message, all copies of the message have been purged from any active processors and communication channels. What originally seemed to be a trivial problem turns out to be not so trivial after all!

Figure 14.3 gives a simple protocol that implements an atomic broadcast that tolerates crash failures. It is similar to the algorithm in Schneider (1986). When a site receives a message for the first time, it retransmits a copy of the message to all the destinations. Hence if a site receives a message and remains operational, all the destinations will receive a copy of the message. Thus atomicity is guaranteed. However, this property is achieved at the expense of increased communication because of the retransmissions. The protocol also takes up memory space because the message (or some part of it) must be stored at a recipient until all the retransmitted copies arrive, otherwise there will be no way of identifying these copies as duplicates of the first one. This protocol could be modified to retransmit messages only if the initiator is seen to fail. Most of the extra communication would then occur only when a failure occurs, which is more reasonable. But even when failures do not occur, this protocol would incur extra storage and communication costs. Each recipient must store the message until it is notified that it has been delivered at all the destinations it was addressed to, and this notification will require some message overhead. In general, depending on the properties that it achieves, a broadcast protocol will incur a cost in terms

At the initiator:

   send message *m* to all sites where there is a destination process

At a site receiving message *m*:

   if message *m* has not been received already
      send a copy of *m* to all other sites where there is a destination process
      deliver *m* to any destination process at this site

Figure 14.3 A simple atomic broadcast protocol

of latency (the time between when a message is sent and when it is delivered at its destinations), communication (because of extra messages or larger messages), and memory consumed.

14.4 More complex protocols

In the previous section a simple broadcast protocol was discussed that achieves atomicity. There are two directions in which one could go to arrive at more sophisticated protocols. One is to expand the class of failures that the protocol tolerates. The other is to consider protocols that provide stronger guarantees than atomicity. An example of a larger class of failures than crash failures is 'omission failures.' In this failure model, a faulty processor could crash as before, or it could remain operational but occasionally fail to send or to receive messages. This is a realistic way to model processors connected by communications links that may lose messages, or that are subject to transmission buffer overflows capable of causing occasional message loss. Interestingly enough, the protocol described above achieves atomicity even with this class of failures. We could go even further, and consider failure models like Byzantine failures, where processes may malfunction by sending out spurious or even contradictory messages. The rest of this chapter, however, is restricted to crash failures, but considers protocols that are more complex because they achieve stronger properties than atomicity. For protocols that deal with omission and Byzantine failures, the reader is referred to Perry and Toueg (1986), and Lamport, Shostak, and Pease (1982), respectively.

14.5 Ordered broadcast protocols

When atomicity was introduced, the example of a number of processes cooperating to maintain a replicated set of items was also considered. Atomicity was seen to be sufficient to ensure that all the copies of the set contained the same items. But what if the processes were maintaining a *queue* of items instead of a set? In this case, the *order* of the items is required to be the same in all the copies. Atomicity is not sufficient here because there are no guarantees of the order in which different broadcasts will be delivered to different destinations (especially if they originate from different senders). Given a broadcast protocol that had the additional guarantee that messages will be delivered in the same order everywhere, implementing a replicated queue is simple: this protocol is used to broadcast items to the processes maintaining the queue, and each recipient adds items to its copy of the queue in the order that it receives them. Atomicity ensures that all operational copies will contain the same set of items; the ordering property ensures that these will be in the same order in all the copies. Without the ordering property, the implementor of a replicated queue will have to include code to ensure that all the copies agree on the order in which items are added to the queue, which makes developing this application a more difficult task. The availability of an ordered broadcast can thus simplify the implementation of many distributed applications, and much work has been done in developing protocols for such broadcasts. A few are described here.

If two sites broadcast messages to overlapping sets of destinations, it is possible for these messages to arrive at the common destinations in different orders. The essential feature of an ordered broadcast protocol, then, is that an incoming message is delivered only when all the recipients have agreed on how to order its delivery relative to other messages. This usually increases the latency, results in additional communication, and requires that the message be stored for the duration of the protocol. The algorithms studied below differ in the way they trade these costs off against one another.

The first protocol we study was proposed by Dale Skeen and is described in detail in Birman and Joseph (1987a) under the name *ABCAST*. It operates by assigning each broadcast a timestamp and delivering messages in the order of timestamps. (These timestamps need have no relation to real time — all that is required is an increasing sequence of numbers.) When a site receives a new message, it stores it in a pending queue, marking it as *undeliverable*. It then sends a message to the initiator with a *proposed timestamp* for the broadcast. This proposed timestamp is chosen to be larger than any other timestamp that this site has proposed or received in the past. (To make the timestamp unique, each site is assigned a unique number that it appends to its timestamps as a suffix). The initiator collects the timestamps from all the recipients, picks the largest of the values it receives, and sends this value back to the recipients. This becomes the *final timestamp* for the broadcast. When a recipient receives a final timestamp, it assigns the timestamp to the corresponding message in the pending queue, and marks the message as *deliverable*. The pending queue is then reordered to be in order of increasing timestamps. If the message at the head of the pending queue is deliverable, it is taken off the queue and delivered. This is repeated until the queue is empty or the message at the head of the queue is undeliverable (if there are deliverable message after this undeliverable one, they remain in the queue until the messages ahead of them are all delivered or moved after them in the queue).

Figure 14.4 illustrates how this protocol works. Let us assume that (processes at) three sites are trying to broadcast messages m_1, m_2 and m_3 to the same set of destinations at sites 1, 2 and 3. Assume that the largest timestamps seen at sites 1, 2 and 3 are 14, 15 and 16 respectively. Step 1 shows the messages arriving at the recipients in different orders. They are all placed in the pending queues marked as undeliverable (u), with proposed timestamps as shown. Notice how the site number is used to disambiguate equal timestamps. In Step 2, the sender of m_1 collects its proposed timestamps (16.1, 17.2 and 17.3), computes the maximum (17.3), and sends this value to the recipients as the final timestamp. The recipients mark the message as deliverable (d) and reorder their pending queues as shown. Since there are no undeliverable messages ahead of m_1 at site 3, m_1 can be taken off the queue and delivered there, but it cannot be delivered at

Site 1   Site 2   Site 3

m_3	m_1	m_2	
15.1	16.1	17.1	$\cdots$
u	u	u	

m_2	m_1	m_3	
16.2	17.2	18.2	$\cdots$
u	u	u	

m_1	m_3	m_2	
17.3	18.3	19.3	$\cdots$
u	u	u	

Step 1

m_3	m_2	m_1	
15.1	17.1	17.3	$\cdots$
u	u	d	

m_2	m_1	m_3	
16.2	17.3	18.2	$\cdots$
u	d	u	

m_1	m_3	m_2	
17.3	18.3	19.3	$\cdots$
d	u	u	

Step 2

m_3	m_1	m_2	
15.1	17.1	19.3	$\cdots$
u	d	d	

m_1	m_3	m_2	
17.3	18.2	19.3	$\cdots$
d	u	d	

m_3	m_2		
18.3	19.3		$\cdots$
u	d		

Step 3

m_1	m_3	m_2	
17.3	18.3	19.3	$\cdots$
d	d	d	

m_3	m_2		
18.3	19.3		$\cdots$
d	d		

m_3	m_2		
18.3	19.3		$\cdots$
d	d		

Step 4

Figure 14.4 The *ABCAST* protocol

sites 1 and 2. Step 3 shows the pending queues after the sender of m_2 sends its final timestamp, and Step 4 shows the queues after the sender of m_3 does the same. At this point, all the messages can be taken off the pending queues and delivered. Observe that the messages are delivered at all sites in the order m_1, m_3 and then m_2, which was the order of their final timestamps.

The *ABCAST* protocol assigns each broadcast a unique final timestamp, and all messages are delivered in the order of their final timestamps. This ensures that broadcasts are delivered in the same order at all destinations. Because the sender picks the *largest* of the proposed timestamps, changing the timestamp of a message from its proposed one to the final one can only cause it to be moved *behind* other messages in a pending queue, and never ahead of them. So a message might have to wait for other messages to be delivered before it gets delivered, but there will never be a situation where it is necessary to deliver a message before one that has already been taken off the queue and delivered (which would cause this protocol to fail).

Let us examine the costs associated with this protocol. First, observe that a message cannot be delivered as soon as it is received; it has to remain in the pending queue until at least a second round of message exchange has occurred, and it has been assigned a committed timestamp. It has also to wait for all messages with smaller timestamps to be delivered. This represents the latency cost. Second, each broadcast results in a higher communication overhead beyond the act of sending the message to each destination site. Each recipient must also send proposed timestamps back to the initiator and the initiator must respond to all of them with the final timestamp. Finally, the message must be saved in the pending queue from the time it is received until the time it is delivered. This represents the storage cost. (Actually, the storage cost is higher than this. Some information about a message has to be maintained at each recipient until it is known that it has been delivered at *all* the destinations.)

How this protocol deals with failures has not been described. If a recipient crashes in the middle of the protocol, the initiator simply ignores it and continues the protocol without it. If the initiator fails, one of the recipients must take over and run the protocol to completion. It doesn't matter which recipient does this, but if several recipients might take over in parallel, steps must be taken to ensure that all arrive at the same outcome even in the presence of further failures. Details of such a mechanism are given in Birman and Joseph (1987a).

Chang and Maxemchuck (1984) describe another family of protocols that achieve ordered reliable broadcasts. Their protocols do not require the transport layer to provide reliable point-to-point transmission — unreliable datagrams suffice because the retransmission of lost messages is built into their protocols. In these protocols, one member of each group of processes is assigned a token and is called the 'token site'. The token site assigns a timestamp for each broadcast, and broadcasts are delivered at all destinations in the order of their timestamps. This ensures that all broadcasts to a group are delivered in the same order at all members of the group. The protocols require that the token be periodically transferred from site to site. The list of possible token sites (called the 'token list') is maintained at each of the token sites, and a token site passes the token to the next site in this list. The protocols operate correctly as long as the number of failures that occur is less than the size of the token list. The sites go through a 'reformation phase' whenever the token list has to be changed — either because of a failure or because a new site is to be added to the list. The different members in this family of protocols have different values for the size of the token list and different rules for when the token is passed to the next site in the token list. These rules also determine the various costs for the protocols.

In the Chang and Maxemchuck protocols, a message may be committed and memory of it discarded only when the token has been passed twice around the sites in the token list. At the end of the first round, it is known that the message has been received everywhere, and at this point it becomes safe to begin delivering copies. At the end of the second round, it is known that the message has been committed (delivered) everywhere, and processes can safely discard any status information needed during the protocol. Thus the rate at which the token is passed from site to site (and the size of the token list) determines the latency cost as well as storage cost (as information about a message has to be stored until it is committed). If the token is passed rapidly, the latency and storage costs are minimized, but unless special hardware can be exploited (such as an Ethernet broadcast), communication costs will go up. The communication costs may be reduced by passing the token infrequently, but this increases the latency and storage costs. In the limit, if the token is never passed, the additional communication goes down to one acknowledgement message per broadcast, but the latency and storage costs go up to infinity and fault-tolerance is lost.

There are several recent developments in this general area. Within the ISIS system, a version of *ABCAST* is being implemented that uses elements of the token-passing approach within a pre-existing ISIS *process group*. In this scheme, a reliable protocol is used to disseminate a message to a set of group members. One of these, the token holder, then performs a second reliable broadcast to inform recipients of the order in which message delivery should take place. The two phases use a weakly ordered broadcast that requires only a single round of communication. The cost is thus comparable to that of *ABCAST*. However, the protocol permits an optimization according whereby the token is passed to the sender of a broadcast as part of the ordering message. If the sender then does a *second* ordered broadcast, it can combine the two rounds into a single one, yielding a very substantial performance improvement. One might wonder how this scheme avoids the token-passing and reformation overhead of the Chang-Maxemchuck scheme. The reason is that these functions are pushed down into the mechanisms that ISIS uses for process-group management and to implement the crash failure abstraction, which impose minimal overhead unless a failure actually occurs.

Spauster and Garcia-Molina (1989) have proposed a third approach to solving the message-ordering problem. In their protocol, a tree is superimposed on the set of processes in the system. To transmit a broadcast, the message is forwarded to the least common ancestor of the destination processes, which in turn uses a reliable FIFO protocol to handle message delivery. As in the modified ISIS protocol, the cost is low unless a failure occurs, in which case a more complex mechanism is required to reform the tree and complete any broadcast interrupted by the failure. In addition, recent work by Peterson *et al.* has resulted in an ordered broadcast implemented on a set of kernel primitives called *Psync*. A detailed discussion of the approach can be found in Peterson, Buchholz, and Schlichting (1989).

Finally, there has been considerable recent interest in the use of 'optimistic' protocols, especially in settings where a small set of senders broadcast to large numbers of destinations. These protocols require the destinations to send negative acknowledgements when packet loss is detected, and often employ special hardware features (such as Ethernet multicast) to reduce the number of messages transmitted. Such approaches make trade offs to reduce communication traffic; for example, very long delivery latencies are a common problem in optimistic schemes. Hybrid schemes have also been proposed, for example using Ethernet multicast for transmission and some modified acknowledgement scheme with constant cost and limited latency to confirm delivery. A good discussion of these approaches appears in Stephenson (1989).

14.6 Weaker orderings

Protocols that place a total order on all broadcasts are useful for many applications, but it has been shown that they entail substantial latency, communication and storage costs. The natural question that arises is whether or not there are less expensive protocols that achieve something less than a total order on broadcasts but which are nevertheless useful for some applications. Within the ISIS system, much work has been done to develop protocols that provided sufficient order to obtain consistency in replicated data, but which are asynchronous in the sense that messages can be delivered as soon as they arrive at a destination (without waiting for further rounds of communication). The advantage of using such a protocol to transmit updates to replicated data is that if there is a copy of the data at the sender site, the latency to update this copy is almost zero (as a message can be sent from one site to itself with very little overhead). As a result, a local copy of replicated data can be updated at almost the same rate as a piece of non-replicated data (with some background overhead becaus? of messages being sent to the sites with the other copies). We begin with an example.

Figure 14.5 shows processes P and Q sending broadcasts b_1, b_2, ... to a group consisting of A and B. (The dotted lines represent the passage of time; the solid lines represent messages being sent.) For some applications, it may not be important that broadcasts from different processes be delivered in the same order, and it may be quite acceptable that A receives b_1 before b_2, while B receives b_2 before b_1, for example. On the other hand, because b_3 and b_4 were sent by the *same* process P and b_4 was sent after b_3, the broadcast b_4 could contain information that depends on b_3. For example, if A and B were maintaining

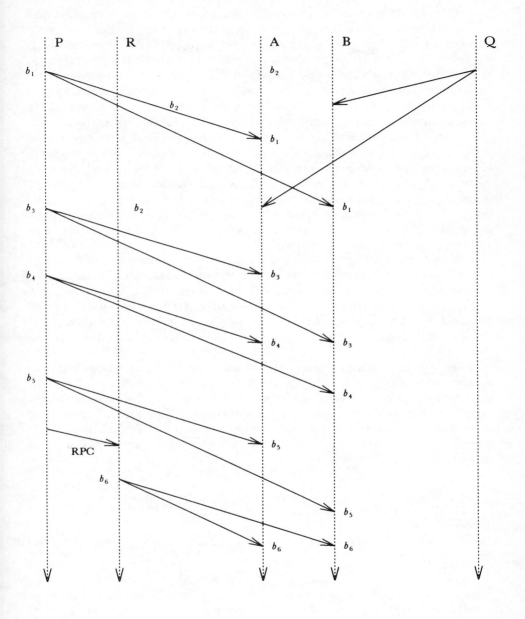

Figure 14.5 Unordered, FIFO, and causal broadcasts

a distributed data structure and b_3 were a message to initialize this structure and b_4 were a message that causes this data structure to be accessed, then b_4 depends on b_3. Because of this causal dependency, it is desirable that b_4 is delivered after b_3 everywhere. The property required here is a FIFO property, namely that all broadcasts made by the same process are delivered everywhere in the order that they were sent. This property is achieved automatically if the transport layer gives sequenced point-to-point communication (provided, of course, that the messages are sent directly from the initiator to the recipients). But what if P does a broadcast b_5, which then does a remote procedure call to R, which then does a broadcast b_6? Broadcast b_6 is logically part of the same computation as b_5 and could have exactly the same causal dependency on b_5 as b_4 has on b_3 (b_5 could be a message to initialize a data structure and b_6 one to access it). Unfortunately, because b_5 and b_6 originate from different processes, the FIFO property gives no guarantee about the order in which they will be delivered. This is especially unfortunate because if b_6 were a broadcast from within a *local* procedure call, a programmer developing this application could take advantage of the fact that the deliveries would be ordered, but just because the procedure call happened to be remote, the task becomes far more complicated. What would be useful here is a broadcast protocol that guarantees that if the initiation of a broadcast b is causally dependent (as described above) on the initiation of a broadcast b', then b will be delivered after b' everywhere. We need to formalize the notion of causal dependency before we can proceed with the protocol.

An event a occurring in a process P can affect an event b in a process Q only if information about a reaches Q by the time b occurs there. In the absence of shared memory, the only way that such information can be carried from process to process is through messages that travel between them. Accordingly, as in Lamport (1978), the potential causality relation $a \rightarrow b$ (b is potentially causally dependent on a) can be defined to be the transitive closure of the two relations $\underset{1}{\rightarrow}$ and $\underset{2}{\rightarrow}$ defined as follows:

1. $a \underset{1}{\rightarrow} b$ if a and b are events that occur in the same process and a occurs before b.

2. $a \underset{2}{\rightarrow} b$ if a is the sending of a message and b is the receipt of the same message.

Informally, if a is an event in process P and b is an event in process Q, then $a \rightarrow b$ if and only if there is a sequence of messages $m_1, m_2, \cdots, m_n$ and processes $P = P_0, P_1, P_2, ..., P_n = Q$; ($n \geqslant 0$) such that message m_i travels from P_{i-1} to P_i and is delivered to P_i before m_{i+1} is sent from there. Also, m_1 is sent from P after event a occurs there, and m_n is delivered to Q before b occurs there. It is the existence of this sequence of messages that enables information about a to be carried to Q and so makes b potentially causally dependent on a.

What is needed, then, is a broadcast protocol that ensures that if $send(b_1) \rightarrow send(b_2)$, b_2 will be delivered after b_1 at all overlapping destinations. The protocol *CBCAST* (for Causal BroadCAST) described in Birman and Joseph (1987a) achieves this. The protocol in Peterson, Buchholz, and Schlichting (1989) is similar. The easiest way to explain the CBCAST protocol is to start with a grossly inefficient version and derive the actual protocol from it. Imagine that for each process P the broadcast layer at its site keeps a buffer containing every message P has ever sent or received (in order). Any time a broadcast b is initiated by P, this buffer will then contain every message that could have causally affected b. Whenever any message m is sent from a site, the protocol sends the entire contents of these buffers along with m (in other words, it piggybacks the buffers onto m). At the receiving site, the broadcast layer adds the piggybacked messages to all its buffers (preserving their order, but discarding duplicates) even if the piggybacked messages are not destined for any process at that site. It then delivers (in order) any messages destined for processes at that site, the last of which will be m.

The reason why the protocol described above works is simple. If b_1 is initiated by process P at site S and b_2 by Q at T and if $send(b_1) \rightarrow send(b_2)$, then there must be a sequence of messages as described above from S to T. The protocol ensures that b_1 will be piggybacked on this sequence of messages (and possibly on other messages as well) and so b_1 will reach T and before b_2 is sent. Since b_1 will be in Q's buffer when b_2 is sent from there, b_1 will be piggybacked on b_2 and will hence be delivered before b_2 at any overlapping destination.

The problem with the scheme described above, of course, is that the amount of information to be piggybacked grows indefinitely. There are a number of ways in which the protocol described above can be improved. First, the buffers can be maintained on a per-site basis instead of on a per-process basis. This reduces the storage overhead. Second, a message does not have to be piggybacked to a site if it has been sent there already. More importantly, messages do not have to be piggybacked once it is known that they have reached all their destinations, because they will be discarded on arrival anyway. This means that a message needs to be piggybacked only from the time a broadcast is initiated until the time it reaches at all the destination sites. If we call this time period δ, piggybacking need occur only if broadcasts are being made at a rate of more than one every δ time units. δ is usually a very small window and so unless broadcasts are being made rapidly one after another, there need be very little actual piggybacking. The initiator can stop piggybacking a message when its transport layer receives an acknowledgement from all the recipients; other sites must continue to do so until they are informed that the message has reached all its destinations. The performance of this protocol thus depends on how effectively this information is propagated to sites that have a copy of this message. This issue can be avoided by piggybacking a message only on messages going directly to the destination sites. Other sites are instead sent a small descriptor that identifies the message. If a destination receives a descriptor before it receives the actual message, it must wait for the message to arrive before delivering any message that may causally depend on it.

Messages sent using the CBCAST protocol can be delivered as soon as they reach a destination site. There is no need to wait for additional rounds of communication and hence no latency cost (except to the extent that transmitting larger messages may take a slightly longer time). The protocol requires no additional messages besides those required to get the message from the initiator to the destinations, but it does increase the message size. In most systems, the *number* of messages (and not their size) is the dominant factor in the communication cost† and so the communication overhead is minimal. The protocol does have a storage cost because the messages have to be buffered while piggybacking is going on.

FIFO broadcasts preserve the order of causality in a computation that runs at one site; causal broadcasts generalize this to distributed computations. Causal broadcasts can be used to order deliveries when all broadcasts to a group arise from a computation with a single thread of control, but this thread of control may span several sites (because of remote procedure calls, for example). They can also be used when broadcasts to a group arise from different computations, but these computations have some other form of synchronization relative to one another. An example of this is broadcasts to a group that arise from within nested transactions whose sub-transactions may run on different sites. Here, the broadcasts arising from sub-transactions of any one transaction will be ordered because they are causally related; broadcasts arising from different transactions will be ordered because of the concurrency control mechanism used to implement nested transactions.

14.7 Real-time delivery guarantees

Another property that may be useful in a reliable broadcast protocol is that delivery will occur within a specified amount of time after the initiation of the protocol. This is especially useful in real-time systems and in control applications, where a broadcast that arrives too late may not produce the desired response. If a broadcast is being made to a set of processes to instruct them to each begin some action, it might also be desirable that broadcast deliveries occur within a known time interval of one another, so that their actions take place with some degree of simultaneity. The protocols described earlier make no such guarantees — they ensure that broadcasts will eventually be delivered to all non-faulty destinations, but delivery could take arbitrarily long.

Cristian *et al.* (1986) describe several broadcast protocols that provide real-time delivery guarantees. For such protocols, one needs to have timing bounds on various aspects of system behaviour, for example, a bound on the time it takes for the system to schedule a process for execution, a bound on the time it

---

† This is true only up to a point. If a message size gets very large, it may have to be fragmented into a number of smaller packets before being transmitted.

takes for a message to travel from one site to another, the ability to schedule an event to occur within a certain time, and so on. Given such bounds, one can devise broadcast protocols by taking into account worst-case timing behaviour. For example, simultaneous delivery can be achieved by timestamping each broadcast with the sending time t and computing Δ, the maximum time it can take for a message to reach a destination. Now, if a broadcast is buffered at each destination and delivered only at time $t + \Delta$, simultaneous delivery is achieved. It should be noted that 'simultaneous' here means that the processors will deliver a broadcast at the same time *as read off their own clocks*. In practice, the clocks of individual processors will differ somewhat from real time, and a broadcast will *not* be delivered everywhere at exactly the same instant. However, by using algorithms such as described in Srikanth and Toueg (1987), the clocks of the various processors can be synchronized to the degree required, thus achieving the desired level of simultaneity.

The calculation of the constant Δ must take into account possible differences in clock values as well as possible scheduling and message transmission delays, and is described in detail in Cristian *et al.* (1986). In addition, this calculation must account for faulty system behaviour. One kind of possible failure is a 'timing fault'. Recall that the protocols were based on timing bounds for certain system activities. If the system violates these timing bounds (such as when a message takes longer to be delivered than the assumed upper bound), a timing fault occurs. Other classes of failures like omission or Byzantine failures could also be considered. Cristian *et al.* (1986) describe protocols to achieve reliable real-time broadcasts that tolerate increasingly higher classes of faults, from no faults at all to Byzantine faults.

There is a basic difference between these protocols and the ones described earlier. The earlier protocols use explicit message transfer to ensure that a broadcast has arrived at all its destinations and to agree on an order for its delivery. These protocols, on the other hand, use the passage of time (and knowledge of timing bounds on system behaviour) to deduce the same information implicitly. As a result, the latter protocols will, in general, have a lower communication cost. However the latency and storage costs are based on worst-case system behaviour. If the variance in the duration of system events (such as message transmission) is low and one has accurate estimates of these times, the latency and storage costs are likely also to be low. On the other hand, if the variance is high (as would happen if the load on the system is variable), then the fact that these costs are based on worst-case behaviour might make them unacceptably high. The latency is especially critical, because the perceived speed of an application performing broadcasts depends on this. For this reason, recent work on real-time protocols has been focused on ways to reduce the delay constant Δ under assumptions that limit the number of various types of faults that can occur while the protocol is executing. With these sorts of assumptions, Δ can be brought down into the 100ms range for a small network of fast machines with closely synchronized internal clocks.

14.8 Broadcasts to dynamically changing groups

Until now, only broadcasts made to a fixed set of destinations have been considered. The protocols described above assume that the set of destinations is known when a broadcast is initiated and that it does not change. For many applications, it is useful to be able to broadcast a message to a 'process group' — a logical name for a set of processes whose membership may change with time. Such a group may implement some service, like a document-formatting service or a compile service. The reason for implementing such a service using a group of processes instead of a single one may be to divide up the work of responding to a user's request over a number of machines, to obtain faster response time by executing a user's request on the machine best suited to that particular request, to have the service remain available despite the failures of some machines, or any combination of these. New members may join the group as the number of requests on the service increases or as idle machines volunteer their cycles for the service. Members may leave the group as the load on the service decreases or when a machine crashes. It is useful if a user of such a service can use the process group name to communicate with the service without needing to know the membership of the group or where the members are located.

To implement broadcasts to process groups, the system must provide a facility for mapping process group names to sets of processes, and provide some semantics for what it means to perform a broadcast to a group whose membership might be changing as the broadcast is under way. The V system (Cheriton and Zwaenepoel (1985)) provides a means to broadcasts to process groups, but there are no ordering guarantees on broadcast message delivery. Also, if the membership changes as a broadcast is in progress, it is possible for the broadcast to be delivered to some intermediate set of destinations that is neither the old membership nor the new one. In Cristian (1988), Cristian discusses the problem of agreeing on group membership in systems that have timing bounds on their behaviour, and describes a solution based on the protocols described in Cristian *et al.* (1986). The ISIS system provides an addressing mechanism that permits ordered broadcasts to be made to dynamically changing process groups. In addition to causal or totally ordered message delivery, ISIS guarantees that if the membership of a process group is changing as a broadcast is under way, the broadcast message will be delivered either to the members that were in the group before the change or to those that were in the group after the change, and never to some intermediate membership. In other words, it is never possible for a broadcast to a group to be delivered to some processes after they have seen a change in the group membership and to other processes before they have seen that change. Let us see why this property is useful.

Figure 14.6 shows processes executing in an environment where broadcast delivery is *not* ordered relative to group membership changes. A process P is using a broadcast to present a task made up of 6 sub-tasks to a group currently

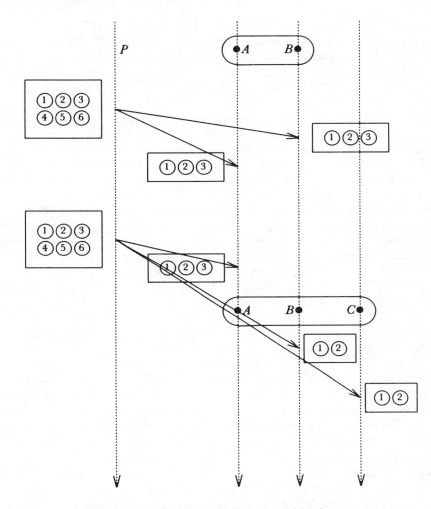

Figure 14.6 Unordered group membership changes

consisting of processes *A* and *B*. The group divides up the task equally, with the first process taking the first set of sub-tasks, and so on. Any deterministic ordering on process names may be used — the lexicographic order has been used in this example. Let us suppose that *P* sends the group another similar task around the same time that process *C* attempts to join the group. The figure shows *A* receiving the task before it knows that *C* has joined the group, while *B* and *C* receive the task after they see *C* join. Consequently, *A* divides the task on the assumption that the group consists of two members, while *B* and *C* do so on the assumption that there are three members. The result is an inconsistent division of the task. In this case, sub-task 3 gets executed twice (which may or may not be acceptable), but if this anomaly arose as a member was *leaving* the group instead of joining, some sub-tasks might end up not being executed by any member (which is clearly unacceptable). The only way to avoid this problem is for the group members to execute some protocol that ensures that they all have the same view of the group membership before they respond to any request. However, if the broadcast delivery had been ordered relative to group membership changes, this problem would not have arisen in the first place.

What the example illustrates is that if broadcast delivery is not ordered relative to group membership changes, and if the members of the group have to coordinate the actions they take in response to an incoming request, then additional protocols are needed to ensure that their response is based on consistent views of the group membership. This would increase the complexity of the algorithms needed and make the task of the person programming such an application a difficult one. On the other hand, if broadcast delivery *is* ordered relative to group membership changes, there are no such problems. Each member can respond to an incoming request based on its view of the group membership, with the assurance that when the other members receive the same request, they will all have exactly the same view, and will consequently take consistent actions. Note that group membership may change not only when a process voluntarily joins or leaves a group, but also when a process drops out of a group because of a failure. To be completely useful, the process group mechanism must order broadcast deliveries with respect to the latter kind of group membership change as well. This might seem impossible to achieve because the system has no control over when failures occur, but in fact it can be achieved because what is important is that each process *observes* group membership changes and broadcast deliveries in the same order, or that each process *detects* failures and broadcast deliveries in the same order, and not that the failure actually occurs in an orderly fashion. Similar observations have been made for database systems that manage replicated data in the presence of failures (Bernstein and Goodman (1983); Bernstein, Hadzilacos, and Goodman (1987)).

To explain how the process group mechanism is implemented in the ISIS system, we will first describe a simplistic mechanism and then show how it may be modified. For now assume that every site in the system has a table containing the names of every existing process group and their current membership. When a process at a site initiates a broadcast to a group, the system simply obtains a list of the current members from the table at that site and executes the relevant broadcast protocol using that list. When a process joins or leaves a group, the tables must all be changed. This is done using a special broadcast protocol whose deliveries are ordered consistently relative to *all* other kinds of broadcasts. In ISIS, the other kinds of broadcast are ABCAST and CBCAST, and the corresponding special broadcast protocol is called GBCAST (for group broadcast). An interlocking mechanism is also required to ensure that broadcasts that have been initiated using the old membership list are delivered before a GBCAST is delivered. When a GBCAST is delivered at a site, the table at that site is changed and all interested processes are notified of the membership change. Since GBCAST is ordered relative to all other broadcasts, all processes observe membership changes in a way that is ordered consistently with respect to other broadcast deliveries.

It is impractical to maintain group membership lists on a system-wide basis and carry out a system-wide broadcast whenever the membership of any group changes. What ISIS actually does is to maintain information about the membership of a group at the sites where members reside (member sites) and optionally at a few other sites (client sites). Membership changes are broadcast using GBCAST only to member and client sites. This ensures that membership changes are ordered relative to broadcasts that originate from member or client sites. If a broadcast is made to a group from a site that is neither a member nor a client site, the system first obtains the current membership list from elsewhere (or uses an old but possibly inaccurate cached list) and then executes the relevant broadcast protocol. This leaves open the possibility that the membership may have changed between when the broadcast message was initiated and when it is about to be delivered. The system detects this if it happens and does not deliver the message. Instead, it sends the new membership list to the initiator site, which then restarts the broadcast protocol with this new set of destinations. This protocol will continue to iterate until the membership list remains unchanged from the time the broadcast is initiated until the time it is delivered. This kind of iteration increases the possible latency cost. This cost can be reduced by increasing the number of client sites, but the trade off is that membership changes now become more expensive.

14.9 Degraded behaviour

The protocols described in this chapter have been designed to be tolerant of various types of failure and by using them one can achieve a certain degree of robustness in a distributed system. At the same time, it is important to be aware of the limitations of these protocols — the assumptions they make, the types of failures they *do not* handle, and the ways in which their performance may degrade when failures occur. Each class of broadcast protocols discussed above makes assumptions about the responsiveness of processors, the way that failures manifest themselves when they occur, and the way that a failed process or processor should be treated subsequent to the failure. Before applying a protocol in a given setting, it is important to evaluate the validity of these assumptions in the intended execution environment.

As an example, consider the protocols that ISIS uses. It was indicated above that ISIS implements a crash failure model. Specifically, ISIS assumes that processors fail by crashing and builds a crash failure detector using a low-level message exchange protocol, as described in Birman and Joseph (1987a). This low level protocol, in turn, is tolerant of message loss and duplicate delivery, but not of partitioning failures. It assumes that processors that continue to send out messages are non-faulty, and operates by having processors send 'Are you alive?' messages to other processors whenever they seem to be unresponsive. These probe messages are sent out sufficiently often to ensure that if a crash does occur, it will be noticed by some operational processor in a timely fashion. Based on this, a two-phase protocol is used to manage the processor status information on which the crash-failure abstraction is based.

From this, it can be seen that ISIS is simply intolerant of failures that cause a processor to continue executing while sending incorrect messages or violating the rules of its protocols. If such behaviour occurs, all bets are off. Moreover, if a processor becomes partitioned from the remainder of the ISIS system, or gets overloaded to such a degree that it ceases to respond to liveness probe messages, it will appear to have failed. ISIS handles these cases exactly as for a genuinely failed processor — by isolating the processor from the rest of the system (any messages appearing to come from that processor are discarded) and by requiring that the processor in question explicitly rejoins and is reintegrated into the system. Processes executing on the 'failed' processor are informed that they have been isolated from the rest of the system, and are expected to react in a way that limits the degree of inconsistent behaviour that can occur during the period before it rejoins the rest of the system. In the current version of ISIS, if several processors find themselves partitioned from the remainder of the system, they may *all* be forced to undergo such a restart: normal execution is permitted only in a partition that has a majority of processors in it. An important area for future work in ISIS is to permit a significant level of processing to continue in such a partitioned mode and to provide useful tools for merging partitions when communication is restored.

What are the practical implications of all this? One is that the ISIS system should probably not span communication links subject to frequent communication partitioning. A preferable approach would be to run one copy of ISIS on each side of such a link, and use other 'long haul' mechanisms to connect applications that run on both sides. Similarly, since the ISIS approach incurs an overhead when a site fails or recovers, there are probably limits on the size of network within which it can be used. However, the ISIS failure detector seems to scale up to at least one or two hundred machines without imposing a severe overhead, and this is without any sort of hierarchical scheme — implementation of this is the obvious next step. On the other hand, the fact that an unresponsive machine could be considered failed is a potential source of concern. If one were to overload a collection of machines running these sorts of protocols, some machines might be treated as if they had crashed, which would serve to exacerbate the load on the system. One could speculate about the use of adaptive methods to deal with this problem more gracefully, but they would certainly increase the system latency in responding to a failure, and in any case it is unclear how one would implement such a scheme in a decentralized fashion. The point here is that serious thought needs to be given to the operational characteristics of an environment and the manner in which it degrades under load as a basic part of a decision to use protocols such as these.

Similar considerations apply in the case of the real-time broadcast protocols. These protocols ensure that processors which do not violate timing constraints will receive broadcasts correctly, but they do not provide a means for a processor that violates these constraints to recognize that it has done so. This is a serious problem because such a faulty processor could be in an inconsistent state, but can continue to communicate with the rest of the system, and its subsequent messages will not necessarily be rejected by the operational processors in the system. Thus these protocols can allow information to propagate out of an inconsistent processor, and this could compromise the entire system. The real-time protocols place a number of timing constraints on the system, including limits on the maximum time before a processor responds to a message, on the time needed to propagate a message through the network, and on the degree to which processor clocks are synchronized. Clearly, these are all constraints that an overloaded system could violate. It can be argued that this whole issue limits the use of real-time protocols to applications where any resulting inconsistent behaviour does not compromise the correctness of the system, or where overloads simply cannot occur. If one adopts the latter assumption, the protocols should only be used in systems known to operate far from the thresholds at which timing faults might become common. Otherwise, were the system load to gradually rise above these thresholds, widespread violations of atomicity might suddenly occur, leading to a catastrophic failure of the distributed application as a whole. Although it seems plausible that one could design a class of adaptive real time protocols immune to this problem, we know of no current research on this topic.

14.10 Conclusion

In this chapter a number of broadcast protocols that are reliable subject to a variety of ordering and delivery guarantees have been considered. Developing applications that are distributed over a number of sites and/or must tolerate the failures of some of them becomes a considerably simpler task when such protocols are available for communication. Indeed, without such protocols the kinds of distributed applications that can reasonably be built will have a very limited scope. As the trend towards distribution and decentralization continues, it will not be surprising if reliable broadcast protocols have the same role in distributed operating systems of the future that message passing mechanisms have in the operating systems of today. On the other hand, the problems of engineering such a system remain large. For example, deciding which protocol is the most appropriate to use in a certain situation or how to balance the latency-communication-storage costs is not an easy question. It is our hope that as our experience with broadcast based systems grows, we will begin to gain insight into some of these problems.

Even lacking these sorts of insights, however, the experience of programming with reliable broadcast protocols can surprising in many ways. An entirely new form of distributed computing becomes practical, one in which teams of processes execute asynchronously but cooperate with one another in a consistent fashion, sharing computational tasks and backing one another up for fault-tolerance. Fredrick Hayes-Roth (also known for his work on speech recognition) recently commented that 'a revolutionary change in how we think about distributed computing is now within our reach, one that will be every bit as striking as the transition from black and white to colour when Dorothy steps out of her aunt's house into the Land of Oz.' Having worked with reliable broadcast protocols and built a system that elevates them to a high level of abstraction, we are now convinced that reliable broadcasts are the key to this change in perspective. In the next chapter, some of the reasoning underlying this conviction is explored.

14.11 References

P. A. Bernstein and N. Goodman (1983). 'The Failure and Recovery Problem for Replicated Databases'. *Proceedings 2nd ACM Symposium on Principles of Distributed Computing*: 114—122, August 1983.

P. A. Bernstein, V. Hadzilacos, and N. Goodman (1987). *Concurrency Control and Recovery in Database Systems*. Addison Wesley, Reading, MA, 1987.

K. P. Birman and T. A. Joseph (1987a). 'Reliable Communication in the Presence of Failures'. *ACM Transactions on Computer Systems* 5(1): 47—76, Feb. 1987.

K. P. Birman and T. Joseph (1987b). 'Exploiting virtual synchrony in distributed systems'. *Proceedings Eleventh Symposium on Operating System Principles*: 123—138, Nov. 1987.

A. D. Birrell and B. J. Nelson (1984). 'Implementing Remote Procedure Calls'. *ACM Transactions on Computer Systems* 2(1): 39—59, February 1984.

Jo-Mei Chang and N. F. Maxemchuck (1984). 'Reliable Broadcast Protocols'. *ACM Transactions on Computer Systems* 2(3): 251—273, Aug. 1984.

D. R. Cheriton and W. Zwaenepoel (1985). 'Distributed Process Groups in the V Kernel'. *ACM Transactions on Computer Systems* 3(2): 77—107, May 1985.

F. Cristian, H. Aghili, R. Strong, and D. Dolev (1986). *Atomic Broadcast: From Simple Message Diffusion to Byzantine Agreement*. IBM Research Report RJ 5244 (54244), July 1986.

F. Cristian (1988). *Reaching Agreement on Processor Group Membership in Synchronous Distributed Systems*. IBM Research Report RJ 5964 (59426), March 1988.

L. Lamport (1978). 'Time, Clocks, and the Ordering of Events in a Distributed System'. *Communications of the ACM* 21(7): 558—565, July 1978.

L. Lamport, R. Shostak, and M. Pease (1982). 'The Byzantine Generals Problem'. *ACM Transactions on Programming Languages and Systems* **4** (3): 382—401, July 1982.

G. Neiger and S. Toueg (1988). 'Automatically Increasing the Fault-Tolerance of Distributed Systems'. *Proceedings Seventh ACM Symposium on Principles of Distributed Computing*, Toronto, Ontario, Aug. 1988.

K. J. Perry and S. Toueg (1986). 'Distributed Agreement in the Presence of Processor and Communication Faults'. *IEEE Transactions on Software Engineering* **SE-12** (3): 477—482, Mar. 1986.

L. L. Peterson, N. Buchholz, and R. Schlichting (1989). 'Preserving and Using Context Information in Interprocess Communication'. *ACM Transactions on Computer Systems*, 1989. (Conditionally accepted.)

R. D. Schlichting and F. B. Schneider (1983). 'Fail-Stop Processors: An Approach to Designing Fault-Tolerant Computing Systems'. *ACM Transactions on Computer Systems* **1** (3): 222—238, Aug. 1983.

F. B. Schneider (1986). 'A paradigm for reliable clock synchronization'. *Proceedings Advanced Seminar on Real-Time Local Area Networks, Bandol, France*, April 1986.

A. Spauster and H. Garcia-Molina (1989). 'Message Ordering in a Multicast Environment'. *Proceedings Ninth International Conference on Distributed Computing Systems*, June 1989.

T. K. Srikanth and S. Toueg (1987). 'Optimal Clock Synchronization'. *Journal of the ACM* **34** (3): 626—645, July 1987.

P. Stephenson (1989). *Ph.D. Dissertation, forthcoming.* Dept. of Computer Science, Cornell University, 1989.

A. S. Tanenbaum (1988). *Computer Networks.* Prentice-Hall, Englewood Cliffs, N.J. 07632, 1988. (2nd edition.)

Chapter 15

Exploiting replication in distributed systems

K. P. Birman and T. A. Joseph

15.1 Replication in directly distributed systems

This chapter examines techniques for replicating data and execution in *directly distributed systems*: systems in which multiple processes interact directly with one another while continuously respecting constraints on their joint behaviour. Directly distributed systems are often required to solve difficult problems, ranging from management of replicated data to dynamic reconfiguration in response to failures. It will be shown here that these problems reduce to more primitive, order-based consistency problems, which can be solved using primitives such as the reliable broadcast protocols discussed in Chapter 14. Moreover, given a system that implements reliable broadcast primitives, a flexible set of high-level 'tools' can be provided for building a wide variety of directly distributed application programs.

15.1.1 Using replication to enhance availability and fault-tolerance

Replication is often central to solving distributed computing problems. For example, modularity and price-performance considerations argue for decentralization of software in factory automation settings. However, many factories contain devices controlled by dedicated processors that require real-time response. Any delay imposed on the controllers by the network must be bounded. In a system where data is not replicated or cached, this would be hard to guarantee because of possible packet loss and unpredictable load on remote servers. Distributed real-time systems thus need ways to replicate information that may be needed along time-critical paths.

Replication can be a powerful tool for solving other types of problems. For example, in a factory automation setting, distributed *execution* may be used by applications that need to subdivide tasks by concurrently allocating multiple processes (or multiple devices) to a single piece of work. In order to distribute the execution of a single request over a set of high-speed processes, however, one must also replicate any information that they use to coordinate their actions. A centralized 'coordinator' would represent a single point of failure and a potential performance bottleneck.

Fault-tolerance requirements are another major reason for replicating data. In a non-distributed setting a failure rarely affects anything but the user of the crashed program or machine. In a network, however, the effects of a crash can ripple through large numbers of machines. A program that will survive the failures of programs with which it interacts must have access to redundant copies of critical resources and ensure that its state is never dependent, even indirectly, on information to which only the failed program had access. It may also be necessary to maintain backup processes that will take over from a failed process and complete time-critical computations or computations that have acquired mutual exclusion on shared resources.

15.1.2 The trade off between shared memory and message passing

At the heart of any distributed system that distributes or replicates information is the problem of *transferring* information between cooperating processes. Broadly speaking, this can be done in one of two ways: by permitting the processes to interact with some common but passive resource or memory, or by supporting message exchange between them. There are advantages and disadvantages associated with each approach, hence the most appropriate style of information transfer for a particular problem must be determined by an analysis of the characteristics of that problem. For example, most database systems use the shared memory paradigm. In other settings, however, a shared resource might represent a bottleneck that could be avoided using replication and direct message-based interactions between the processes using that resource.

This point is important because the approach used to replicate data depends strongly on the way in which processes will interact. For example, considerable recent work (Rashid *et al.* (1987)) has been invested in the development of distributed virtual memory schemes, an approach introduced in the Apollo Domain operating system (Apollo (1985)). Synchronization in such systems is often based on transactional approaches, such as the database replication techniques described in Chapter 12. The shared-memory approach to replication and synchronization thus leads to a whole school of thought concerning distributed program design and development.

As noted earlier, in this chapter applications in which processes interact directly with one another and where the actions taken by one process may be explicitly coordinated with those taken by another process are of particular interest. The style of distributed programming needed to support this sort of application, and the most appropriate tools for implementing it, are substantially different than for the shared memory and transactional case.

Below, we start by identifying a set of characteristics of problems that call for direct interactions or cooperation between the processes that solve that problem. This characterization leads to a list of services that a directly distributed system may require. Next, we look at a number of systems in order to understand how they address the problems in this list. Finally, we examine a particular model for solving these problems in a message-passing environment and a set of solutions that can be easily understood in terms of this model.

15.1.3 Assumptions and limitations

Although this chapter explores a number of approaches to replication and distributed consistency, some assumptions are made that limit the applicability of the treatment. The model used here is intended to match a typical local area network or a loosely coupled multiprocessor. The programs and computers in such systems fail benignly, by crashing without sending out incorrect messages. Processors do not have synchronized clocks, hence the failure of an entire site can only be detected *unreliably*, using timeouts. Message communication is assumed to be reliable but bursty, because packets can be lost and may have to be retransmitted.

Two major problems that arise in LAN settings will not be considered here. The first is network partitioning, where the network splits into subnetworks between which communication is impaired (for example, if a LAN bridge fails). Providing replication that spans partitions is a difficult problem and an active research area. Secondly, problems that place real-time constraints on distributed algorithms or protocols will not be discussed here. Real-time issues are hard to isolate; once they are introduced, the entire system must often be treated from a real-time perspective. That is, although our methods are potentially useful in systems for which a real-time constraint leads the designer to dedicate a computer to some device, it will be assumed that the real-time aspects of such problems do not extend beyond the control program itself.

15.2 Consistent distributed behaviour in distributed systems

When processes cooperate to implement some distributed behaviour, an important issue is to ensure that their actions will be 'mutually consistent'. Not surprisingly, the precise meaning that one attaches to consistency has important implications throughout a distributed systems that presents coordinated behaviour. As shown in previous chapters, transactional serializability is a widely accepted form of consistency. In intuitive terms, a transactional system acts as if processes execute one by one, with each process modifying data objects in an atomic way that can be isolated from the actions taken by other processes. This leads to a natural question: should *all* types of distributed consistency be viewed as variant forms of transactional consistency, or are there problems that can only be addressed using other methods?

Looking at the factory automation setting, one finds that whereas shared shared memory problems fit well into the standard transactional framework, directly distributed problems generally do not. Consider the following two examples:

> ● *Build software for monitoring job status and materials inventories. Updates will be done by the warehouses (quantities on hand), 'cell controllers' (requests for materials and changes in job status), and from a central management site (changes in prices, deliveries from suppliers, changes in job priorities, and so on). Queries will be done from managerial offices throughout the factory complex.*

> ● *Develop software for a cell controller operating a set of drills. Each drill is independently controlled by a dedicated microprocessor. The cell as a whole receives a piece of work to do, together with a list of locations, sizes and tolerances for the holes to be drilled. It must efficiently schedule this work among the drills. Drills can go offline for maintenance or because of bits breaking, or come online while the cell is active, hence the scheduling problem is dynamic. Some drills are better suited to heavy low-precision work, while others are suitable for lighter high-precision work. Finally, it is critical no hole is drilled twice, even if a drill bit breaks before it is fully drilled, because this would result in a very low precision. Instead, an accurate list of partially drilled holes should be produced for a human technician to check and redrill manually.*

These two problems illustrate very different styles of distributed computing, and distributed consistency means something different for each. The former clearly lends itself to a transactional shared memory approach. One would configure the various programs into a 'star', with a database at the centre, perhaps replicated for fault-tolerance. Programs throughout the network interact through the database. Transactions are the natural consistency model for this setting. The essential observation to make is that the processes share data but are *independent*. By adopting a transactional style of interaction, they can avoid tripping over one another. Moreover, transactions provide a simple way to ensure that even if failures occur, the database remains intact and consistent.

Now consider the second problem. A star configuration seems much less natural here. The processes in a decentralized cell controller will need explicit knowledge of one another in order to coordinate their actions on a step-by-step basis. They need to reconfigure in response to events that can occur unpredictably, and to ensure the consistency of their views of the system state and one-another's individual states. When a control process comes online after being offline for a period of time, it will have to be reintegrated into the system, in a consistent way which may have very little to do with its state at the time of the failure. When a process goes offline, the processes that remain online need to assume responsibility for finishing any incomplete work and generating the list of holes to be manually checked. Moreover, it is not reasonable to talk about 'aborting' partially completed work, since this could result in redrilling a hole.

What should consistency mean in problems like this? All of the above considerations run contrary to the spirit of a transactional approach, where the goal is serializability — *non*-interference between processes. A process in a transactional system is encouraged to run as if in isolation, whereas the cell controller involves explicit interactions and interdependencies between processes. Transactions use aborts and rollback to recover from possibly inconsistent states, but in this example, rollback is physically impossible. On the other hand, although the kind of consistency required here may not be transactional, one would not want to go to the extreme of concluding that there is no meaningful form of consistency that applies in this setting. Certainly, there should be a reasonable 'explanation' for what each control process is doing, and this explanation should be in accordance with the cell controller specification. However, the explanation should be one that holds *continuously*, not just for 'committed' operations as in case of transactions. That is, a set of drills that operate concurrently should behave in mutually consistent ways *at all times*.

This leaves us with two choices. One option is to look at how the transactional model could be extended to cover these new requirements. The idea of extending transactions is hardly a new one, and has previously led to mechanisms like *top-level* transactions† (Liskov *et al.* (1987)), mixtures of serializable and non-serializable behaviours (Herlihy (1986a); Lynch, Blaustein, and Siegel (1986)), and specialized algorithms for concurrently accessing data structures like B-tree indexes. The trouble is that these introduce complexity into a model that was appealing for its simplicity. Moreover, these methods have been around for some time, and have proved appropriate only for a narrow set of problems. The second option — pursued here — is to develop a different style of distributed computation better matched to problems like the ones arising in a cell controller. The focus of this style of computation will be on enabling programs to reason consistently about one-another's states and actions.

15.3 A toolkit for directly distributed programming

One can think of a system that implements transactions as a collection of tools for solving problems involving shared data. These tools provide for synchronization, data access and update, transaction commit, and so forth. In this section, the problem of building directly distributed software by postulating a set of tools for helping directly distributed processes to coordinate their actions is discussed. Later, a variety of systems will be examined in the light of how close they come to solving these problems.

† A top-level transaction is essentially a way of sending a message from 'within' the scope of an uncommitted transaction to other transactions running outside that scope. It provides an escape from the shared memory paradigm into the message passing one. The fact that such a mechanism is needed within transactional systems is strong evidence that no single approach addresses all types of distributed system.

15.3.1 Components of the toolkit

What sorts of tools would the builder of a directly distributed system need? Although not exhaustive, the list of tools that follows is intended to be fairly extensive.

- Process groups: A way to form an association between a set of processes cooperating to solve a problem.

- Group communication: A location-transparent way to communicate with the members of a group or a list of groups and processes. In some systems, group communication consists only of a way to find some single member of a named group. In others, communication is broadcast-oriented† and *atomic*, meaning that all members of the destination group receive a given message unless a failure occurs, in which case either all the survivors receive it or none does. A problem that must be addressed is how group communication should work when the group membership is changing at the time the communication takes place. Should the broadcast be done before the change, after it, or is it acceptable for some group members to observe one ordering and some the other? Should message delivery to an unresponsive destination be retried indefinitely, or eventually interrupted — with the attendant risk that the destination was just experiencing a transient failure and is actually still operational? We will see that the way in which a system resolves these issues can limit the type of problems that process groups in the system can be used to solve.

- Replicated data: A mechanism permitting group members to maintain replicated data. Most approaches provide a 1-copy consistency property, analogous to 1-copy serializability.

- Synchronization: Facilities for synchronization of concurrent activities that interact through shared data or resources.

- Distributed execution: Facilities for partitioning the work required to solve a problem among the members of a process group.

- State monitoring mechanisms: Mechanisms for monitoring the state of the system and the membership of process groups, permitting processes to react to the failure of other group members.

- Reconfiguration mechanisms: Facilities with which the system can adapt dynamically to failures, recoveries, and load changes that impact on work processing strategies.

---

† A group broadcast should not be confused with a hardware broadcast. A group broadcast provides a way to communicate with all members of some group. It may or may not make use of hardware facilities for broadcasting to all the machines connected to a local area network. Here, unless it is explicitly indicated that a hardware broadcast is being discussed, the term broadcast will always mean broadcast to a group.

• Recovery mechanisms: Mechanisms for automating recovery, which could range from a way to restart services when a site reboots to facilities for reintegrating a component into an operational system that is actively engaged in distributed computations.

15.3.2 Consistency viewed as a tool

Let us return to the issue of consistency. In the context of a set of tools, a mechanism that provides for consistent behaviour can also be understood as a sort of tool, but it is a more abstracted one than the sorts of 'tools that do specific things' listed above. For example, in a shared memory setting, consistent behaviour generally means that the accesses made to the data by client programs are serializable (Bernstein and Goodman (1981)), and that some invariant holds on the state of programs themselves. Serializability is thus a tool for building transactional systems. In a directly distributed setting, there is no data manager or shared data items, and hence the serializability constraint is lost. Nonetheless, one needs a way to establish that the processes in the system, taken as a group, satisfy some set of system-wide invariants in addition to local ones on their states.

Any notion of distributed consistency will be incomplete unless it takes into account the *asynchronous* nature of the systems in question. In particular, a definition of consistency based on respecting global properties or invariants must somehow take time into account. When one says that two actions taken at different locations are in accord with a global predicate, that statement will have no meaning until it is decided *when* the predicate should be evaluated. This temporal dependency is particularly striking if the notion of consistency changes while the system executes. Thus, consistent behaviour in an idle cell controller is quite different from consistent behaviour while work is present. Taking a more extreme example, consistent behaviour of a distributed program for controlling a nuclear reaction means one thing during normal operation, but something entirely different if a cooling pump malfunctions. Since the switch from one rule to another cannot occur instantaneously, a notion of consistency both simple and 'dynamic' is needed.

Distributed systems designers have approached the consistency issue in several ways. Much theoretical work starts with a rigorous notion of distributed consistency. However, this work often relies on simplified system models that may not correspond to real networks. For example, the theoretical study of Byzantine agreement establishes limits on the achievable behaviour of a distributed agreement protocol. The failure modes permitted include malicious behaviours that real systems do not experience, and the model assumes that all processors share a common clock (so that they can run in lock-step). Unfortunately, however, real systems generally have multiple, independent processor clocks. Even if this were not the case, the cost of Byzantine agreement turns out to be very high. Similarly, innumerable papers have presented complex protocols to solve distributed problems, remarkably few of which have ever been implemented. Any practitioner who scans the literature discovers that many of these are in fact not 'implementable' because they make unrealistic assumptions.

At the other extreme, most existing 'distributed' operating systems provide little more than a message-passing mechanism, often only available through a cumbersome and inflexible communication subsystem. Systems like this simply abandon any rigorous form of consistency in favour of probabilistic behavioural statements. When attempts have been made to formally specify the behaviour of real distributed systems, the results have often included so much detail that it becomes hard to separate the abstract behaviour of the system from the implementation and interface it provides. Thus, a formal specification of a distributed system often includes details of how the message channels work, how addressing is handled, and so forth. While this information is unquestionably of value in designing applications that depend on a precise characterization of system behaviour, high level issues such as 'consistency' are obscured by such a treatment. As we will see, few of the problems in our list could be solved using a message-passing approach, and a highly detailed formalism describing exactly how the message-passing mechanism works offers little help.

An intermediate approach, which will be adopted here, restricts system behaviour in order to simplify the solutions to problems like the ones that arise in the toolkit. On the one hand, these restrictions must be efficiently implementable. On the other, it must be possible to talk in abstract terms about how distributed programs execute in the system, what it means for them to behave consistently, and how consistency can be achieved. Specifically, given a distributed system, it should be possible to describe its behaviour formally in a way that will help establish the correctness of algorithms that run under it. If this requires restrictions on the permissible behaviour of the system, it will be necessary to understand how those restrictions can be enforced and how weak they can be made.

15.3.3 Other properties needed in a toolkit

More will be needed than a set of tools if the intention is to solve real-world distributed computing problems. Questions of methodology, efficiency of the implementation, and scalability must also be addressed. For example, it is easy to solve database problems using transactions. To be able to say the same about directly distributed software, one would need to demonstrate that the tools lead to a natural and intuitive programming style in which problems can be isolated and solved one by one, in a step-wise fashion. Also, it must be easy to establish that the solutions will tolerate the concurrency and configuration changes characterizing asynchronous distributed systems. That is, given a notion of consistency, it should be reasonably easy to establish that a particular system in fact achieves consistent behaviour.

We will also want to pose questions about the extent to which the tools influence each other. Ideally, one would want tools that operate completely independently from one another. Otherwise, by extending the functionality of a system in one way, one would risk breaking the preexisting code. As we will see, 'orthogonality' of a set of tools is arrived at using mechanisms closely related to the ones by which consistency is achieved.

Efficiency is also an important consideration. Nobody will use a set of tools unless it yields programs that perform as well (or better) than software built using other methods. Moreover, the absolute level of performance achieved must be good enough to support the kinds of applications likely to employ direct distribution.

A final issue relates to questions of scale. Our tools treat direct distribution as a problem 'in the small'. One also needs to construct larger systems out of components built using these tools, in a way that isolates the larger-system issues from the implementation of the directly-distributed components of which it is built. Otherwise, it may be impractical to talk about system design and interface issues without simultaneously addressing implementation details.

15.4 System support for direct interactions between processes

A variety of existing systems provide facilities that could be used when building directly distributed software. Below, we look at how close these come to addressing the major items in our list of tools.

15.4.1 Basic RPC mechanisms and nested transactions

Most operating systems provide *remote procedure calls* (Birrell and Nelson (1984)). The technological support for remote procedure calls has advanced rapidly during the past decade, and sub-millisecond RPC times for inter-site communication should be common in operating systems in the near future. RPC does not, however, address any of the problems in the above list. Thus, the programmer, confronted by a direct distribution problem, would be in a very difficult situation when using a system in which RPC is the primary communication mechanism. Short of building a complex application-level mechanism to resolve these problems, there would seem to be no way to build directly distributed software using an unadorned RPC facility.

To make this more concrete, let us consider a specific problem that might arise in the context of the toolkit. Among the many issues that the tools must address, a key problem is to synchronize the actions of a set of processes that are performing some action concurrently. This is an instance of the well-known 'mutual exclusion' problem, and there is no doubt that any system supporting direct interactions between processes will need a mutual exclusion mechanism. A typical solution might implement a token managed with rules like the following:

> *A set of processes shares exactly one copy of a token, using operations to pass and request it. If the holder of the token fails, a pass is done automatically on its behalf, in such a way that the token is never permanently lost unless all processes fail, and duplicate tokens never arise within the operational set. New processes can join the set dynamically.*

How would one go about solving this problem using remote procedure calls? Typical RPC implementations detect failures using timeouts. Since timeouts can be inaccurate, an agreement protocol is needed to deal with token-holder failures. For example, one could try to inform all operational processes of each pass so that they know which process to request the token from. However, in addition to the inaccuracy of the failure detection mechanism, the solution must deal with the possibility that the token could be in motion at the time of a request. Dynamic group membership changes make these problems even more complicated.

Although there are several systems that extend RPC to deal with failures and concurrency, their orientation has been towards the shared memory paradigm, by extending RPC into a form of *nested transaction*. In a sense this is not surprising, since RPC is a pairwise mechanism in which the caller is the active participant and the called process is passive until it receives a request from the caller — a structure strongly evocative of the relationship between a transaction manager and a set of data managers on which it performs operations in a database setting. The ARGUS language and the CAMELOT system both take this approach, with ARGUS focusing on linguistic aspects of the problem and CAMELOT on performance and on creative use of virtual memory mechanisms. For brevity, neither of these systems will be discussed in detail here. However, it is important to recognize that the token passing problem remains difficult to solve in either system, and the same can be said for many (not all!) of the other tools in our list. The reader may want to try and design a token passing protocol using any of these approaches (pure RPC, ARGUS or CAMELOT): although feasible, it isn't easy!

Token passing is just a simple example of the sorts of problem that a directly distributed system would have to solve. In a setting where token passing is difficult, the implementation of complex directly distributed systems will surely be impractical. Some experimental evidence to support this claim exists: many systems support RPC but few provide mechanisms like the token passing facility outlined above. One system that does, at least internally, is Digital Equipment's VAX-Clusters system, which uses a locking facility similar to the token mechanism (Kronenberg, Levy, and Strecker (1986)). However, the lock manager implementation is complex, and few application designers could undertake a similar effort.

15.4.2 Quorum replication methods

Many database systems manage replicated data using quorum schemes (see Chapter 13). Quorum mechanisms support replicated data without the added 'baggage' of a full-blown transactional system. Do they offer an appropriate primitive on which to base a complex directly distributed program?

To answer this question, let us briefly review the mechanism that a quorum replication facility requires. The basic idea of a quorum replication scheme is that read and write operations must be performed on enough copies of the replicated data object to ensure that any pair of writes overlap on at least one replica and that any read overlaps with the most recent write.

When a quorum scheme is implemented, update operations require two phases, while read-only operations can be done in one phase. An update is transmitted during the first phase, and then committed in the second phase if a quorum of copies were updated and aborted otherwise. The abort is needed to avoid an uncertain outcome if some processes failed just after doing the update but before getting a chance to reply. Consequently, recovering processes must start by determining the status of uncommitted operations that were underway at the time of the failure.

Now consider the implications of this in a fault-tolerant setting. It will be impossible to avoid running both reads and writes synchronously (meaning that neither can be performed on any single data item). The problem is that if we don't want writes to block whenever a failure occurs, the write quorum will necessarily be smaller than the full set of replicas; for example, in a scheme that will provide continued availability in the presence of two failures, the write quorum size must be at least two smaller than the total number of copies. To ensure overlap with the writes, it follows that the read quorum must be larger than the number of simultaneous failures that that must be tolerated, three copies in the above example. Thus, although read operations can be done in one phase, they cannot be done on any single copy of the data item. In light of this, one sees that although quorum schemes are conceptually easy to describe, they have important drawbacks.

Specifically, a quorum replication mechanism can be expected to run slowly, because of the need to execute both reads and updates synchronously (that is, replies are needed from remote copies of data items before these operations can be completed). And, a fairly complex recovery mechanism must be implemented to support the multiphase commit done on writes and to handle the recovery of a process that had a copy of a data item that was being updated at the time of a failure. If every approach to these problems were equally synchronous, this objection would not be an important one. However, as we will see below, there are asynchronous alternatives of comparable complexity, and would normally outperform a fault-tolerant quorum scheme.

Could quorum methods be used to solve the general set of direct distribution tools enumerated earlier? Consider the token passing problem. It would certainly be possible to use quorum methods to update variables identifying the current token holder and request queue. However, one would be faced with the issue of maintaining a list of processes holding copies of this information. The problem here is that database systems are fairly static; a copy of a replicated database may be online or offline, but the set of copies doesn't change very often. Thus, databases usually define quorum sizes statically, taking both failed and operational replicas into account. In contrast, the problem under consideration requires that the set of processes involved change dynamically, with new processes joining in an unpredictable manner and old members dropping out permanently. We know of no quorum-based scheme that explicitly supports this sort of dynamicism, although some of the extended quorum algorithms developed by Herlihy (1986b) may be capable of solving this problem. Thus, a fault-tolerant quorum-based token passing algorithm is likely to be costly both in terms of code required and the performance that it can achieve, and may prove restrictive with regard to the degree of dynamic behaviour it can accommodate.

Just as transactions have begun to appear in higher-level systems and languages, so have quorum replication techniques. In particular, the AVALON language, which was built on top of CAMELOT, provides mechanisms for maintaining quorum-based replicated objects in which quorum sizes change dynamically (Herlihy (1986b)). The approach works well in settings with frequent communication partitioning, site failures and recoveries — in contrast to some of the methods that will be discussed below, which perform better than quorum schemes when problems of these sorts do not arise, but may block during communication partitioning and impose a high overhead when site failures and recoveries occur.

15.4.3 The V system

Until now, the systems discussed in this chapter have been those that do not really support direct interactions between processes. V is an RPC-based system that simultaneously places a strong emphasis on performance and on providing system support for forming process groups and broadcasting requests (Cheriton and Zwaenepoel (1985)). By virtue of supporting process groups, V is able to address many of the problems in our toolkit. However, V was not designed with fault-tolerance or distributed consistency as a primary consideration, and provides little support for the application designer for whom these are major issues. For example, recall the problem of how a group broadcast mechanism should work when group membership is changing or processes fail. Although V makes a 'best effort' to deliver messages to all members of a process group, V makes no absolute guarantees that all receive a given broadcast, or that messages are received in some consistent order relative to a membership change.

A V-style broadcast is well suited to some types of directly distributed applications. If an application is broadcasting to a network resource manager, for example, to find the mailbox for a user, it may not matter very much if some processes fail to receive the request. It is easy to program around the uncertainty, ensuring that behaviour is correct in all but the most improbable scenarios. Thus, when broadcasting mailbox location updates, it may not matter if some processors miss occasional updates (Lampson (1986)). In this example, and in others with a similar character, the V broadcast primitive is suitable for implementing replication.

Our token passing problem is no easier to solve in V than in a standard RPC setting. Similarly, replicated data with a 1-copy behaviour constraint would be hard to implement on top of the standard V broadcast: if an update fails to get through, or two updates arrive in different orders at different group members, the copies could end up with inconsistent values. To solve either problem, a non-trivial mechanism would be needed at the application level, and, as noted earlier, few application designers would be capable of undertaking such a complex and uncertain development effort.

15.4.4 The Linda kernel

One problem with using shared memory in a directly distributed application is that the processes interacting through the memory are also faced with a complex synchronization problem. At Yale, Carriero and Gelernter have developed a set of language extensions that solves both of these problems simultaneously (Carriero and Gelertner (1986)). This enables them to use shared memory as a tool for building directly distributed software. Before discussing the system in any detail, it should be noted that the present implementations of Linda are designed for a different environment than the one that interests us here: parallel processors, where failure is less of an issue and concurrent execution is paramount. Of course, this does not rule out a Linda implementation for loosely coupled distributed systems subject to failure, but substantial re-engineering would be needed. What makes Linda interesting is that it permits simple solutions to some of the toolkit problems that the mechanisms reviewed above are unable to handle, and this makes the system particularly interesting in the light of the objectives in this chapter.

The Linda approach is based on the idea of a shared collection of *tuples*. The operations provided are *out* (add a tuple to the space), *in* (read and remove a tuple) and *read* (read a tuple without deleting it). Tuples can be extracted by specifying the values of some fields and just the data types for others. In this case Linda performs a pattern-matching operation that finds some tuple matching the specified fields and returns the values contained in the remaining fields. The caller can specify whether or not an *in* operation should block if it cannot be immediately satisfied. The basic idea of Linda is to allow a set of processes to execute tuple-space operations concurrently, but to perform those operations in a logically (but not necessarily physically) serialized fashion.

There have been several implementations for Linda. Among these is one in which *in* and *out* are broadcast using an ordered protocol and executed in parallel by all processes, one in which *out* is performed locally, and *in* broadcast to all processes, and one that operates by dividing tuple space among the various processes in such a way that one can map a tuple to its handler using a simple hash function. That process then resolves the *in* or *out* requests presented to it in the order they arrive. Thus, although the tuple space is conceptually shared, it is not necessarily physically replicated, and different data objects may be managed by different processes.

One could easily build a solution to the token-passing problem in Linda. The token would be represented by a tuple, and the processes would use the blocking version of *in* to request it and *out* to pass it. The solution would be subject to some limitations, but here one needs to distinguish intrinsic issues from consequences of the engineering decisions made as part of the Linda implementation.

```
NewBatch(hole_list)
  {
     /* Load workspace with hole descriptions */
     for(each hole in hole_list)
         out("to_do", hole.x, hole.y, ...);

     /* Wait for all to be processed */
     for(each hole in hole_list)
     {
         /* in will block until outcome is known */
         in("done", hole.x, hole.y, int status);
         if(status == MUST_CHECK)
             print("Must check hole at ...'n", hole.x, hole.y);
     }
  }
```

Figure 15.1 Generating work for a cell controller in the C-Linda

For example, the dynamic group membership aspect of the problem could be solved easily in a version of Linda that performs *out* locally and broadcasts *in* operations, but would be much more difficult in a version of Linda that requires that the set of processes managing the tuple space be static. Another problem that arises is that none of the present implementations of Linda can tolerate failures. If the process that manages some fragment of tuple space process crashes, that part of tuple space is simply lost. Although one could solve this by replicating the tuple space, to do so would just push the issues that were identified above into the Linda implementation, since Linda itself would now need to implement a correct and fault-tolerant replication mechanism. Thus, the Linda primitives somehow embody a property that makes it easy to solve problems like the token passing one. However, solutions to problems like the replicated data problem are still needed before we can apply this successful aspect of the Linda system in the general setting of our toolkit.

Linda has been applied successfully in several settings. In the area of parallel simulation (that is, simulations run on distributed or parallel systems), Linda has been used primarily to build parallel solutions to a range of problems. Nearly full utilization of the processors is often cited.

For example, Figure 15.1 and Figure 15.2 illustrate a skeletal solution to the drilling problem introduce at the start of this chapter, using Linda tuples to describe the work to be done and the outcome. Each hole to be drilled is described by a 'pending work' tuple. A drill control processor selects a tuple on which to work, drills the hole, and then outputs a tuple describing the outcome.

Because Linda was not designed to address fault-tolerance, the above code lacks the mechanism needed to detect failures and generate a list of holes that a technician should recheck. That is, there is no good way to generate a MUST_CHECK tuple on behalf of a crashed control process in present versions of Linda. Likewise, it is hard to see how one could handle dynamic scheduling

```
/* A typical drill controller */
DrillControl()
  {
    forever
    {
        in("to_do", int x, int y, ...);

        /* Position the drill, then make the hole */
        PositionDrill(x, y);
        outcome = DrillHole(HoleSpecs);

        /* Record outcome */
        out("done", x, y, outcome);
    }
  }
```

Figure 15.2 A control process for a single drill

using Linda's tuple-matching mechanism. The problem here is that the language lacks a way for the user to provide a tuple selection criteria. Thus, to pick the optimal hole subject to some user-specified metric, such as the hole that minimizes the total expected drilling time, it would seem necessary to examine the full set of tuples. (Of course, there may well exist a clever encoding of the problem into a tuple-space data structure that would efficiently solve this.) One could also certainly imagine extensions of the language in which this problem could be addressed.

Linda is intriguing because it points to a possible structure for the kind of problems we are interested in. The essential observation is that when all processes in a system cooperate through a mechanism that orders elementary operations that might interfere with one another, distributed consistency is surprising easy to achieve. As shown below, by substituting ordered reliable broadcasts for ordered tuple-space operations, one can implement fault-tolerant solutions to most of the issues that the toolkit raises. Just as the partial solution to the drilling problem shown above arises naturally out of the structure that Linda suggests, fault-tolerant solutions to the other problems in the toolkit result from this extended approach.

15.4.5 The HAS system

At IBM, the HAS project explored a closely related approach. HAS supports Δ-*common storage*, which is much like the Linda tuple space but defined in terms of abstract operations on a shared memory. As in the case of the real-time broadcast protocol discussed in Chapter 14, updates are completed within a period of time bracketed by upper and lower bounds expressed in terms of a computed parameter, Δ. That is, no update can be completed in *less* than a certain minimum time, but neither will any be delayed for longer than a specified maximum time. In addition to the shared memory abstraction, HAS provides a processor grouping mechanism on top of this layer of protocols, like the one suggested for individual processes but at a coarser granularity (Cristian *et al.* (1986); Cristian (1988)).

In contrast to Linda, HAS was designed for use in loosely coupled processors communicating on high speed point-to-point channels as well as broadcast media such as token rings, and subject to a variety of failure modes. Moreover, the HAS methodology provides tolerance to a range of failures including Byzantine failure modes in which processes can behave in arbitrary malicious ways and experience bizarre clock failures. However, any protocol that would actually tolerate worst case behaviour for a wide range of possible failure modes would perform very poorly, translating to a very long minimum delay when updating the shared memory. To arrive at a practical facility, the group exploited the observed failure characteristics of this environment, which permitted them to make a trade off between the types of failures that their implementation actually tolerates and its performance. For a realistic scenario, with relatively high speed processors on a fast token ring, this approach resulted in a real-time atomic delivery protocols in which the minimum delay to update the shared memory was fairly small — of the order of 100ms.

With current technology, the HAS approach would not scale well to very large networks because the real-time performance characteristics of such a system would be very poor in comparison to the small, closely coupled machines used to achieve the sort of performance cited above. An open question relates to how changes in communication hardware and increased processor speeds could impact on the way the system scales.

15.4.6 The ISIS system

Like Linda and HAS, the ISIS system adopts an approach based on synchronous execution, whereby every process sees the same events in the same order (Birman and Joseph (1987a)). However, ISIS simultaneously seeks to provide fault-tolerance, effective replication mechanisms, and good performance in larger local area networks. The system starts with the observation that synchronous execution models offer strong advantages. Their primary disadvantage is one of cost: without hardware support, a distributed lock-step execution performs poorly. Even with hardware support, a lock-step style of computation does not scale.

To address this, ISIS provides an *illusion* of synchronous execution, in much the same sense that transactional serializability provides the illusion of a sequential transaction execution. Whenever possible, ISIS relaxes synchronization in order to reduce the degree to which processes can delay one another and to better exploit the parallelism of a distributed environment. We use the term *virtual synchrony* to refer to this approach, because the system appears to be synchronous but is actually fairly asynchronous. For example, processes are permitted to initiate an operation asynchronously, by broadcasting a request without pausing to wait for a reply.† When this is done, ISIS behaves as if such messages were delivered immediately, preventing any action that occurs 'after' the broadcast was sent from seeing a system state from 'before' the broadcast was sent. Similarly, ISIS delivers broadcasts with common destinations in the same order everywhere — except when it is possible to infer that the application does not need such strong ordering. In such cases, ISIS can be told to relax the delivery ordering rules, which permits it to use a cheaper broadcast protocol.

ISIS differs from Linda and HAS in that it provides a message-oriented (rather than a shared-memory interface). The basic ISIS facilities include tools for creating and managing process groups, group broadcast, failure detection and recovery, distributed execution and synchronization, etc. A Linda-style replicated tuple space is easy to implement in ISIS, as is 1-copy replicated data. Moreover, the implementations can readily be customized to address special requirements of the application program, such as the selection of the optimal next hole for a controller to drill. These mechanisms will be examined in more detail below, and then an example illustrating how ISIS could be used to solve the drill control problem will be discussed.

15.5 An execution model for virtual synchrony

One desirable feature of systems like ARGUS, CAMELOT, Linda, HAS and ISIS is that one can write down a model describing the execution environment they provide. In the case of ARGUS or CAMELOT, the model is based on nested transactions, and the lowest-level elements are data items and operations upon them. Models for the latter systems are similar but oriented towards the representation of synchronous executions. Before looking at virtually synchronous algorithms for the tools enumerated earlier, it will be helpful to start by defining such a model and giving virtual synchrony a more precise meaning.

The elements of the execution model we will be working with are processes, process groups, and broadcast events. Broadcast events include more than group communication. Point-to-point messages are treated as a broadcast to a singleton process-group. Failures are treated as a kind of broadcast too: a last message from the dying process informing any interested parties of its demise. Data items are not explicitly represented, although one can superimpose a

† Note the difference between this and an RPC, where such a pause is built in even if no reply is desired. For example, on the SUN 3 version of ISIS a program that issues an asynchronous broadcast to 5 destinations would resume executing after a delay lasting for a small fraction of a millisecond. The remote message deliveries occur within 5-10 milliseconds. With RPC, which has a 10 millisecond round-trip time under UNIX on a SUN 3, the caller would be delayed by 50 milliseconds, plus any costs associated with the group addressing protocol. Delivery would take as long as 45 milliseconds between the start of the broadcast and the arrival of the last message. On systems with faster processors and cheaper RPC costs, the costs here might scale, but the same argument could still be made. The advantage is that when ISIS sends acknowledgement messages, it overlaps them with concurrent execution in the sender, winning improved performance.

higher level on top of this basic model in which operations and the values of data become explicit.

15.5.1 Modelling a synchronous execution

One way to understand a model is as a formalism for writing down what an 'external observer' might see when watching the system execute from somewhere outside of it. The external observer provides a notion of global time to relate the actions taken by distinct processes. One defines an execution to be *synchronous* if the external observer can confirm that whenever two processes observe the same event, they do so at the same instant in time. This is illustrated in Figure 15.3, where time advances from top to bottom.

In a synchronous model it is easy to specify the meaning of an *atomic* ('all or nothing') broadcast to a process group. At the time at which a broadcast is delivered, it must be delivered to all *current* members of the group. Thus the set of destinations is determined by the event sequence (processes joining or leaving the group) that occurred prior to that time. This does not tell us how to implement such a broadcast, but it does give a rule for deciding whether a broadcast is atomic or not. We will be making use of this rule below.

Of the systems discussed above, Linda comes closest to providing a synchronous execution. However, a genuinely synchronous execution would be

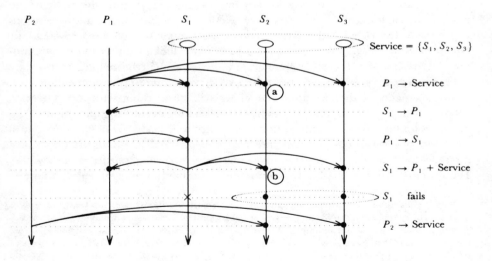

Figure 15.3 A synchronous execution. A pair of client processes, identified as P_1 and P_2 interact with a process group containing three server processes. Execution advances from top to bottom in a lock-step manner. Several message exchanges and a failure are shown.

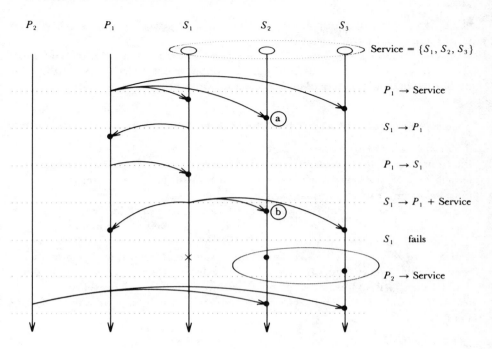

Figure 15.4 A loosely synchronous execution

impractical to implement in a local area networking environment. To do so, all the processes would need access to a common clock and to execute at fixed speeds, neither of which is normally possible.

15.5.2 Modelling a loosely synchronous execution

An execution is said to be *loosely synchronous* if all processes observe events in the *same order*. Figure 15.4 illustrates such an execution. An external observer who notes the time at which events are executed may see the same event processed at different times by different processes. However, the events will still be executed in the same order as they would have been in a truly synchronous execution. Hence, if the system is not a real-time one (and this is something we assumed at the outset), processes that behaved correctly in a truly synchronous setting should still behave correctly in a loosely synchronous one (Neiger and Toueg (1987)).

More formally, for every loosely synchronous execution E, there exists an *equivalent* truly synchronous execution E'. The two executions are equivalent in the following sense. Let E_p be the sequence of events observed by process p in an execution E. Then $E'_p = E_p$ for all p, that is, every process observes the same sequence of events in E and E'. Unless a process has access to a real-time clock, it cannot distinguish between E and E'. Figure 15.4 is indistinguishable from Figure 15.3 by this definition.

Any synchronous system is also loosely synchronous. Thus, Linda and HAS are both loosely synchronous systems; the global event ordering being imposed by hardware in the former case, and by a software protocol in the latter.

15.5.3 Modelling a virtually synchronous execution

A *virtually synchronous* execution is related to a loosely synchronous one in much the same way that a *serializable* execution is related to a serial one. The characteristic of a virtually synchronous system is that although an external observer may see cases in which events occur in different orders at different processes, the processes themselves are unable to detect this. For example, Figure 15.5 is a copy of Figure 15.4 with the delivery of event a delayed to occur after b at one destination. This execution would be called virtually synchronous if, after both a and b have terminated, no process in the system can contradict a claim that a executed first everywhere. Evidence of the order in which operations took place could be explicit in the value of some variable, or it could be reflected in the response to one of the requests or the actions that a process took after receiving some request.

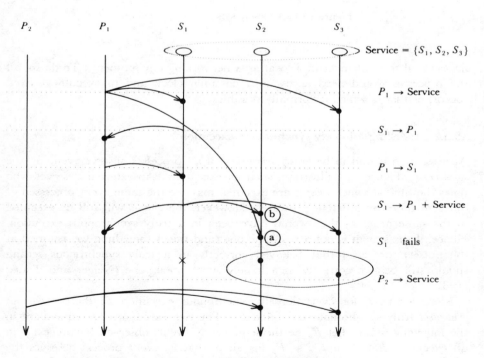

Figure 15.5 A virtually synchronous execution

One problem with the sort of relaxation of order seen here is that it looks very narrow in applicability. For it to be of interest, one needs to be able to identify relaxations that can be applied in a systematic manner and actually correspond to protocols of different cost. In particular, it is highly advantageous to substitute a one-phase broadcast protocol for a two-phase protocol, and this is the sort of relaxation of ordering that we are after here. The idea in building a virtually synchronous system is to look for such cases and to exploit them. This was also our hidden motive in introducing a list of tools. Whereas it is unlikely that one could systematically find ways to relax order in arbitrary applications, it is entirely reasonable to do so in applications that are uniformly structured and interact primarily through standard 'toolkit' interfaces. In such a setting, one could optimize the tools as a way of optimizing all the application software that later gets built on them.

Recalling the definition of loose synchrony in the previous section, an execution E is *virtually synchronous* if there exists some truly synchronous execution E' equivalent to E. However, we broaden our notion of equivalence between executions by requiring only that $E'_p \approx E_p$, for all p. Here '$\approx$' means that two event sequences are *indistinguishable*, but not necessarily identical. The determination of which event sequences are distinguishable depends on the semantics of the individual events in a particular application. A formal definition of this sort of equivalence and a theory of virtual synchrony have been developed by Schmuck (1988).

15.6 Comparing virtual synchrony with other models

15.6.1 Transactional serializability

Is our model really any different than a transactional one? We argue that virtual synchrony is a substantial generalization of transactional serializability.

Clearly, if a system is serializable, it is virtually synchronous. On the other hand, a virtually synchronous execution need not be serializable. First, there is nothing like a *transaction* in a virtually synchronous system. Consider a pair of processes, executing concurrently, that interchange a series of messages leading to a dependency of each on the state of the other. In a transactional setting, this could only occur if each interaction was a separate top-level transaction — a series of atomic actions with no subsuming transactions at all. However, transactional work has generally not considered this case directly, and it is normally not even stated that the serialization order for such top-level actions should be the order in which they were initiated. For many concurrency control schemes, such as two-phase locking, there is no a priori reason that this would be the case: a single transaction might asynchronously initiate two top-level transactions, first T_1 and then T_2, which would be serialized in the order T_2 followed by T_1.

---

† For example, T_1 might block waiting for a lock and then update variable x, while T_2 acquires its locks and manages to update x before T_1.

Virtual synchrony imposes an explicit correctness constraint on sequences of interactions like this, namely that unless the order is irrelevant, the events must be observed in the order they were initiated, even if they were initiated asynchronously, and even if order arises through a very indirect dependency of one action on another. Moreover, virtual synchrony talks about process groups and distributed events (broadcasts, failures, group membership changes, and so forth). None of these issues arise in a conventional transactional setting. In light of their importance within the directly distributed tools we listed earlier, and the apparent difficulty of layering them on top of transactions, these are significant differences.

Transactions and virtual synchrony both depend strongly on the semantics of operations. In the case of transactions, this was first observed when an attempt was made to extend transactional serializability to cover abstract data types (Schwarz and Spector (1984)). Whereas it is easy to talk about concurrency control and serializability for transactions that read and write (possibly replicated) data items, it is much harder to obtain good solutions to these problems for transactions on abstract data types. In the case of virtual synchrony, the problem arises because the model lacks data items or any other fixed referent with well-known semantics. One can only decide if an execution is virtually synchronous if one knows a great deal about how the system executes. This is an advantage in that the definition is considerably more powerful than any data-oriented one. There are many virtually synchronous systems that could not be interpreted as synchronous by somehow making the model knowledgeable about data. On the other hand, the presence of semantic knowledge makes it hard to talk about correct or efficient system behaviour in general terms, without knowing what the system is doing. As we will see shortly, one can only do this through a detailed analysis of those algorithms on which a particular system relies.

15.6.2 Virtual synchrony in quorum-based schemes

Earlier, some examples were given of how a quorum scheme might be used to obtain consistent behaviour in a relatively unstructured setting. Such an approach can be understood as a form of virtual synchrony. The basic characteristic of a quorum scheme is its *quorum intersection relation*, which specifies how large the quorums for each type of operation must be (Herlihy (1986b)). If two operations potentially conflict — that is, if the outcome of one could be influenced by the outcome of the other — then their quorums will intersect at one or more processes. Thus one can build a partial order on operations, such that all conflicting operations are totally ordered relative to one another, while non-conflicting operations are unordered. Since non-conflicting operations always commute, the executions of a quorum-based system are indistinguishable from any extension of this order into a total one. Such a total order can be understood as a description of a synchronous execution that would have left the system in the same state as it was in after the quorum execution. Thus, a quorum execution is virtually synchronous.

15.7 System support for virtual synchrony

15.7.1 The ISIS virtually synchronous toolkit

Let us now return to the ISIS system and look more carefully at some of the virtually synchronous algorithms on which it is based.

15.7.2 Groups and group communication

The lowest level of ISIS provides process groups and three broadcast primitives for group communication, called CBCAST, ABCAST and GBCAST. The primitives were discussed in Chapter 14, and their integration into a common framework supporting group addressing is covered elsewhere (Birman and Joseph (1987b)). We therefore focus on their joint behaviour while omitting implementation details.

In ISIS, a *process group* is an association between a group address and some set of members. Membership in a process group has low overhead, so it is assumed that processes join and leave groups casually and that one process may be a member of several groups.

A *view of a process group* is a list of its members, ordered by the amount of time they have belonged to the group. ISIS includes tools for determining the current view of a process group and for being notified of each view change that occurs. All members see the same sequence of views and changes.

The destination of a broadcast in ISIS is specified as a list of groups. Group membership changes are synchronized with communication, so that a given broadcast will be delivered to the members of a group in the same membership view.

Recall that a broadcast is *atomic* if it is delivered to *all* members of each destination group. Here, 'all' refers to all the group members listed in the process group view in which delivery takes place, which may not be the same as the membership when the broadcast was initiated.† A *virtually atomic* delivery is one in which all group members *that stay operational* receive the message in the same view. The ISIS broadcast primitives are all virtually atomic. Thus, the recipient of an ISIS broadcast can look at the 'current' group membership (in a virtually synchronous sense) and act on the assumption that all of the listed processes also received the message. It may subsequently see some of them fail, perhaps without having acted on the message.

CBCAST, ABCAST and GBCAST differ in their delivery ordering properties. Before we review these differences, recall the definition of the potential causality relation on events, $\rightarrow$ introduced in Chapter 14: $e \rightarrow e'$ means that there may have been a flow of information from event e to event e' along a chain of local actions linked by message passing.

---

† In ISIS, it will be the same or a subset of the initial membership.

Let *bcast(a)* denote the initiation of broadcast *a* and *deliver(a)* the delivery of some *a* to some destination. All three types of broadcast ensure that if *bcast(a)* → *bcast(b)* for broadcasts *a* and *b* (below, *a* → *b*), then *deliver(a)* will precede *deliver(b)* at any common destinations. In fact, they satisfy an even stronger property, namely that if *a* → *b* then, even if *a* and *b* have no common destinations, *b* will be delivered only if *a* can be delivered too. This ensures that if some subsequent broadcast *c* is done, with *b* → *c*, and *a* and *c* have common destinations, the system will be able to respect its delivery order constraints. The ISIS delivery ordering constraint can be thought of as a FIFO rule based not on the order in which individual processes transmitted broadcasts, but on the order in which threads of control did so. Here, a thread of control is any path along which execution may have proceeded.

CBCAST satisfies exactly the above delivery constraint. If *a* and *b* are concurrent, then CBCAST might deliver *a* and *b* in different orders. ABCAST provides a delivery order that extends → so that if *a* and *b* are two concurrent ABCASTs, a delivery order will be picked and respected at all shared destinations. However, ABCAST and CBCAST are unordered with respect to each other. GBCAST, in contrast, provides totally ordered delivery with respect to *all* sorts of broadcasts. Thus, if *g* is a GBCAST and *a* is any sort of broadcast then *g* and *a* will be delivered in a fixed relative order to all shared destinations.

A system that uses only ABCAST to transmit broadcasts is loosely synchronous. For this reason, ISIS uses ABCAST as its default protocol unless told otherwise by the programmer. However, ABCAST is costly. Like the quorum protocols, it sometimes delays message deliveries in a way that would be noticeable to the sender. CBCAST is much cheaper, especially when invoked asynchronously.† This leads to the question of just when synchronization can be relaxed by changing an ABCAST to a CBCAST in a broadcast-based algorithm.

15.7.3 When can synchronization be relaxed?

Let us examine the degree to which some specific algorithms depend on the ordering characteristics of the broadcasts used for message transmission. We begin with some examples drawn from a single process group with fixed membership:

- A replicated tuple space, supporting the Linda *in*, *out* and *read* operations but using replicated data to achieve fault-tolerance.

- A shared token, supporting operations to *request* it, to *pass* it, and to determine the current holder.

---

† The implementation of ISIS is more complex than the earlier discussion of these protocols made it appear. For reasons of brevity, the associated issues are not discussed here. However, the reader should be aware that to make effective use of protocols such as these, a substantial engineering investment is needed. This ranges from the requirement for a system architecture that imposes low overhead to heuristics for scaling the protocols to run in large networks and to avoid thrashing when communication patterns overload the most costly aspects of the protocols (Birman, Joseph, and Schmuck (1989)).

- Replicated data. There are two cases: a variable that can be updated and accessed at will, and a variable that can only be accessed by the holder of a token (lock) on it. We look only at the second case, as the first one is essentially the same as for the Linda tuple space.

15.7.4 Shared tuple space

Say that we wish to replicate a Linda tuple space (refinements such as fragmenting the space using a hashing rule could be superimposed on a solution to this basic problem). In ISIS, this would be done by having the processes that will maintain replicas form a process group. What kind of ordering would be needed here? Except for the *read* operation, which can be done locally by any process managing a replica, all operations change the tuple space. Consequently, they all potentially conflict with one another, suggesting that ABCAST is the appropriate protocol.

Notice that it is possible to relax the relative ordering when two operations that affect independent tuples. Could we take advantage of this to replace ABCAST with a cheaper protocol? Such a protocol would look at the type and arguments of each operation. It would chose a global order for operations that actually conflict with one another, while permitting non-conflicting operations to execute in arbitrary orders. At first glance, it may sound like one could design a hybrid protocol that would run in two phases in the case of a conflict but deliver in one phase if no conflict were found. However, on closer examination one sees that if the *possibility* of conflict exists, a two phase protocol is always needed. The problem is that when an operation *o* arrives at a replica *r*, it is not sufficient to know that no conflicting operations are underway at *r*; one needs to know that none are underway at *any* replica. This precludes delivery during the first phase. But, if two phases will be needed, there is no benefit to be gained by including a test for conflict. It seems more reasonable to just use a normal ABCAST.

15.7.5 Shared token

The shared token is interesting because it admits a variety of possible implementations. The most synchronous implementation is the easiest to understand. In this algorithm, both *request* and *pass* operations are transmitted using a globally ordered group broadcast. Members maintain a queue of pending requests. A token holder wishing to do a pass operation first waits until at least one request is pending, then broadcasts the pass operation. On receiving such a broadcast, all processes mark the request at the head of the queue as having been granted.

What if we wanted to use a cheaper broadcast primitive? Since the algorithm depends on a totally ordered request queue, we cannot use a cheaper protocol for sending requests without major algorithmic changes. On the other hand, it might be possible to use a less ordered protocol for transmitting *pass* operations. This, however, raises a subtle issue. It may be possible for a *request* message to

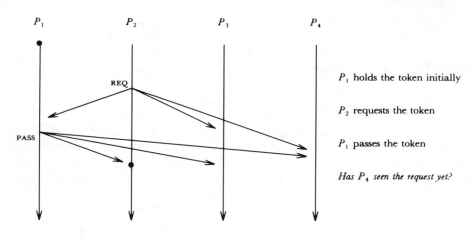

Figure 15.6 A race could develop when using a weakly ordered broadcast

reach one group member much earlier (in real time) than some other. If we change the broadcast primitive, such a sequence could result in a race, where a subsequent *pass* operation arrives at a slow process before the request from which it will be satisfied (Figure 15.6).

Likewise, a process about to pass the token could decide to satisfy a request that has already been granted, for example, if it were to receive the token before receiving the pass message corresponding to that earlier request. Clearly, this would lead to error.

Fortunately, although the situations described above could arise when using a totally unordered protocol, or one that is FIFO on a point-to-point basis, it cannot occur with a CBCAST protocol. To illustrate this, notice that a process cannot try to pass the token unless it has first requested it and then received it from some other holder. Let R_i denote the i'th token request to be satisfied and P_i the pass done by the process that issued R_i. This results in $R_i \rightarrow P_i$ and $\forall j < i: P_j \rightarrow P_i$. Thus, $\forall j < i: R_j \rightarrow P_i$. In other words, when CBCAST delivers a particular *pass* message, the destination will always have received the prior *request* operations and *vice versa*, eliminating the source of our concern.

This reasoning inspires a further refinement. Why not transmit *request* operations using CBCAST as well? The preceding analysis shows that any process receiving a *pass* will have received the *request* to which that pass corresponds. Thus, the only problem this change would introduce would be due to the loss of a global request ordering: different processes could now receive requests in different orders. This means that it would no longer be possible for each process to determine, in parallel with the others, who is the new holder of the token: they would have no basis for making consistent decisions. On the other hand, the decision could be made by the process about to send a *pass* message. If there

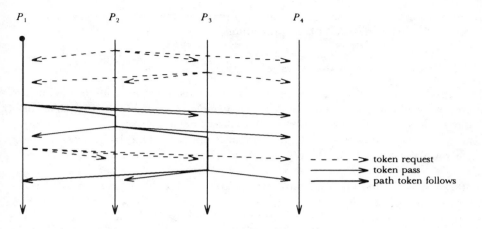

Figure 15.7 A virtually synchronous token-passing algorithm

is no pending request, that process will have to defer its *pass* until a request turns up. Given a *pass* message that indicates the identity of the new holder, all processes can find and remove the corresponding request from their set of pending requests, where it will necessarily be found.

Figure 15.7 illustrates this behaviour schematically. The darker lines show the path along with the token is passed, which is precisely the equivalent of the $\rightarrow$ relation used in the above argument.

To summarize, a token-passing problem admits a variety of correct solutions. The cheapest of these, from the point of view of message transmission, is the third. It depends only on the ordered delivery of messages that relate to one another under $\rightarrow$. A slight price is paid when a *pass* operation is carried out and there is no pending *request*: the broadcast corresponding to the *pass* must be delayed, and this will have the effect of introducing a delay before the *request* can be satisfied when it is finally issued. In the ISIS system, the benefits of using an asynchronous one-phase protocol to implement the broadcast far outweigh any delay incurred in this manner.

Token passing is an especially interesting problem because it captures the essential behaviour of any system with a single locus of control that moves about the system, but remains unique. Many algorithms and applications have such a structure. Thus, if the token passing problem can be solved efficiently, there is some hope for solving a much larger class of problems efficiently as well. Notice in particular how the final optimization replaced a global ordering decision (in the ABCAST) with a local one in the sender, and then took advantage of the fact that the sender holds mutual exclusion to propagate the decision using an inexpensive protocol. Viewed in this manner, one sees that the original algorithm was discarding ordering information and then paying a price to regenerate it! The underlying lesson is clear: in constructing efficient order-based algorithms, one must make every effort to preserve and exploit any sources of distributed order available to the application.

15.7.6 Replicated data with mutual exclusion

The usual reason for implementing tokens is to obtain mutual exclusion on a shared resource or a replicated data item. In an unconstrained setting, like the Linda tuple space, it has been shown that correct behaviour may require the use of a synchronous broadcast. What if updates are only done by a process that holds mutual exclusion on the object being updated, in the form of a token for it?

If W_i^k denotes the kth replicated write done by the ith process to hold the token, we will always have $R_i \rightarrow W_i^0 \rightarrow \cdots W_i^n \rightarrow P_i$. Now, since P_i denotes the passing of the token to the process that will next obtain it, it follows that if a process holds a token, then all *write* operations done by prior holders precede the *pass* operation by which the token was obtained. Thus, if CBCAST is used to transmit *write* operations, any process holding the token will also see the most current values of all data guarded by the token.

It follows that 1-copy behaviour can be obtained for a replicated variable using a token-passing and updating scheme implemented entirely with asynchronous one-phase broadcasts. Any process holding the token will 'know' it also possesses an up-to-date state. This kind of knowledge is formalized in Taylor and Panangaden (1988). Moreover, execution can be done by reading and writing the local copies of replicated variables without delay — just as for a non-replicated variable — and leaving the corresponding broadcasts to complete in the background.

Figure 15.8 illustrates replicated update using token passing in this manner. All the updates occur along the dark lines that highlight the path along which the token travels, which is the $\rightarrow$ relation used in the above argument. Although the system has the freedom to delay updates or deliver them in batches, it can never deliver them out of order or pass a token to a process that has not yet received some pending updates. The algorithm is thus executed as if updates occurred instantaneously.

What about an application that uses multiple data items, and multiple locks? The algorithm described above can yield very complex executions in such a setting, because of delayed delivery of update messages and deliveries that can occur in different orders at different sites. Nonetheless, such a system always has at least one synchronous global execution that would have yielded the same outcome. To see this, observe that $\rightarrow$ for this system is a set of paths like the one seen in Figure 15.8, each consisting of a sequence of *write* and *pass* operations. These paths cross when a token is passed to some process p that subsequently receives a second token (Figure 15.9). Such a situation introduces edges that relate operations in the former path to operations in the latter. Similarly, if a process reads a data item, all the subsequent actions it takes will be ordered after all the previous updates to that data item. Although it may be hard to

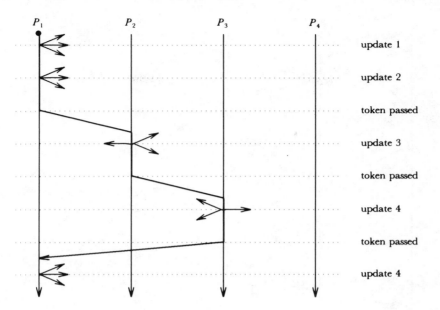

Figure 15.8 A virtually synchronous replicated update algorithm

visualize, the resulting → relation is an acyclic partial order. It can therefore be extended into at least one total order, and in general many such orders, each of which describes a synchronous global execution that would yield the same values in all the variables as what the processors actually saw.

Thus, although the update algorithm is completely asynchronous and no process ever delays except while waiting for a token request to be granted, the execution is indistinguishable from a completely synchronous one such as would result from using a quorum write (Herlihy (1986b)) for each update. The performance of our algorithm is much better than that of a synchronous one, because a synchronous update involves sending messages and then waiting for responses, whereas an asynchronous update sends messages without stopping to wait for replies. No process is ever delayed in the execution illustrated by Figure 15.9, except when waiting for a token to be passed to it.

A similar analysis can be undertaken for replicated data with local read- and replicated write-locks, although we will not do this here. The existence of local read-locks implies that write-locks must be acquired synchronously, with each process granting the lock based on its local state, and the write-lock considered to be held only when all processes have granted it. This leads to an algorithm in which read-locks are acquired locally, write-locks are acquired using a synchronous group broadcast, and updates and lock releases are done using asynchronous broadcasts. In a refinement, the breaking of read-locks after failures can be prevented by asynchronously broadcasting information about pending

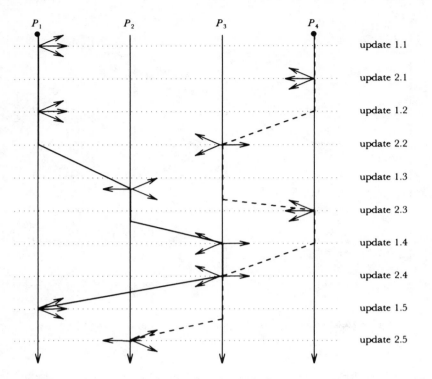

Figure 15.9 Replicated updates with multiple tokens

read-locks in such a way that any updates that depend on a read lock are related to the read-lock broadcast under →. This method was first proposed by Joseph and Birman (1986).

15.7.7 Dealing with failures

The analysis of the preceding section overlooks failures and other dynamic group membership changes. In many applications one wishes to deal with such events explicitly, for example by granting the token to the next pending request in the event that the current holder fails. Recall that group membership changes must be totally ordered with respect to other events in order to ensure the virtual atomicity of broadcast delivery. Since ISIS does this, any broadcast sent in the token or update algorithm will be received by all members of the group that stay operational, and in the same view of the current membership.

Say that the rule to be implemented is:

> *All group members monitor the holder of the token. If the holder fails, the oldest process in the group takes over and passes the token on its behalf.*

For a solution to be correct, it is necessary to be able to establish two things about the system. First, because the rule depends on the ordering of group members by age, this information must be consistent from member to member. Group views have this property in ISIS.

Secondly, it must be known that any view change reporting a failure will be ordered after all broadcasts done by the failed process. This ensures that if the failed process did a pass before dying, either no process saw it happen or all processes saw the broadcast and are already watching the new holder. That is, if X_p^i is the ith action taken by p and F_p denotes the event reporting the failure of p, we need $\forall p, i: X_p^i \to F_p$. Certainly, in any synchronous execution a failed process takes no further actions, hence this condition will also hold for any virtually synchronous execution.

Thus, one could readily implement a fault-tolerant token-passing algorithm in a virtually synchronous environment.

Notice that the failure ordering property links the atomicity of one broadcast to the atomicity of a subsequent one. A conventional atomic broadcast places an all or nothing requirement on broadcast delivery. But, this does not rule out the transmission of a broadcast a that will not be delivered anywhere because of a failure, followed by the transmission of a broadcast b from the same sender that will be delivered. In a virtually synchronous system, such behaviour is not permitted.

15.8 Other virtually synchronous tools

Virtually synchronous solutions have been illustrated to two of the problems in the list of tools enumerated at the start of this chapter: replicated data management and synchronization. Let us briefly address the other problems in the list.

15.8.1 Distributed execution

There are several ways to distribute an execution over a set of sites in a virtually synchronous setting. The ISIS toolkit supports all of the following:

Pool of servers: The Linda system illustrates a style of distributed execution that called the *pool of servers*. In this method, a set of processes share a collection of work-description messages, extracting them one at a time, performing the indicated operation, and then placing a completion message back into the pool for removal by the process that initiated the work. The approach is simple and lends itself to environments where the processes composing a service are loosely coupled and largely independent of one another. It can be made fault-tolerant by maintaining some sort of 'work in progress' trace that can be located when a process is observed to fail. On the other hand, this method of distributed computing is potentially costly because it relies so heavily on synchronous operations. Were such a system to access its tuple space frequently, a bottleneck could develop.

Redundant computation: A redundant computation is one in which a set of processes perform identical operations on identical data. The approach was first proposed by Cooper for use in the Circus system (Cooper (1985)). Redundant computation has the advantage of fault-tolerance, and when the operation involves updates to a replicated state it is often the most efficient way to obtain a replicated 1-copy behaviour. On the other hand, it is unclear why one would want to use a redundant computation for an operation that does not change the state of of the processes involved. With the exception of a real-time system operating under stringent deadlines, where it might increase the probability of meeting the deadline, such an approach would represent an inefficient use of computational resources. And, in a computation that is at all deterministic, the method is clearly inapplicable.

Redundant computation is easily implemented in a virtually synchronous environment. The event initiating a computation is broadcast to all the processes that will participate in the computation. They all perform the computation in parallel and respond to the caller, sending identical results. The caller can either continue computing as soon as the first result is received, or wait to collect replies from all participants.

ISIS does not permit redundant computations to be nested unless the application makes provisions to handle this possibility. In contrast, the Circus system supports nested redundant computations in a way that is transparent to the user, even permitting replicated callers to invoke non-idempotent operations and operations implemented by a group with a replication factor different from that of the caller. Cooper discusses these problems, as well as mechanisms for guarding against incorrect replies being sent by a faulty group member, in Cooper (1985).

Coordinator-cohort computation: A coordinator-cohort computation is one in which a single process executes a request while other processes back it up, stepping in to take over and complete the request if a failure occurs before the response is sent (Birman and Joseph (1987a)). Such a computation could make good use of the parallelism inherent in a group of processes, provided that different coordinators are picked for different requests (in this way sharing the load). Moreover, it can be used even in non-deterministic computations. However, if the distributed state of the processes involved is changed by a request, the coordinator must distribute the updates made to its cohorts at the end of the computation. In situations where a redundant computation was a viable possibility, the cost of this style of updating should be weighed against that of running the entire computation redundantly and eliminating the communication overhead.

Implementation of a coordinator-cohort computation is easy in a virtually synchronous setting. The request is broadcast to the group that will perform the computation. The caller then waits for a single response. In many applications, the broadcast can be done using a one-phase protocol such as CBCAST, although this decision requires analysis similar to that used for the token passing example. The participants take the following actions in parallel. First, they rank themselves using such information as the source of the request, the current membership of the group doing the request, and the length of time that each member has belonged to the group. Since all see the same values for all of these system attributes, they all reach consistent decisions. The coordinator starts computing while the cohorts begin to monitor the membership of the process group. The coordinator may disseminate information to the cohorts while doing this, or use mechanisms like the token for synchronization. When the coordinator finishes, it uses CBCAST to atomically reply to the caller and (in the same broadcast) send a termination message to the cohorts. If a coordinator fails before finishing, its cohorts react as soon as they observe the failure event (a broadcast sent prior to the failure is delivered before the failure notification). The cohorts recompute their ranking, arriving at a new coordinator that terminates the operation. If the original coordinator sent this information while computing, there are a number of options: the cohorts can spool this and discard it if a failure occurs, or could apply it to their states and take over from the coordinator by picking up from where it died.

Unless the application is sensitive to event orderings, this algorithm can be implemented with asynchronous CBCASTs. As in the case of the token algorithm, a highly concurrent execution would result.

Subdivided computation: A subdivided computation arises when each participant does *part* of a requested task. The caller collects and assembles these to obtain a complete result. For example, each member of a process group might search a portion of a database for items satisfying a query, with the result being formed by merging the partial results from each subquery. As in the case of a coordinator-cohort computation, the participants in a subdivided computation can draw on a number of properties of the environment to divide the computation. Provided that they all use the same decision rule, they will reach the same decision. Dealing with failures, however, is problematic in this case. A simple solution is to identify the results as, for example, 'part 1 of 3'. A caller that receives too few replies because some processes have failed can retry the whole query, or perhaps just the missing part.

15.8.2 System configuration and reconfiguration

Above, the term 'configuration' was used as a synonym for the view of processes groups and processors in the system — that is, a list of the operational members, ordered by age. However, some systems have a software configuration that augments this view-based configuration and is also used for deciding how requests should be processed. This suggests that software designers need access to a broadcast primitive like the one ISIS uses to inform process group members of group membership change. The GBCAST primitive can be used for this purpose. Because GBCAST is atomic and totally ordered with respect to both CBCAST and ABCAST, one can use it to transmit updates to a replicated configuration data structure shared by the members of a process group. Such an update would otherwise be implemented just like any other update to replicated data, but because of the strong ordering property of the GBCAST, all processes see them in the same order with respect to the arrival of other messages of all kinds. Thus, when a request arrives or some other event is observed, the extended configuration can be used as part of the algorithm for deciding how to respond.

15.8.3 Recovery

When a process recovers, it faces a complex problem, which is solved in ISIS by the *process-group join tool*. A recovering process starts by attempting to rejoin any process groups which the application maintains. When invoked, the tool checks to see if the specified process group already exists and if any other process is trying to recover simultaneously. A given process will observe one of the following cases:

1. The group never existed before and this process is the first one to join it. The group is created and the caller's initialization procedure invoked. If two processes restart simultaneously, ISIS forces one to wait while the other recovers.

2. The group already exists. After checking permissions, the system adds the joining process to the group as a new member, transferring the state of some operational member as of *just before* the join took place. The transfer is done by repeatedly calling user-provided routines that encode the state into messages and then delivering these to user-provided routines that decode the messages in the joining process. The entire operation is a single virtually synchronous event. All the group members see the same set of events up to the instant of the join, and this is the state that they transfer. After the transfer, all the members of the group (including the new member) see the membership change to include the new member, and subsequently all see exactly the same sequence of incoming requests (subject to the ordering constraints of the protocol used to send those requests).

3. The group previously existed but experienced a total failure. The handling of this case depends on whether or not the group is maintaining non-volatile logs and, if so, whether or not this process was one of the last to fail and consequently has an accurate log; Skeen (1985) gives an algorithm for deciding this. The former case is treated like case (1). In the latter, a recovery is initiated out of the log file. If the process is not one of the last to fail, the system delays the recovery until one of the last group members to fail has recovered, and then initiates a state transfer as in case (2).

    In ISIS, a log file consists of a checkpoint followed by a series of requests that modify the state. The checkpoint itself is done by performing a state transfer (see above) into a log file. Thus, recovery out of a log looks like a state transfer from a previously operational member, followed by the replay of messages that were received subsequent to the checkpoint and prior to the failure. Management and recovery from logs in a virtually synchronous setting has been examined by Kane (1989).

ISIS obtains its join mechanism by composing several of the tools described earlier. For example, the state transfer is done using the coordinator cohort tool, described above. To ensure that this is done at a virtual instant in time, a GBCAST is used to add the new member to the existing process group, and the transfer is triggered just before reporting the membership change to the group members (including the new member). The mechanism is not trivial to implement, but is still fairly simple. Similarly, solutions to the other aspects of the problem are constructed out of broadcast protocols and reasoning such as what we described above for the token passing algorithm.

The ISIS recovery tool illustrates an interesting aspect of virtual synchrony. On the one hand, the designer thinks about recovery as a series of simple steps: a site restarts, the recovery manager executed the user's program, the program requests that it be added, the request is authenticated, a series of state transfer messages arrive and finally a new view becomes defined showing the new member. The sequence is always the same, and no other events ever occur while it is underway. On the other hand, the same designer treats state transfer as an atomic event (a sort of 'transaction') when writing software that may interact with a group while a recovery may be taking place. The recovery either has not happened yet or it is done, seen from outside there are no other possibilities. Because this eliminates a huge number of possible race conditions and cases to deal with, a complex mechanism is rendered simple enough for a novice to use correctly.

15.9 Orthogonality issues

It was observed that for a set of tools to be of practical value they must permit a step-by-step style of programming. For example, if a distributed program is built using some set of tools, and it is extended in a way that requires an additional replicated variable, the only code needed should be for managing and synchronizing access to the new variable. It should not be necessary to re-examine all the previous code to ensure that no unexpected interaction will creep in and break some preexisting algorithm. We say that a set of tools are orthogonal to one another if they satisfy this property.

A desirable characteristic of the virtually synchronous environment is that orthogonality is immediate in algorithms that require just a single broadcast event, because these broadcasts are virtually synchronous with respect to other events in the system. For example, since updates to a replicated variable appear to be synchronous, introducing a coordinator-cohort computation for some other purpose in a program that uses such updates should not 'break' the replicated data mechanism. More complex mechanisms, such as the ISIS recovery mechanism, are made to look like a single synchronous event, even when they involve several distinct subevents. A consequence is that one can build software in ISIS by starting with a non-distributed program that accepts an RPC-style of interaction, then extending it into a distributed solution that uses a process group and replicated data, introducing a dynamically changing distributed configuration mechanism, arranging for automated recovery from failure, and so forth. Each change is virtually synchronous with respect to the prior code, hence no change will break the pre-existing code. The same advantage applies in a setting like the Linda system: software here can be developed by debugging a single process that uses the tuple-space primitives, and once it is operational replicating this process to the extent desired.

15.10 Scaling, synchrony and virtual synchrony

It has been observed that a genuinely synchronous approach to distributed computing will have scaling problems. Of the framework, listed bove, only HAS implements such an approach, and its performance degrades quite explicitly as a function of the number of sites in the network, because a larger network has larger expected delays over its communication links. This increases the minimum delay before a broadcast can be delivered, and, because HAS does not support an asynchronous broadcast, the performance of application software is directly impacted.

A system like ISIS has a slightly different problem. Here, the basic protocols are essentially linear in the size of process groups (see Birman, Joseph, and Schmuck (1989)). However, several parts of ISIS involve algorithms that scale with the number of *sites* in the network. To address this issue, a recent version of ISIS introduced a notion of scope into the system. The idea of this is to restrict these algorithms to small collections of sites in a way that does not compromise the correctness of the overall system. The resulting system has been scaled up to more than one hundred sites without imposing a severe load on any machine, although process *groups* must not grow to include more than 20 or 30 members (here, we assume a 10 Mbit network and 2—5 MIPS workstations). Current research is now focused on introducing a notion of hierarchy for use when process groups get very large. These figures are based on current experience with those aspects of the ISIS system that will not change when better algorithms are installed. Thus, ISIS potentially scales to moderately large networks, but is unlikely to scale up into geographically distributed settings with tens of thousands or millions of sites. An open question is whether there exists some other architecture that would yield virtual synchrony and high levels of concurrency, as does ISIS, but would scale without limit.

Finally, consider the quorum schemes, which also achieve virtual synchrony. These degrade in a way that is completely determined by the quorum size and the number of failures to be tolerated. While process groups stay small, one would expect bounded performance limited by RPC bandwidths, and poorer than what can be achieved using asynchronous protocols. The quorum approach is clearly unsuitable for systems that replicate data at very large numbers of locations.

To summarize, there seems to be good reason to view virtual synchrony as an effective programming tool for small and medium size networks, and with the use of hierarchical structuring techniques should even be able to encompass a typical medium-size factory or company. In much larger settings, other approaches yielding weaker correctness guarantees would be needed.

It should also be noted that our collection of tools focuses on programming 'in the small'. The design and implementation of software for a factory requires something more: a methodology for composing larger systems out of smaller components, and perhaps a collection of tools for programming in the large. The former would consist of a formalism for describing the behaviour of system components (which could themselves be substantial distributed systems) and how components interact with one another, independently of implementation. The latter would include software for cooperative application development, monitoring dependencies between components of a large system and triggering appropriate action when a change is made, file systems with built in replication, and mechanisms with which the network can be asked to monitor for arbitrary user-specified events and to trigger user-specified actions when those events occur. These are all hard problems, and any treatment of them is beyond the scope of this discussion. Moreover, the current state of the art in these areas is painfully deficient. Substantial progress is needed before it becomes practical to talk about building effective and robust network solutions to large-scale problems.

15.11 An example of ISIS software and performance

It might be interesting to see a sample of a typical ISIS program. The program shown below solves the drilling problem in ISIS. In contrast to the Linda solution, the method is fault-tolerant and supports dynamic process recovery. As before, the code will be in two parts: the code for a process that issues the original work request to the cell controller, and the distributed algorithm run in parallel by the control processes. We start with the code for making a request:

```
/* Define a type called hole_t for describing holes */
typedef struct
{
    /* Description of hole */
    int     h_x, h_y, ....;        /* Description of the hole */

    /* Runtime variables set by algorithm */
    address h_drill;               /* Process that will drill it */
    int     h_state;               /* Status, see below */
} hole_t;

#define     H_NULL       0         /* Initial state */
#define     H_ASSIGNED   1         /* h_drill has been set */
#define     H_DRILLING   2         /* Drilling underway */
#define     H_DONE       3         /* Hole completed */
```

```
main()
  {
    address driller;
    int nholes, nreplies, checklist[MAXHOLES], ntocheck;
    hole_t holes[MAXHOLES];

    ... initialize nholes and holes[0..nholes-1] ...

    /* Lookup address of drill service */
    driller = pg_lookup("/bldg14/cell22-a/driller");

    nreplies = cbcast(driller, WORK_REQ,
                      /* Message to broadcast */
                      "{%d,%d,...,%a,%d}[]", holes, nholes,
                1     /* One reply wanted */,
                      /* Reply format */
                      "{%d}[]", checklist, &ntocheck);

    if(nreplies != 1)
        panic("Drill service is not available\n");
    if(ntocheck != 0)
    {
        printf("Job requires manual recheck.  Please check:\n");
        for(i = 0; i < ntocheck; i++)
        {
            hole_t *h = &holes[checklist[i]];
            printf("Hole at %d,%d ..\n", ...);
        }
        printf("Type <cr> when finished rechecking: ");
        while(getchar() != '\n') continue;
    }
    ... etc ...
  }
```

This program imports the list of entry points from the drill service, which defines the WORK_REQ entry to which the work request is being transmitted. To a reader familiar with the C programming language, the code will be self-explanatory except for the arguments to cbcast, which are the group to transmit to (a long form accepting a list of groups is also supported), the entry point to invoke in the destination processes, the format of the data to transmit (here, an array of structure elements), the array itself and its length, the number of replies desired (1), the format of the expected reply (an array of integers), a place to copy the reply, and a variable that will be set to the length of the reply array.

The cell controller requires more code:

```
/* A typical drill controller */

# include "hole-desc.h"

main()
  {
    /* Bind the two entry points to handler routines */
```

```
        isis_entry(WORK_REQ, work_req);
        isis_entry(DRILLING, drilling);
        /* Start ISIS lightweight task subsystem */
        isis_mainloop(restart_task);
    }

/* Task to restart this process group member */
restart_task()
    {
        /* Join or create group, obtain current state */
        driller = pg_join("/bldg14/cell22-a/driller",
            /* On first time create, call first_time_init */
                PG_INIT, first_time_init,
            /* On joining an existing system, do state transfer */
                PG_XFER, state_xfer_out, state_xfer_in,
            /* Call monitor_routine on membership changes */
                PG_MONITOR, monitor_routine,
            0);
    }

/* Global variables */
int     checklist[MAXHOLES], ntocheck;

/* Reception of a new work request (WORK_REQ entry) */
work_req(msg)
    message *msg;
    {
        int nholes;
        hole_t holes[MAXHOLES];
        pgroup_view *pgv = pg_getview(driller);

        msg_get(msg, "{%d,%d,...,%a,%d}[]", holes, &nholes);
        for(n = 0; n < nholes; n++)
        {
            hole_t *h = &holes[n];
            h->h_who = schedule(h, pgv);
            if(<first hole assigned to this process>)
                h->h_state = H_DRILLING;
            else
                h->h_state = H_ASSIGNED;
        }
        t_fork(drill_task);
        ntodrill = nholes;
        ntocheck = 0;
        cur_req = msg;
        send_rep();
    }

send_rep()
    {
        t_wait(&work_done);
        if(pg_rank(my_address, driller) == 1)
            /* Oldest process replies for group */
```

```
                reply(cur_req, "{%d}[]", checklist, ntocheck);
        cur_req = (message*)0;
    }

int drill_task_active;

/* How many failures we can tolerate at a time */
#define    N_FAULTS_TOLERATED    1

drill_task()
    {
        int done_with, n;
        char answ[N_FAULTS_TOLERATED];
        ++drill_task_active;
        n = next_hole(my_address, holes);
        while(n != -1)
        {
            hole_t *h = &holes[n];
            drill_hole(h);
            done_with = n;
            n = next_hole(holes);
            /* Async. broadcast to inform others of my next action */
            cbcast(driller, DRILLING,
                    "%a,%d,%d", my_address, n, done_with,
                   N_FAULTS_TOLERATED+1,
                  "%c", &answ);
        }
        --drill_task_active;
    }

/* Invoked when a DRILLING cbcast is done */
drilling(msg)
    {
        msg_get(msg, "%a,%d,%d", who, &next, &done);

        /* Update status of holes list */
        holes[done].h_state = H_DONE;
        if(next != -1)
            holes[next].h_state = H_DRILLING;

        /* When done, awaken send_rep() */
        if(--ntodrill == 0)
            t_signal(&work_done);

        /* Confirm that we got the message */
        reply(msg, "%c", '+');
    }

/* When a process fails, reassign its remaining work */
monitor_routine(pgv)
  pgroup_view *pgv;
    {
        int must_drill = 0;
```

```
        if(pgv->pgv_event != PGV_DIED)
            return;
        for(h = holes; h < &holes[nholes]; h++)
            if(h->h_who == pgv->pgv_died)
            {
                if(h->h_state == H_ASSIGNED)
                {
                    h->h_who = schedule(h, pgv);
                    if(addr_ismine(h->h_who))
                        ++must_drill;
                }
                else if(h->h_state == H_DRILLING)
                {
                    h->h_state = H_DONE;
                    checklist[ntocheck]++ = h-holes;
                    if(--ntodrill == 0)
                        t_signal(&work_done);
                }
            }
        if(must_drill && drill_task_active == 0)
            t_fork(drill_task);
}
```

The above code is certainly longer than for the Linda example, and it looks far more more complex than the Linda example. However, the Linda example was not fault-tolerant and did not address the scheduling aspects of the problem. Moreover, our solution is actually quite simple. It works as follows.

Each controller process joins a driller process group. The group as a whole receives each request by accepting a message to the work_req entry point. In parallel, all members schedule the work, noting which hole each of the other processes is currently drilling and marking all others as assigned. A lightweight task is forked into the background to do the actual drilling; it will share the address space cell controller with the task running work_req, using a nonpreemptive 'monitor' style of mutual exclusion under which only one task is executing at a time, and context switching occurs only when a task pauses to wait for something. The work_req task now waits for drilling to be completed.

The drill_task operates by drilling the next assigned hole, then broadcasting to all group members when it finishes this hole and moves on to the next one. The broadcast must be done synchronously, waiting until enough replies are received to be sure that the message has reached at least N_FAULTS_TOLERATED remote destinations (because the sender will receive and reply to its own message, we actually wait for one more reply above this threshold). The point here is to be sure that even if N_FAULTS_TOLERATED drill processes crash, the broadcast will still be completed because some operational process will have received it. Each group member marks the previous hole as H_DONE and the next one as H_DRILLING when this broadcast arrives.

If a process fails, the other group members detect this when their monitor routines are invoked by ISIS. They reassign work, moving any hole that the failed process was actually drilling to the check list. Any process that has ceased

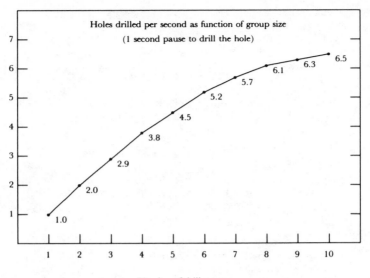

Figure 15.10 Holes drilled per second with a one-second per-hole delay.

drilling (and hence no longer has an active `drill_task`) spawns a new one at this time.

A normal ISIS application would also include code for initializing the group at cold-start time and for transferring the state of the group to a joining member, by encoding it into one or more messages. This code has been omitted above.

What about performance? Figure 15.10 and Figure 15.11 graph the performance of this application program, in holes-per-second drilled by the entire group as a function of the number of members. These figures were generated on a network of SUN 3/60 workstations, otherwise idle, running release 3.5 of the SUN UNIX system and communicating over a 10Mbit Ethernet. Figure 15.11 was based on a control program for which the simulated delay associated with moving the drill units and drilling holes was 1-second per hole. Figure 15.11 used a delay of zero. In the absence of any ISIS overhead, the first graph would show a linear speedup and numbers would all be infinite in the second graph. Thus, the communication overhead imposed by this version of ISIS becomes significant when the group reaches six members, limiting the attainable speedup for drilling holes with this delay factor. Since the number of messages sent per second grows as the square of the size of the group in this example, these curves are not unreasonable ones. More detailed performance figures for ISIS are available in Birman and Joseph (1987a), and Birman, Joseph, and Schmuck (1989).

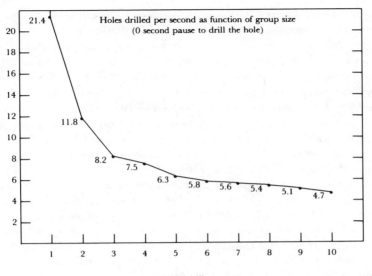

Figure 15.11 Holes drilled per second with a zero-second per-hole delay.

15.12 Theoretical properties of virtually synchronous systems

This chapter concludes with a review of some theoretical results relevant to the behaviour of virtually synchronous systems.

15.12.1 How faithful can a virtually synchronous execution be to the physical one?

A system like ISIS seeks to provide the illusion of a synchronous execution while actually executing asynchronously. Moreover, unlike Linda or HAS, failures are 'events' in the virtually synchronous execution model used by ISIS. This leads to limits on the extent to which the model can be faithful to reality. For example, it is impossible to ensure that a virtually synchronous execution will present failures in the precise sequence that physically occurred with respect to other events. Specifically, in a situation where the system is about to deliver a broadcast, it cannot prevent a physical failure from occurring just as the broadcast delivery is taking place. At one destination, the failure has occurred 'after' delivery, but at the other it is 'before' delivery. From this it can be seen that a system like ISIS might sometimes be forced to claim that a message was delivered to a process that had actually crashed before delivery took place.

A relevant theoretical result (Fisher, Lynch, and Patterson (1985)) shows that it is impossible to reach distributed agreement in an asynchronous system subject to failures. Additional work along these lines was done by Hadzilacos and reported in Hadzilacos (1984). These results limit what is achievable in a virtually synchronous system. In particular, this establishes that ISIS cannot avoid all risk of incorrectly considering an operational site to have failed.

On the other hand, it is possible for a system to avoid claiming anything inconsistent with the *observable* world. This is done by introducing agreement protocols to decide what picture of a fundamentally uncertain event to provide in its synchronous world model, and then present this to its users in a consistent manner. This is what ISIS does. Unless a failed site or process recovers and can be queried about what it observed just before failing, code that runs in ISIS can never encounter an inconsistency. Moreover, when there is some doubt about ensuring that all processes have really observed a broadcast or other event, this can be arranged by briefly running the system synchronously — for example, by asking those processes to reply after they have seen the event and waiting for the replies. This is comparable to deferring external actions in a transactional system until the transaction has reached the prepared-to-commit stage.

15.12.2 State machine approach

It was suggested above that virtual synchrony be viewed as an extension of transactional serializability that introduces process groups and atomic group addressing while eliminating the transactions. Virtual synchrony is at least as closely related, however, to work that was done on a theoretical abstraction called the *state machine* approach to distributed computing. State machines were originally introduced by Lamport, and work in the area is surveyed by Schneider (1986). In this approach, a (static) set of processes interact through a logically centralized service termed the *state machine*; the machine chooses an order in which requests should be executed and delivers them to the participants. In the terms of this chapter, a state machine implements a closely synchronous environment. In most theoretical treatments, state machines are used as a fault-tolerance mechanism, and described in terms of a Byzantine failure model. This may be one reason that their practical value was not immediately perceived. ISIS can then be understood as a state machine implementation that uses a series of optimizations to make the approach viable in an environment subject to a less difficult class of failures. To the best of our knowledge, this issue was never examined directly in a state machine context.

15.12.3 Representing and using IPC context information

There has been other work on communication mechanisms that preserve some form of 'context information', which CBCAST does by constraining the order in which messages are delivered. For example, Jefferson's *virtual time* approach implements a causal delivery ordering constraint using rollback (Jefferson

(1985)). The mechanism operates in a point-to-point communication setting where messages are timestamped and must be delivered to each process in increasing timestamp order (this is common in event-based simulation systems). The problem that arises is that although processes are constrained to use monotonically increasing timestamps for their transmissions, it is impossible to predict just when any given process will need to transmit to any other. If a message is received with timestamp t, it should be delayed if some other process might send a message with timestamp $t' < t$ to the same destination. But, without waiting for all processes to advance beyond time t, how can this property be insured? A virtual time system operates by making the 'optimistic' assumption that no such earlier message will be sent, permitting the delivery of interprocess messages as soon as they arrive. After delivering a message at time t, if a message does arrive with timestamp $t' < t$, the system simply rolls the destination process back to a time prior to t' ('unsending' any messages it issued during this period, which may trigger further rollbacks), then delivers t' and t in the correct order. The scheme requires the system to be able to make checkpoints and that rollback be cheap. The system of Strom and Yemeni (1985) implements a closely related programming language.

Notice that the timestamping scheme described above is really intended to represent time during a discrete simulation, and hence has a different purpose than the $\rightarrow$ operator introduced earlier. In contrast, Peterson (1987) (Peterson, Buchholz, and Schlichting (1989)) has developed a communication mechanism that represents $\rightarrow$ explicitly and then uses this to enforce causal delivery orderings. His system, Psync, includes a small amount of event ordering information in messages that are sent. On reception of a message, a process can invoke simple primitives to test whether there may be outstanding prior messages, or to compare the orders in which two messages were sent. In effect, they permit the interrogation of $\rightarrow$. Peterson has completed an implementation of these primitives in the X-kernel, and used this to build several Psync applications. These include reliable broadcast protocols with the ordering properties of CBCAST, ABCAST and GBCAST, although lacking dynamic process group addressing.

15.12.4 When can a problem be solved asynchronously?

Schmuck has looked at the question of when a system specified in terms of synchronous broadcasts can be run correctly using asynchronous ones (Schmuck (1988)). He defines a system to be *asynchronous* if it admits an implementation in which every broadcast can be delivered immediately to its initiating process, with remote copies of the message being delivered sometime later. Failure broadcasts are not considered, although they could be added to the model without changing any of the results. Thus S_{async} is the class of all system specifications describing problems that can be implemented in this efficient, asynchronous manner. He also introduces the concept of a *linearization operator*, a function that maps certain partially ordered sets of events to legal histories. In a theorem he shows that for all specifications S:

$$S \in S_{async} \iff \exists \text{ a linearization operator for } S.$$

He proves the only-if direction by showing how to construct an implementation for a specification S, based on its linearization operator, using a communication primitive similar to CBCAST. The other direction is proved by contradiction. The result establishes that Schmuck's implementation method is *complete* for the class S_{async}, that is, the method yields a correct implementation for all specifications $S \in S_{async}$.

Schmuck's construction method depends on finding a linearization operator for a given specification. Unfortunately, whether a given specification S is in S_{async} is undecidable. It is immediately clear that there exists no general method for finding a linearization operator for S. However, Schmuck does propose methods for solving this problem for certain subclasses of S_{async}. The basic characteristic of these subclasses is that they have linearization operators determined entirely by commutativity properties of the broadcasts done in the system. Moreover, Schmuck shows how to construct mixed specifications, in which CBCAST is used as often as possible, but ABCAST is still available for situations in which CBCAST cannot be used. These results can be used to 'automatically' construct a linearization operator, and hence an optimal asynchronous broadcast protocol, for a problem like the token-passing ones described above. Interestingly, when we showed that token request, token passing and replicated updates could be totally ordered along the path the token follows, we essentially described the construction of a linearization operator for that problem. Thus, Schmuck's work formalizes a style of argument of important practical relevance.

Herlihy and Wing have also looked at the cost of achieving 'locally' ordered behaviour in distributed systems. This work develops a theory of linearizability, a property similar to serializability, but observed from the perspective of the objects performing operations rather than from the perspective of the processes acting upon those processes (Herlihy and Wing (1987)).

15.12.5 Knowledge in virtually synchronous systems

Some recent work applies logics of knowledge to protocols similar to CBCAST and ABCAST. The former problem was examined by Taylor and Panangaden (1988), who develop a formalism for what they refer to as *concurrent common knowledge*. This kind of knowledge is obtained when an asynchronous CBCAST is performed by a process that subsequently behaves as if all the destinations received the message at the instant it was sent. In ISIS, such a process will never encounter evidence to contradict this assumption. Taylor and Panagaden formally characterize the power of this style of computation, and then use their results to analyse algorithms like the concurrent update discussed above.

Neiger and Toueg have examined the relationship between the total ordering of events in an ABCAST protocol and the total ordering that results from incorporating a shared real-time clock into a distributed system (Neiger and Toueg (1987)). They characterize the settings under which a broadcast algorithm written to use a distributed clock could be implemented using an ABCAST protocol and a logical clock (Lamport (1978)).

15.13 Acknowledgements

We are grateful to Frank Schmuck for detailed comments and suggestions that lead to substantial revisions to this text. Nick Carriero's comments about the discussion of Linda and Ray Strong's comments about recent work on the HAS systems were extremely valuable. The above treatment also benefited from discussions with Ajei Gopal, Ken Kane, Keith Marzullo, Gil Neiger, Pat Stephenson, Kim Taylor, Sam Toueg, Doug Voigt, and many others.

15.14 References

Apollo (1985). *The Apollo Domain File System*. Apollo Computers, Inc., 1985.

P. A. Bernstein and N. Goodman (1981). 'Concurrency Control in Distributed Database Systems'. *ACM Computing Surveys* 13 (2): 185—221, June 1981.

K. P. Birman and T. Joseph (1987a). 'Exploiting virtual synchrony in distributed systems'. *Proceedings Eleventh Symposium on Operating System Principles*: 123—138, Nov. 1987.

K. P. Birman and T. Joseph (1987b). 'Reliable Communication in an Unreliable Environment'. *ACM Transactions on Computer Systems*: 47—76, Feb. 1987.

K. P. Birman, T. Joseph, and F. Schmuck (1989). Issues of Scope and Scale in the ISIS Distributed Toolkit. 1989, In preparation.

A. D. Birrell and B. J. Nelson (1984). 'Implementing Remote Procedure Calls'. *ACM Transactions on Computer Systems* 2 (1): 39—59, February 1984.

N. Carriero and D. Gelertner (1986). 'The Linda S/Net's Linda Kernel'. *ACM Transactions on Computer Systems* 4 (2): 110—129, May 1986.

D. R. Cheriton and W. Zwaenepoel (1985). 'Distributed Process Groups in the V Kernel'. *ACM Transactions on Computer Systems* 3 (2): 77—107, May 1985.

E. C. Cooper (1985). 'Replicated distributed programs'. *Proceedings Tenth Symposium on Operating System Principles*: 63—78, Nov. 1985.

F. Cristian, H. Aghili, R. Strong, and D. Dolev (1986). *Atomic Broadcast: From Simple Message Diffusion to Byzantine Agreement*. IBM Research Report RJ 5244 (54244), July 1986.

F. Cristian (1988). *Reaching Agreement on Processor Group Membership in Synchronous Distributed Systems.* IBM Research Report RJ 5964 (59426), March 1988.

M. Fisher, N. Lynch, and M. Patterson (1985). 'Impossibility of Distributed Consensus with One Faulty Process'. *J. ACM* **32**(2): 274—382, Apr. 1985.

V. Hadzilacos (1984). *Issues of Fault Tolerance in Concurrent Computations.* Ph.D. Thesis, Harvard University, June 1984. (Available as Technical Report 11-84.)

M. Herlihy (1986a). 'Optimistic Concurrency Control for Abstract Data Types'. *Proceedings 5th Symposium on Principles of Distributed Computing*: 206—217, Calgary, Alberta, Canada, 1986.

M. Herlihy (1986b). 'A quorum-consensus replication method for abstract types'. *ACM Transactions on Computer Systems* **4**(1): 32—53, Feb. 1986.

M. Herlihy and J. Wing (1987). 'Linearizable abstract types'. *Proceedings ACM Symposium on Principles of Programming Languages*, Munich, Germany, Jan. 1987.

D. R. Jefferson (1985). 'Virtual Time'. *ACM Transactions on Programming Languages and Systems* **7**(3): 404—425, July 1985.

T. Joseph and K. Birman (1986). 'Low Cost Management of Replicated Data in Fault-Tolerant Distributed Systems'. *ACM Transactions on Computer Systems* **4**(1): 54—70, Feb. 1986.

K. Kane (1989). *Log-based recovery in asynchronous distributed systems.* Ph.D. Thesis , Dept. of Computer Science, Cornell University, Ithaca, NY, Expected Dec. 1989.

N. P. Kronenberg, H. M. Levy, and W. D. Strecker (1986). 'VAXclusters: A Closely-Coupled Distributed System'. *ACM Transactions on Computer Systems* **4**(2): 130—152, May 1986. (Presented at the Tenth Symposium on Operating System Principles, Orcas Island, Washington, December, 1985.)

L. Lamport (1978). 'Time, Clocks, and the Ordering of Events in a Distributed System'. *Communications of the ACM* **21**(7): 558—565, July 1978.

B. Lampson (1986). 'Designing a Global Name Service'. *Proceedings 5th ACM Symposium on Principles of Distributed Computing*: 1—10, Calgary, Canada, Aug. 1986. (1985 Invited Talk.)

B. Liskov, D. Curtis, P. Johnson, and R. Scheifler (1987). 'Implementation of Argus'. *Proceedings of the Eleventh Symposium on Operating System Principles*: 111—122, Austin, TX, 8-11 November 1987.

N. Lynch, B. Blaustein, and M. Siegel (1986). 'Correctness conditions for highly available replicated databases'. *Proceedings 5th ACM Symposium on Principles of Distributed Computing*: 11—28, Calgary, Canada, Aug. 1986.

G. Neiger and S. Toueg (1987). 'Substituting for realtime and common knowledge in asynchronous distributed systems'. *Proceedings 6th ACM Symposium on Principles of Distributed Computing*: 281—293, Vancouver, Canada, Aug. 1987.

L. L. Peterson (1987). 'Preserving Context Information in an IPC Abstraction'. *Proceedings 6th Symp. on Reliability in Distributed Software and Database Systems*: 22—31, Williamsburg, VA, March 1987.

L. L. Peterson, N. Buchholz, and R. Schlichting (1989). 'Preserving and Using Context Information in Interprocess Communication'. *ACM Transactions on Computer Systems*, 1989. (Conditionally accepted.)

R. Rashid *et al.* (1987). 'Machine-Independent Virtual Memory Management for Paged Uniprocessor and Multiprocessor Architectures'. *Proceedings 2nd ASPLOS*: 31—39, Palo Alto, Ca., Oct. 1987.

F. Schmuck (1988). *The use of efficient broadcast protocols in asynchronous distributed systems*. Ph.D. Thesis, Dept. of Computer Science, Cornell University, Ithaca, NY, Aug. 1988.

F. B. Schneider (1986). *The State Machine Approach: A Tutorial*. Technical Report 86-600, Cornell University, December 1986.

P. M. Schwarz and A. Z. Spector (1984). 'Synchronizing Shared Abstract Types'. *ACM Transactions on Computer Systems* 2 (3): 223—250, August 1984. (Also available in Stanley Zdonik and David Maier (Eds.), *Readings in Object-Oriented Databases*. Morgan Kaufmann, 1988, and as Technical Report CMU-CS-83-163, Carnegie Mellon University, November 1983.)

D. Skeen (1985). 'Determining the Last Process to Fail'. *ACM Transactions on Computer Systems* 3 (1): 15—30, Feb 1985.

R. Strom and S. Yemeni (1985). 'Optimistic Recovery in Distributed Systems'. *ACM Transactions on Computer Systems* 3 (3): 204—226, April 1985.

K. Taylor and P. Panangaden (1988). 'Concurrent Common Knowledge: A New Definition of Agreement for Distributed Systems'. *Proceedings Seventh ACM Symposium on Principles of Distributed Computing*, Toronto, Canada, Aug. 1988.

PART VII

Methodology and Architecture

In Chapter 16, Weihl describes how to specify distributed programs. As examples, he uses a simple distributed dictionary system and the well-known Grapevine system.

Chapters 17, 18, and 19 are about the ANSA project. The ANSA project, based in Cambridge, UK, is a research project on finding an architectural structure of distributed systems. Such a structure is necessary before any standardization of distributed systems can be attempted and it is useful because it creates a framework for collaboration between different areas of distributed systems research.

Herbert, ANSA's chief architect, describes the project in Chapter 17, the ANSA Architecture in Chapter 18, and the computational model for distributed applications in ANSA in Chapter 19.

Chapter 16

High-Level Specifications for Distributed Programs

W. E. Weihl

In this chapter we discuss how to specify distributed programs. Such programs often have a number of performance requirements that make them difficult to specify. First, they are typically concurrent and may require a high degree of concurrency. In addition, they may need to be highly reliable (unlikely to lose information entrusted to them) or highly available (needed information is likely to be accessible), and they may need to have fast response time. These requirements often have an effect on the functional behaviour of the system, resulting in different behaviour from what a user might expect from a centralized system, and making that behaviour more difficult to specify.

It is easy to describe a distributed system by giving a detailed description of its implementation, for example, where data is located, how many replicas there are, how requests are processed, and how the pieces of the system communicate. However, such a specification includes many details that are frequently not of interest to a user of the system. Like user-oriented specifications of sequential programs, specifications of distributed programs should be expressed in user-oriented terms and should be free of implementation detail. In this section, it will be shown, through a series of examples, how to give high-level specifications of complex distributed systems with stringent concurrency, reliability, availability, and response time requirements. The examples illustrate how such requirements can affect the functional behaviour provided by a system.

A distributed system is an abstract object that can be used by calling various operations. Thus, the system is an instance of an abstract data type (Guttag, Horowitz, and Musser (1978); Liskov and Zilles (1974); Liskov *et al.* (1977)). The specification of a system describes all relevant constraints on its observable behaviour; this includes the behaviour of the operations called by users and, if the system is active, internal operations that are run by the system itself. The user of a system could be a program or, if the system is interactive, a person. A system may have concurrent users, and these users may invoke its operations in parallel.

In our specifications, each operation is viewed as an atomic action. Atomic actions have been widely studied in recent years as a way of organizing programs that must cope with concurrency and failures (see Chapter 11). Atomic actions have two important properties: serializability and totality. *Serializability* means that the concurrent execution of a group of actions is equivalent to some sequential execution of the same actions. *Totality* means that each action is all-or-nothing: either it executes successfully to completion (in which case it *commits*), or it fails and has no effect on the state of the system (in which case it *aborts*).

Viewing each operation as atomic greatly simplifies specifications. It means that operation invocations, even those executing in parallel, never appear to overlap; instead two such calls appear to occur in some sequential order. Furthermore, if for some reason it is impossible to complete a call, it aborts. This means that the specification is simpler and easier to understand for both the users and the implementers of the system.

Note that a specification that views each operation as an atomic action does not require the implementation to execute each operation atomically. Several authors (e.g., see Birrell *et al.* (1982), Fischer and Michael (1982), Garcia-Molina (1983), Lamport (1976), and Schwarz and Spector (1984)) have claimed that atomicity is incompatible with satisfying various requirements such as high availability or high concurrency. These authors are right that atomicity at the level of the implementation is sometimes incompatible with some performance requirements (such as availability and concurrency); however, this does not preclude using atomicity in the specification. It will be shown here how such systems can be specified using atomic operations.

A user might ordinarily expect a service to be deterministic; for example, if a name is inserted and then looked up, the user would expect the look-up operation to see the effects of the prior insertion. When a system has stringent availability and concurrency requirements, however, services may behave in a more non-deterministic manner. For example, a look-up operation might not see the effects of a prior insertion if the two operations overlap in time, or if the look-up is run at one replica and the insertion at another. The basic technique used in writing specifications is to introduce non-determinism in the specifications of operations to model the delay in propagation of information among replicas and the 'non-serializable' effects of concurrent operations. The examples given in this chapter illustrate how non-determinism can be used to hide irrelevant detail from users while still providing useful information about the behaviour of the system.

It is also useful to structure specifications to distinguish expected and desirable effects from undesirable ones. (A similar approach was proposed by Lampson (1981).) This distinction is an important one for both users and implementers of a system, and it makes the specifications easier to understand.

The specifications given will be informal, in the sense that a precise mathematical meaning for them will not be presented. An important open problem is to provide a precise meaning for these kinds of specifications.

Most of the rest of this chapter consists of specifications of example systems. In each case the way in which atomicity can be used to write a high-level specification that avoids implementation details will be illustrated. In all of the examples considered here, the primary goal is to achieve high availability along with fast response time. Example specifications of systems with high concurrency requirements can be found in Liskov and Weihl (1986).

A very simple example, taken from Fischer and Michael (1982), serves to introduce the issues and the basic approach we take. Next, we look at a real and very complicated system, Grapevine (Birrell *et al.* (1982)). Not all of Grapevine is specified here; more details can be found in Liskov and Weihl (1986). Finally, we conclude with a discussion and a summary of our approach.

The approach taken here is essentially bottom-up: we start with a description of the implementation of a system, and then discuss how to specify that system in user-oriented terms. This approach is taken to illustrate the expressive power of the specification technique. In designing and implementing a system, a more top-down approach is recommended.

16.1 A distributed dictionary

Our first example is a simple distributed dictionary, taken from Fischer and Michael (1982). They present an efficient algorithm for maintaining a replicated distributed dictionary, with *insert*, *delete*, and *list* operations. The dictionary is modelled as a set, with *insert* adding an element to the set, *delete* removing an element from the set, and *list* returning the current members of the set.

The dictionary is to be implemented on a distributed system, consisting of a collection of nodes connected by a network; both the nodes and the network may be unreliable. The goal is to make the system highly available, in the sense that any operational node should be able to perform any of the three operations at any time, regardless of the status of the network or of other nodes.

The implementation works by processing each operation at a single node. Each node has a copy of the dictionary. If an insert or delete operation is executed at a node, only that node's copy of the dictionary is updated. Messages are sent between nodes periodically to propagate information about updates. A list operation executed at a node returns exactly those elements known by the node to have been inserted and not known to have been deleted. (A node knows about a previous operation if either the operation was executed at the node, or the node has received a message from another node that knew about the operation at the time the message was sent.) Because one node may not know about some operations performed at other nodes, users are required to ensure that any given element is inserted at most once, that an element is deleted only if it has been inserted at some point in the past, and that the node at which a deletion occurs knows about the prior insertion.

Notice that this replicated dictionary does not meet the usual specification of a dictionary. In particular, a list operation does not return exactly those elements

that have been inserted and not yet deleted. Instead, it returns only those elements that are known at the node at which it is executed. Thus, a specification
of this system must reflect the replicated nature of the implementation in some
way.

Fischer and Michael's specification, however, contains implementation details
that are unlikely to be of interest to a user of the system. For example, a user
cannot see or control the internal communication, yet their specification of the
dictionary depends heavily on this communication. These implementation
details also introduce the possibility of over-specification, placing unnecessary
and possibly undesirable restrictions on implementations.

In FIGURE 16.1 an alternative specification of the dictionary that hides these
details is presented. In the specification, the dictionary is treated as a logically
centralized resource; its distributed implementation is irrelevant. The state of
the dictionary is modelled as a pair of sets, Members and ExMembers.
Members contains all elements that have been inserted, while ExMembers contains all elements that have been deleted. Each of the three operations described
by the specification is viewed as an atomic action. The operations preserve the
following invariant on the state:

$$\text{ExMembers} \subset \text{Members}$$

The figure illustrates the form used for specifications. The specification of
each operation consists of a *header* followed by a number of clauses. The header
describes the types of the arguments and results. The optional *requires* clause
describes the assumptions that the operation makes about its arguments and the
state of the system when it is called. For example, the requires clauses for the
insert and delete operations define two assumptions needed for Fischer and
Michael's algorithm. Finally, the *effects* clause describes the behaviour of the
operation when the assumptions stated in the requires clause are satisfied; if the
requires clause is not satisfied when the operation is called, then the specification
places no constraints on the behaviour of the operation.

insert = **proc** (x: element)
    requires $x \notin$ Members.
    effects Adds x to Members.

delete = **proc** (x: element)
    requires $x \in$ Members.
    effects Adds x to ExMembers.

list = **proc** ( ) **returns** (sequence[element])
    effects Returns a subset of Members.

Figure 16.1 Specifications of the dictionary's operations.

The figure also illustrates the way we approach specifications. We begin by introducing an abstract model (Liskov and Zilles (1974)) for the system state; this model is used in defining each of the operations. The operations are then specified operationally, that is, they modify or read the state. (An axiomatic approach could also be used, but in writing informal specifications this kind of operational approach is easier to use.)

As with any abstract data type, the operations of the dictionary can be classified as *constructors*, which modify the state, and *observers*, which read the state. (Sometimes an operation is both a constructor and an observer.) For the dictionary, *insert* and *delete* are constructors, and *list* is an observer. To write a specification, we think of the constructors as having an instantaneous effect on the state. For example, *insert* adds the new element to Members. However, users can only observe the state by calling the observers. These typically have non-deterministic specifications, modelling the delay in propagating information among replicas. For example, *list* only returns a subset of the state. Thus, while constructors are specified to 'happen' immediately, users do not necessarily see their effects right away. Using nondeterminism in this way enables us to hide both the existence of multiple copies of the dictionary at different nodes, and the communication among nodes.

The specification in the figure does not match the specification given earlier in one respect: the requires clause of *delete* does not state the constraint that the node at which the deletion is executed must know about the insertion of the element to be deleted. To state this requirement, it would be necessary to expose the existence of nodes in the specification. It would not be difficult to add the nodes to the specification. (We would model the multiple copies in the state. In addition, the operations would all have as an extra argument the node at which the call is to run.) We chose not to do this because of our desire to suppress information about replicas that is unlikely to be of interest to users.

When it is impossible to give an accurate description of a system without exposing information that is not relevant to users of the system, it should be considered whether different decisions should be made, so that the specification need not expose such details. One virtue of specifications is that they serve as a warning flag by bringing such questions to our attention. They help the designers to make an informed decision, where the impact on the user is well-understood.

Of course, a specification is of interest only if it can be implemented efficiently. For example, can the specification in Figure 16.1 be implemented as efficiently as the algorithm of Fischer and Michael? We have done such an efficient implementation for a system very similar to the dictionary. Our system is part of an orphan detection algorithm (Liskov (1984)); its specification is essentially the one given in Figure 16.1. Its implementation must store information about deletes explicitly, where Fischer and Michael need not do this, but we can use garbage collection to discard this information as soon as all nodes know about the delete. (A general description of this replication technique can be found in Ladin, Liskov, and Shrira (1988).)

16.2 Discussion

The specification given above describes the behaviour of the dictionary in high-level, user-oriented terms, but does not capture some important aspects of its behaviour. In particular, it does not indicate what a list operation is likely to return. What is needed is an approach that permits us to distinguish the normal, expected behaviour (for example, that *list* returns exactly those elements that have been inserted but not deleted) from other kinds of behaviour that, although still possible, are less likely and less desirable.

The following simple approach is suggested: divide the effects clause of a specification into two parts, the *normal* and the *abnormal* effects. The normal effects describe what the user can ordinarily expect to observe, for example, when all nodes are up and information is being propagated among nodes fast enough. In effect, it describes an ideal system in which all modifications are observable immediately. The abnormal effects describe unlikely events, for example, what happens when there is a problem like a network partition that prevents messages from being sent from one node to another. It describes situations where the implementation only approximates the ideal system.

In Figure 16.2, a revised specification is shown for the list operation of the replicated dictionary; the specifications of the other operations remain unchanged. Notice that the normal behaviour of *list* is to return exactly those elements that have been inserted and not deleted. It is still possible for it to return some elements that have been deleted, or not to return some elements that have been inserted; this behaviour is described as the abnormal effects. Notice also that the abnormal effects simply repeat the normal effects but in a 'fuzzier' way. All our specifications will be like this; the abnormal effects happen when the normal effects can only be approximated.

A specification using this notation should be interpreted as defining a non-deterministic choice between the normal and abnormal effects. The normal effects are intended to be much more likely to occur than the abnormal effects, but a user of the operation must be prepared for either. A reader would mostly pay attention to the normal effects, since this is what would happen most of the time. He would have to be aware of the abnormal effects, but would not expect them to happen very often.

To really understand how to interpret 'normality', a reader needs to know the relative likelihoods of the various outcomes of an operation. A problem with our specifications is that they do not provide this kind of information. For example,

list = **proc** ( ) **returns** (sequence[element])
    normal effects Returns Members — ExMembers.
    abnormal effects Returns a subset of Members.

Figure 16.2 Revised specification of *list*.

it should be very likely that an element that was inserted a long time ago and has not been deleted will be returned by a call of the list operation, and similarly if an element was deleted a long time ago it should be unlikely that it will be returned. Intuitively, the normal effects should be likely to happen provided the call happens long enough after all other calls whose effects it is supposed to observe, but we do not know how likelihood should be expressed formally. We discuss this issue further in Section 16.5.

16.3 Grapevine

In this section, we provide a partial specification of the Grapevine system (Birrell *et al.* (1982)). In contrast to the previous example, Grapevine is a real, complex system. The main performance issues here are high availability and quick response time.

In this section, we concentrate on the naming environment, and ignore other aspects such as the mail system and the rules for access control. Our specification defines a number of operations that are intended to model the actions that Grapevine users can perform. Grapevine does not actually provide these operations, but instead provides an interactive interface with the same functionality. Also, only some of the permitted actions are illustrated; the ones shown should be sufficient to indicate how the entire interface would be specified. (A more detailed specification of Grapevine, including the mail system and the rest of the naming environment, can be found in Liskov and Weihl (1986).)

Grapevine runs in a distributed environment consisting of computers connected by a network. Some of the computers are classified as *clients*: these are used by people and make use of services provided by the other category of machines, the *servers*. Grapevine runs on both clients and servers. All its information (such as the users' mail) is stored at the servers. The clients run a front-end program that interacts with the servers to make information available to users.

Grapevine provides a name space of two level names called *rnames*. An rname is written

     x.y

where *y* names a *registry* and *x* identifies an *entry* within registry *y*. Thus, the name space consists of entities called registries, and every rname is a member of some registry.

The entry named by an rname can be either an *individual* or a *group*. An individual entry records information about a person or a server. An entry for a server contains information about how to connect to it. Information recorded about people includes their passwords and the rnames of mail servers that store their mail. An entry for a group simply lists the rnames of members of the group.

Grapevine provides operations to look up an rname, to modify the rname's entry, and to add and delete rnames. It is also possible to add and remove registries and servers. The behaviour of these operations does not quite match our intuitive expectations, but instead is influenced by the performance requirements of the implementation. As in the previous example, the behaviour will be explained by describing the implementation first, and then presenting high-level specifications that hide much of the implementation detail.

Grapevine was designed to be highly available and to have a good response time. If all Grapevine information were stored at just one server, then the system could not be used if this server crashed or became inaccessible. Therefore, information is replicated at several servers. However, only one of these servers is needed to use or modify the replicated information. In this way, each access has both high availability and good response time. Grapevine provides operations that allow a user to change the set of servers that stores a particular registry.

To provide access to the registries, there is one special registry called *gv*, which serves as the root of the name space. Each registry (including gv) is an entry in gv. In this way, information about registries can be accessed using rnames that are just like other rnames. Each registry entry is a group; the rnames in this group identify the servers that store replicas of the registry. The servers themselves are also stored as entries in gv. Thus every registry and server has a name of the form *x.gv*.

To look up rname *x.y*, the first step is to find a server that stores registry *y.gv*. To avoid searching for such a server (thus adding to the response time of the access) and to ensure that this first step will have no impact on availability, the gv registry is stored at every server. Thus to access a particular rname, it is necessary to communicate with at most two servers, first to find a server that stores the registry, and then to communicate with that server.

Every operation provided by Grapevine, even one that modifies a registry, interacts directly with just one of the servers that stores a replica of the registry. That server modifies its local information, and then, in background mode, propagates the change to the other replicas. The result of this policy is that the replicas can contain inconsistent information. For example, one replica may contain a new rname *x.y*, but that information may not have propagated to a second replica. If a user attempts to access *x.y* at this point, it is possible that the result will indicate that *x.y* does not exist.

As in the previous example, we use nondeterministic specifications to describe situations in which the effects of an update operation are not necessarily visible to later operations. The normal effects of an operation will describe what should happen when all needed information is available and everything is working properly, while the abnormal effects will describe what might happen if, for example, the effects of an earlier operation have not yet become known throughout the system. The implementation of Grapevine ensures that the normal effects are extremely likely, and that the abnormal effects occur only rarely.

The state of the system will be modelled as a pair:

Info × ExRnames

ExRnames is a set containing all rnames that were created and then deleted. Info is a partial function that maps rnames to their associated information:

Info = [rname → [Indiv + Group + Server]]

(The + notation means a disjoint union.) A mapping exists in Info for every rname that has ever been created. This mapping reflects the fact that some rnames are individuals, some are groups, and some are servers (although servers are similar to individuals, different information is stored for them, so they are treated differently here). Rnames for registries are included in Info; they are simply rnames of the form *r.gv* where the associated information is a group. However, there is no mapping for gv.gv; for convenience, gv.gv is treated specially rather than making it an entry in the system.

The notation

Info(n)

is used to stand for the information stored for rname n in Info, and we will often write an rname using the Grapevine notation *x.y*. The following abbreviations will also be useful:

isDef(n)	is true iff a mapping for n is defined in Info.
isIndiv(n)	is true iff Info(n) is an individual.
isGroup(n)	is true iff Info(n) is a group
isReg(x.y)	is true iff y = 'gv' & [x = 'gv' ∨ isGroup(x.y)], i.e., iff *x.y* is a registry.

The operations will preserve the following invariants on the state:

1. Rnames must be created before being deleted:

    $n \in$ ExRnames $\Rightarrow$ isDef(n)

2. Rnames of entries must be members of existing registries:

    isDef(x.y) $\Rightarrow$ isReg(y.gv)

As in the previous example, the idea of the specifications is that update operations have an instantaneous effect on the state, but this effect need not be visible to later operations. This uncertainty is reflected in the specifications as a nondeterministic choice between the normal and abnormal effects; the abnormal effects describe the behaviour when not all needed information is available. In the specifications in this section, a nondeterministic choice is allowed to be made among the alternatives within the normal or abnormal effects. This nondeterministic choice is expressed using guarded commands (Dijkstra (1976)) with the form

$$g_1 \Rightarrow e_1$$
$$g_2 \Rightarrow e_2$$
$$\cdots$$
$$g_n \Rightarrow e_n$$

where the g_i (the 'guards') are predicates and the e_i (the 'effects') describe results and state changes. The meaning of a guarded command is that the effects described by e_i will occur only if g_i is true; if more than one guard is true, then a nondeterministic choice is made among their associated effects.

We begin by defining some operations for individuals. Operation *add_indiv* adds a new individual rname; the name must be of the form *x.y*, where $y \neq$ gv. Operation *remove_rname* removes an rname (for any kind of entry), and operation *get_indiv_info* returns the information associated with an rname for an individual. For all these operations, normal termination is possible only under certain conditions, for example, a new rname can be created only if a registry exists for that rname. To model this situation, each operation can terminate normally or by signalling an exception. The exceptions that can be signalled by an operation are listed in its header. The specifications for these operations are shown in Figure 16.3.

A good specification to look at first is the one for *get_indiv_info*. Intuitively, we would expect this operation to return normally if and only if there is a mapping defined for *n* in Info, $n \notin$ ExRnames, and *n* is an individual; otherwise it should signal the appropriate exception. This is the behaviour indicated by the normal effects. However, because updates do not happen everywhere instantaneously, *get_indiv_info* cannot give such a precise result. It can be guaranteed that it will not return information if *n* has never been entered in the system. Otherwise, however, as indicated by the abnormal effects, it may or may not return information. It might return information about an rname that has been deleted or signal even though the rname exists.

The specifications for the other two operations are similar. Again the guarantees that can be made are relatively weak. In the case of *remove_rname* we can guarantee not to delete an rname that has never been added to the system. However, we may be unable to delete an rname that has been added. The reason for this, of course, is that the information about the addition may not yet have propagated to the replica of the registry that is used to implement the operation.

The situation for *add_indiv* is even stranger. We can guarantee to add the name if it has not already been added, provided *y* is a legitimate registry name. However, the abnormal effects indicate that it may be possible to add *x.y* even if it has already been added. Again, the reason is that the information about an earlier addition may not have propagated to the replica used for the later addition. Also, *no_such_registry* may be signalled even if *y* is a legitimate registry name because this information may not have propagated to the server used to look up *y*.

add_indiv = **proc** (*x.y*: rname, *i*: Indiv)
        signals (name_in_use, no_such_registry, wrong_form)
   normal effects
      if *y* = 'gv' then signals *wrong_form*
         elseif ¬isReg(*y.gv*) $\vee$ *y.gv* $\in$ ExRnames then signals *no_such_registry*
         elseif isDef(*x.y*) then signals *name_in_use*
         else adds [*x.y* $\rightarrow$ *i*] to Info and returns normally
   abnormal effects
      y $\neq$ 'gv' & isReg(*y.gv*) $\Rightarrow$ adds [*x.y* $\rightarrow$() *i*] to Info and returns normally
      y $\neq$ 'gv' $\Rightarrow$ signals *no_such_registry*

get_indiv_info = **proc** (*n*: rname) **returns** (Indiv) **signals** (no_such_indiv)
   normal effects
      if ¬isIndiv(*n*) $\vee$ *n* $\in$ ExRnames then signals *no_such_indiv*
         else returns Info(*n*)
   abnormal effects
      isIndiv(*n*) $\Rightarrow$ returns Info(*n*)
      true $\Rightarrow$ signals *no_such_indiv*

remove_rname = **proc** (*x.y*: rname) **signals** (no_such_name)
   normal effects
      if isDef(*x.y*) then adds *x.y* to ExRnames and returns normally
         else signals *no_such_name*
   abnormal effects true $\Rightarrow$ signals *no_such_name*

Figure 16.3 Specifications of some operations for individuals.

The uncertainty in adding and removing rnames is an acknowledged problem in Grapevine. The most serious problem is that the same rname may be added 'simultaneously', for example, by users using two different client machines. In this case, it is not defined which addition prevails. (Our specification does define the effect; the later addition prevails.) The 'solution' proposed in Birrell *et al.* (1982) is to require that 'simultaneous' additions of the same rname cannot happen.

Grapevine also provides operations to add and delete groups, and to modify the membership of a group. Other operations are provided for reconfiguring the system (adding and deleting registries and servers, and adding and deleting servers that hold replicas of a registry). Specifications of these operations can be found in Liskov and Weihl (1986). They are similar to those shown above, and suffer from similar problems. For example, Grapevine has trouble ensuring that a new replica contains the same information as previously existing replicas. The problem is that a change to a registry is made at one replica and then forwarded by that replica to the others. To know which are the others, that replica consults a copy of gv (probably the one at its server). However, this copy might not have received information about a new replica yet, in which case the change will not be forwarded to the new replica. A similar problem arises when a new server is added to Grapevine.

Like the simultaneous addition of rnames, these are problems that Grapevine 'solves' by requiring users to avoid them. For example, no new rname should be entered in a registry until it is known that information about a new replica has propagated 'sufficiently'. It is not clear, however, how a user would ever know for sure that sufficient propagation had occurred.

It would be possible to capture Grapevine's solution to these problems by adding a requires clause to the specifications of some operations, e.g., to *add_indiv*. To do so, however, would involve including more details in the specification. For example, the replicas could be included in the model explicitly, and require that the replica used for the call of *add_indiv* contain information at least as recent as all other replicas. However, as mentioned in the discussion of the dictionary, whenever a specification must include details that seem intuitively not to be user-oriented, the decisions that led to the need should be questioned.

In Figure 16.4 a new specification for *add_indiv* is shown that avoids adding duplicate rnames without exposing unwanted details. The main point to notice is that the specification no longer includes the clauses in the abnormal effects that caused problems before. The earlier specification permitted *add_indiv* to add a name even when it was already defined; now this is no longer possible. By having similar specifications for all operations that modify the name space, the uncertainties mentioned above can be avoided entirely. Such specifications are shown in Liskov and Weihl (1986).

Of course, as mentioned earlier, a specification like this is only of interest if it can be implemented efficiently. Notice first that operations like *get_indiv_info* that only read the name space remain unchanged. This means that operations with severe response time constraints, such as for sending and receiving mail, are not affected by the change. The response time constraints for operations like *add_indiv* are less severe since they are executed relatively infrequently.

add_indiv = **proc** (*x.y*: rname, *i*: Indiv)
    signals (name_in_use, no_such_registry, wrong_form)
    normal effects
        if *y* = 'gv' then signals *wrong_form*
            elseif $\neg$isReg(*y.gv*) $\lor$ *y.gv* $\in$ ExRnames then signals *no_such_registry*
            elseif isDef(*x.y*) then signals *name_in_use*
            else adds [*x.y* $\rightarrow$() *i*] to Info and returns normally
      abnormal effects *y* $\neq$ 'gv' $\Rightarrow$ signals *no_such_registry*

Figure 16.4 New specification of *add_indiv*.

However, these operations must not represent an availability bottleneck. It is shown below that a reasonably efficient implementation satisfying this constraint is possible.

Since the abnormal effects in Figure 16.4 indicate that *add_indiv* can signal *no_such_registry* even if the registry exists, its implementation need read only one replica of gv. However, the implementation must read and modify more than one replica of the rname's registry. For example, *add_indiv* signals *name_in_use* exactly when the rname is defined. Therefore, if an rname *r* is added and then added again, the second call must terminate with the *name_in_use* exception. This means that the replicas read in the second call must intersect the replicas modified in the first call. This can be accomplished if each operation uses a majority of the replicas. (The majority could be defined simply by number or by weighted votes (Gifford (1979)).) In addition, the exception *name_in_use* must occur even if a new replica for the registry was added in between the two calls. Techniques developed in recent years (Herlihy (1984), among others) can be used to cope with this kind of reconfiguration efficiently. Finally, the implementation should not add an rname if the rname's registry has been deleted; this can be avoided by having the replicas contain information about deletion of their registry.

It may appear that having the name space modification operations use a majority of replicas can lead to a loss of concurrency. However, this loss can be quite small. For example, it is possible to implement a registry in such a way that adding a new rname excludes only other operations that use *that* rname. It would still be possible to look up or insert some other rname in the registry without having to wait for an *add_indiv* operation to complete. Implementations like this are discussed in Weihl (1984) and Weihl and Liskov (1985).

Another problem is deadlock. The additional concurrency discussed above avoids some deadlocks but not all. For example, adding a replica is likely to exclude the adding of rnames for that registry. If two such operations start simultaneously, they may lock replicas in opposite orders and thus deadlock. However, the chance of such a deadlock is extremely small, since the operations, especially to add a replica, are executed so rarely. Therefore, a simple approach such as assigning priorities and aborting the lower priority operation if there is a conflict should be sufficient.

16.4 Limiting non-determinism

The specifications given in the last three sections have substantial non-determinism: an observer might see the effects of an arbitrary subset of the prior constructors. This is really a problem of the systems being described, not just with how we have written the specifications. Unless the user knows how many replicas there are, and can tell when an update has been propagated to all replicas, there is no way a user can know whether an observer operation will see a given update.

It would be useful for a system to allow a user to indicate how up-to-date the answer to a query must be, or for the user to be able to tell which updates are guaranteed to be included in the answer. Several replication techniques (Ladin, Liskov, and Shrira (1988); Lampson (1986)) designed recently allow the user to determine a bound on how out of date an answer can be, or to require the answer to be current as of some point in time. The answer may include more recent information also, but the effects of all constructors before the bound are accounted for in the answer. In effect, the non-determinism is limited to the updates that happened after the bound. These systems work by keeping track internally of how many replicas know about a given update, and allowing the user to determine whether all the replicas know about the update.

To illustrate how one might specify these systems, we will show how the specification of the dictionary from Section 16.1 could be modified. The idea is to assign a logical time to each operation. The state has four components, Members, ExMembers, Clock, and Bound. As before, Members and ExMembers are used to keep track of the insertions and deletions that have occurred. Now, however, we also need to remember the 'time' at which each update happened. Thus, we model each as a partial map from elements to times. Clock is a time used to generate times for updates. Bound keeps track of the updates that are guaranteed to be seen by an observer: all updates with times less than Bound will be seen, along with some subset of the later updates.

insert = **proc** (x: element)
    requires Members(x) is undefined.
    effects Adds [$x \rightarrow$ ()Clock] to Members and advances Clock.

delete = **proc** (x: element)
    requires Members(x) is defined.
    effects Adds [$x \rightarrow$ ()Clock] to ExMembers and advances Clock.

list = **proc** ( ) **returns** (sequence[element])
    normal effects
        Returns $\{x \mid x$ is mapped by Members$\}$ —
            $\{x \mid x$ is mapped by ExMembers$\}$.
    abnormal effects
        Let $I = \{x \mid$ Members(x) $<$ Bound$\}$ and
            $D = \{x \mid$ ExMembers(x) $<$ Bound$\}$.
        Let I' be a subset of $\{x \mid$ Members(x) $\geqslant$ Bound$\}$ and
            let D' be a subset of $\{x \mid$ ExMembers(x) $\geqslant$ Bound$\}$.
        Then returns $(I \cup I') - (D \cup D')$.

Figure 16.5 Specification of the dictionary with limited non-determinism.

A specification of the operations is given in Figure 16.5. In addition to the specifications given there, we add the requirement that Bound can either stay the same or increase when an operation is executed, but that it can never be larger than Clock. The specification of *list* states that it normally returns exactly the elements that have been inserted and not deleted. However, it can also return an approximation to this answer, computed by including the effects of all updates that occurred before Bound as well as the effects of some of the updates that occurred after Bound.

The specification given in Figure 16.5 does not allow a user to tell whether the effects of a given update are guaranteed to be included in an answer returned by an observer. In Figure 16.6 it is shown how the specification of list could be changed to permit this. It is assumed that the specifications of the update operations are changed so that each update operation returns the time assigned to it. In the specification shown in Figure 16.6, *list* returns Bound along with the sequence of elements. Given the time returned by an update and the time returned by *list*, a user can tell whether the update is guaranteed to be reflected in the answer returned by *list*.

list = **proc** ( ) **returns** (time, sequence[element])
    normal effects Advances Bound to equal Clock;
        returns Bound and
        $\{x \mid x$ is mapped by Members$\} - \{x \mid x$ is mapped by ExMembers$\}$
    abnormal effects
        Let $I = \{x \mid \text{Members}(x) < \text{Bound}\}$ and
            $D = \{x \mid \text{ExMembers}(x) < \text{Bound}\}$.
        Let I' be a subset of $\{x \mid \text{Members}(x) \geqslant \text{Bound}\}$ and
            let D' be a subset of $\{x \mid \text{ExMembers}(x) \geqslant \text{Bound}\}$.
        Then returns Bound and $(I \cup I') - (D \cup D')$.

Figure 16.6 Alternative specification of *list*.

16.5 Conclusions

In this section, how to give user-oriented specifications for several distributed systems has been discussed. In each case, the system has some performance requirements: Fischer and Michael's dictionary requires high availability, and Grapevine requires high availability and fast response time. These requirements led the designers to relax their constraints on the system's behaviour. For example, instead of requiring all modifications to be known everywhere instantaneously, they have allowed changes to become known at different times in different parts of the implementation. Nevertheless, we were able to describe the behaviour of these systems in high-level terms without including low-level details that are not of interest to users of the systems.

In our specifications, we used a format in which normal and abnormal effects were specified separately. As discussed earlier, the idea is that a reader will mostly pay attention to the normal effects, since this is what should happen most of the time. He will have to be aware of the abnormal effects, but should not expect them to happen very often. To really understand how to interpret 'normality', however, the reader needs to know the relative likelihoods of the various outcomes of an operation. It might be useful to associate probabilities with the different outcomes of an operation, or to rank them in order of preference. It is not clear, however, how to give a precise mathematical meaning to such specifications. This is an area where more work is needed.

Herlihy and Wing (1987) have generalized our structure; instead of having 'normal' and 'abnormal' effects, they propose a lattice structure for specifications. The top of the lattice corresponds to our 'normal' effects, and is the most constraining. The bottom of the lattice corresponds to a non-deterministic choice between our 'normal' and 'abnormal' effects, and is the least constraining. Intermediate points in the lattice represent specifications that are less constraining than the 'normal' effects, but more constraining than the 'abnormal' effects. Herlihy and Wing also discuss how a 'constraint' lattice can be associated with the lattice of specifications, where the constraints might describe the number of available replicas, the constraints on quorum intersection, or the level of concurrency. Their approach allows a user to deduce the behaviour of the system when it satisfies a subset of the possible constraints, such as when no more than k transactions execute concurrently. This approach gives the user some information about when certain behaviour can occur, but may require the user to know about details (for example, the number of replicas and how they communicate) in order to understand when a particular constraint is satisfied. A higher level way of describing constraints would be useful.

Another way of specifying systems like these is to use the 'eventually' operator of temporal logic (Owicki and Lamport (1982)) to require that the results of an update will eventually be visible to later operations. This gives a result similar to that obtained using nondeterminism, since nothing is said about *when* the results will become visible. However, there are several problems with using 'eventually'. The first is that it may be too strong, since if enough failures occur at inopportune times it is possible (though, perhaps, extremely unlikely) that something might *never* happen. This should not mean, however, that the system has failed to meet its specification. For example, in Grapevine, a message might never be delivered, and no trouble message sent either, but this does not means that the system is broken. A specification that required all messages to be delivered eventually would not be satisfied by Grapevine, or by any realistic implementation.

The second problem with 'eventually' is that it does not say enough. Simply requiring that something happen 'eventually' does not tell a user how long it can be expected to take to happen. This is also a problem with our specifications, since they do not indicate how long one should wait to be reasonably certain that the normal effects will happen. This, too, is an area that deserves further study.

Another problem is that a specification that requires something to happen eventually does not indicate which results are more desirable than others. We believe that the distinction between normal and abnormal effects made in our specifications is important for both users and implementers of a system. For example, such specifications could serve as a basis for comparing implementations. One implementation might be considered better than another if the abnormal effects occur less frequently in it, or if the normal effects happen more quickly. Again, this is an area where more work is needed.

In our specifications, each operation was viewed as an atomic action. As mentioned earlier, this greatly simplifies specifications, yet does not overly constrain implementations. Multi-step behaviour, as in spooling mail for later delivery, can be modelled by appropriate non-determinism in the operations that ultimately observe the state (such as the operation that allows a user to read his mail), or by viewing the system as active, and introducing 'internal' operations that model the multi-step behaviour. In Liskov and Weihl (1986), we took the latter approach in specifying the mail delivery component of Grapevine.

Occasionally, one will encounter an operation that is best viewed as a sequence of several atomic operations; for example, an operation that waits on a queue for a signal from another operation could be specified as a sequence of two atomic actions. A recent paper by Birrell *et al.* (1987) discusses how formal specifications of such operations might be written. Although some operations might need to be viewed as a sequence of atomic actions, the specification of a system is likely to be simpler and easier to understand if most operations are specified as single atomic actions.

We claim that our specifications accurately describe the aspects of each system's behaviour that are relevant to the system's users. For instance, in the Fischer-Michael example, knowing that the replicas send messages to one another does not help the user understand how quickly a given addition or deletion will propagate. Similarly, in Grapevine, knowing that servers communicate by sending messages does not help the user understand how soon mail will arrive. Therefore, our specifications, in which the delay in information propagation is modelled by nondeterminism, are as informative to the user as this extra detail. (The extra detail is clearly of interest to a system implementer or maintainer, but our specifications are not intended for them.)

The advantage of specifications is that they make it clear exactly what interface a program provides. Specifications provide valuable information not only to users of a system, but to designers. Users, of course, need to know what behaviour they can expect to see. For example, a user of Grapevine needs to know all the situations that might happen, even if some are unlikely to occur (e.g., the problems with adding and deleting rnames, registries, and servers). Similarly, designers need to decide if they have made the right decisions. Given the specifications, they can decide whether the interface is what is wanted. Different designers might make different decisions; the important point is that

they need a clear understanding of a system's interface in order to decide if the
trade-offs made during design are justified.

As stated at the beginning of this chapter, our approach has been primarily
bottom-up: we started with a description of the implementation of each system,
and then described how to specify that implementation in user-oriented terms.
Program design, however, should be driven primarily by the user's requirements,
and thus should take more of a top-down approach. For example, one might
start with a relatively strong specification (without any nondeterminism), and
gradually weaken it by introducing nondeterminism and abnormal effects as the
implementation constraints become better understood. At each stage, the
specification could be used to help evaluate decisions, since it makes evident the
effects on the users.

16.6 References

A. D. Birrell, R. Levin, R. M. Needham, and M. Schroeder (1982). 'Grapevine:
An Exercise in Distributed Computing'. *Communications of the ACM* **25**:
260—274, April 1982.

A. D. Birrell, J. Guttag, J. Horning, and R. Levin (1987). 'Synchronization
Primitives for a Multiprocessor: A Formal Specification'. *Proceedings of the
Eleventh Symposium on Operating System Principles*: 94—102, Austin, TX, 8-11
November 1987. (In *ACM Operating Systems Review 21*:5.)

E. W. Dijkstra (1976). *A Discipline of Programming*. Prentice-Hall, Englewood
Cliffs, NJ, 1976.

M. J. Fischer and A. Michael (1982). 'Sacrificing Serializability to Attain High
Availability of Data in an Unreliable Network'. *Proceedings of the Symposium on
Principles of Database Systems*, 1982.

H. Garcia-Molina (1983). 'Using Semantic Knowledge for Transaction Processing in a Distributed Database'. *ACM Transactions on Database Systems* **8**(2):
186—213, 1983.

D. K. Gifford (1979). 'Weighted Voting for Replicated Data'. *Proceedings of the
Seventh Symposium on Operating System Principles*: 150—162, December 1979.

J. Guttag, E. Horowitz, and D. Musser (1978). 'Abstract Data Types and
Software Validation'. *Communications of the ACM* **21**(12): 1048—1064, 1978.

M. P. Herlihy (1984). *Replication Methods for Abstract Data Types*. Ph.D. Thesis,
MIT, 1984.

M. Herlihy and J. Wing (1987). 'Specifying Graceful Degradation in Distributed Systems'. *Proceedings of the Sixth Annual Symposium on Principles of Distributed
Computing*: 167—177, Vancouver, 1987.

R. Ladin, B. Liskov, and L. Shrira (1988). *A Technique for Constructing Highly Available Services*. Technical Report-409, MIT Laboratory for Computer Science, 1988.

L. Lamport (1976). *Towards a Theory of Correctness for Multi-User Data Base Systems*. CA-7610-0712, Massachusetts Computer Associates, 1976.

B. Lampson (1981). 'Atomic transactions'. In Goos and Hartmanis (Ed.), *Distributed Systems — Architecture and Implementation*, Volume 105, pages 246—265. Springer-Verlag Lecture Notes in Computer Science, Berlin, 1981.

B. Lampson (1986). 'Designing a Global Name Service'. *Proceedings 5th ACM Symposium on Principles of Distributed Computing*: 1—10, Calgary, Canada, Aug. 1986. (1985 Invited Talk.)

B. Liskov and S. N. Zilles (1974). 'Programming with Abstract Data Types'. *SIGPLAN Notices* **9**(4): 50—59, 1974. (Proceedings of the ACM SIGPLAN Conference on Very High Level Languages.)

B. Liskov (1984). *Overview of the Argus Language and System*. MIT Laboratory for Computer Science Programming Methodology Group Memo, 1984.

B. Liskov and W. E. Weihl (1986). 'Specifications of Distributed Programs'. *Distributed Computing* **1**: 102—118, 1986.

B. Liskov *et al.* (1977). 'Abstraction Mechanisms in CLU'. *Communications of the ACM* **20**(8): 564—576, 1977.

S. Owicki and L. Lamport (1982). 'Proving Liveness Properties of Concurrent Programs'. *ACM Transactions on Programming Languages and Systems* **4**(3): 455—495, 1982.

P. M. Schwarz and A. Z. Spector (1984). 'Synchronizing Shared Abstract Types'. *ACM Transactions on Computer Systems* **2**(3): 223—250, August 1984. (Also available in Stanley Zdonik and David Maier (Eds.), *Readings in Object-Oriented Databases*. Morgan Kaufmann, 1988, and as Technical Report CMU-CS-83-163, Carnegie Mellon University, November 1983.)

W. E. Weihl (1984). *Specification and implementation of atomic data types*. Ph. D. Thesis, MIT, Cambridge, MA, 1984. (Available as Technical Report MIT/LCS/Technical Report-314.)

W. E. Weihl and B. Liskov (1985). 'Implementation of Resilient, Atomic Data Types'. *ACM Transactions on Programming Languages and Systems* **7**(2): 244—269, April 1985.

Chapter 17

The ANSA Project and Standards

A. J. Herbert

17.1 The ANSA project

17.1.1 Background

The Advanced Networked Systems Architecture (ANSA) originated as a project within the UK Alvey Programme for advanced research and development in Information Technology. Eight major IT companies came together to sponsor a project which would propose an architecture for networked computer systems to support distributed applications and to promote the acceptance of the results as an industry-wide standard.

The method adopted was to harvest the state-of-the-art in published and ongoing research into a consistent and modular architectural framework. Key features of the framework are portability, scaling and evolution from current industry standards such as Unix and OSI.

The ANSA project was set up in what was, for Alvey, an unique way. Rather than carry out disjointed work at each of the sponsors' sites, a single laboratory was set up in Cambridge, under the technical guidance of a Chief Architect who was hired specifically for the task. His team was formed partly by long-term secondment of staff from the sponsors and partly by direct hiring. This approach to shared collaborative working has been found to function efficiently and effectively by insulating team members from individual corporate pressures and in establishing cohesion and dedication in the team: benefits which are perceived and valued by all of the sponsors.

As a working laboratory, ANSA is just over three years old. In that time the team has developed the architectural framework, and described it in the *ANSA*

Reference Manual which has been widely distributed. The project has carried out a major awareness programme by means of workshops, seminars, teaching and participation in national and European planning bodies. The project has also been active in standardization: over half of the current ISO Open Distributed Processing (ODP) working documents originated from ANSA. The project has contributed to the ECMA RPC standard and the new work in CCITT on Distributed Applications Framework (DAF).

A further major achievement of the project is the ANSA Testbench — a suite of software which provides a reference implementation to demonstrate the use of ANSA principles. The Testbench provides an advanced remote procedure call and distributed system management facility and software tools to simplify the task of writing distributed applications. As time goes by, more functions are being added to the Testbench, both in terms of additional mechanisms and in additional tools. This software has been a major means of transferring technology back to the sponsors and others: the Testbench currently runs on top of various Unix systems and MS-DOS. Ports to Apollo Domain, VMS and VME are in development at present. The Testbench has been used for applications as diverse as intelligent networks, office systems, telephone exchange control and factory automation.

Good working links and relationships have been built with many other projects including those in Alvey and Esprit as well as with academic groups in Europe, the USA and the Far East.

Both the Testbench and the *ANSA Reference Manual* are developing activities. There is still much to be added and defined, for example, in widening the functionality of the architecture, in the areas of security and replication techniques, and in modelling the corporate enterprise and its use of information technology to provide a seamless integration of business requirements and technological solutions.

From this base, the ANSA laboratory is now moving onwards into its second stage of development, firstly as a major player in a major Esprit project on Integrated Systems Architecture (ISA) and secondly by widening its collaborative base in Europe. The ISA project will form the focus for ANSA over the next four years; with EEC funding and Europe-wide collaboration it will continue with its main theme of building an effective and timely path from research to standards. This increased collaboration will bring a wider input from application domains and provide an opportunity to demonstrate and evaluate the architecture in these domains, generating requirements and feedback to the architectural core. To facilitate this process the ANSA laboratory has become a non-profit company supported by the sponsoring companies. The ANSA laboratory currently exploys about eighteen people.

Additionally to ISA, the laboratory is involving itself in other relevant projects and programmes extending the architecture, enhancing and supporting the Testbench and participating in standards work. These are a mix of industry-led, government-funded and collaborative projects, all aligned with the ANSA themes:

- distributed systems and applications

- timely and effective open standards

- technology transfer from research into standards and products

The ANSA collaborators are: British Telecom, Digital Equipment Corporation, The General Electric Company/Marconi, Hewlett Packard, International Computers Limited, Information Technology Limited, Olivetti Research Ltd, Plessey Office & Networked Systems, and Racal.

The ISA collaborators are: AEG Modcomp, British Telecom, Digital Equipment Corporation, Ellemtel A/B, The General Electric Company, GEC-Plessey Telecommunications, Hewlett Packard, International Computers Limited, Information Technology Limited, Philips NV, SEPT, Siemens AG, and STC Technology Limited.

17.2 Activities

The ANSA project has two themes: *integration* and *standards*. It is intended to enable the integration of application systems from multiple vendors both by creating a set of common architecture for distributed computing systems and by utilizing this architecture in the development of standards.

The project concentrates on *enabling* rather than *providing* integration; that is, it concentrates its efforts on defining models, interfaces and standards based on work already done by others so as to create a common infrastructure or platform through which separate applications can achieve true interworking.

The mission of the ANSA project has three aims:

- to provide a nucleus of concepts around which the architectural ideas of distributed processing can crystallize, thus enabling integration

- to provide a reference model for open distributed processing in order to enable standards to be defined, and to develop those standards for open distributed processing which are common to all areas of application

- to demonstrate the practical feasibility of integration through adherence to the standards, based on prototype implementations of the new protocols and services.

These aspects are reflected in the two categories of objectives for the ANSA team: *coordination* and *technical* objectives.

Coordination objectives

Standards: building and sustaining project-wide consensus on technical contributions into the international standards process.

Technology transfer: acting as a 'clearinghouse' providing precompetitive technical knowledge to assist the partners to formulate industrial exploitation of open distributed processing.

Dissemination: publishing annually the project results in the form of updated and extended versions of the *ANSA Reference Manual* and further releases of the *ANSA Testbench*. Participation in international standards bodies is another form of dissemination. Emphasis is also placed on participation in workshops and presentations at seminars.

Technical objectives

Foundations: developing architectural concepts, modelling techniques and taxonomies by which distributed processing systems can be described consistently.

Engineering: developing and specify engineering methods that will be needed by designers of applications of distributed processing.

Productivity: improving productivity in the construction and interconnection of integrated processing applications by the provision of a base set of building blocks both for the ANSA partners and for cooperating groups.

17.3 Standards

Standards first emerged in the field of engineering. Bodies were formed to agree dimensions for parts and to agree engineering practices. In this form of standardization, the issues are well understood and the task is one of choosing between obvious alternatives.

The IT industry in Open Systems Interconnection (OSI) standardization started in a similar way. The OSI Reference Model was developed by analysis of extant proprietary and CCITT communications and many of the layer standards were achieved by selecting from protocols that existed at the time with only minor modification.

OSI has assumed importance in the IT industry since it opens up an alternative communications platform to the dominant proprietary communications architectures. Before OSI, vendors of communications related applications typically announced them for proprietary architectures. This had the effect of making the dominant vendors application rich and other vendors application impoverished. With OSI, vendors have joined together to achieve an OSI platform as important to application providers, if not more so, than proprietary ones.

There has been a consequent effort to extend OSI standards into areas such as transaction processing, electronic mail and office document transfer. Many of these are new areas with which there has been little practical experience. Consequently ISO committees find themselves *inventing* standards rather than *choosing* them. This is a dangerous strategy, since all vendors who align themselves to

OSI depend upon the technical expertise of standards committees. Unfortunately, it is often the case that these committees have changing memberships that meet three or four times a year and are distracted from their technical goals by the intense politics of international standards making.

Within Europe, a new approach to standards making has begun, illustrated by X/Open. Here the industry has come together and funded a technical group to develop and extend Unix within the forum of X/Open members. In this way momentum and excellence are maintained since there is a permanent group devoted to technical progress.

ANSA is similar to X/Open in approach, but different in scope and scale. The scope of ANSA is distributed processing. The aim of distributed processing is to achieve a distributed applications platform that is independent of communications, operating systems and computer instruction sets.

X/Open is trying to develop an applications platform based on Unix. Unix is a mature system and its origins are as a stand-alone machine operating system. A new generation of operating systems has emerged that is oriented towards distributed processing (Mach, Chorus, Amoeba, V and so on). These operating systems are qualitatively different from Unix and place greater emphasis on performance and distribution. It is these sorts of operating systems that will be the foundation of distributed processing. It is imperative that work be done, in a similar fashion to X/Open, for this next generation so that they can be developed into products sooner rather than later. Fortunately for product evolution, most of these systems are able to emulate Unix with no loss of function (and sometimes increased performance).

A new force for standardization is the Open Software Foundation (OSF). This is an international consortium of IT suppliers who have come together to agree and develop an open applications environment. Their first release is targetted at Unix and compatibility with X/Open. However, for the future, OSF has ambitious aims to include many features of advanced operating systems, including distribution into their offering. A difference in approach between OSF and previous standardization is the introduction of the concept of a *reference implementation* as the primary mode of dissemination, rather than volumes of abstract specification.

17.4 Standards for distributed processing

Standards for distributed processing are necessary for two reasons: firstly because of the diverse range of requirements to be satisfied by current and future integrated IT systems and secondly from fragmentation of the IT supply industry.

17.4.1 Diversity

Human organizations are distributed in nature: people work in different places and information is acquired and stored at different locations. People increasingly rely on computers in their work. To achieve good human-computer interfaces, fast response and independence it pays to locate computers close to the people that use them. This leads to the philosophy of personal computing. However, people do not work in isolation and need to share data with one another and engage in cooperative processes. Therefore people are best served by a distributed computer system which reflects the distribution of the human organization it serves.

But human organizations are subject to changes and these too must be accommodated by the computer systems supporting those organizations. Also, technology will provide opportunities to develop computers with new functions and improved performance. Whilst enterprises may wish to replace old equipment with new from time to time, the related costs and effort involved are likely to become prohibitive. Instead, owners will call for gradual and continual evolution of their IT systems and, consequently, IT systems will be thought of as integrated collections of distributed components, rather than a single resource.

Integrating multiple computers of the same type is relatively easy. Such computers can be combined so that, to the application designer, they appear to be one very large computer. Application designers in the distributed environment can then continue to exploit existing non-distributed application design processes.

This approach does not always lead to a satisfactory solution, however, because different applications lead to different operational requirements. For example, factory automation applications require real-time response and a high degree of reliability; applications in office automation require high security but place fewer constraints on real-time response. Thus the many applications that form an integrated system will place different emphases on quality attributes such as response time, throughput, security, and reliability. This diversity of application requirements demands a diversity of hardware and software support. This heterogeneity complicates, in turn, the design of a distributed system and the integration of its parts.

17.4.2 Fragmentation

At the moment there is no open architecture for building distributed systems on a multi-vendor basis which can span multiple application domains. It is just about possible to install a multi-vendor system in a single application domain where standards are relatively mature (office applications, computer integrated manufacturing) and where the users and suppliers have a common forum for determining agreement (MAP, TOP). However, the increasing importance of value-added network services and the extension of the computing arena from offices and factories into homes and schools means that there is a real need for a common architectural approach which incorporates the very significant differences in policies and patterns of communication arising from these extensions. Currently these different domains are serviced by different communities of suppliers who have no common forum in which to establish a common agreed base of technology. There has therefore been no opportunity to integrate the technology used in the domains of computing, telecommunications, and value-added networks.

Another aspect of the problem of fragmentation is that many IT companies are at a disadvantage in the breadth of products they can supply to meet the new demands in the expanding areas, by virtue of their size compared with the market leaders. Since such companies are not able to compete in breadth, they concentrate on their undoubted capacity for specialization in depth. In many cases, however, this specialization has been done in isolation. There is now a need to provide some common architectural framework that will enable system integrators to focus on a particular market area. The IT industry therefore needs an enabling mechanism to provide scope for market-specific suppliers to survive by selling to a wide range of industries and system integrators, and a structure to aid integration of market-specific components from different suppliers servicing different application domains.

It is important to recognize that the scope of this problem is wider than that of mere communications interworking, a sub-problem which can be solved (at least at the lower levels of the OSI Reference Model) by building subsystems conforming to the standard protocol definitions. Integration at the system level requires careful attention to issues such as information, processing, communications, distribution, management and administration, specification, human factors, and the applications environment. Currently these are treated piecemeal whereas what is required is an architectural approach which treats them all as facets of a single problem.

17.4.3 Limitations of OSI

The objective of OSI has been to create standards for the interconnection of two or more systems, without prescribing the internal organization of these systems. The aim has been to enable communication between different sorts of systems and from different manufacturers without requiring changes in the philosophy of those systems. Therefore OSI avoids making statements about the kinds of interface that might exist within a system or the position of the interfaces in the structure of a system. OSI is defined relative to the physical points of interconnection as shown in Figure 17.1.

OSI abstracts from the physical medium by repeated application of the model of two service users communicating through a supporting service. The service user concept is the projection of the system onto the points of interconnection as a set of requirements for a particular type of communication service.

The step of projection is both the strength and the weakness of OSI (Linington (1988)): it provides the necessary abstraction to decouple communication from the internal structure and behaviour of the systems involved, but it also makes discussion of any other relationships between the interconnected systems difficult. This accounts for the problems that have arisen in parts of the OSI work programme such as the application layer structure, the management framework and naming and addressing structure. To tackle these problems it is necessary to be able to describe other relationships beyond communication.

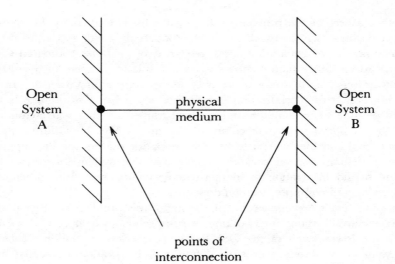

Figure 17.1 Open systems interconnection

17.4.4 Open distributed processing

Work on distributed processing in ISO started two years ago in a Rapporteur Group within SC21/WG1, the Working Group responsible for architectural issues of OSI, but has recently been formed into a full Working Group (WG7) within SC21. This is a clear recognition of the significant and far-reaching scope of the work on distributed processing and the difference between this work and that on OSI. By the end of 1990, it is expected that the SC21/WG7 will have produced a basic reference model for open distributed processing (ODP), having completed definition of the terms of reference and scope of the work.

The work on a reference model for ODP aims to provide the necessary structural framework for standardization. Four reference points have been identified at which conformance can be claimed (ISO, 1987)):

(a) programmatic interfaces allowing access to a defined function, as, for example, in the standardization of a database language,

(b) human-computer interfaces, as for example in some graphics standards,

(c) interconnection interfaces, as in OSI standards,

(d) external physical storage media formats, as in information exchange standards.

Moreover, the ODP work has recognized the need to be able to describe the requirements for consistency between interfaces. For example, Figure 17.2 shows

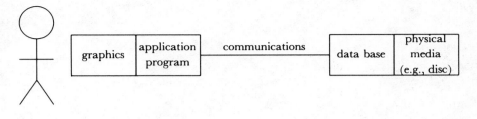

Figure 17.2 Multiple interfaces

a system in which a user interacts with an application that accesses a remote database via a graphical interface. ISO standards exist, or are in progress, for all the interfaces identified in the picture, but there is no architectural basis for showing how a user action might correlate with a modification to the database. The goal of the ODP reference model is to allow the expression of requirements for consistency between interfaces. Specific models for specific functions will remain the responsibility of other groups within ISO, but the use of the ODP reference model will facilitate the combination of standards from various areas.

17.5 References

ISO (1987). *Proposed revised text for the NWI on Basic Reference Model of Open Distributed Processing.* ISO/IEC JTC1/SC21/WG1 Basic Reference Model of Open Distributed Processing Rapporteur Group, ISO, April 1987. (ISO/TC97/SC21 N1889, Geneva.)

P. Linington (1988). 'OSI Networks — Problems and Future Trends'. In R. Speth (Ed.), *Research into Networks and Distributed Applications (EUTECO 85).* North Holland, Amsterdam, 1988.

Chapter 18

The Advanced Networked Systems Architecture

A. J. Herbert

18.1 Introduction

The purpose of the Advanced Networked Systems Architecture is to support the design, implementation, operation and evolution of distributed information processing systems where the different components that make up the systems, such as applications packages, operating systems, computers and networks, come from different vendors. The complexity that arises from this heterogeneity of hardware and software can only be managed if information technology vendors adopt a common approach to the design and interconnection of the components they offer.

Common design principles provide for a consistent model of information processing across the system which, in turn, eases the task of integrating diverse applications packages into a coherent, extensible system.

For the system operators, common design enables a consistent approach to the day-to-day management of the system and the incremental growth of the system to accommodate new requirements and changes in the information technology policies of the system owners.

For the system implementors, common design principles enhance productivity by enabling software re-use and facilitating the automatic generation of system-specific software from declarative statements of requirements. The latter point is particularly important since it frees applications implementors from the need to understand the specifics of how particular functions are achieved in every target system. Use of common design principles also reduces the conceptual gap that must be bridged when otherwise separate systems are to be interconnected, simplifying the complexity interconnection and extending the range of components which can be interconnected.

The approach adopted for ANSA was first to formalize and systematize research and development experience in distributed processing into a framework of concepts, design rules and implementation recipes.

18.2 ANSA and the system design process

This chapter introduces a number of design schemas for distributed processing. Each of these schemas has its own purpose; the aim of this chapter is to explain how, when and by whom the various schemas are to be used. The explanation necessarily begins with an analysis of design and implementation processes.

System development is often described as the repeated application of a single canonical step, where each step has the same general form. Each step takes the currently latest description of the system and produces the next description by means of a transformation. The word 'transformation' is used here in its widest sense: it may be entirely automated, as when performed by a compiler, semi-automated, or entirely manual. Each step is constrained to be sufficiently small that it will succeed with some confidence. The canonical step is illustrated in Figure 18.1.

The initial and final description for each step will be termed the 'base' and 'target' respectively. Each description is expressed in some symbolic form — that is a linguistic system of notation and defined concepts — which is appropriate to its position in the sequence of steps and the intended readers of that particular description.

Transformations, particularly those performed manually, are often subject to checks. Two kinds of incremental check of the target can be distinguished, namely *verification* and *validation*.

Verification is the process of showing that the target is internally consistent and displays all the properties required by the base. The term 'verify' is used here in the mathematical sense of 'increase confidence in the correctness of'. (Formal mathematical verification is neither explicitly assumed, nor excluded from this analysis; the objective is simply to have as much confidence as possible that the target is correct with respect to its base before embarking upon the next step in the sequence).

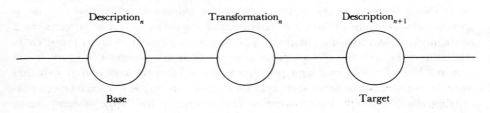

Figure 18.1 Canonical design step

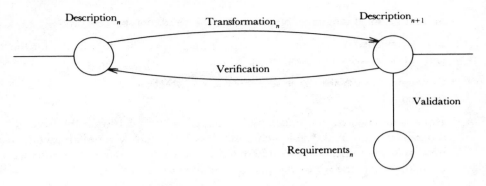

Figure 18.2 Verification and validation

The fact that a target has been verified does not guarantee that it provides a good basis for further development. At any step, a large number of descriptions could have been produced, all equally correct, but showing different trade-offs and design judgements. Some of these descriptions will be entirely satisfactory; others will have brought undesirable properties into the design. Thus, in addition to verification, there is a need to check that the target is fit for its purpose. Such a check is termed *validation*.

The major difference between verification and validation is that verification is analytic: it can be performed on the basis of the base and target alone, whereas validation is synthetic: it requires reference to the requirements of the system owners and the enterprise into which the system is to be placed. To put it another way, verification is a check on the process of development, and validation is a check on the (current design state of) the product, and its suitability to meet the requirements upon it. This is illustrated in Figure 18.2.

A transformation step can be be thought of as two activities: *analysis* of the base and *generation* of the target.

Analysis of the base is essentially the process of determining which features of the base have to be preserved across the transformation. In general, these will be structural features of the system as a whole, rather than descriptive features of the individual components. This requires dialogue with the system owner to resolve ambiguities and correct errors uncovered in the analysis: the faults are not necessarily with the description themselves, but may reside in the system owners' and system implementors' understanding.

Generation of the target is essentially the process of taking the structure determined by the analysis and elaborating it using the concepts and structuring rules governed by external constraints such as cost, compatibility with other systems, and availability of technology to make appropriate trade-offs between the options available in the target language.

Bringing together all of the foregoing analysis it becomes clear that an architecture for distributed system designers has to provide two different things:

(a) an architectural language for use during the validation process; and

(b) sets of concepts, design rules and design principles, or design schema, for the generation activity in a design step.

- **Concepts** specify the basic elements from which a model can be constructed.

- **Rules** state how the concepts may be combined: they constrain the freedom a designer has to make design choices. A system which violates an architectural rule may operate as required but could be more difficult to enhance or modify than one which did not, or it may not work at all.

- **Design principles** suggest useful compositions of concepts to meet particular needs. Principles aid the design of structures that achieve particular effects. They are compiled so as to provide effective ways to do things while remaining within the rules. It is not mandatory to follow the principles but the use of principles reduces design effort. It is likely that components adhering to design principles will become the most widely available, since following the principles will be a quick way to design a system.

- **Guidelines** explain the problems that can be encountered in design and how they can be avoided: they give general techniques for constructing models of systems rather than the more explicit instructions that are contained in the recipes.

Figure 18.3 shows how all of the elements of a canonical design step fit together.

The architectural language can be formal or informal; ANSA has gradually developed a formal notation called *object engineering* to represent systems designs. At the outset of the project it had been intended to use established formal methods such as LOTOS, CSP, Z and VDM but it was found that none of them was sufficient in itself to meet all needs, and there was no pathway between the different notations. Section 18.3 explores some of the aspects of modelling which are not well covered by current formal methods.

The design schema that make up ANSA are termed *projections* of the architecture. The concepts, rules and principles in each projection are defined using the object engineering notation.

18.3 Modelling requirements

Techniques for the design and modelling of many kinds of social and physical systems have common features. These features have been noted by many distinguished authors (Alexander (1964); Checkland (1981); Le Corbusier (1954); Liskov and Guttag (1986); Simon (1962)). The intention of all design techniques has been to assist the system designers and builders by making designs and descriptions manageable. The essence of the various approaches is to reduce

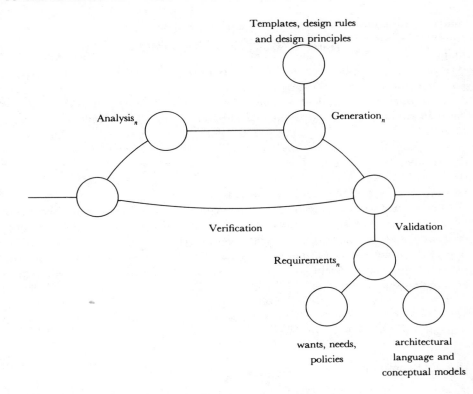

Templates, design rules
and design principles

Analysis$_n$

Generation$_n$

Verification

Validation

Requirements$_n$

wants, needs,
policies

architectural
language and
conceptual models

Figure 18.3 Canonical design step

complexity and to identify and classify common patterns.

Designers of all kinds choose to ignore some of the details in order to cope with complexity and this deliberate omission of detail is called *abstraction*. The detail that is considered establishes a point of view or projection of the system and several different projections may be appropriate at different design stages. The projections that comprise ANSA are described in Section 18.4.

The following sections explore some ways in which designers use abstraction.

18.3.1 Classification and types

Classification involves looking at systems as compositions of parts and ignoring detail so that several components can be characterized by a single description. A set of components characterized by a single description is called a *class*. Many classification schemes are hierarchical by nature with components grouped into classes which are themselves grouped in classes and so on. Some schemes permit a component to be assigned to more than one class. Some schemes insist there must be a single universal class to which all components belong. These are all matters of organizational convenience for the classifier. The term *type* is used for classes whose descriptions are constrained to avoid circular definitions. A particular component which is an element of a type is known as an *instance* of that type and the description that is common to all the potential instances of a type is known as the *type specification*.

A component can be described by reference to its type specification, together with an outline of the additional features that make that component unique, thereby reducing the size of the specification for each component. The use of classification stimulates sharing of specifications which can reduce effort in design and manufacture. The use of classification also helps to organize the description of components; types are frequently used to check the consistency between designs and their implementation.

In computer science, classification has become an important tool in areas such as formal specification, database organization, programming languages and operating systems, under the umbrella label of 'object-orientation'. The application of the same label to different specializations can cause problems when people compare what is meant by terms such as 'object'. In ANSA these differences are made clear by relating objects to the projection in which they are defined. The notations used in ANSA for describing concepts are neutral to the various interpretations of 'object'. This enables the relationship between objects in different projections to be explained.

18.3.2 Decomposition and epochs

Even though in abstraction much of the detail is ignored, the remaining description of a problem or solution may still be overwhelming. A rational way of tackling complex problems or expressing complex solutions is to think of the problem or solution as a composition of several parts. The nature of each of the parts can be discussed individually, repeating the decomposition process if necessary, and then other, separate, discussions can focus on how the components fit together.

This raises an important point for these designer of a system because some of the structure in a design may be necessary to satisfy the requirements placed upon the system, whereas other parts of the structure may be merely an artifact of the way in which the designer has chosen to think about the problem. Examples of necessary structure may be representations of geographical location — 'The system is to have three computers, one each in London, Paris and Munich' — or of security — 'There is no communication path between trusted and untrusted processes.' The latter example also indicates that in some cases requirements are phrased in terms of what is not, or should not be, possible.

Some components may appear in several projections of a system and be decomposed quite differently in each projection to explore different aspects of the components. The designer then has to relate these different decompositions to explain all the features of that component.

In addition to the spatial decomposition of a component into parts, the lifetime of a system can be divided (or decomposed) into time periods called *epochs*.

The operation of a system can then be studied in one epoch at a time. In any one epoch, some components are inactive and can be ignored. Each epoch is then an abstraction, in which a simplified system description is valid. Epochs play an important role in the discussion of distributed computer systems, since there is the potential for different things happening in different places at the same time and some activities may depend upon a long chain of previous events. For example, the transition of a program from source code to executing binary may be broken into several stages — compilation, linking, loading and execution — and there is a need for communication and consistency between all of the stages.

The design of distributed systems often involves trade offs between space and time. For example, data can be transmitted serially or in parallel. All other things being equal, serial transmission takes longer, but only requires one communications link; whereas parallel transmission is faster, but needs more links. Sometimes the designer wants to be explicit about these matters, but at other times only the existence of communication need be discussed. Thus the designer needs to be able to treat space and time as a continuum.

18.3.3 Physical realizability

Designs are descriptions of proposed systems. Eventually a builder will be given the task of building the system from physical components. A design created through the imagination of the designer is not subject to the constraints of the physical world. Every aspect of the design has to be built into some physical form and will be subject to the basic constraints described in physics. Therefore, designers must check that their designs are physically realizable.

Only two physical constraints are of widespread importance. These are that the propagation of physical effects takes time and that something cannot be created from nothing. Designers will often assume the instantaneous operation of equipment, even though this is not physically feasible. This assumption leads them to neglect taking into consideration the speed of operation and performance of systems and to assuming that consequences of actions occur simultaneously in different places and leads them to ignore possible transient inconsistencies in the system; it leads designers to neglect the kind of causal loops that result in deadlock or livelock; and it causes designers to ignore the consequences of design changes, such as increasing the number of connected systems or the physical extent of a system, that modify the rate of propagation of effects and hence the performance of their system, often to the worse.

When compiling a system design it is convenient to disregard the need for the construction of system parts. For example, files are conveniently thought of as being infinitely extensible and stacks as being infinitely long. No system has unlimited resources and attention needs to be paid to the deployment of resources and the actions to be taken when resources are fully consumed.

A feature of physical components, often caused by a lack of knowledge, human error, or poor manufacture, is that they fail and the designer must be aware of which failures are likely to occur and which of these are significant and the kind of effects that can arise.

18.4 Viewpoints on distributed processing

To derive the architecture, the ANSA team studied current practice and research in distributed computing and system design techniques.

The study revealed that different distributed processing experts have different viewpoints about what are the crucial concerns that make up 'distributed processing'. Further examination revealed that five viewpoints were dominant and that each viewpoint in some way or other acknowledged the concerns addressed in other viewpoints but with a lesser priority. As a consequence, ANSA has been structured in terms of these five viewpoints. A similar structure has been adopted by the ODP Reference Model standards group. A distributed system can be described in any one of these projections, and the resulting descriptions, or models, reveal different facets of the system. Each model is self-contained and complete. The difference between models is not how much of the system they describe, but rather what aspects of the system they emphasize. Thus each projection contains within it some abstraction of each of the other projections. It is therefore incorrect to think of the viewpoints as a series of service layers like the OSI Reference model.

Designers used to working with one projection often have difficulty assessing the relevance of the concepts used in any of the other viewpoints. It is important to realize, however, that a system has ultimately to be described from each viewpoint; all of the viewpoints are equally valid and it is a mistake to argue which is the more fundamental.

18.4.1 Enterprise projection

The purpose of the enterprise projection is to explain and justify the role of a computer system within an organization. An enterprise model describes the overall objectives of a system in terms of roles (for people), actions, goals and policies. It specifies the activities that take place within the organization using the system, the roles that people play in the organization, and the interactions between the organization, the system and the environment in which system and organization are placed.

Enterprise models provide managers of the enterprise with a description showing how and where the system is placed within the enterprise. The interactions between the organization and the designers of the system can be included in this projection so that the process of procurement, installation, maintenance and evolution is included as part of the system design.

Design decisions made using the enterprise projection concern *what* a system is to do and *who* it is doing it for. The design concepts defined in the enterprise projection allow the designer to develop a closed (bounded) model which represents all the real world requirements which the designer is prepared to incorporate into the structure of the system.

For distributed systems the major purpose of enterprise models is to determine the management style and dependability requirements for the system. Some organizations are highly centralized whereas in others, parts of the organization are largely autonomous. In the first kind of organization, a central authority can be in charge of naming and security, and exercise control over what services are provided on the network. In the second kind of organization a more fluid, federated structure is required so that each part of the organization can manage its own affairs independently. Many of the arguments that occur concerning the design of directory services stem from different assumptions at this level. With distributed systems, there are opportunities to exploit redundancy to obtain enhanced levels of dependability — performance, reliability and security. However, these attributes do not come free and so the designer needs to understand where to apply redundancy to best effect. Related to dependency is the question of consistency. It is well known that global shared memory does not scale well and that the designer has to partition the memory of a large system. This leads to problems of consistency. In general, the weaker the guarantees required, the more freedom the designer has to produce systems that scale. Therefore the designer needs guidance on what are the real consistency constraints on information and what failure models are acceptable to the final users of the system.

The current state-of-the-art in enterprise modelling lags behind technology by a considerable margin. Most established system design techniques are oriented towards a central database which is assumed to always be up to the minute. Indeed this lag is probably one of the biggest hindrances to the uptake of distributed systems outside of the academic and research community.

18.4.2 Information projection

The purpose of the information projection is the identification and location of information, and the description of information processing activities. An information model describes the structure, flow, interpretation, value, timeliness and consistency of information held within a system. An important feature of distributed systems is that information can be collected, processed and presented in different places and at different times. Consequently information models regard the system as a collection of information resources and information processes. The asset value attached to information in modern business makes these models important to managers as well as designers.

Designers use information models to explore the nature and role of information in the system. They take design decisions that are epistemological in nature: Who knows what? Where can information flow? Information projections describe conceptual models of a solution to the functional requirements given by an enterprise model. The people in the organization may also figure in the information model so that the impact of a system on the organization that is to use it can be properly analysed.

In terms of distributed processing, the main issues to be addressed in the information projection are how to breakdown a system into separate information-bearing objects and to choose the sorts of transparency constraints on interactions between those objects that provide the levels of consistency and acceptable fault behaviour identified in the information projection. It is at this level that the designer begins to discuss the use of replication, atomic transactions, servers and overall management of the system configuration. Thus it is in this projection that ANSA begins to make contact with much of the research done by the distributed systems community over the past decade.

18.4.3 Computational projection

The purpose of the computational projection is to show the organization of a distributed system as a set of linked applications programs. A computational model provides programmers with a description of a system that explains how distributed application programs may be written for it. This description is in terms of data representations, programming languages, system services and program specifications. Computational models show how programmers have structured systems for modularity and parallelism, for linking separate applications into integrated packages and for making programs independent of the computers and networks on which they run.

The computational projection necessarily takes account of systems in which computations can proceed in parallel, which can fail independently and which are configured dynamically.

In terms of distributed processing, the main issues to be addressed in the computational projection are how programmers should see distribution. Many systems expose the applications programmer to the raw engineering mechanisms of process creation, network communications and so forth. This level of complexity overwhelms the application programmer and also has the unfortunate effect of locking an application into a particular operating system and communications environment. The solution is to provide the application programmer with a simple model of distributed computation which gives control over transparency but hides the workings of the mechanisms. In the same way that fourth generation languages provide a declarative style of interface to databases for applications programmers, languages are required in which programmers can state declaratively what transparency mechanisms and failure models are to apply to particular applications and to have these automatically transformed into calls to low level libraries that drive the mechanisms. Chapter 19 explores in more detail the kind of facilities required in these sorts of languages.

18.4.4 Engineering projection

The purpose of the engineering projection is to describe distributed systems in such a way that designers can reason about the performance of the systems built to their designs. The engineering projection describes processing, memory and communications structures that can be used to support the transparency requirements of programs structured according to the computational projection.

A designer uses an engineering model to make decisions that concern trade-offs between quality attributes such as performance, dependability and scaling. Designers, system management and maintenance staff all use these sorts of models as a basis upon which to predict the consequences of possible system reconfigurations.

There is no discretion in the engineering projection over the sorts of information processing components the system is to contain: design is restricted to the sorts of coupling between components and the management of computer and network resources to achieve desired quality attributes.

Thus the distributed systems issues that arise in the engineering projection concern which mechanisms should be used to provide particular transparencies. This aspect is the one that is discussed in most depth by the other lecturers in this course: each is exhibiting the abstractions thay are most proud of. The role of the other projections is to put these abstractions in context.

The large variety of techniques found for solving different kinds of distributed processing problems requires ANSA to take a building block approach since it would clearly be impractical to specify a universal distributed operating system that was capable of supporting all the applications of distributed processing.

Figure 18.4 provides a simplified illustration of the relationship between the engineering components in a typical ANSA system. The base systems represent

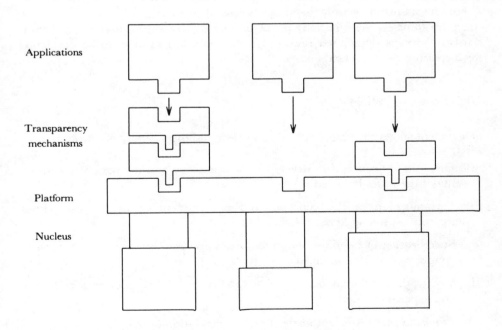

Figure 18.4 The engineering model

the computers and networks used to provide the processing, memory and communications capability. The components in each nucleus cooperate to provide an applications platform spanning the base systems offering basic access and location transparency. The components that provide transparency mechanisms make use of the platform functionality and provide a transparent interface to the applications. The classes of transparency mechanism under development in ANSA include concurrency transparency (via atomic transactions), replication transparency, failure transparency (by combining replication and atomicity techniques) and migration transparency. A consistent model of interaction is applied between applications, transparency mechanisms and the platform, differing at each level only in the classes of fault that might occur.

Note that the figure shows that different applications may select different transparency stacks, since different guarantees may be required. This emphasizes the need for a building block approach rather than a monolithic distributed operating system.

18.4.5 Technology projection

The purpose of the technology projection is to describe the physical components, in terms of hardware and software, that make up the distributed system so that they may be related to the architecture concepts defined in the other projections. Technology models act as blueprints of systems during their construction and maintenance, showing how architectural concepts have been implemented in practice.

For the industrial world, this projection is of great importance for it enables designers to assess the suitability of the current generation of products and standards to support distributed processing and enables a strategy to be developed for increasing their applicability.

18.5 Scope of ANSA

Self-evident stages that are involved in the establishment of any architecture are:

(a) **Definition** of concepts to develop the terminology and the basic understanding of the issues involved

(b) **Formalization** of the concepts and development of models, to permit rigorous reasoning about systems.

(c) **Specification** of standard design templates and rules that describe how these templates may be combined.

(d) **Verification** of the adequacy and suitability of the templates by prototyping and experimentation.

(e) **Provision** of tools to automate the implementation of templates for particular systems.

(f) **Maintenance** of the architecture to support its continued validity and to allow for evolution.

(g) **Exploitation** of distributed systems built using the architecture in new products.

(h) **Investment** in education to disseminate the architecture to distributed systems designers and implementors.

The set of projections on the one hand, and the stages described above on the other, provide a 'map' of the field of distributed processing given in Figure 18.5.

	Definition of concepts	Formalization of concepts	Specification of templates	Verification	Provision of tools
Enterprise	●	○			
Information	●	○	○	○	
Computational	●	●	●	○	○
Engineering	●	●	●	●	●
Technological	●				

Figure 18.5 Scope of distributed processing The areas of distributed processing currently included within ANSA are shown by '●'. The areas to be developed within ISA are shown by '○'

To date, the ANSA team have concentrated on the computational and engineering projections, since they have a large degree of independence from both application domains and technology trends. These projections provide an environment for the creation of stable specifications for the interface between distributed applications and the hardware and software that support them.

18.6 Conformance

Architectures can vary in the emphasis they place on their prescriptive or descriptive function: the more prescriptive an architecture is, the smaller the possible set of systems that are valid implementations of the architecture. Thus a primarily descriptive model can capture a wide range of systems whereas a strongly prescriptive model will only capture a small number of systems. In consequence, a design goal of ANSA has been to set conformance criteria at a sufficiently high level of abstraction so that as wide a range as possible of systems can conform, yet at the same time the complexity of interconnecting systems that have chosen different implementations at lower levels of abstraction remains manageable.

Conformance is a concept which can be applied at any level of abstraction. To avoid confusion between conformance at higher levels and conformance of physical components, the term 'compliance' is sometimes used for the notion of conformance at higher levels. The distinction being made is that compliance is the acceptance of design rules, principles and conceptual models, whereas conformance is the acceptance of particular physical representations.

In fact, the concept is the same at all levels; it is that a system conforms to a standard if, and only if:

(a) All conformance requirements expressed in the standard are true of that system; these requirements consist of some or all of:

    (i)   statements of necessary correspondences from the architectural model of the system to the physical world,

    (ii) statements of necessary architectural properties,

    (iii) statements requiring information to be provided by the implementor.

(b) Any assertions made by the implementor are true, and do not themselves violate the conformance requirements.

The *ANSA Reference Manual* defines the conformance criteria for ANSA projection by projection. It is possible for a system to conform in any number of the projections and conformance to each projection brings different benefits.

The enterprise and information projections of ANSA can be used to establish a design model of information sources, sinks and processes that meet the requirements of the enterprise that requested the system. Conformance requirements at this level identify constraints on the conceptual schema of the system information base and on system management policies necessary to enable distributed processing.

The computational projection can be used to transform an information projection model into a network of interfacing computer programs. Conformance requirements at this level identify constraints on programming language structures to enable distributed processing. Programs that conform to this projection will have the potential to interwork with other conforming programs and will be portable across all machine environments that conform to the projection.

The engineering projection can be used to transform a computational projection model into a model in terms of processing, memory and communication functions. The conformance requirements here identify constraints on systems that independently conform to the architecture necessary to enable their interconnection.

18.7 References

C. Alexander (1964). *Notes on the Synthesis of Form*. Harvard University Press, Cambridge, MA, 1964.

P. B. Checkland (1981). *Systems Thinking, Systems Practice*. Wiley & Sons, 1981.

Le Corbusier (1954). *The Modulor*. Faber & Faber, 1954. (First English Edition.)

B. Liskov and J. Guttag (1986). *Abstraction and Specification in Program Development*. MIT Press, Cambridge, MA, 1986.

H. A. Simon (1962). 'The Architecture of Complexity'. *Proceedings of the American Philosophical Society* **106** (6): 467—482, Dec 1962.

Chapter 19

The Computational Projection of ANSA

A. J. Herbert

19.1 Introduction

19.1.1 Background

The computational projection of ANSA is concerned with the requirements of distributed application programs. It provides the concepts needed to define a computational model for distributed applications programming languages. This computational model specifies the programming language features that are necessary to be able to write applications programs for a distributed environment.

Since ANSA is an architecture for open systems it is not viable to impose a single language as the conformance criteria for the computational model. Parts of a large application may be written in different languages for reasons of history or suitability and any scheme for distributed applications programming must face this reality. The approach adopted for ANSA has been to identify the functions that must be provided and the constraints on program structure necessary to enable distribution, rather than a particular syntax. The outcome of this approach is that all programs, in whatever language, are written for the same abstract (distributed) machine as their target. Porting a program from one system to another is then only a matter of changing the local representation of the abstract machine as it appears in the application programming language, which does not require any changes to be made to the application program itself.

To make the description of the computational projection clearer, the ANSA team have defined a programming language, called DPL (Distributed Programming Language) which has syntactic representations of all the concepts in the computational projection. A DPL compiler and run-time system is currently under development, so that those who wish to can write applications programs in a language oriented towards distributed processing. It had originally been intended to take an existing language and add features to it to support distribution, but it was found early on in the design of the computational projection that it is also necessary to impose constraints on programming languages, as well as adding new features. Rather than impose constraints by convention, or pay the cost of run-time checking for violation of them, it was decided to have a purpose-built language. In its semantics, DPL is close to Emerald (Black *et al.* (1987)), and Argus (Liskov and Scheifler (1983)).

19.1.2 Interface definition language

The first requirement of any environment for distributed programming involving multiple languages is to have a common interface definition language (IDL). An IDL is used to describe the sorts of interactions permitted between, for example, a client and a server and the kinds of data that may be passed in these interactions. The description of the sorts of interactions possible enables appropriate protocols for supporting the interaction to be inserted into the program automatically. The description of data enables the encoding required to transmit information between the objects to be inserted automatically. (It is worth noting that OSI standards include a notation for describing data and their encoding rules — Abstract Syntax Notation One, or ASN.1 for short — but ASN.1 does not include representation of OSI service primitives and therefore cannot be used to define interface, but merely the contents of protocol-data-units).

Thus two immediate questions that face the designer of a distributed programming language are: (a) what are the permitted kinds of interaction, and (b) what are the sorts of data that can be included in them?

19.1.3 Automatic target language mapping

It is necessary to find a representation of each of the kinds of interaction and each of the kinds of transmissible data permitted by an IDL in every potential applications programming language so that invocations of interfaces described in IDL can be programmed.

Some systems, such as the SUN RPC system, have made the programmer do all of the work by providing library routines that correspond to the interaction primitives and routines that convert and pack data application language data types into their IDL encodings.

Other systems, such as that reported in Birrell and Nelson (1984) have provided stub generators that scan an interface definition and automatically generate routines in the application programming language to marshal the data and drive the protocol. This approach works well if the programming language and the IDL are close to one another in concept. If, however, the IDL supports a richer range of interaction types or a wider range of data types than the application language, problems can arise. A particular example is exception signalling: exceptions are the natural way to reflect communications problems and other failures, but many languages do not have exception handling facilities and those that do differ in the details.

The need to overcome this problem was one of the stimuli behind the development of DPL by the ANSA team. It was decided that a standard syntax would be used for making invocations of operations defined in ANSA's IDL in all application languages. (ANSA's IDL is in fact the type specification component of DPL). For each language supported by ANSA, a pre-processor has been written which scans for DPL invocations and translates them into whatever arcane series of procedure calls is necessary to drive the stubs for that language.

There are two advantages to this approach. The first is that remote invocations are distinguishable from local procedure calls and this reinforces in the programmer's mind the need to think about the additional failure modes of remote invocations over local ones. The second is that the pre-processor is sometimes able to spot optimizations from the static structure of the invocation which could not be easily detected at run-time. For example if a sub-process is created which makes a remote invocation and then terminates it is not necessary to allocate a local stack for it, or assign a local (virtual) processor. Making these sorts of optimization can be very important, because while the 'threads and procedures' model is a very convenient one for the programmer, worries about resource consumptions often lead language designers to complicate their languages with non-blocking calls and various unstructured forms of message passing.

19.1.4 Distributed application building

There are two styles of distributed application programming. In the first the application is treated as a single large program. The program may be divided up into separately compiled parts for reasons of efficiency and modularity. Once compiled, the program is then loaded into an appropriate configuration of computers and allowed to execute. In the second, an application is treated as a number of separate programs which are independently compiled and loaded into individual computers. Programmers who work in this style often refer to 'client' programs and 'server programs' to indicate whether a program expects to be invoked by others, or whether it is responsible for invoking others. This second style is dependent upon some form of system directory that enables servers to register their presence in the network and for clients to locate servers. The distinction between these two styles is one of early versus late binding.

In the first style, as program modules are loaded into separate computers they have the network address the other program modules bound into them by the program loading system (called a configuration manager by some researchers). The configuration manager must take care not to start modules executing until the modules they invoke are themselves started, otherwise interactions will be lost.

In the second style, clients contain names for servers and servers know their own name. When a server starts it tells the system directory of its name and its network address. When a client wants to locate a server, it looks up the name in the directory and retrieves the address. If the server is not yet started, the client must poll the directory until the server's address is registered. In some systems the directory is itself a server, in others it is decentralized and broadcast algorithms are used to locate servers.

The first program style is potentially more flexible that the first, since the programmer can change the configuration arbitrarily by altering the assignment of modules to computers. However, this style does not permit an application to be constructed in which some modules are developed independently of others. This requirement is inevitable in an open systems context, because it is unlikely two organizations will be willing to lock together their programming environments in order in interwork over a network! On the other hand, the second style tends to lead to a rather rigid assignment of modules to computers, since externally visible names have to be invented and this can be inconvenient if the system supporting the application is re-structured. It can be concluded that both styles are appropriate in different circumstances, and a distributed programming language must provide for both.

19.1.5 Objects and interfaces

It is very hard in a networked system to achieve a workable, let alone efficient, implementation of distributed storage. It is therefore necessary to look for a programming model which partitions and encapsulates state. Such a model is found in the object-oriented programming languages. In these languages each object provides a set of operations by which it can be manipulated. Externally these operations are known by their names. The binding of operation names to procedures that perform operations is an internal property of each object. Thus it is possible for different objects to respond to the same operation names, but to have different implementations of those operations. This indirection from operation name to implementation has useful properties for distributed computations. Firstly it allows for heterogeneity: two interacting objects need not share the same infrastructure; they merely require communication between their infrastructures. Secondly the indirection provides a point to transparently insert the mechanisms that provide for communications. Thirdly the indirection it possible to substitute replacement objects, or to change the implementation of an object without requiring any actions by the users of the object's operations. This has important benefits for software maintainability and evolution.

In an open systems environment it is frequently necessary to group the operations of an object into sets intended for different classes of user. In the computational model these sets are called interfaces. An object may, for example, have a normal user interface and a system manager interface with extra privileges. Thus DPL uses objects as the unit of distribution and interfaces as the units of structuring.

Every data type in the computational model is defined by an interface. For example, an integer, such as 305, has operations add, subtract, multiply and so on that compute the result of applying the arithmetic operation to the integer. A file might have an interface with operations called read and write that transfer vectors of characters to and from the file. A vector is an object with indexing operations for reading and writing data into the vector.

A conformance relationship can be defined between interface types. Where a programmer requires an interface of some type T to be provided, an interface which has at least the same operations are are defined in T must be provided. The provided interface may have more operations than those required, but they are not available in this instance. For the required operations is it permitted for the argument types in the interface provision to be of a richer type than required, and for the results to be of a poorer type than required.

19.2 Operations

19.2.1 Synchronous operations

The simplest kind of invocation catered for in the computational model is the synchronous operation, which is like a procedure call in other languages. A calling thread of control is transferred to the nominated operation together with a bundle of arguments; when the execution of the operation terminates the thread of control returns, bringing with it a bundle of results.

Arguments and results
The argument and result passing paradigm of the computational model is interface sharing. Prior to transferring control, all the arguments are evaluated and therefore yield a set of interfaces. The formal arguments of the called operation are then bound to these interfaces (and hence the interface is shared by both caller and callee). For immutable abstract types, the effect is essentially similar to call-by-value; for mutable abstract types the effect is call-by-reference.

It is important to note that while a synchronous operation may not return any result interfaces, there is still required to be a synchronization between caller and callee. The caller cannot resume until the operation has terminated.

The computational model permits an operation to return multiple results for symmetry with the ability to pass multiple arguments. (DPL includes a syntax for multiple assignment and provides various ways of constructing a multiple result).

Terminations
Sometimes there may be a variety of possible terminations of an operation. In many programming languages, the programmer indicates this by returning some kind of discriminated union which is then unpicked by the caller. As an alternative to this the computational model provides for named terminations which are

a generalization of the exception handling schemes found in many programming languages. Each named termination may have its own list of result types, possibly different from the result types of other named terminations. When an operation terminates it is bound to deliver either its result — its anonymous termination or one of the named terminations. Thus a termination has both a control and a data aspect. Separating these two aspects can be used to achieve a number of useful effects, particularly in the control of concurrency and atomicity (see Sections 19.2.4 and 19.3.2). In addition to the terminations named by the programmer, there are a number of implicit terminations which may be generated by the system when there are communication problems that prevent an invocation from being started.

An interface requirement can put a constraint on which 'system' terminations are acceptable. If there is a system problem — for example communication with a remote interface fails persistently — the runtime system will attempt to generate a termination to signal the condition. If the interface requirement has opted not to take the termination, the runtime system will leave the invoking thread blocked. Thus by opting out of accepting system terminations, the programmer is forced to organize time-outs or user break signals to recover control: any call is guaranteed to be exactly-once, but no call is guaranteed to terminate. If system terminations are accepted, the runtime system will offer them as soon as the condition is encountered and the programmer has an at-most-once guarantee, unless operations are made atomic. The choice between the two options is essentially one of programming style and this is why the computational model allows for both.

Deadlines

A frequent requirement in many systems is to put bounds on the amount of time an operation may take so that response guarantees for external events can be given. This is done in the computational model by including deadlines for operations in interface type requirements. A deadline may be soft, or hard. A soft deadline provides purely advisory information to help the infrastructure schedule threads. No action is taken if the invocation overruns its deadline. Hard deadlines are more severe: if the operation is still executing when the deadline passes, the operation (and all the sub-operations within it) is aborted and the top level invocation results in a termination.

If the invoked operation was atomic (see Section 19.3.2), the abort mechanism will undo the effects of the partial execution, giving an exactly-once semantics to the invocation. If the invoked operation was not atomic, orphans may be created and the effects of partial executions not undone, giving an at-most-once semantics to the invocation.

Example interface requirement

The following is an example of the definition of the abstract type of an interface, known as its requirement, showing the DPL syntax for the various forms of synchronous operation described above:

```
x = requires {
    a = op () result ()
    b = op (Int, Real) result (Bool)
    c = op (File) result (Char, Int, Bool)
    d = op (File) result (Char) result eof ()
}
```

and invocations of an interface i of type x might appear thus:

```
i.a()
p = i.b(1, pi)
c, i, b = i.c(logFile)
c = d.f(logFile) accept eof {"*"}
```

Handlers

The last example indicates the use of a handler to intercept a named termination. The termination scheme for the computational model is more-or-less the same as CLU and Argus. If an expression (of which only type and invocations have been met so far) results in a named termination and that expression is followed by an accept clause for that termination, the result of evaluating the accept clause will be substituted in place of the anonymous termination of the expression. Thus if operation d.f generates an eof termination, instead of generating a character result, an asterisk will be assigned to c.

An invocation may result in a termination in one of three ways: because of some system failure, such as network communication difficulties; because a nested invocation terminates and the termination is not handled; or because a terminator operator is used to force the termination of an expression. (The termination operator corresponds to result and signal operators in other languages).

19.2.2 Sequential invocations

Like other programming languages the computational model has the concept of sequential execution in which one action is dependent upon the results of another. Thus there is in the computational model an operator to define a sequence of expressions (of which invocations are the only example that have been discussed so far). In a sequence, each expression is evaluated one after the other. Evaluation of the next expression in a sequence does not begin until evaluation of the current expression terminates. If the evaluation of an expression results in a named termination for which there is not an attached handler, the evaluation of the sequence is stopped and the termination promoted to being the termination of the sequence as a whole. The result of a sequential expression, if it does not have a named termination, is a multiple result composed of the individual results of each of the sub-expressions within it, in order. Often only the final result of a sequence is required: to this end there are operators defined to reduce the size of a multiple result.

19.2.3 Parallel invocations

In a distributed system there is considerable scope for exploiting inherent parallelism available in a network of computers and so a means of permitting parallel
executions to occur is needed. However, managing parallelism costs resources,
particularly in terms of scheduling overheads and protocol state. Therefore the
programmer needs be in a position to control the degree to which parallelism is
sought. To this end, the computational model has an operator which constructs
a parallel composition of expressions. A new thread of control is established for
each expression in the composition and the threads are evaluated independently.
The parallel expression itself terminates when all of the sub-expressions within it
have terminated and the result is a multiple value composed of all the results
from the sub-expressions.

Sometimes parallelism is used to try alternative strategies for a task and once one
of the strategies has completed the task, its alternates can be discarded. This is
accomplished in computational model by the interplay between terminations and
the parallel operator. If any of the sub-expressions in a parallel expression ends
with a named termination, the parallel expression itself is terminated the same termination and the sibling threads become orphans. The underlying infrastructure
is permitted to kill orphan threads: this is represented as the occurrence of a termination in the orphan for which the programmer cannot write a handler.

Thus, it can be seen that only tree-structured parallelism is possible for synchronous operations in computational model. This is a deliberate constraint to
enable the use of nested transactions as a mechanism for atomic operations.

19.2.4 Atomic operations

Distributed systems permit parallel evaluation and may suffer partial failure.
To cope with these features it is often convenient to have the abstraction of
atomic operations. Atomic operations are all-or-nothing in effect and are indivisible in the sense that the evaluation of one atomic operation cannot depend
upon the partial evaluation of another. An operation in an interface can be
marked as having the atomic property (and there are features elsewhere in the
computational model to help the programmer implement atomic operations —
see Section 19.3.2).

The treatment of atomicity in the computational model is very similar to the
nested transactions approach taken in the Argus system.

19.2.5 Asynchronous operations

Sometimes it is the case that there is an activity which is required to be done,
but for which there is not an immediate dependency, for example, routine
house-keeping or taking a checkpoint. These are represented in the computational model as operations which have no terminations (as distinct from a synchronous operations with a termination containing no results).

Such an operation runs in parallel with the thread that invoked it, but there is no way for the invoker to rendez vous with completion of the activity. Thus asynchronous operations provide a way to obtain non-tree structured parallelism, but any synchronization between asynchronous operations must be built by the programmer through the use of shared objects between the operations.

Asynchronous operations, like synchronous ones can be atomic. An atomic asynchronous operation invocation within an atomic operation is treated as creating a new independent nest of atomic transactions, much like the concept of a topaction in Argus.

Optional invocation

Often the situation arises where it would be useful to perform some housekeeping, but only if there are resources available to do so. For example, a memory allocator may want to begin garbage collecting a heap in advance of running out of memory if there are spare CPU cycles available. This notion is supported in the computational model by giving asynchronous operations in an interface requirement an attribute to indicate that they can be ignored if there are not resources to handle them.

Ordering and sequencing

Other constraints can be placed on asynchronous operations to achieve useful effects. The first is serialization. If a set of asynchronous operations are marked as being serial in an interface requirement, invocations of those operation will be serviced one at the time. (Without the constraint they can be processed in any order and potentially simultaneously). This essentially establishes a pipe into which interactions are pushed. The second constraint is sequentiality. This constraint requires that remote invocations are dispatched in the same order at the called interface as they leave the caller. (Invocations due to multiple threads may be interleaved, but the sub-sequences due to individual threads maintain their order). By combining serial and sequential constraints, the programmer can establish a stream-like protocol from client to server. Operations enter and leave the stream in FIFO order, one at a time. The stream can be buffered to overcome delays due to latency: the caller can assemble a batch of invocations and send them in a single network message. If a synchronous operation is included in a set of serial operations the programmer is guaranteed that all the asynchronous operations in the pipe will have been completed before the synchronous invocation begins — in other words, the synchronous operation will flush the pipe. Thus asynchronous operations, serialization constraints and sequentiality constraints provide for ANSA an analogue to the streams proposed by Gifford and Glasser (1988).

Clocked operations

A final variant of asynchronous operations are clocked operations. These operations are tied to an external clock; an invocation is held back until the next tick of that clock. This variant is used to handle isochronous channels of the kind used for transmitting real-time voice and video in multi-media systems. It is the responsibility of the programmer to ensure that the program goes around fast enough to keep up with the clock; the effect of missing a clock tick is implementation dependent. Some implementations retransmit the last invocation, others send rubbish.

19.2.6 Secure operations

The common idea that appears over and over again in the computational model is that as many properties as possible of an interaction are determined by the declarative type requirements of an interface rather than by adding imperative primitives to the language. There are two motivations for this: the first is that the declarative approach can be made extensible (see Section 19.7); the second is that all the distribution aspects of a distributed application program are decided by type requirements; code as such defines the application semantics. This gives a clear separation of concerns: application programmers can concentrate on application issues, systems programmers can concentrate on the distribution of the application. The applications programmer and the systems programmer must negotiate what sorts of distribution transparency they want for an interface. The result of the negotiation is then declared in the interface requirement.

It is proposed to extend this idea to include security in the ANSA computational model, although the experiment has yet to be tried. The major requirements for security are authentication, confidentiality and integrity. Authentication gives client and server a guarantee that both are what they claim to be. Thus a client can put in an interface requirement a statement of what set of principals it recognizes as trustworthy servers of the interface. A server can similarly declare in an interface provision the clients it is willing to act on behalf of. Only if both constraints are met will the interaction occur. (This can be easily mechanized using the sort of secure RPC protocols proposed by Birrell (1985)).

Confidentiality and integrity require that data is encrypted so that it cannot be read or modified in transit. Often the confidentiality relationship is between client and server and so encryption under a key used to establish authentication is sufficient. Sometimes, however, an argument is not for the server, but for a sub-server. The classic example of this is a print spooler which accepts documents for both an insecure and a secure printer. Secure documents must not be exposed to the spooler in plain text, though it must be possible for the spooler to store and forward coded text. This is easily done by labelling each argument in an interface requirement with its intended recipient.

The treatment of the label depends upon the way in which the argument is encoded on the wire (see Section 19.3.2). If the argument is sent by value, the label should be used to establish encryption key for the data sent. If the argument is sent by reference, the label should be used to construct a delegation for the argument. A delegation is an interface reference encrypted in a private key of the server for that reference together with the identity of the recipient. A server will only honour a delegation if it is authenticated as being sent from the delegated principal. (The operation however will be accounted the delegating principal in many cases.)

Delegations can be made quite general, to include lifetimes, sub-delegation privileges and other dynamic features. From the computational model point of view, a delegation is a migrating object which can only execute at its birth site, and which implements an access control algorithm for some other object known to the birth site.

19.3 Interface provision

The description so far has focused on the client perspective of the computational model in terms of the kinds of invocations that can be made of operations in interfaces. This section presents the other side of the coin, namely how servers set about honouring interface requirements.

The basic building block is an operator which takes a set of denotations for procedures and a set of constraints to construct an interface. This is analogous to the requirement operator which takes a set of operation signatures and constraints to define a type.

Each procedure definition necessarily has a name, and each name must be unique within an interface. A definition may have formal arguments and these must be typed. If the definition has results and/or named terminations it defines a synchronous operation. If no results or terminations are specified the operation is assumed to be asynchronous. Result and termination specifications must state the types of results they return.

Following the argument and termination definitions comes the implementation of the operation. This must be an expression which evaluates to the same set of results as are required by the definitions. If when this expression is evaluated a named termination occurs, which is not accepted within the expression, the action taken depends upon the terminations listed if any. If the occurring termination is in the listed terminations of the operation it is offered as the termination of the operation. Otherwise a distinguished termination is substituted to flag 'unhandled termination' (and if the operation is asynchronous it quietly disappears).

The operation expression is a composition of declarations, invocations, atomic expressions and terminate expressions. (The computational model follows the Smalltalk example in treating if statements and loops as syntactic sugaring of operation's types such as Boolean and integer-sequence).

19.3.1 Synchronization

There may be several concurrent activations of operations in an interface, due to parallel invocations and asynchronous invocations. This raises the problem of synchronization. As elsewhere, it was desired to find a declarative form for expression synchronization constraints. This gave a choice of either monitors or path expressions. The latter were chosen as being more general and offering greater flexibility. The form of path expressions used are *extended open predicate path expressions* (EOPPEs). An EOPPE is similar to a regular expression indicating permitted sequences of operation invocations. As well as simple sequences, EOPPEs can express constraints on concurrency (for example, in producer-consumer situations) and fairness policies (for example, writer precedence). The runtime support of EOPPEs consists of eventcounts and sequencers (Reed (1977)). The compiler converts a path expression into a prologue that is evaluated before the operation it protects and an epilogue that runs after. The prologue checks to see if the conditions required before the operation can be executed have been met. The epilogue advances eventcounts to indicate that the operation has completed, which may in turn release other invocations blocked in their prelude.

19.3.2 Operation properties

An operation defined in an interface can be given properties which affect its failure modes, analogous to the ability to set constraints in interface type definitions.

Atomic operations

An operation can be labelled as having the property of atomicity — that it is all or nothing in effect. The label is an assertion by the programmer, rather than an instruction to the compiler to make the operation atomic. If the programmer desires to have an expression made atomic, there is a special operator to do so which converts an expression to use version stores for intermediate results so that the expression can be rolled back if the operation is aborted. Handlers to an atomic expression can have an 'undo' property attached to them: if the exception occurs, the effects of the expression are undone before evaluating the handler; otherwise, the results of the expression will be committed if the atomic invocation within which they occur commits.

As an alternative to asking the compiler to make an expression atomic, the programmer may choose to write a careful program that is inherently atomic, in which case the operation definition will assert that the operation has the atomic property, but the expression will not be versioned. However, asserting the atomic property will put in place all the machinery for the commit/abort protocol. In the main, this feature is used by the authors of the library of basic atomic abstract types for use by other programmers.

To maintain the independence of atomic operations it is necessary sometimes to take out synchronized use of shared data either by taking out locks of by comparing timestamps. This is handled by adding the concept of *conflict predicates* to EOPPEs. Whenever an operation name is referenced in an EOPPE it can be qualified by assigning mode names to each of its arguments. The EOPPE must then be followed by a mode table which specifies the scheduling actions to be taken by the atomic operation manager in the infrastructure when particular conflicts arise. Simple read/write lock modes are provided in the default library.

Replicated interfaces

The computational model supports the concept of server groups: that is to say a group of interfaces that appear externally as one interface. Groups come in three forms. First there are *functionally distributed* groups in which each member performs some part of the requested operation and prepares some part of the result. Secondly, there are *coordinated replica* groups in which only one member of the group accepts and performs invocations and the others act as hot standbys (Birman and Joseph (1987)). Thirdly, there are *parallel replica* groups in which all members process the request. The members may be exact copies of the same program, or in some applications they may be, for example, different programs for the same function (i.e., *N*-version programming).

The essential differences between these different sorts of group are how messages are collected and collated. Collection is the process of receiving messages from some subset of the group (one, majority or all are typical cases) and collation is the conversion of multiple results into a single result (merge and identity being typical cases).

The ANSA model of replication is that inter-group communications are the same as ordinary communications, and so for any group there is a coordinator which accepts requests from clients and distributes them to the group, using intra-group communications (which are handled optimally by various kinds of specialized atomic broadcast protocols when available).

Given this model, collection and collation is a local issue within the group and so the selection of a collection and collating scheme is done in interface provisions. Various standard schemes are provided for the cases specified above and the means exist for programmers to write their own. To help with the latter, every operation is assumed to have an implicit argument, in addition to the arguments provided by the client, which represents the group as an object. The argument has operations to determinate the current size of the group and the index of the a member within the group, and operations to add and remove members from the group.

A further complication of groups is that it is not always necessary for all members of the group to see operation invocations in the same order. Birman explains how a variety of weaker consistency constraints can be used to increase the efficiency of broadcast protocols. These constraints are on the ordering of operations: do all servers see all operations from each client in the same order (destination ordering) and do all servers see operations from all clients in the same order (source ordering). They can be given as constraints on the interface provision to select the appropriate underlying protocols.

Argument passing

The semantics of argument passing are call-by-sharing. Therefore a naive implementation would be to encode arguments in messages as a 'call-back' address for accessing the argument at its home site. For some sorts of interfaces, files in a file server for example, this is quite suitable. For things such as integers and Booleans it is excessive. For some objects, such as a user's mailbox, a strategy of migrating the argument to the server for the duration of an operation might give better performance. Consequently it is made possible for the programmer to decide on how to represent different sorts of interface 'on the wire'. The computational model assumes that some set of basic immutable interfaces is available representing integers, Booleans and so forth, together with constructor types for concrete data types such as immutable arrays and records. A set of concrete encodings is defined as the transmissible representation of these types: they will be transferred by simple copying and will not incur the overheads of call-back. For mutable interfaces, the call-back scheme is available as the default. However, it is also possible for the programmer to instruct the compiler how to make a concrete representation for any interface and to transmit this as the argument. Building upon this facility it is possible to provide call-by-visit argument passing where required. A problem that can arise will call-by-visit is that the interface is lost if the server crashes in mid-operation. There are two solutions to this problem: operations on the interface can be made atomic, so that the server's version is aborted; alternatively, the client and server can set up a coordinated replica group to represent the interface, so that if the server fails, the client's replica will be able to continue in service.

Lifetimes

A problem that arises with the sharing model is that of garbage collection. Garbage collection within an open system is not a tenable option, since there is not a guarantee that nodes will cooperate. Consequently interface references are expiry-dated. If an interface reference is not used for some specified period it is assumed that all remote copies of the reference have decayed and that the interface is no longer required externally. If there are no internal references, the interface can be garbage collected. The lifetime can be specified by the programmer. Clearly there is a trade-off to manage between space in local tables and the complication of forcing periodic refreshing of stale references. If an interface reference has a lifetime of zero, a callee will only have guaranteed access to the interface for the duration of the operation to which it is an argument.

(At the time of writing, the relationship between lifetimes and persistent objects is under exploration. It may be desirable for an object to progress through various stages of passivation before it is eventually expunged, in which case rather than a simple lifetime, it would be necessary to name the passivation strategy.)

Embedded code

In DPL, the body of an operation can be either an expression in DPL or else an embedded fragment of another language. Thus DPL can be used to configure applications written in languages other than DPL as servers in a distributed system. Embedded code is restricted to being the body of an operation rather than an general expression so that the normal kinds of multi-language linkage editor facilities can be used to separately compile and then link together the various parts of a program. There is a problem however, if the embedded code is also a client: how can operations be invoked from within embedded code? The solution is to provide a simple pre-processor for each embedded language so that DPL-like invocations and handlers can be written within the code. The DPL fragment and the code section can then be separately compiled as external procedures and then subsequently linked together. Obviously these contortions are only necessary for a language which has a very different computational model to ANSA. In a situation where the default programming language is close to the computational model, it would be better to invest effort in providing libraries and other language extensions or restrictions to bring it into line, rather than embedding the language in DPL. DPL with embedded code is seen very much as a means to carry forward existing programs, rather than a development vehicle for new ones, where writing entirely in DPL, or an equivalent language, is more sensible.

19.3.3 Nested interfaces

The interface provision operator is dynamic: in implementation terms it builds a closure of the operations grouped by the operator and the surrounding environment. Thus it is possible to nest interfaces. An outer interface can possess an operation which dynamically constructs new interfaces sharing some of the parent's state. This is illustrated in the following example:

```
Int total := 0;
Int start := 0;
Counter = requires { next = op () result (Int) };
counters = provide {
    new = op () returns (counter) {
        Int from := start;
        start := start + 1000;
        provide {
            next = op () result (Int) {
                Int this = from;
                from := from + 1;
                total := total + 1;
                this
            }
        }
    }
}
Counter a = counters.new();
Counter b = counters.new();
a.next();
```

Counters is an interface with an operation new which constructs an interface to a simple counter. The first counter is initialized to zero, the next to one thousand, the next to two thousand and so on. Each counter has a `next` operation which advances that counter by one. The variable `total` will record how many times `next` has been called in all counters.

Sometimes, often for reasons of access control, it is desirable to partition an interface so that different clients see different subsets of the possible operations on some piece of state. This is made possible by enabling an operation definition in one interface to be a reference to an operation in some other interface that is in scope, illustrated by the following example:

```
producerconsumer = provide { put = op (...)... get = op (...)... };
producer = provide { give = producerconsumer.put };
consumer = provide { take = producerconsumer.get };
```

This facility can also be used to produce variants of an interface with different transparency constraints.

19.4 Binding

State is introduced into the computational model by providing for the binding of interfaces to identifiers. An identifier has scope and range and extent. The scope is the block within which the identifier is declared (and defines the duration for which storage must be provided). The range defines that part of the scope where the identifier is not hidden by a nested declaration in an inner scope. The extent defines that part of an identifier's range in which it is bound to an interface. It is forbidden to evaluate an identifier outside its range, but to permit definition of mutually recursive interfaces an identifier can be referenced outside its scope in interface requirements and interface provisions.

Two kinds of binding are recognized: constant and variable. A constant binding is one where the identifier can only be ascribed to one interface in its range, whereas an identifier subject to variable binding can be ascribed to many interfaces in its range. Bindings can be written anywhere with an expression.

Constant bindings are provided for two reasons: firstly they increase the safety net available to the programmer and secondly the compiler can make local copies of constant bindings when programs are distributed over multiple machines.

For updating variable bindings there is an assignment operator. All interfaces assigned to an identifier must be of the same type. A declaration can be optionally given a type constraint to force the type of the identifier, otherwise it takes the type of the expression assigned to it.

19.5 Objects

The principal difficulty in distributed systems is the lack of global shared memory. Memory has to be partitioned into disjoint regions and to configure those regions to different computers. each region encapsulates some piece of abstract state. Encapsulation in the ANSA computational model is achieved by an object operator. The operator defines a scope boundary: any expression within an object (including interface provisions) can only access identifiers with constant bindings outside of the encapsulation. Identifiers with variable bindings become inaccessible (hence the distinction between the two forms of binding made in Section 19.4).

Thus the ANSA object model is one in which an object has interfaces rather than operations. Interfaces are views of the potential operations of an object. This gives the model useful scaling properties since it can, within the same framework, encompass in the term 'object' something simple like an integer and something complex like a server with several user and manager interfaces. Dynamic interface creation gives support for fine-grained access control and synchronization.

An object can contain subobjects. There is not, however, a requirement that subobjects be located on the same computer as their parent and so the configuration of a program need not be identical to the way it is structured. This is an important point since the block structure of a program is an artifact of the programming methodology and is orthogonal to the dependability issues of how best to distribute the program.

19.6 Abstract types

The computational model assumes strong typing so that all possible checks on program structure and linkage can be made as early as possible in the life cycle of a program. Thus every interface has a type. All formal parameters and formal results are required to state the type of acceptable interfaces that can be bound to them. Declarations can also specify a type for an identifier if the expression to which the identifier is being bound yields a 'bigger' type than that desired. There is a library of built-in types defined by the computational model — including the immutable types for which the architecture defines an on-the-wire representation.

An interface requirement specifies an abstract type: abstract types are represented in the computational model as interfaces with an operation getSpecification which returns an interface of type Specification as its result, where Specification is a built-in type. Any interface which conforms to this behaviour is acceptable as an abstract type. Thus it is possible to define an interface that acts as both an abstract type and a factory for a class of interfaces, much like the classes in other object-oriented languages. This is illustrated by the following revision of the counters example given above:

```
Int total := 0;
Int start := 0;
Counter = {
    type = requires { next = op () result (Int) };
    provide {
        getSignature = op () returns (Specification)
        type.getSignature ()
        new = op () returns (type) {
            Int from := start;
            start := start + 1000;
            provide {
                next = op () result (Int) {
                    Int this = from;
                    from := from + 1;
                    total := total + 1;
                    this
                }
            }
        }
    }
};
Counter a = Counter.new();
Counter b = Counter.new();
```

The only difference between the two examples is that in the first the type and
the factory have different identifiers, where as in the second there is one
identifier that acts as both, in a style familiar to programmers in other object-
oriented languages.

Programs can compute with abstract types to provide generics such as lists
and stacks etc. The following trivial example defines an interface variable which
can be used to make containers with put and get operations for particular types.

```
OBJECT (Generic)
SEQ {
    Variable = INTERFACE {
        of = OP (AbstractType ElementType) RESULT (vartype)
        SEQ {
            VAR ElementType state := ();
            vartype = TYPE {
                put = OP(ElementType)RESULT(),
                get = OP()RESULT(ElementType),
                getSpecification = OP()RESULT(Specification)
            };
            INTERFACE {
                put = OP(ElementType value)RESULT() {
                    state := value
                },
                get = OP()RESULT(ElementType) {
                    state
                },
                getSpecification = OP()RESULT(Specification) {
                    vartype.getSpecification()
                }
```

```
                }
            }
        };
        v = variable.of(Integer);
        v.put(1);
    }
```

This mechanism provides much of the functionality of inheritance found in other object-oriented systems. The principle here however is one of encapsulation, rather than inheritance.

19.7 Interface constraint processing

Specification is itself an abstract data type and provides operations to interrogate the signatures and constraints in the interface requirement from which they were derived. In fact, this is the basis of constraint processing in DPL. All constraint expressions have the structure of an operation invocation (a name followed by arguments). Whenever the compiler translates an invocation of a constrained requirement, it invokes the operation on an interface called constraints (of which a default version is available in the standard library) with the supplied arguments and an interface to a parse tree for the invocation. The constraint operation can then modify the parse tree to provide the additional processing required by the constraint and return it to the compiler. A similar technique is used for applying constraints to interface provisions and the definition of operators such the ones for atomicity and replication. Here the task is more complex since version stores, locking managers, commitment protocols, group coordinators have to be set up. Thus by exposing the parse tree as a DPL interface the means for (systems) programmers to define constraint processing operations is provided. Applications programmers need only be informed of the available constraints and their qualitative effects; they need not be embroiled in the provision of constraints. By providing a general mechanism, rather than a specific list of constraints, the system becomes extensible, permitting other constraints to be applied beyond the standard set defined by ANSA. This mechanism is the DPL version of the stub-processing found in other systems.

19.8 The trader

There is one other important aspect of the computational model and that is the *trader* which is an interface available to every program that provides a means for separate halves of a program to rendez-vous. The trader is basically a directory structure which can be searched by path name, by property of some combination of both. A server can export an interface to the trader to make it accessible to other programs. An import function is provided to clients so that they can retrieve interfaces from the trader.

The trader performs type matching of imports and exports. This is done by maintaining a type name space in the trader. The name space is an acyclic graph showing the sub-typing relationships between types. The trader provides operations for programs to add and retrieve types by name from the type graph.

Imports and exports are typed: trader operations are parameterized by types and the trader will only search through exports of the required type (and its sub-types) when attempting to make a match. The import operation returns an interface reference to the caller. These references are arranged to be unambiguous for all time within a trading domain (a trading system can be structured as a federation of autonomous trading domains managed by separate authorities, and a domain can be partitioned into a hierarchy of sub-domains). The importer can retain the reference for as long he likes. Interface references may be location transparent, in which case the system infrastructure includes a (distributed) locator objects which search the system to find the interface whenever it is referenced. If the node supporting the object has crashed or is otherwise inaccessible, the client will be informed that while the interface reference is apparently valid, the interface cannot currently be reached. To speed up the task of location, interface references include an address hint for the interface and the interface reference of the locator for the interface. (If there is no location transparency, the address hint is actually an absolute).

There are a number of ways of organizing the locator: one is to follow the Amoeba strategy (Mullender (1985)) and have a single locator replicated across all sites communicating by a broadcast protocol. Another is to search the trader, using the interface reference as a property. These are, however, engineering issues, transparent to the application programmer.

19.9 References

K. P. Birman and T. Joseph (1987). 'Exploiting virtual synchrony in distributed systems'. *Proceedings Eleventh Symposium on Operating System Principles*: 123—138, Nov. 1987.

A. D. Birrell and B. J. Nelson (1984). 'Implementing Remote Procedure Calls'. *ACM Transactions on Computer Systems* **2** (1): 39—59, February 1984.

A. D. Birrell (1985). 'Secure Communication Using Remote Procedure Calls'. *ACM Transactions on Computer Systems* **3**: 1—14, Feb. 1985.

A. P. Black, N. Hutchinson, E. Jul, H. Levy, and L. Carter (1987). 'Distribution and Abstract Types in Emerald'. *IEEE Transactions on Software Engineering* **SE-13** (1): 65—76, Jan. 1987.

D. K. Gifford and N. Glasser (1988). 'Remote Pipes and Procedures for Efficient Distributed Communication'. *ACM Transactions on Computer Systems* **6** (3): 258—283, August 1988. (Also available as MIT LCS TR-384.)

B. Liskov and R. Scheifler (1983). 'Guardians and Actions: Linguistic Support for Robust, Distributed Programs'. *ACM Transactions on Programming Languages and Systems* 5(3): 381—404, July 1983.

S. J. Mullender (1985). *Principles of Distributed Operating System Design.* Ph. D. Thesis, Vrije Universiteit, Amsterdam, October 1985.

D. P. Reed (1977). 'Synchronization with Eventcounts and Sequencers'. *Sixth Symposium on Operating System Principles*, November 1977.

PART VIII

Conclusions

Chapter 20

How robust are distributed systems?

K. P. Birman

I started writing this chapter in November 1988, shortly after a 'worm' was unleashed in the internet; by exploiting network security loopholes it penetrated and crashed large numbers of machines.† Coincidentally, newspapers were filled with retrospective analyses of the 1987 stock market crash seemingly exacerbated by a flurry of program-driven trading. Both events gave rise to speculation concerning the robustness of contemporary distributed systems, and it is to this topic that I address myself.

Before beginning, it is important to recognize that these episodes also touch on rather deep ethical questions. One can and should ask about the propriety of writing and running a program that has no constructive purpose, or even of pitting small investors against massive institutions armed with supercomputers.

Personally, I feel that the running a worm shows a deplorable lack of judgement, and entertain some doubts about the modern stock market. Nonetheless, these conclusions are debatable, and strongly dependent on questions of taste. The present discussion focuses on a more technical issue, namely the robustness of distributed computing systems — against intrusions, but also in the presence of events that commonly arise in distributed settings, such as failures and overloads. Because these issues are basically technical, one can hope to arrive at a more or less technical answers to them. To the extent that these lead back to philosophical speculations, the questions raised concern implications of more technical conclusions, and hence one might hope that they will be less

---

† The program was designed to penetrate as many machines as possible using bugs and loopholes in UNIX communication and mail-handling software. Although apparently intended to unobtrusively maintain a low level of 'infection', a programming error caused the worm to replicate much faster than intended. It gained access to nearly 6000 systems during a 48-hour period, overloading and crashing a large percentage.

controversial than conclusions arrived at using, for example, ethical principles that might not be universally accepted.

20.1 Predicting the behaviour of a distributed system

Consider the problem of predicting how a distributed system will behave while it is executing. Such a system will be made up of large numbers of components, operating asynchronously from one another and hence with incomplete and inaccurate views of one-another's state. Moreover, few distributed systems operate in a steady state: load fluctuations are common as new tasks arrive and active tasks terminate. Jointly, these aspects make it nearly impossible to make accurate detailed statements.

For example, feedback can arise in an automated stock trading system because programmed trade decisions are based on market indexes that change rapidly to reflect recent trading. If all trading programs operate independently, this feedback effect is minimal. However, if a condition provokes sell decisions in large numbers of programs, or exceptionally large sell orders, it can reinforce itself by driving those indexes down, triggering waves of sales. Such a sequence apparently led to the 1987 crash. Whether or not one questions the use of trading systems in general, it seems obvious that one could question the use of trading programs subject to such behaviour. What is less obvious is that these sorts of behaviours are unpredictable and can arise from seemingly trivial mechanisms.

A behaviour prediction problem also arose as an issue in the 1988 worm incident. One way to design a worm would be to write a distributed protocol that maintains a replicated list of currently infected sites, by having worm programs communicate directly with one another and monitor one another's status to detect failures. Using this approach, one could maintain a very stable population of worms, infecting new sites in a highly controlled manner. However, the protocol would be hard to design — similar problems were discussed in Chapters 14 and 15. An easier solution is to implement such an algorithm given atomic group addressing and broadcast primitives, but the designer of a worm cannot (yet) assume that such primitives are available.

In an ill-fated decision, the designer of the 1988 worm evidently turned instead to a random algorithm. Under this approach, each worm independently makes decisions to infect neighbouring sites based on probabilistic mechanisms. The resulting worm population is influenced by factors that include the current population, the rate of new infections, the death rate, and the probability of a successful penetration of a system. For certain values of these parameters, the worm population might well remain stable and small. However, for other values, an *unstable* solution results, whereby the worm population will die out or grow uncontrollably. The question is thus how to pick parameter values that will definitely give stable populations. Unfortunately for the designer of the worm, problems of this sort are often intractable, and this one almost certainly is. Current mathematics gives little insight into how one might pick the parameters to ensure stability, or even test for stability given particular choices of parameters. The 1988 worm thus had an intrinisic and probably insurmountable flaw.

It is striking that whereas the worm provoked much discussion of distributed systems security, and some attention was been given to the ethical implications of running such a program, rather little was paid to the broader issue of which the worm was just a manifestation. Many systems contain feedback mechanisms, for example, in schedulers and in the flow-control mechanisms used by the communication layer. There is growing interest in applying these sorts of systems in a wide range of critical settings. How can one be sure that a given system is secure and immune to chaotic behaviour? Lacking this knowledge, should one not expect other such incidents, perhaps with catastrophic consequences?

Until recently, a laboratory rarity, distributed systems have become increasingly widely used, and our society has come to rely on them during the last five years. Increasingly, systems such as these replace humans who cannot provide the sorts of predictable realtime responsiveness of a computer. Yet, as these episodes illustrate, however bright the *promise* of distributed computing, the technology is also associated with significant risks.

20.2 Technology and social responsibility

I believe that the inventors of a technology assume an obligation to overcome flaws in that technology, especially flaws that could exact a direct human cost. Too many technologies have been turned loose without adequate thought being given to where they might lead. The more critical a technology, the more important it is that its weaknesses be anticipated before they become stumbling blocks. To fail to confront this issue in the context of distributed computer systems invites haphazard interconnection of machines using mechanisms capable of interacting in unanticipated ways. Lacking explicit actions to the contrary, one must anticipate that confidential data will be increasingly often exposed to intrusions, that critical control facilities will increasingly often be subject to disruption, and that failures of all sorts will be increasingly common.

This argument can be carried even further. In many cases, sober analysis leads to the realization that a technology simply cannot be perfected to the degree needed in the time available, if ever. A good example, strongly dependent on distributed computing technologies, is launch-on-warning software for controlling the nation's strategic weapons systems. These systems have been proposed because human beings cannot function rapidly enough to make launch decisions in response to a surprise attack. Unfortunately, the proponents of new weapons technologies have often overlooked the weaknesses of a technology, and the limits on the degree to which it can be perfected. Can one really build a large distributed system that is sufficiently robust to entrust it to perform such a crtical task? Based on the arguments that I will advance below, I think the answer is a negative one. It seems to me that there is an applicable 'impossibility' result; every bit as serious a limitation as any theoretically provable one. And, similar arguments seem to apply in many other settings. To establish this, however, one must first ask how robust a distributed system can reasonably be expected to be.

In the case of more mature technologies, such as transportation and power generation, organizations exist to ensure the safety of systems that enter widespread use. The measures mandated in some areas are astonishing in their pessimism about human potential for error and for assuming that unlikely events will not only occur, but will do so at the worst possible time. For example, nuclear reactors incorporate the most extreme measures to minimize risk. This has clearly reduced the potential for disaster. Yet, incidents continue to occur, and in many cases the ways in which they occur raise new questions about the whole assumption that systems of this sort can ever be made safe.

In contrast, the engineering of even the most widely used distributed systems has been fairly informal. If trains crash and nuclear 'excursions' (leaks) occur despite every countermeasure that designers with years of experience have managed to devise, should one not expect frequent disruptions in distributed systems designed with only minimal attention to robustness? The most common form of regulation for distributed systems has been through low-level standards, as for the ISO data transport protocols. However, the problems identified above arise at the application level, and to the extent that applications-level standards have been developed, they have been premature and overly restrictive. Clearly, one cannot define a standard for aspects of a system that are still experimental. Yet, it seems equally clear that ignoring these issues only encourages the construction of complex, fragile software.

20.3 Principles for distributed computing

One thing that we lack is a set of guiding principles to encourage the development of sound solutions to distributed computing problems. Let me propose a set of such principles now.

- *Assume responsibility.* Those who produce distributed computing software should make every effort to ensure that the software is safe for its intended mode of use and that it can only be used in the intended way. And, we must accept our responsibility to apply the highest standards of ethical behaviour in our individual research and to instill these standards in our students and colleagues.

- *Interconnect for good reasons.* Systems should be interconnected to achieve concrete objectives, not in the abstract belief that interconnection is a good thing. Systems that are incapable of interacting are incapable of compromising one another.

- *Support only necessary services.* When systems are interconnected, the default should be to support the smallest possible set of services. Services should be enabled selectively and because there is a good reason to support them. This minimizes the probability that a loophole in the large (and ever increasing) set of communication services could have widespread consequences. Also, it makes it more likely that the services that are enabled will be properly maintained.

  This is especially important for services implemented anonymously and provided as executables (without source). For example, the 1988 worm made use of a bugs in the Unix remote finger and mail-handling utilities. One might ask just what purpose was served by enabling these on the majority of the machines that were compromised. Many users maintain a primary account on just one of the machines with which they work, and neither receive mail nor maintain finger databases on other machines. Many machines, in fact, are used in ways that preclude reception of mail or finger queries. Yet, the default has been to enable every possible service whether needed or not, and substantial expertise is often required to selectively *disable* an unwanted service. This pursuit of uniformity and flexibility has had a paradoxical outcome: resources are consumed to run services that are not useful, and the machines on which they run are made less robust.

- *Include self-diagnosis and authentication mechanisms.* When communication is permitted and a service is supported, authenticate the origin and legality of requests. Many current networks make 'punning' (misrepresentation of origin information) too easy, giving the illusion of security where there is actually none.

  Authentication is an issue beyond its security implications. It is widely accepted that procedures should authenticate their arguments. Large distributed systems should carry this principle further. Mechanisms are needed by which whole system components can monitor themselves continuously, actively looking for inconsistencies and shutting themselves down if problems are detected. The reasoning here is that although software bugs may be inevitable, if they are detected rapidly the consequences can often be limited, for example by explicitly halting and restarting affected programs. This approach has long been used successfully in electronic circuit switching.

- *Design for fault-tolerance.* Far too many distributed systems are designed as if failures will not occur, or give undefined behaviour in the presence of failures. This is precisely the converse of the attitude needed when building software to survive a wide range of communication and hardware disruptions, especially in light of the self-checking mechanism proposed above. To build a robust distributed system, one must assume that failures will occur. The choice is to try to survive such events, or to detect them and shut down before an inconsistent or erroneous action could result.

  What faults should be treated? It is generally agreed that human behaviour will violate any rules one attempts to impose. Thus, the traditional approach in systems that must interact with humans is to design for tolerance of the largest conceivable class of behaviours. In contrast, designers of distributed systems generally assume independent, benign machine failures, and that communication failures involve only packet loss, duplication, unsequenced delivery or partitioning — not message corruption, forgery, or protocol violations.

Although one can question whether failures are always benign and independent, there are practical difficulties with using more demanding failure models. Most wider classes of failures turn out to be equivalent to the *Byzantine model*, in which arbitrary, correlated and even malicious behaviour are all treated as plausible. Computation in this model requires such costly consensus algorithms as to preclude the use of these algorithms in all but the most demanding settings. Moreover, the model requires that all interactions with the outside world be through a Byzantine agreement, which is often impractical. For example, if a system is capable of unlocking a door, the door would have to be controlled at least in quadruplicate, such that three out of four actuators would have to be operated simultaneously to perform the task.† Even in extreme settings, such as the control of the space-shuttle cargo hold, triple redundancy was felt to be adequate. Few mundane applications can afford to adopt the most pessimistic approach.

To summarize, there seems to be little hope for building practical day-to-day systems capable of tolerating severely incorrect or malicious behaviour on the part of some components. Yet, if benign behaviour is assumed, one must also consider the possibility that a system will experience failure modes that violate assumptions, and ask what the impact will be and how damage can be minimized.

● *Design for scale.* Just as it is common to oversimplify issues of fault-tolerance in distributed systems, questions of scale are often neglected. Contemporary distributed systems become hopelessly difficult to manage when more than a few dozen machines are interconnected. Systems that will interconnect hundreds or thousands of machines will require a completely different design mindset, in which scale is viewed as a design feature rather than an aspect that can be dealt with as an afterthought.

● *Avoid mechanisms that can cascade failures.* In many current systems, failures can cascade under heavy load or when plausible (but unlikely) failure modes occur. For example, recall the realtime protocols discussed in Chapter 14. In these protocols, a failed component may experience non-atomic broadcast deliveries that corrupt its software state. If such a program were *later* to interact with programs that remained operational, their

---

† In practice, triple modular redundancy is adequate for most applications. Nonetheless, the Byzantine approach requires that there be at least $3T + 1$ total participants in any protocol that will tolerate up to T failures while it is running.

states could be corrupted too. Many such protocols include lack mechanisms to solve this gradual contamination problem, although some do provide notification if an obvious error is detected.

A different kind of cascading can occur when machines are declared faulty due to overload. If the operational ones try to take over interrupted tasks, they risk becoming overloaded themselves. This, in turn, would trigger further failures. To avoid such problems one must either design substantial excess capacity into a system (which is often too costly to be practical) or detect overload and react by invoking load-shedding mechanisms. The latter approach is familiar from telephone systems.

- *Avoid using 'magic' mechanisms.* When a large system is built out of large numbers of interacting components, the superficially simple algorithms they embody can misbehave in surprising ways. This poses special problems to the designers of distributed systems, where it is often difficult to predict exactly how a mechanism will behave under real loads. For example, there is a strong temptation to include scheduling heuristics and adaptive mechanisms in low levels of a system; my group did this in some parts the ISIS system for purposes of load balancing. Yet, short of accurately modeling a system, there is no way to know if local optimization decisions will yield globally good behaviour, or simply cause the system to 'thrash'. Given the choice, a simple, well-understood mechanism is always preferable to a fancier but poorly understood one.

- *Robustness is expensive.* Systems builders often believe that robustness is a desirable objective, but at the same time insist that software systems should be constructed using the highest performance technologies available. To the (limited) extent that a robust solution to a problem is practical, one must be prepared to pay a price. Unfortunately, this price will often take the form of performance limits, limits on the functionality of the system and limits on the convenience of using it. One can certainly decide that a given 'price' is simply too high to tolerate. However, one must also recognize that the cost of such a decision will often be a less robust system.

20.4 Future directions

The principles enumerated above raise a tremendous number of questions about current and future distributed systems. It is interesting to examine some of the application areas that were covered in the text in this light.

20.4.1 Scaling and administration of file systems

The major focus of recent work on distributed file systems has been on performance. Systems like Andrew and Sprite represent major advances over, say, the SUN NFS, because they make more effective use of network resources and caching, where effectiveness is typically measured in terms of file transfer bandwidth, access latency, and the number of users the file server can support. These are extremely important issues. But, is it not somewhat narrow to orient file systems so strongly towards performance considerations?

For example, consider the problem of scaling and administering a large distributed file system. Whereas current file systems use a star architecture, future distributed systems will contain large numbers of file servers of varying capacity, and the performance and capacity of local disks will grow so large that using them just for caching and temporary files will be unacceptably wasteful. Yet, if a file system is assembled out of *multiple* servers, current systems provide little support for management of the ensemble, or for optimizing the assignment of files to available resources. For example, no existing file system maintains the primary copy of a file on the disk local to a user's machine, migrating updates to a remote file server at periods of low load to permit backups from the server and for fault-tolerance. While there has been considerable work on file replication, file systems to date have taken a fairly restricted approach to this whole issue.

This problem is not a purely abstract one. The Cornell Department of Computer Science recently placed an order for 25 workstations which are configured with 350Mbyte local disks. A decision was made to use the local disks only for swapping, temporary files and storage of immutable binaries, because the available file systems otherwise require a great deal of human engineering to manage, and the backup problem would become a major source of overhead. The administrative group was forced to do this because it lacked the personnel to support other general purpose uses of the local disks.

In addition to making more effective use of replication, it is likely that future file systems will need to look hard at semantic information in order to optimize the handling of each file based on its usage patterns. For example, current Unix-based file systems ignore information about file 'type', which forces distributed implementations to guess the best file management policies to use. This policy dates from a period when the Unix file system was touted for its simplicity. One could question whether simplicity of this sort remains desirable. Most Unix applications encode information about file type through standard extensions to file names, and the step from this to genuinely typed files is not a huge one. Moreover, information about file type is of great value in a distributed Unix file system, since it helps in predicting typical modes of access, the likely lifetime of a file, the importance of maintaining availability despite failures, compression methods to use, etc. This list of attributes will surely grow with the widespread use multimedia systems.

Tremendous advantages could be gained by implementing more sophisticated file system architectures. An architecture is needed in which the various servers are knowledgeable about one another and cooperate directly to optimize file distribution in response to patterns of access. Moreover, since this will require some amount of distributed state, the solution must be one which is fault-tolerant and gives well-defined consistency guarantees to file users. Lacking these possibilities, the extent to which file systems can be scaled is inevitably limited.

20.4.2 Security and authentication in transactional contexts

Interesting questions of security and authentication arise in a transactional context.

Consider the authentication issue. In addition to conventional problems of access control and protection, transactional systems depend on the correct use of concurrency control by their components. Moreover, the concurrency control mechanisms must be compatible ones. For example, if a module that uses timestamped concurrency control is called from one that uses locking, applications that include calls to both modules may execute non-serializably. The authentication problem that then arises is to detect concurrency control errors and mismatches in a large system composed of independently developed transactional components.

In current transactional systems, these issues do not arise because components share a common concurrency mechanism. However, in the future, one can easily envision large-scale transactional systems in which no single component provides this function. For example, one may wish to perform transactions under the aegis of Camelot on a set of databases managed by multiple commercial database systems. Similarly, one can imagine vendors supplying software packages with transactional interfaces.

Not only is the transactional authentication problem difficult to solve, it is not even clear how one can write down concurrency control requirements or behaviour as part of an interface specification. For example, in a module that implements locking and read/write access to a set of variables one might require that a caller acquire a write lock before calling write and a read lock before calling read — *except* when such locks are not needed because some other lock of coarser granularity was previously acquired. How can this even be expressed, much less formally verified?

Next, consider the security problem. Say that a transactional service is accessed by an anonymously implemented caller. Even given a compile-time interface check, one must ask what information can be trusted at runtime. A caller that performs concurrency control incorrectly could contaminate any service that trusts it, and by indirection any other programs that interact with that service. One solution to this problem would employ validated concurrency control and commit 'services' accessible over secure RPC. But, one can question whether this is the most efficient and practical solution to the problem. Until system designers begin to ask these sorts of questions and to build systems that include mechanisms such as this, major problems will arise in attempts to move these technologies out of the laboratory.

20.4.3 Replication-based systems

Chapter 15 discussed the sorts of group addressing mechanisms and group broadcast mechanisms needed in systems that maintain replicated state. The protocols used for this are complex, and bugs in them could crash large numbers of machines. It would be hard to imagine a failure mode in which a transactional system might shut down every machine on a network, but it is fairly easy to imagine how bugs in a complex protocol could have this effect.

This complexity has several implications. Certainly, work is needed on simplifying the protocols used in replication-based systems. Might there not be a way to build these up from simple, verifiable mechanisms? Another issue is that, to the extent possible, these protocols should be implemented as part of the operating system. My reasoning is that if operating systems lack support for the sorts of mechanisms needed in application software, those applications either will not get built, will be built using less than ideal methods or will be forced to individually reproduce the missing mechanisms. Moreover, security and trust considerations would limit the composition of large systems out of smaller components: it will be too hard to agree on protocol specifications and implementation details.

It is clear that a substantial number of applications will need replication. Given this situation, it seems that one would be better off providing such services in a standard way. If individual application builders are asked to take on an effort of this scale, a large amount of duplicated effort will surely result, leading to application software that is less robust, less portable, and harder to maintain than desired.

20.5 Changing the way people think about distributed computing

Not long ago I met with a vice president of a major corporation who expressed interest in ISIS. This individual explained that within his company, known primarily for its mainframe systems, a perception had arisen that we need to 'change the way people think about distributed computing'. This comment is intriguing at several levels: how *do* people think about distributed computing? Why change this? And how?

For too long, distributed computer systems have been viewed primarily in terms of interconnection. We have tended to think about such systems as a way to run a program on one machine that uses resources on another and to send mail to our colleagues, and have generally treated workstations as if they were terminals connected to a mainframe. The benefit of a using a workstation is often seen primarily in terms of its ability to offload computation from a centralized resource.

Perhaps the time has come to recognize that centralized servers and transparent distribution are not always good things. It seems clear that the real advantages to distributed systems come about only when one begins to treat the fact of distribution as a positive element that can contribute to the solution of an application, rather than as an annoyance that should be concealed. This does change the requirements that one places on the communication support of the operating system, but the problems that arise can be solved. It is entirely possible that the future successes of distributed computing will be in applications where decentralization, autonomy, fault-tolerance and cooperative behaviour are critical.

Whereas many of these applications are today viewed as either too difficult or too costly to solve, the technology for building such systems is finally at hand.

Recall Fredrick Hayes-Roth's comments, quoted in Chapter 14. Like Dorothy who steps out of her aunt's house and suddenly sees the world in color, the revolution in thinking that awaits us is enormous. The potential to solve new problems and take on new applications that this will enable staggers the imagination.

In accepting the challenges offered by these new applications, however, one must be honest concerning just how robust technological solutions to problems can possibly be. And, in situations where analysis of the technical barriers to a solution reveals that the available technology is not adequate to the task, it is necessary to accept the reality of these limitations. Blind faith in technology can simply no longer be justified in the face of the increasingly long list of technical failures that the world has compiled. Those who create these technologies must, for their part, accept the responsibility to do all that they can to ensure that their products will be used in appropriate and reasonable ways.

It has been common to believe that with sufficient financial resources, any problem can be overcome. It appears that this will not be the case for software robustness. The price of robustness is often a system with much reduced functionality, if a robust solution is possible at all.

The era of distributed computing is just beginning. In writing this textbook, a group of us have come together to survey the field and point in some of the directions that it has to offer. In rereading the material that we have produced, it is encouraging to see both the progress that has been made throughout the field and the accelerating *rate* of progress. At the same time, a tremendous range of problems remain to be solved. In this respect, distributed computing seems to be special within computer science as a whole. Whereas many other areas have flowered rapidly only to stagnate rapidly, new directions keep opening up in distributed systems, and revolutions keep occurring in even the most 'traditional' areas of the field. Meanwhile, more and more applications depend on some form of distribution, and these also pose new challenges. The potential applications of distributed computing technology have hardly been tapped. Provided that this is done in a careful, considered manner, distributed computing could change the way that we deal with computer systems in a profound and beneficial way.

It is unfortunate that the potential for abuse of this technology is a real as for any other technology that civilization has devised. Nonetheless, that potential *is* real, and will have increasingly important consequences. Our field must accept the responsibility for this technology: even as we create these new forms of computing, it falls upon us to control them through new and more demanding ethical standards.

20.6 Acknowledgments

I am grateful to Robert Cooper, Ajei Gopal and Barbara Simons for commenting on drafts of this material. Several of the ideas put forward here emerged from discussions with Prof. Jacques Neirynck, who has written extensively on the relationship between science and society. I also feel that an apology is due to the authors of papers and books germaine to this discussion. I could certainly have cited relevant technical material, but felt that this would be inappropriate given the theme of the chapter. And, I know of little material on ethics in relation to technologies of this sort. I would be grateful for any references that readers knowledgeable about the subject might care to recommend.

Index

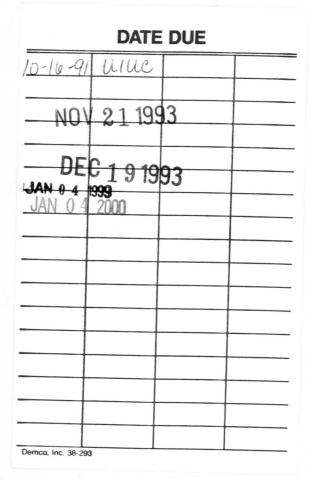